James W. Neville
November 1993

FROM AUTOTHANASIA
TO SUICIDE

FROM AUTOTHANASIA TO SUICIDE

Self-killing in Classical Antiquity

Anton J. L. van Hooff

London and New York

First published 1990
by Routledge
11 New Fetter Lane, London EC4P 4EE

Simultaneously published in the USA and Canada
by Routledge
a division of Routledge, Chapman and Hall, Inc.
29 West 35th Street, New York, NY 10001

Typeset in 10/12pt Baskerville by
Columns Ltd, Berkshire
Printed in Great Britain by
MacKays of Chatham Ltd, Kent

British Library Cataloguing in Publication Data
Van Hooff, Anton J. L.
From autothanasia to suicide: self-killing in classical
antiquity.
1. classical world. Suicide
I. Title
362.2
ISBN 0-415-04055-8

Library of Congress Cataloging in Publication Data
Van Hooff, Anton J. L.
From autothanasia to suicide: self-killing in classical antiquity
Anton J. L. van Hooff.
00 p.   cm.
Translation from Dutch.
Includes bibliographical references.
ISBN 0-415-04055-8
1. Suicide—Greece—History. 2. Suicide—Rome—History.
I. Title.
HV6543.H66   1990
362.28'0938—dc20   89-70139
                                          CIP

Andreae, Claudiae, Mirjam,
causis vivendi

CONTENTS

ILLUSTRATIONS

ix

FIGURES

PROLOGUE

This study about a sinister but 'vital' theme had its origin several years ago when I gave some lectures about the theme for branches of the Netherlands Classical Association (Nederlands Klassiek Verbond). It was much helped by a working-group I conducted at the University of Nijmegen consisting of advanced students in Ancient History in the autumn of 1983: Peter Beelen, Tim Dijkstra, Ad Franken, Steef Geurden, Fred Hendriks, Léon Hermse, Elena Janner, Burgie Koopman, Harry de Korte, Kiek Offermans and Marc van der Velde laid the foundations for the collection of cases and helped to develop the interpretations of the facts.

Several colleagues who heard of my 'hobby' told me about interesting cases and literature: in this respect I have to thank my colleagues in the Department of Classics in Nijmegen: A. Bastiaensen, L. de Blois, J.-J. Flinterman, A. Kessels, P. Leunissen and W. van Loon. P. van Minnen and H. S. Versnel in Leyden and E. Eyben (Leuven-Belgium) drew my attention to some interesting literature.

The Netherlands Organization for the Advancement of Pure Research (Z.W.O.) contributed to this study by conferring a travel grant which enabled a stay at the Fondation Hardt in Vandoeuvres-Geneva during the spring of 1988.

My British colleague in Classics Teacher Training at Durham University, Richard Smith, undertook the painstaking task of removing Dutchisms and outright faults from my English. In June 1989 I enjoyed the hospitality of his home and the discussions we had then were very helpful in clarifying many ideas.

Finally, many thanks are due to Mariken van Groenestijn, *dimidium animae vitaeque meae*, who critically and conscientiously read the first Dutch draft and helped considerably to improve the work in style and thought.

xi

LESS THAN AN ANIMAL,
MIGHTIER THAN A GOD

If there really was a single and perfect god, would he be able to do absolutely anything? When the Homeric pantheon was being replaced by monotheistic ideas, ancient philosophy came across this tricky theological problem. Homer's Olympic gods had overcome the manifest limitations of human existence; in accordance with the Homeric epithet *easy living* they were unacquainted with the toiling of man. As *always living* they were not to fear death. But after the idea of a single god had got a firm footing, the omnipotence which had to be accorded to *the god – ho theos –* remained a disturbing attribute. Christian theologians who conformed to ancient thinking later will wonder whether God is able to undo what has been done: can he bring back an ex-virgin to her former integrity? Before that, in the first century AD, Pliny discovers tragedy in God's almightiness:

> But the chief consolation for nature's imperfection in the case of man is that not even for God are all things possible – for he cannot, even if he wishes, commit suicide, the supreme boon that nature has bestowed on man among all the penalties of life
>
> (*Natural History* 2,27)[1]

According to this ancient view at least in one respect man is mightier than god.

But is man obedient to nature, *physis*, when using this superdivine power? The argument that suicide is not 'in accordance with nature', *physei*, was advanced by Flavius Josephus among many other considerations which prompted him to renounce suicide when he and other Jewish fighters had hidden themselves

xii

from the Romans in a cavern under Jotapata. During his whole remaining life he was vexed by self-criticism and reproaches from his fellow-Jews: why had he not shared the heroic end of his comrades? During the Jewish War Massada had not been the only instance of collective self-destruction. That is why self-killing plays such a conspicuous part in the books Josephus wrote in Greek as a favourite of the Flavian emperors[2]. Most comprehensive is the speech Josephus put into his own mouth at Jotapata. In that *apologia pro vita* he uses very diverse arguments against self-killing which have been borrowed from Jewish as well as ancient thinking: it is not allowed to tear apart body and soul. Falling in action brings honour, but self-destruction is a cowardly and outrageous act. A suicide is like a pilot who fearing a tempest sinks his own ship before the storm.

> Suicide is alike repugnant to that nature which all creatures share, and an act of impiety towards God who created us. Among the animals there is not one that deliberately seeks death or kills itself; so firmly rooted in all is nature's law – the will to live[3].

Is man really placing himself outside nature by laying hands upon himself? If Josephus had had a better knowledge of Aristotle he would have been acquainted with one case of animal suicide: a Scythian horse-breeder tried to have a young stallion mate with its mother. The animal refused, but later it was cheated when the mare's head had been covered. Discovering the truth, it jumped into an abyss. So already the ancient world borrowed its argumentation from animal behaviour. Only the ancients did not use the lemmings as an example to refute the conviction that self-killing is an exclusively human ability. They had at their disposal tigers, a bird that watched over the fidelity of the wife and the Scythian horse[4].

Pliny and Josephus show that Camus' words also apply to antiquity: 'There is only one serious philosophical problem: suicide'[5]. At the same time it becomes apparent from the amalgam of Jewish and Greek counter-arguments in Josephus that the ancient attitudes have more ambiguity than is assumed in the modern myth of *Roman death*. This syndrome of tolerance and respect towards self-killing appears both in novels and in public discussion. In Ambrose Bierce's 'One officer, one man' the Roman way of death comes to the mind of an American captain during the

Civil War. For the first time he was going to be confronted with real battle. His nerves were tense;

> . . . suddenly he grew calm. Glancing downward, his eyes had fallen to his naked sword, as he held it, point to earth. Foreshortened to his view, it resembled somewhat, he thought, the short heavy blade of the ancient Roman. The fancy was full of suggestion, malign, hateful, heroic!

At last he cannot get rid of this fascination and he throws himself on his sword[6].

At the end of 1986 a curious discussion suddenly arose in the Netherlands about the self-killing of an antifascist writer in 1940 when the Germans invaded: could his suicide be called a Roman death? Different positions were taken by leading literary personalities. A quotation from Martial was used to demonstrate that the whole idea was absent in Roman culture: Fannius committed suicide in order to escape from the enemy. 'Now I ask you: is it not sheer madness to expire in order not to die?' But the same Martial has – in another poem – the very expression *Romana mors* as a respectful denomination for a noble suicide[7]. So both glorification and scorn were part of the ancient attitude.

It is not difficult to dwell at length on ancient *ideas* with respect to self-killing; this is the way some older studies have treated the problem. In this respect *Altertumswissenschaft* distinguishes itself favourably from other fields of historical research in that some work has already been done; for other past societies studies of suicide are rare[8]. But a serious defect of existing studies, e.g. those of Hirzel and Geiger, is that they are mainly concerned with the history of ideas: concepts of ancient thinkers are explained and systematized, but the implications of ideas for reality are shown only if a philosopher has suited the act to his word. In this type of publication some folklore serves mainly as a picturesque illustration and gives only a glimpse of reality.

Reality, as far as it can be reconstructed, is the basis for a study which hopes to do justice to the 'experience' of self-killing. A really integral history should start with concrete *phenomena*. We try to sort out the facts in Part I, chapter 1, under the title *casus moriendi*, in which we discuss first the methods of research, the global figures gathered and the representativeness of the data. Under the same heading 'cases of dying' attention is paid to suicidal behaviour among specific groups: cultures, sexes and age groups. After that the ways of committing suicide are treated under *modi moriendi*. The signature of ancient suicide is completed by a study into the motives of dying, *causae moriendi*.

Having processed this concrete material we have laid a foundation for further investigation into the attitudes with respect to self-killing in antiquity. Those will be discussed in Parts II and III. In the metaphor used by Vovelle to clarify the principles of the *history of mentality* he calls counting, measuring and weighing – activities which sometimes have been called cliometry – constructing a cellar for a complete historical building. On the ground floor we are in the level of popular morality. There we come across all kinds of material that expresses the general attitude: words, sayings, jokes, folklore, burial habits, pictures and the like. Finally we reach in Part III, in what Vovelle calls the discourse, the attic in his simile. On this level of reflection we find philosophy and theology, activities of the mind which have a dialectical relation with reality, that is to say to a great extent they legitimize existing values and furnish them with an ideology, but sometimes the sages distance themselves from prevailing attitudes, when they act as utopians and advocate changes.

For instance, the development of the idea of self-killing as an act of murder cannot be traced back to any – demographic – reality. In this sense phenomena are not the all-determining 'substructure'. The Christian taboo on self-murder, which gets its classical formulation by St Augustine, emerges only in late antiquity. The concept of *suicidium*, which was to have such a formidable impact on mentality as well as reality in Christian Europe, is an instance of an idea which descends from the high level of the *discours* to the layers of mentality and reality.

Before acquiring the status of an ideology, self-killing in antiquity met with very diverse attitudes. At first the Greek concept was 'killer of his own', i.e. killer of his own people (family, clan). In a narrow sense an *authentes* could become the killer of himself (*autothanatos*). Apart from the extremes of complete indifference and outspoken respect there always existed horror, doubt and condemnation. Disapproval gets the upper hand only in late antiquity when the idea of self-*murder* takes shape. The idea of *suicidium* originates 1250 years before the word comes into being[9].

Part I

PHENOMENA OF SELF-KILLING

1

CASUS MORIENDI

A certain morbid collector's mania is required for making a file of suicides in the Graeco-Roman world[1]. For research of this type the *klassische Altertumswissenschaft* is well equipped; it has many instruments available. In the tradition of classical scholarship philology and history never lost contact; therefore it is possible to trace many cases by means of reference books: various terms for self-killing in lexicons disclose many a passage in ancient literature. Greek and Latin have at their disposal a much richer vocabulary on suicide than dictionaries and lexicons suggest. As a by-product of our heuristic activities a suicidal vocabulary was developed which has been relegated to Appendix C. It may not only be useful as an instrument for further investigation; the corpus of expressions makes it possible also to see the nuances in ancient thinking on self-killing, the more as a central word (and idea) like 'suicide' is lacking (see II.4.A *'suicidium*, a non-word' and Appendix B).

Exploring usage is part of the history of mentality in a narrow sense. Apart from the use of lexicological instruments reading of 'promising' authors like Seneca, Plutarch and Diodorus of Sicily enriched the corpus of cases – this type of investigation was helped by the fact that suicides usually figure at the end of a life-story. At first it seemed only necessary to collect the data on *Greek* suicide as Yvonne Grisé has published several articles and a book on Roman self-murder which includes an impressive list of cases. That was the reason why in the autumn of 1983 when I was working with some students on ancient suicide, special attention was given to the collecting of Greek data. For the Roman situation Grisé's list was used as the basis for generalization. Working on this book and checking Grisé's materials I discovered deficiencies in her data: some passages could not be found in modern editions. It seems that the authoress copied many a reference from older publications. More serious are misinterpretations of sources she claims to have consulted[2]. Several weeks had to be spent doing her homework over again. Also many a conclusion she draws is debatable, as will become apparent when we compare our views with hers on several major points.

Data were also added to the stock by way of academic communication: colleagues who came across cases in their reading of classical authors passed them on to me; I have thanked them in the prologue.

The material gathered in these ways is mainly literary in the ancient broad sense of 'literature'. As 'realistic' genres historiography and biography account for 484 out of 960 cases. Suicides also figure in other prose: they illustrate philosophical points of view or they serve as exempla in rhetorical texts. An ancient book on dreams has some fine cases taken from the practice of an interpreter. Mythical and purely fictional cases have been collected from epic, drama, lyrical poetry, novels and even from jokes. Special attention has been paid to direct sources: do inscriptions mention suicide as a cause of death and are there cases in the papyri from Greek Egypt? The – meagre – harvest of this research will be presented in Part II as material which demonstrates ancient attitudes to self-killing[3].

This collector's work resulted in a file of 960 cases which are presented in Appendix A without the claim of covering all ancient suicides. Further research would certainly disclose some more cases: the magical limit of 1000 is already in sight. On the other hand I would be surprised if the number ever surpassed 2000 or even 1500. Far more time was spent on gathering the last tens of cases than the first hundreds, which indicates that the law of diminishing returns is already operative. There is no need to aim at completeness, for the list of the Appendix does not have real statistical significance: several filters determined the appearance in ancient sources. Therefore certain types of suicide were recorded with zeal by ancient authors whereas others are demonstrably under-represented. For instance hanging as a method arguably does not emerge in the cases as often as one would expect. Another filter accounts for the fact that Roman women do not have the place in the statistics they should have. Before we tackle the problems connected with suicidal patterns of specific groups such as women, cultures and age-groups it is necessary to make it clear why in this study absolute numbers of individuals have not been chosen, but that the case has been chosen as the basic element.

A WHAT'S IN A CASE?

Ischomachos' daughter had been married to a priest of Demeter and Persephone. This holy man, devoted to Mother and Maid (*Kore*), as Andokides describes in his speech on the *Mysteries* (1,125), seriously misbehaved: he took his wife's mother as well into his house and bed. Thereupon the young woman tried to hang herself, but was stopped in the act. Then, when she recovered, she ran away from home (later the mother was driven out by her lover as well). This *attempt* at suicide has also been included in the corpus of cases because it enables us to analyse means as well as motives. Basically it is impossible to trace the real motive of a suicide[4]. In fact the ratio of attempted to committed suicide in the ancient corpus remains far below the proportions which are regarded as standard in modern times: instead of eight to ten attempts for each suicide committed, in our material the ratio is one attempted self-killing to four or five accomplished acts (see Appendix B 2).

Just because on the whole the ancient information remains on the surface of events the few cases of *intro- and retrospection* deserve special attention. A couple of people write that they once considered suicide because bodily or mental pain made life unbearable. As an adolescent Seneca contemplated his exit because he suffered from weak lungs. But he realized the grief it would cause to his old father and he abandoned the plan. St Augustine speaks about his 'aversion to life', *taedium vitae*, dominating his mind when he had lost 'his soul's half', his best friend[5].

The *longing* for another's suicide may also clarify in which circumstances a person in antiquity was expected or supposed to take his life. In this category of people wishing suicide on others there is a case which has come to us on solid stone. In an inscription in Rome a girl is bewailed: 'Her father miserable by missing her dragged himself weeping through evil life'. In the next lines the father is speaking about the arrangements for his own burial: 'My bones mixed with those of my daughter must repose in an altar'. Then the speaking person imagines how his emancipated slaves, men and women with their children, will crown with garlands the altar. But one person is excluded, Atimetus the freedman 'by whose guile I lost my daughter'. Grief is obstructing pure Latin in the next lines, but the general meaning is clear: 'nail and rope to fasten his neck to'. What is meant by 'guile', *dolus*, can only be guessed at. Was the former slave held responsible for the death of the girl by practising black magic?[6]

When an ancient source expresses *doubt* about the reality of a suicide saying 'it is said that', 'rumour has it that', 'some spokesmen say', the case has been included (with a ? for 'reality' in Appendix A). In further 'maximal' counting also the many cases in the fiction of epic, novel and myth have been included. It is possible to discuss endlessly and fruitlessly whether Ajax really fell on his sword when Achilles' weapons were not assigned to him. Did Iokaste really hang herself on discovering her shameful marriage with her son Oidipous? Epic and myth especially express the ideals and nightmares of ancient people: this highly significant material must not be left out. In this way beneath the neat figures of 960 cases with 9639 individuals there are layers of different solidity. To reassure the historian, who in spite of everything wishes to know 'wie es eigentlich gewesen', on those occasions where it makes sense to distinguish between hard and soft cases, the real figures are given explicitly or put between brackets after the hard number. Soft cases are all of the 960 cases where only an attempt, a consideration, a wish/curse is mentioned in the sources. Apart from that, all fictional suicides have been excluded in the solid figures. The remaining number has been reduced by three non-human suicides which, because of their very human motivation, are suitable for analysing the general experience of suicide in antiquity: Erigone had hanged herself on finding her father Ikarios dead; Maira her female dog pined away, refusing food, and finally jumped into a well[7]. Finally, there is one lifeless case: the *dikaios logos*, Right Reason, curses itself in Aristophanes' *Clouds* to underline its words; its 'May I hang if' is one of the 'softest' instances which have been included in the corpus[8]. Such 'fabulous' cases may disturb the critical mind as sheer fantasy; therefore they have not been regarded as belonging to the hard core. This includes only the cases which meet Durkheim's standard: 'tout cas de mort qui résulte directement ou indirectement d'un acte, positif ou négatif, accompli par la victime elle-même et qu'elle savait devoir produire ce résultat'[9].

By these reductions we reach a kernel of 564 hard, historical cases, i.e. in which *according to the source beings have killed themselves*[10]. This number of 564 cases (out of 960) comprises 494 individual suicides and 70 collective self-killings. *Collective suicides* are in all respects very difficult to assess; what is the element of personal will? Most often – to use Durkheim's terminology – an 'anomic' fit of mind has overpowered a group. In establishing the motives in most cases we have to satisfy ourselves with the inarticulate 'despair', *desperata salus* in the Latin denomination we use on purpose (see I.3 on motives). A recent parallel in the difficulty of assessing the motivation of a group was the mass suicide by the adherents of Jim Jones' Temple of God in French Guyana on 18 November 1978: what exactly were their personal motives? Among the 76 collective self-killings which are part of our file a disproportionate share, 35, is taken by groups of non-Greeks and non-Romans, 'barbarians' in ancient usage. They generally belong to the type which Durkheim styles 'suicides obsidionaux', self-killings by the inhabitants of a beleaguered city. In most cases the victor watches with satisfaction the fatal humiliation brought upon his enemies. This attitude is in principle not different from the way in which triumphant commanders have their opponents depicted as killing themselves. Thus Decebalus completes Trajan's victory as he stabs himself as shown on one of the last panels of the column in Rome. More subtlety characterized the monument Attalus I erected in Pergamum commemorating his victory over the Gauls: some compassion mingles with the satisfaction of the victor (see II.5.D for the iconography of suicide). In a similar fashion Xenophon relates that the Ten Thousand looked on with bewilderment as the Armenian Taochians chose to commit suicide by hurling themselves from their fort onto the rocks below. In the first place the women threw their children from the heights. They jumped next and their men followed suit. One of the Greek soldiers, Aineias from Stymphalos, tried to stop one desperate individual but he was dragged along with the person he wanted to save[11].

Collective suicide does not lend itself to precise analysis: with respect to motive it falls under the heading of despair, the least distinctive category. In sheer number of (countable) persons group suicide would determine the totals if we counted individuals: 8785 (out of 9639 in total) self-killers were involved in the 11 (out of 76) cases of mass suicide where a specific number is given. The effects on the relative frequency of methods and motives would be enormous if we counted each participant in a collective self-murder as one item. In another respect too the conclusions would be distorted. A disproportionate share of group suicides is furnished by barbarians. Here the special attention by Greek and Roman historians devoted to the humiliation of enemies accounts for the over-representation. Leaving them completely out of account – an option contemplated for a while – would rob us of some valuable insights into what 'civilization' expected from defeated enemies. That is the reason why it figures in this study, whereas e.g. king Saul's suicide has been left out: this case has not been 'observed' by a Greek or Roman[12].

B WHAT'S IN A NUMBER?

What is the general relation between the figures taken from our material and historical reality? In Appendix A there are 960 cases. As was explained above one case can comprise quite a lot of people if it refers to a collective suicide by troops who despaired of survival or if a mass of barbarians is involved who destroyed themselves together with wives and children. In most cases we simply do not know how many persons were involved in the 65 out of 76 cases of group suicide where the number of individuals is only indicated by Greek and Latin equivalents for 'many', 'numerous', 'hundreds' and the like. They only count as one case; in no way is it feasible to estimate the number of persons. Also in cases where the number is indicated by 'a few' etc. no attempt has been made to establish a figure. But wherever an ancient source gives a precise number it has been taken as factual. Thus St Jerome (*Letters* 123,7) gives three hundred as the number of the wives of Teutones and Cimbri who died by self-destruction. They had in vain asked Marius the Roman commander to guarantee their bodily integrity by putting them under the protection of the Vestal Virgins. To escape (sexual) humiliation they killed themselves 'by reciprocal wounds or they hanged themselves by a rope made of their own hair on trees or the yokes of waggons'. Other participants in mass suicides were calculated in thousands: the absolute top are the five thousand inhabitants of Gamala who, in Flavius Josephus' description, jumped into the abyss when the Roman took their city. Their number even exceeds the famous 960 defendants of Massada[13]. Adding up numbers like these exact three hundred we reach a total of 9639 countable individuals. This seems quite an impressive number.

But it has no significance for the suicidal reality of the ancient world. Modern Britain has about 5000 suicides per year out of a population which is comparable to that of the whole of the ancient Mediterranean world. If we take the earliest mythical and epic Graeco-Roman cases as happening about 1500 BC and regard as the last ancient instance the Byzantine lady (*matrona ornata*) who in the sixth century AD jumped into the water to escape violation by pirates, we have on average some five individuals each year from a population which at its peak is reckoned at 50 to 60 million people; so no figure can be produced that is comparable to modern statistics which reckon in 'x cases per 100,000 per annum'. On the basis of the numbers it is impossible to answer the question whether suicide in antiquity was more or less frequent than in the modern world[14].

There is a general belief among modern experts that suicide rates in literate societies are higher than those in primitive cultures. But among the latter there are some which exceed the lowest rate of some European countries. Neither is it demonstrable without question that industrialization and urbanization cause an increase of suicide as the myth of the dehumanizing metropolis has it. Do the modern statistics say anything about the suicidal calibre of a society? At first glance the rates of modern Greece and Hungary differ shockingly: 5 to 55 (out of 100,000 per annum); it looks as if the Magyars are eleven times more suicidal. But looking upon it from the point of view of survival one could say just as well that in Greece each year 99,995 out of 100,000 prefer to live on compared to 'only' 99,945 people in Hungary. The ratios of survival are not markedly different: 1.0005:1[15]. Using suicide rates as an indication for mental health of a nation is unjustified in the same way as once the rates of illegitimate births were mistaken as signs of the moral level of a people.

On a closer look modern suicide statistics are not too solid. In some countries shame accounts for silence or unbelievably low figures; only in 1989 did the Soviet Union publish its rates for 1987 (19 per 100,000). But even the numbers in 'open societies' can raise doubt. There is a school of radical 'rejectionists' among the suicidologists who fundamentally distrust all published figures. Taylor, who has a moderately sceptical attitude, took a closer look at the way London Transport reported a case of death on its premises as an accident or a suicide. Starting from the figures he went way back to the officials behind the desks who classified a death one way or the other. All were sure they made their decision without prejudice or theory. But in his interviews Taylor found that the observer was led by 'systematic biases'. Unconsciously influenced by 'values, beliefs, theories, common-sense-understandings, etc.' he will not readily decide for suicide in the case of a young person with a future ahead, whereas the questionable death of an older person will promptly be attributed to self-killing. To illustrate his point the sociologist makes comparisons with historical thinking: both the official of London Transport and the historian are reconstructing the facts in such a way that *to the observer a logical structure emerges.* All sorts of events which happened on the eve of a catastrophe – a revolution or a sudden death – become meaningful in retrospect[16].

If even the establishing of facts about modern suicide is subject to selective perception and interpretation, a historian is entitled to use a corpus of 960 cases comprising at least 9639 individuals as the foundation of a study about the *values* of a past society with regard to self-killing. For those 960 cases have not been reported by chance. Looked upon as a reservoir of selected materials they may help us to come to grips with the way ancient society tried to understand suicide.

C THE PEAKS OF REPUBLICAN AND MYTHICAL SUICIDE

The selective mechanisms operative in Roman observation are also visible in the distribution in time: peak years are 48 and 43 BC, the years in which the last of the republicans were destroyed: Pompey and the pair of tyrannicides Brutus and Cassius. The whole of the period 49–42 BC is prominent with 58 cases and 1048 countable individuals. A solid basis to these 1048 is laid by the thousand comrades of Vulteius, Caesar's loyal adherents. The real figure of victims is arguably higher; we have five group suicides with undetermined numbers of participants. Out of the cases which can be dated, the year 43 BC has 22. The year of Philippi, 48 BC, shows 11 instances with 12 (countable) victims.

The tragic downfall of the *res publica libera* has its poet in Lucan. As 'The Poet of Suicide' in his *Pharsalia* he wallows in macabre scenes of voluntary death by the defenders of the Republic[17]. The last champions of the old constitution committed suicide because life seemed impossible under the triumviri, Mark Antony, Octavian and Lepidus. The numerous self-killings of those years have been recorded as symbolic of the death of political freedom.

They have been commemorated with melancholy by the historians of the Empire who relished the minimal liberty they did at least have in describing the republican past. The suicide peaks are accounted for solely by attempts to foster the memory of the dying days of the republic. According to theory years of turmoil should have markedly less suicides[18].

Again and again it becomes evident that the figures contained in the collection of ancient suicides primarily reflect the way of looking. They do not express reality or trends. So it has become clear why the Late Republic has been represented so well. Late Republic is taken as the time from after the Hannibalic War till the beginning of Octavian's monarchy (200–27 BC). In absolute figures that period has 2433(1408) (countable) individuals covered by 164(133) cases (Figure 1.1, p.12). This disproportion only confirms in a cumbersome manner the well-known fact that the period has been recorded more extensively by ancient historiography with its almost exclusive attention to noble politicians and generals: in this period they had many an occasion to get a reputation by dying. The same epoch also has a fair amount of group suicides, sometimes with (pseudo-)exact numbers[19].

The total of persons who committed suicide during the Early Empire (27 BC–200 AD) is considerably larger, 6624(6575), than those registered for the last centuries of the Republic, but here the figures of the 5000 Gamalani and the 960 Jews at Massada count heavily. But the period has also the highest score in cases, 255(202). They cover mainly the many suicides among the social elite of the Empire; many personal tragedies or epics have been recorded with full details. The ruin of the Senate as the counterbalance to the emperor's autocracy is symbolized in the numerous freely chosen deaths among the aristocracy. That is the reason why suicides on the orders of the princeps are mentioned and described by Tacitus and others with a certain eagerness.

Apart from the Late Republic and the Early Empire the distribution of cases over the other domains of antiquity does not require much explaining: the 250 years we reckon as the Archaic Period, which in our rough division comes after the Time of Myths and Heroes (1500–750 BC), have only a few cases, namely 38(18) regarding 44(20) individuals. For this period there is simply not much material; the same factor is operative in the data for Early Rome and Early Republic[20]. The Classical Period, 500–334 BC, (Alexander starts on his campaign against Persia) shows in

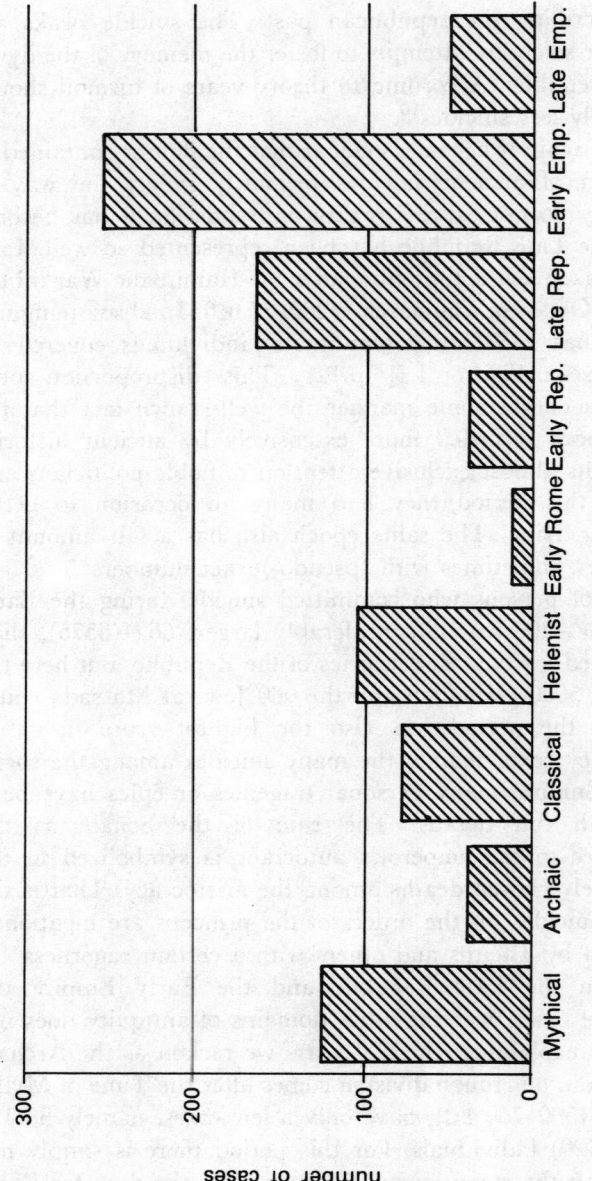

Figure 1.1 Distribution of datable cases over the periods of antiquity

conformity with the richer sources somewhat more instances: 78(54) cases with 74(50) individuals. For the era of Hellenism[21], 334–27 BC (the end of Ptolemaic Egypt and the establishing of Augustus' monarchy), 105(59) cases have been attested with 95(50) individuals. When comparison is made over time this result does not indicate a growth in suicide rates, neither absolutely nor in the recording.

Does the meagre revenue of the investigations into the Later Roman Empire (from 200 AD) have any meaning apart from a confirmation of the well-known fact that the richest category of source material, historiography, is not so well represented? There are 51(41) cases regarding 71(61) individuals. A complementary explanation can be that discretion has grown. During that period we notice a shifting of attitudes, especially among the intellectual elite. This change in mentality, which is prepared for by Neo-Platonic abhorrence, accounts for the development of the idea of suicide as murder of the self among Christian theologians; even some stories of martyrs have been adapted as compared with the primary versions in order to free the saints of all suspicion of self-murder[22].

So Figure 1 mainly depicts the availability of sources and the attention they pay to the phenomenon of self-killing. The surprisingly high first column that stands for mythical cases asks for some explanation. Suicides occurring in the mythical sphere are regarded by antiquity as happening in the olden days. But in fact they are above any time: mythology is the mental universe of the ancient world. Wherever it is possible to follow the development of a myth the interaction becomes apparent between the reality of contemporary society and the world of fiction constituted by myth. Myth is a very pliable medium[23]. A concrete example of adaptation is to be found in the replacement of the Greek rope by the Roman sword in the stories of Iokaste and Phaidra. By its nature mythical material belongs to the sphere of 'mentality'. It will be specifically discussed in connection with tragedy, but it is present under many headings in this study, because it furnishes us with insights on several topics. No mythical suicide can be classified as real; the story of Arachne who hanged herself because of the destruction of her fabric by the enraged Athena was not told primarily to record a suicide. We would get entangled in 'Homeric questions' if we tried to establish the truth of Ajax's self-killing. But the evolution of the evaluation of the self-destruction by this hero reflects changing attitudes in the course of many centuries. In the same respect the well documented self-burning of Heracles is a valuable track in the history of ancient suicide.

Therefore it is impossible to put hard figures between brackets behind the numbers for the section 'myth-epic'. The extent of the file reflects the fact that myth is the domain where the ancient world comes to grips with essential problems like suicide: in numbers only the historical periods of Late Republic and Early Empire surpass the mythical 'era'. In this study 125 cases of mythical suicides have been incorporated in which 130 individuals were involved, including Erigone's dog Maira. The mythical cases are highly valuable as they explore ancient attitudes: they represent excessive behaviour which clarifies human codes.

The many cases that were recorded for the Late Republic and Early Empire are exemplary of a different aspect: they demonstrate what is expected of the aristocrat when put to the final test. Of course they constitute the tip of the suicidal iceberg and it is evident that we should always be aware of the mechanisms of ancient perception, but on the other hand they disclose the values which regulated ancient suicidal behaviour: in many respects the tip of the iceberg represents the whole.

It has turned out that the grouping of figures according to periods disclosed rather the nature of attention than the frequency of suicide. What will come out if we no longer compare eras, but turn to larger entities? In the second part of this section I.1, which treats the phenomena, we will look for specific features of certain groups, such as sexes, classes, age-groups and, first of all, cultures.

D BARBARIANS, GREEKS, ROMANS

'Barbarian' cases are only a small part of all the instances: 113(93). But in this 12 per cent of the cases are included no fewer than 6431(6412) individuals, by far the majority of all countable persons (Appendix B 4a). The figures are heavily influenced by the exact number of 5000 for the inhabitants of Gamala, the 960 Jews who killed themselves in Massada and 300 wives of the Teutones. The first two figures were recorded by Flavius Josephus, who wished to demonstrate the extent of the Jewish catastrophe. Other 'exact' figures were recorded by historians who looked upon the self-destruction by barbarians from the point of view of Graeco-Roman civilization; as argued before, their records give more evidence about the society which is looking on, than about the culture outside the *oikoumene* being observed.

More reflection is necessary on the discrepancies between Greek and Roman data. The difference between the numbers of recorded cases is not dramatic: 403 Greek and 444 Roman. But if we purge the Greek material of all 'soft' cases, i.e. the attempts, the fictional accounts in novel and myth, the picture changes: only 137 hard Greek cases remain against no fewer than 334 real Roman ones. On a closer look we can account for these marked differences. Roman cases have mainly been recorded by historiographers who by profession claim to describe reality[24]. Greek sources comprise much more differentiated material: apart from historiography and biography with their pretensions to truth many cases are furnished by epic, tragedy, comedy and novel; in coming to grips with the various styles of self-killing these genres are in many respects richer than historiography which concentrates on the behaviour of the elite.

During the Late Republic and the Early Empire committing suicide becomes something of a moral duty for the nobleman who loses face or the favour of the emperor. The ritual scenes are duly recorded by the historian of that age. Tacitus' literary talent prevents the descriptions from becoming wearying to the reader's mind (*animum fatigant*) as he feared they would do. He uses all the registers of language and style to convince his readers that 'in a continuous slaughter' (*caede continua*) the senatorial elite destroyed itself by order of the emperor. Simple counting proves that it is not just Tacitus' powers of description that leave an unforgettable impression. In no fewer than 85 cases he is the primary source, i.e. the first to inform us or – in some cases – the writer who has the most detailed description[25]: 85 cases is about 9 per cent of all the instances on which this study has been based. A century later Cassius Dio writes the history of the Early Empire with more detachment, more 'without grudge and prejudice' (*sine ira et studio*). He has at his disposal far fewer stylistic means; the only way in which he tries to emulate Tacitean variety is by using new expressions to denote the act: dying 'own-handedly', voluntarily, willing, by free choice (*autocheiriai, ethelontes, hekontos, ethelontedon, hekon apothneiskein*)[26]. But he too is part of a Roman tradition that had attention only for the suicide of aristocrats who saved their honour by using weapons against themselves. The Greek material is more variegated and more evenly distributed over different

15

genres. Therefore they record far fewer authentic cases, but on the other hand, by the sheer fact of their variety, they probably reflect social reality better. This applies for instance to the frequency of hanging as a method. Paradoxical as it may sound, fiction is often more realistic than historical record.

In one respect Greek and Roman authors share the selective perception. They disregard suicide among common people, the first of the social groups that deserve a closer look.

E THE LOWER CLASSES SHOW THE WAY OUT

There is general consensus among suicidologists that self-killing occurs more often both at the top and the bottom of society than in the middle-class. Psycho-analytic theory has an explanation for a higher frequency among the upper classes. It sees self-killing as an act of aggression that is directed inwards. Members of the elite resort to self-destruction because they can attribute failure solely to themselves (people of the lower strata can hold those on top of them responsible for their reverses; their pent-up rage may find an outlet in murder). This psychological approach (by Henry and Short, 1954) arrives at the same conclusions as the macro-sociological perspective of the *fin-de-siècle*. Durkheim was convinced that suicide most afflicted 'les classes les plus cultivées et les plus aisées'. Also the ancient world took little notice of self-killing among the common people. But recent studies indicate that the lower classes are not behind the people in the most prestigious occupations with respect to suicide. Do we find some traces of a similar situation in the ancient world?[27]

Prisoners of war and slaves who took their own life in order to escape misery on the whole remained nameless. In AD 133 during one of the numerous dirty wars Rome waged on the Iberian peninsula, Spaniards who had fallen into the hands of the victors could not bear the outrage. In AD 393 twenty-nine Saxon gladiators ingeniously broke their necks without resorting to the rope; they did not wish to die ignominiously in the Eternal City confirming the Roman 'Herrenvolk' in its feeling of superiority[28]. Their refusal to play the game was very painful to Symmachus, who was in charge of the show. In a letter, however, he exhorts himself to bear the blow with Socratic endurance. Barbarians in captivity aroused in Seneca a certain respect by their *audacia*. Some reluctant fighters of Germanic origin preferred an exit from life above a triumphal 'Einzug der Gladiatoren'.

Seneca often chooses extreme situations to explore the scope of the Stoic attitude to life[29]. A beastfighter furnishes him with an example of a common man who behaved audaciously. For a moment he retired to a closet; it was the only chance for privacy offered to him. He took the stick with the sponge attached to it which was in collective use for cleaning the anus, and thrust it down his throat. Seneca calls him a 'tough man' (*virum fortem*). He gets a place among the men of lowest position (*vilissimae sortis homines*) who achieved a release from life with 'enormous energy' (*Letters* 70,19). In this way the Germanic *bestiarius* was included in the *exempla* of impetuosity[30]. They confirm Seneca's thesis 'where there is a will, there is a way out' (*Nihil obstat erumpere et exire cupienti*).

Along these lines people of the 'vilest' status only emerge when an observer needs them to make a specific point. Anonymity is the rule in the category of self-murderers with low status. In 87 cases I have established the status of the suicide as low. These 87 'sordid examples' (Seneca, *Letters* 70,22) are less than ten per cent of the corpus of cases (960); however, they comprise a considerable part of individuals who can be counted: 2491 out of the 9639, which is the total number of countable persons. This impressive number of 2491 'humble' suicides is based on the few cases where a figure is given for victims. In most instances, as we saw, the sources only use indefinite numerals: a few, some, several, many, etc.

So it is clear that collective suicide is dominant among the cases of 'vulgar' suicides. Groups of self-murderers consist of loyal eunuchs, soldiers and the plebeians who refused to work on Tarquinius Priscus' cloacae[31], beleaguered barbarians and run-away or rebellious slaves. In AD 104 Sicily's revolting fugitive slaves came into the hands of the Roman troops as a result of treason; they escaped into death. No specific figure is given. There are some neat ciphers: 1000 soldiers at Opitergium who remained loyal to Caesar till death. Another 1000 were comrades of Satyrus; they refused to die as gladiators and slaughtered each other on the public altars. Those 2000 added to the 400 Roman soldiers who in AD 28 slew themselves with 'reciprocal stabs' to escape the Frisians, give a basis of 2400 persons to the figure 2491 for individual self-murderers of low status: the figures are to be found in Appendix B 9. (To avoid unnecessary overloading with notes in this book, which by its nature has many references, from now on the reader will not be referred to the appendices on every occasion: when names of suicides are mentioned they can be found in Appendix A. Appendix B presents the figures and percentages, and Greek and Roman words relating to self-destruction are listed in Appendix C.)

The authors of antiquity who write for an elite readership raise from anonymity only those self-killers of low status who have some exemplary value. Demonstration of moving loyalty to a leader or master in particular makes it worthy of being included in the annals. Thus the female slaves Charmion and Eiras die together with Cleopatra their queen. It is noticeable that before the period of Hellenism no cases of 'servile' self-killing are attested; was there no need to ideologize about the fidelity of slaves in ages in which slavery was not so strikingly prevalent?

Fides, loyalty, and *devotio* are virtues of servants. Among subordinates loyalty till death generally does not have an abstract object like the fatherland. In almost all cases there is a personal relationship in which the lesser partner sacrifices himself on behalf of the master. In the military sphere examples of fidelity are noticeably concentrated in the Year of the Four Emperors (AD 68–9). One centurion, Sempronius Densus, plunged into the rebellious mass and in this way distracted attention from Piso (Lucius Licinianus). By this behaviour the 'noble hero' – Tacitus' predicate – performed in an exemplary way the duty which was allocated to him by Galba the emperor: he had to protect the successor designate. For the moment Piso was safe, but later he was produced from his hiding place, the temple of Vesta, and slaughtered in front of the temple (by a Briton who only recently had become a Roman citizen and by his act satisfyingly demonstrated his lack of civilization). In the eyes of Tacitus this case of self-sacrifice by a centurion of the praetorian guard was an encouraging sign that even his own time, *aetas nostra*, was not completely devoid of old Roman *virtus*. Sadly it had to be the *humiles* who taught the old nobility this lesson.

Otho, Galba's short-lived successor, also received proof of loyalty to death. Next to his pyre some soldiers slew themselves 'not because of any fault or from fear, but prompted by a desire to imitate his glorious example and moved by affection (*caritate*) for the princeps.' Otho did not have to wait until death to elicit exemplary deeds of loyalty; both Suetonius and Plutarch tell the story of the messenger who came to announce the defeat of Bedriacum, but was not believed. He was even suspected of desertion, whereupon he fell on his sword at the emperor's feet. According to Plutarch his last words were: 'Know, O Caesar, that all of us stand in this fashion at thy side'[32].

There is some repetition both in history and historiography in treatment of that year of crises; not every author attributes the same anecdotes to the same pretender. It seems that Plutarch picked up the fine last message of Otho's faithful courier from a scene Tacitus ascribes to a centurion of Vitellius, the third emperor in the series of ephemeral *principes*. After the defeat of Cremona this leader refused to face the reality of a situation which was not completely desperate, but 'by foolish dissimulation delayed the remedies for his misfortunes rather than the misfortunes themselves'. Only Tacitus mentions by name the centurion who put an emperor to shame. He was Iulius Agrestis. After much pleading he was allowed to inspect the situation in Cremona. Reporting his findings he was not believed by Vitellius, who preferred to dissimulate the truth and even accused him of having been corrupted. Then Agrestis spoke: 'Since I must give you a convincing proof of my statements, and you can have no other advantage from my life or death, I will give you evidence that will make you believe me'. With these words he left the emperor's presence, and made good his words by suicide (*voluntaria morte dicta firmavit*)[33].

It was not only the military and other males who made themselves a name by self-sacrifice. A humble woman also put aristocrats to shame: Epicharis remained loyal to (Caius) Piso who had been the centre of a plot against Nero, whereas the other conspirators tried to save themselves by betraying comrades. During the first round of torture she had remained silent. On the next day, as she was being dragged back in a chair to a repetition of her agony – her dislocated limbs were unable to support her – she fastened the breast-band (which she had stripped from her bosom) in a sort of noose to the canopy of the chair, thrust her neck into it, and, throwing the weight of her body into the effort, squeezed out such feeble breath as remained to her.

Her example shone the brighter while she, an emancipated slave and a woman at that, under this dire coercion shielded men unconnected with her and all but unknown, whereas persons freeborn and male, Roman knights and senators, untouched by the torture, were betraying each his nearest and dearest.

Tacitus stresses the circumstance that it was a lowly woman who accomplished this noble deed. Without a noble motive self-hanging by common women is merely ridiculous. What Diogenes the philosopher saw may have been a familiar spectacle in ancient cities. Seeing some women hanged from an olive-tree, he said 'Would that every tree bore similar fruit'. Probably these were not gentlewomen who afforded to the Cynic this satisfactory sight ('hanging women', *feminae pendentes* in Appendix A[34]).

Roman law explicitly pays attention to suicide among slaves; the legal aspects deserve to be treated separately (see II.5.B). Here it suffices to establish the fact that self-killing among slaves as a way of escape was so frequent that it attracted attention by jurists.

Like Tacitus Seneca looks for *exempla* in the underworld of society. We have already quoted from his seventieth letter to Lucilius which gives some shocking instances of audacity by common individuals such as unwilling gladiators. In spite of their infamy they confirm his point that there is always a way out of life if one needs it. The meanest slaves gather strength in cases of unbearable bodily suffering and they outwit their guards in finding an opportunity for dying[35]. Will those who by their noble souls are obliged to outdo the common man falter in choosing death in the face of the inevitable? Thus Seneca and Tacitus exploit suicide by humble people to underline their message to the elite.

Ancient drama plays upon a more general attitude among the public. Time and again the plot depicts slaves in desperate situations; promptly the idea of suicide comes into their minds, a reaction which is intended to be recognizable and as such to raise laughter. There is even opportunity for special fun: Staphyla contemplates making herself a capital letter 'I', a metonymy for hanging. Acroteleutium threatens to kill herself if 'he' is unwilling to marry her[36].

Ideological and dramatic exploitation of suicide among humble people once again makes it clear that self-killing was common in all classes of ancient society. But in the materials handed down to us, upper-class males dominate the scene; they are the bulk of the individual cases where the victims have a name. The unhappy few of the elite are of course only the tip of the iceberg of suicide.

Beneath there is the great mass of anonymous desperate people. Similar selection accounts for the under-representation of women.

F *VIRTUS* OF WOMEN

Women are strikingly well represented in the mythical material: there are 71 cases of female suicide against 51 male ones in the world of myth, or, when we count only the number of individuals who according to the tales actually put an end to their lives, we have 56 women and 37 men[37]. That sex ratio is not a reflection of reality. It is more the case that myth is the medium through which the more problematical nature of female existence is handled. So only in this limited sense is Steiner right in ascribing 'an aura of the feminine' to ancient sensibility with respect to suicide[38]. Sometimes the mythical woman who kills herself confirms the specific values for which she stands. The life of man is less problematic; that is the reason why male suicide is less represented in mythology.

In its selective perception the Roman material constitutes the opposite of myth: in every respect it is characterized – also with regard to motives and means – by *virtus* in its essential meaning of manliness. The number of suicides shows a big preponderance of men: 358(269) cases of male self-killings against 69(48) female ones, a ratio of 5:1 (Appendix B 10a). With respect to individuals the disproportion is unbelievably great: there are 1727(1643) countable men against 88(69) women who destroy themselves, which means a ratio of 20:1, even 24:1 if only the hard figures are considered. In fact the situation is even less 'favourable' for female suicide among the Romans when we realize that Roman collective suicide of unknown numbers is mainly furnished by soldiers. It is more than evident that Roman perception focuses on men in their 'moment suprême'. When we look at motivation the selective perception also appears. Even the few Roman women whose self-killing is recorded are said to have demonstrated manly qualities. According to Valerius Maximus (6.1.1) in the case of Lucretia there had been implanted a male soul into a female body by a freak of nature. Only in this way could the editor of the lexicon of *Memorable Facts and Sayings* account for her noble suicide.

The Roman numbers cannot be the reflection of reality; in all older societies women fall behind men – solely in the Western world have women almost emancipated themselves in this respect –

but never in such a dramatic way as the Roman figures suggest. Only a century ago the ratios for male to female suicide were 4:1 in France and 3:1 in England[39]. In non-Western societies the ratios given vary between 2:1 and 8:1. These proportions are reported from West Nigeria, Rhodesia/Zimbabwe and Uganda. A study of a limited number of medieval cases establishes a ratio of 3:1[40]. For lack of more historical studies these numbers must figure as an indication of the situation in pre-industrial societies. For the whole of the material – Greek, Roman, barbarian (as observed by the ancients) – the ratio is in line with the African numbers; in 683(429) cases men are the suicides, in 229(91) women, which gives a ratio of 3:1(5:1). A summation of countable individuals gives 3117(1883) men against 555(412) women: 6:1(5:1). Because of the disproportion in the data for the Romans, the Greek figures deserve a closer look.

They are based on diverse literary genres; historiography is far less dominant than in the Roman material. In the Greek sphere the record is 246(95) cases of male suicide against 143(33) female ones. At first sight the numbers between brackets are most significant, because they are 'immune' from the rich fiction in myth, epic, tragedy, comedy, epigram and novel. They give a ratio for men against women of 3:1. But as will become clear in this study, in many respects fiction is more true than the filtered material of the realistic genres; the 'unpurified' numbers of 246 male against 143 female self-killings have also a claim to trustworthiness[41].

The Greek figures may be indicative of the real situation: they fit well in a pattern which emerges from pre-industrial societies with respect to the rate of male and female suicide. When we come to discuss the ancient means and motives in I.2 and I.3 we will regularly compare the behaviour of men and women and confront the findings with what is known about the pre-modern world.

G VIRGINS AS A RISK GROUP

Did the condition of women's life in Greece indeed elicit more self-killings or had the Hellenes more empathy with females, even up to the point of understanding *autothanasia*? Both hypotheses can be supported by evidence. In the writings which have come to us under the name of Hippocrates there is a short text 'About maidens' (*Peri parthenion*). Arguing from medical *practice* the ancient doctor establishes the fact that women hang themselves more often than men. Women, he explains, are more sensitive to delusions. Their nature is known to be more 'little-minded' (*athumotere kai ologotere*). Among females girls especially are a risk-group; their virginity stands in the way of fulfilling the feminine fate; women are 'Bound to bleed'[42]. Not finding a complete exit blood accumulates near the heart and the diaphragm. Because of the pressure exercised on these vital organs a fatal sombreness takes possession of the *parthenia*; they feel the inclination to hang themselves or to jump from heights and in general they are fascinated by death. This diagnosis points the way to the therapeutic advice: 'Whenever girls suffer from these affects I recommend (*keleuo*) them to live with men as soon as possible'.

Such a physiological interpretation is essentially Greek. In as far as ancient science generalizes about human behaviour the causes are sought in the nature of the body; the predominance of one fluid causes people to be melancholic or phlegmatic. Blood which cannot flow in accordance with the female destiny may darken the mind. A modern interpretation of the phenomena observed by writers of the corpus Hippocraticum will stress the fears which must have dominated the life of girls in antiquity.

On rare occasions ancient onlookers show a certain awareness. In one epigram a (male) poet expresses his empathy with the fate of girls. While boys enjoy a social life girls must sit at home; 'we on the contrary are not even allowed to see the daylight, but are kept hidden in our chambers, the prey of sombre thoughts'[43]. The great event in female life was marriage. Only then could the girl fulfil herself as a *gyne*. There is more to it than just evoking compassion among the public when in a tragedy Antigone or Elektra complains or is complained of for never having children. They will remain a 'femme manquée'. About 540 BC Phrasikleia says in an epitaph:

I will always be called a virgin[44].

Tensions could arise if a marriage was impossible, for instance because the household could not afford a dowry[45]. Marriage was the only occasion in woman's life when she was 'seen' by the polis. At her transition from the *oikos* of her father to that of her groom she appeared in public for a moment. The transfer from one family to another also meant a change in private cult; familiar family-gods were left behind for new ones. Many an edifying *exemplum* stresses the ideal of complete loyalty to the new *oikos* by the young woman. Such is the message of Euripides' *Alcestis*. Taken on its own the

story is undeniably rather bizarre and the drama has some
burlesque features: Admetus will not have to die on the destined
hour if somebody is willing to take his place. His old parents both
refuse, in an attachment to life which enrages Admetus. Without
hesitation he accepts the offer of his young wife. But after her death
he bursts into grotesque laments. What can life be after she has
passed away? On her side Alcestis is fully aware of her noble
sacrifice in order to save the *oikos* of her husband; in exemplifying
this loyalty the tragedy is absolutely serious. The parts of the play
where Alcestis, conscious of her dignity, makes preparations for her
end are free from the pleasantry which is present in Admetus'
words, for instance when he considers sharing his bed with a doll
made like Alcestis. Euripides does not specify her way of death; it
simply comes on the destined day[46].

Many an ancient woman must have been confronted with the
urgent question whether she would be able to identify herself with
the new *oikos* like Alcestis. Marriage meant the dignity of a *gyne*,
but also the irretrievable loss of the old identity. Fears of the
disclosure of the mysteries of sex may have contributed to a crisis.
One bride was devoured by watch-dogs as she fled the house in the
wedding-night 'dreading the first coupling of love'; such fear, the
poem says, is common among young girls[47]. Especially for girls
who entered married life at an early age the threshold of the new
oikos must have been dreadfully high. An example of the age of
marriage is furnished by Domitilla, one of the rare female self-
killers, whose suicide is attested in an epitaph. She was only
fourteen years and had already been married for seven months
when she killed herself in AD 262/3, to escape being raped by
Gothic invaders. Her parents glorify her death in the inscription:

> She did not fear death;
> preferred it above shameful violation[48].

Alcestis is not the only woman in myth who exemplifies loyalty to
the *oikos*. She is only special because of her devotion to the
household of her husband. The old stories often explore the values
of female life, which in general raises more problems than that of
males. In two cases however – Makaria and the daughters of
Antipoinos – females represent the importance of the polis by
sacrificing themselves; in this way they put to shame the man who is
expected to demonstrate this kind of communal behaviour. An oracle
had said that the noblest citizen of Thebes had to sacrifice himself.

The person qualified, Antipoinos, refused the honour, but then his daughters showed the standards expected of their family. When king Demophon of Athens was not willing to sacrifice his own child in order to assure victory in the war against the Argives, Heracles' daughter Makaria presented herself.

These acts of *devotio* to the community are the exceptions to the female code of behaviour which requires before all loyalty to one's own family. Selene mythically meets this standard by jumping from a height in grief for her brother's death. Erigone takes her own life having found her father dead. Phyllis hangs herself believing dead – wrongly as it turns out – her affianced (or young husband in other versions). And Oinone hangs herself when her beloved Paris is no more. This case already has 'romantic' traits: a young woman cannot exist without her lover. The woman left behind is unable to live on: Kallirhoe could not bear being deserted by Diomedes whom she had saved from her father (who conforming to Libyan customs used to sacrifice to Ares all the strangers washed ashore). It was love which caused Skylla to cut off her purple hair which was the guarantee of the safety of Megara when king Minos beleaguered the city. But the Cretan king sailed away leaving her and she jumped into the sea. There is even a version of the story of Theseus and Ariadne according to which the princess left behind on Naxos was not comforted by Dionysus, but hanged herself from grief. This reading, recorded by Plutarch in the second century AD, is a striking example of retelling and re-interpretation.

In those late versions of ancient stories romantic motives increase. Tradition had it that Polyxena was sacrificed on the grave of Achilles. This is the story which the mythographer Hyginus still tells. Therefore there is no place for her in his list of *Women who killed themselves*. But Philostratos the rhetor says that the Trojan princess stabbed herself at Achilles' tomb from unfulfilled love[49]. Such retouching within the frame of the old story bears the colour of the love-novels which became immensely popular in the Greek 'renaissance' of the second and third century AD. Myth remains a flexible genre up to the end of antiquity; as such it reflects changing values. Myths do not only codify woman's behaviour (which sometimes has to be confirmed by suicide), they also give specific information about methods and motives of self-killing. In not a few mythical stories which end in suicide the problem of sex inside the family is explored. The mythical answer to the question whether relations between father and daughter or brother and sister are permitted is negative without reserve; those stories where the taboo has been neglected have an unhappy ending. Byblis hanged herself, not being able to satisfy her love for her brother. Pelopeia killed herself having had intercourse with her father Thyestes. Harpalyke committed suicide having been violated by her father Klymenos. The myth of Kanake can be followed in its evolution. Homer tells without disapproval about the marriages of Aiolos' children, but Euripides sees incest: Kanake became pregnant by her brother Makareus. When their father Aiolos discovered the shame he sent her a sword which she used without hesitation in the tragedy. The story was popular in Nero's days as the theme of an opera. Kanake giving birth was the favourite role of the emperor who appalled the Roman aristocrats by appearing in person on the stage as this infamous character[50].

So ancient myth prescribes that a woman should leave the house of her childhood in order to fulfil herself as a *gyne* in another *oikos*. Stories about young women stress family virtues. The attention given to suicide which confirms female virtue, is in an indirect way an indication of the crisis which must often have happened in the life of a young woman; in this respect the evidence given from practice by a Hippocratic doctor and that furnished by myth are complementary. The interest in suicide among young females is shown by the fact that they are nearly as numerous as young males, with eighty-two against eighty-four cases. This is a remarkably high ratio in the light of the general under-representation of women.

H ANCIENT WERTHERS?

Were male adolescents a risk-group in the same way as the *parthenoi*? This question is related to the problem of youth in general. Was it a phase of life in its own right as Eyben holds or did the young always participate in society as younger versions of their adult counterparts?[51] A markedly higher frequency of self-killing among males at the threshold of adulthood would be a strong argument for the existence of youth as a special domain. Eyben mentions some cases, but in my view they lack the elements connected with problems of self-acceptance and fear of adult life.

Lucius Scribonius, Dolabella and Lucan the poet were *forced* to commit suicide in a very 'adult' way. It is debatable whether Dolabella and Lucan can be regarded as young[52]. The number of young male suicides cannot give an answer to the question what *proportion* they are of the whole of the material; only where there are clear indications of being young has a case been marked as such. Appendix B11 has 84(25) cases of male self-killing at an early age.

Among the 25 hard cases there is one occasion when the motive is shame at incest. Sextus Papinius had been forced by his mother into having intercourse. From shame he threw himself out of a window and in this way chose an 'infamous death'. For once we come across the pressing intimacy of the nuclear family which according to Stephen Kern could lead to suicide among children in Victorian England[53]. In general neither in reality nor in myth is incest a problem which causes suicide among males.

On the other hand the romantic motive of frustrated love leading to self-destruction is not exclusively a motive for women. Propertius complains that his beloved does not permit him to enter her house even after ten days waiting. Embittered he roams in the night and exclaims:

> Now gladly, impious maid, would I cast myself from
> some hard rock or take distilled poison into my hands[54].

In a pastoral Lycidas is described as contemplating hanging himself on the tree that was the witness of the treason by his beloved girl, whereas in a novel Chaireas makes several attempts at suicide in a row, wrongly believing that Kallirhoe is in love with Dionysios. Just in time he is untied from the noose, but then he draws his sword (which is duly wrested from him). Suicide because of frustrated (heterosexual) love was committed actually and historically, if we are to believe Plutarch, by one Straton. He tried to lay hands on Aristokleia, Kallisthenes' bride, by kidnapping her. The girl did not survive the action and then 'Straton slew himself in sight of all upon the body of the maiden'. (Kallisthenes had a sorry fate as well; he vanished without a trace. Maybe he too committed suicide, Plutarch comments.) Homosexual love could lead to a series of self-killings. Meles challenged his lover Timagoras to give proof of his passion by jumping from a rock. The *erastes* showed his love as he was asked. Then, too late, the *eromenos* realized that life was impossible without Timagoras and he jumped after his lover.

In cases like these the relation between youth and killing does not justify more than the plausible statement that young people are inclined to get entangled in erotic dramas. Other cases of suicide accomplished by youthful individuals demonstrate the willingness to sacrifice oneself for the well-being of the community – the motive of *devotio* – or shame over being humiliated[55]. Exemplary in this category is the Spartan slave of king Antigonos, a young person – if *pais* does not mean 'boy' in the sense of slave. He refused to do what was not becoming to a free man, fetching a chamber-pot, and he dashed out his brains against the wall. According to Seneca he explained the motive for his action by crying: 'I will not serve' (*non serviam*)[56]. Losing face in general is a major motive in recorded suicide for the ancient world. With respect to self-killing by the young one could say that they are more sensitive to being humiliated. One of Pythagoras' pupils could not bear being rebuked by the master in the presence of others. His suicide caused Pythagoras henceforth to make his criticisms privately.

Among the 'hard' cases there are no clear instances of Wertherian suicide. If we take into account attempts and contemplated attempts we come across the two specimens of intro/retrospection by Seneca and St Augustine. Both declare that on one occasion in their youth they were sick of life. Seneca suffered from asthmatic affliction, the bishop of Hippo confessed to having considered self-killing after losing his friend. Meditating self-destruction in cases of unbearable bodily suffering is a well-known phenomenon among men of advanced age. In this respect Seneca's motive falls in the category 'intolerable pain' (*inpatientia doloris*) and as such is not typical for youth. Also Augustine's grief over the loss of his 'soul's half' is only indirectly connected with his young age. It is just another way of saying that in antiquity too the young were more sensitive to friendship than the old, hardly a surprising claim.

In a society where the members of the elite had to prove themselves one would expect an accumulation of self-killings among young males afraid of not meeting expectations. Ancient, especially Roman, society ought to have a Japanese pattern of suicide with a first peak around the age of twenty. The high degree of integration which is required of Japanese youngsters is held responsible for the statistical peak at that age[57]. Such an apex does not become visible in our material. Unless there is a conspiracy of silence the conclusion must be that either the ancient world did not have an eye for that Wertherian motive or that age-specific reasons did not exist in a society where young gentlemen were smoothly introduced into the world of adults from their early years. The special clubs for the young and other forms of ancient scouting-for-boys were all directed at developing the skills and attitudes which were expected of a gentleman. The litmus-test of suicide appears to contradict the view that adolescence, at least for the elite, was a specific stage in life. The young in the lower strata of society could not indulge at all in what Sartre calls the bourgeois illness of youth[58].

A. Methods of the young in the 120 cases where these have been specified

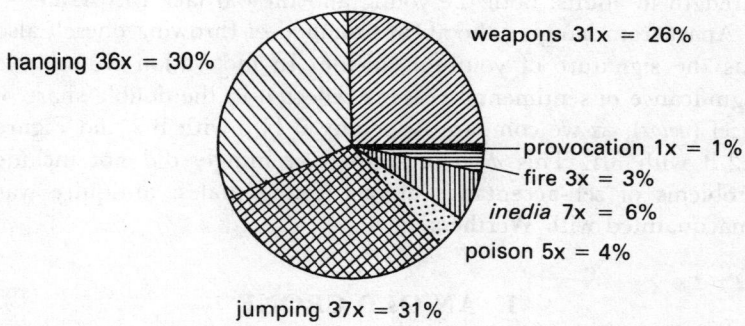

B. Motives of the young in the 153 cases where these have been specified

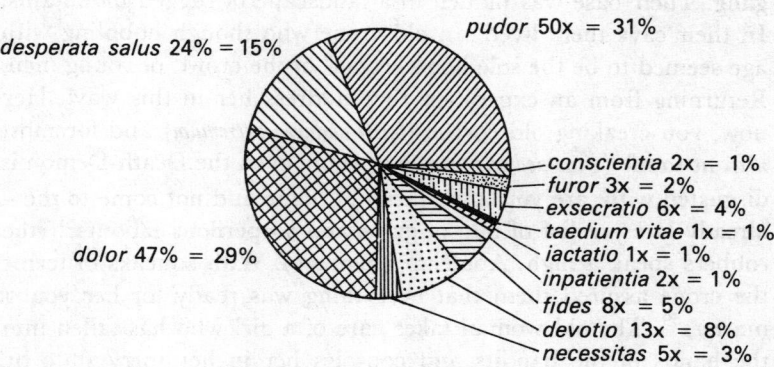

Figure 1.2 Methods and motives of the young; to be compared with Figure 2.1 (methods in general) and Figure 3.1 (motives in general)

Taken together young males and females show patterns of suicide which are different from the general trends. The figures of Appendix B 11 which refer to them are graphically pictured in Figure 1.2 A. Comparing them to the ciphers (Appendix B 11 b) and graphics (Figure 2.2) about methods in use, we see that jumping from heights and hanging are far more used by the young. A generalization by Aristotle runs parallel to our findings. The young, he says, make more use of the rope, as do the aged (as compared with middle-aged men). They do not yet possess the vital warmth which the old already have lost. That is the reason why they are liable to despondency, *athymia*. Aristotle has only a physiological explanation at his disposal: vital heat is the source of strength in adults; both the young and the old lack this flame.

Apart from hanging the abrupt method of throwing oneself also has the signature of youthful suicide. In motivation we see the significance of sentimental reasons reflected in the double share of grief (*dolor*), as we compare Appendix B 11 c with B 7 and Figure 1.2 B with 3.1. This *dolor* or despair seemingly did not include problems of self-acceptance among young males: antiquity was unacquainted with Werthers.

I AN OLD CRONE

To get acquainted with the feelings of ordinary people we need, lacking autobiographical documents, the empathy of the novelist. In his *Metamorphoses* Apuleius introduces his readers to a robber-gang. Their base was hidden in a landscape of rugged mountains. In their cave there lived 'an old crone who though hobbling with age seemed to be the sole housekeeper' of the crowd of young men. Returning from an expedition they address her in this way: 'Hey now, you creaking old corpse (*busti cadaver extremum*) and foremost affront to life (*vitae dedecus primum*), whom even the Death-Demon is disgusted with, are you to sit lazily at home and not come to the – already late – relief of our so great and so perilous labours?' (the robbers speak a high, Apuleian language). With squeaks of terror the crone assured them that everything was ready for her young masters[59]. The old woman takes care of a girl who has fallen into the hands of the bandits and consoles her in her sorry state by telling the charming tale of Cupid and Psyche. After an unlucky attempt to escape the girl and Lucius, the donkey who tells the story, return to the cave:

and there we found the old woman with a rope round her neck, hanging from the branch of a tall cypress. The thieves cut her down, and at once dragged her by her own rope to the cliff-edge, over which they tossed her. Then, putting the girl in chains, they wolfishly attacked the dinner which the hapless old woman had prepared for them – so that she still served them, dead as she was.   (*anus quaedam* in Appendix A)[60]

Self-killing by old women does not attract the attention of ancient authors. Old women are even less visible than women in general[61]. Out of thirteen cases only five are historical (Appendix B 12). The other eight are sacrificed by writers of fiction to the 'values' which an old woman represents, such as being the doormat of the young.

She appears as an old desperate slave in comedy and threatens to make a long letter of herself, in a wink to the public which is so literate that it knows the 'I' (p.20)[62]. The despairing old mothers of Habrokomes and Anthia, the pair of lovers in Xenophon's novel, understandably commit suicide when they believe their children dead, just as their husbands do. The ancient novel flourishes from the second century AD; it is not only there that sentimental reasons are presented as motives for suicidal behaviour. Ancient myths too acquire a touch of sensitivity. Odysseus' mother Eurykleia becomes one of the 'women who killed themselves' in Hyginus. According to the mythographer she ended her life on hearing the (false) news of her son's death.

Euripides is known for his ability to penetrate into the souls of women. In his tragedies many a woman contemplates suicide or commits the deed. His Leda is so struck by the misconduct of her daughter Helen that she puts an end to her life. Phaidra's old nurse contemplates jumping from a height on hearing from her ex-suckling the terrible confession of her shameful passion for Hippolytos her stepson:

> Woe, child! What wilt thou say? Thou hast dealt me death!
> Friends, 'tis past bearing. I will not endure
> To live. O hateful life, loathed light to see!
> I'll cast away, yield up, my frame, be rid
> Of life by death! Farewell, I am no more.
>
>   (*Hippolytus* 353–7)

Sentimental reasons for self-killing among the few women who have been recorded in history, can only be found in the aged mother of Darius III. During her captivity she had been treated with great respect by Alexander the Great. When, after she had lost so much in her life, her protector finally died in 323 BC, Sisyngambris put an end to her life because of the death of this substitute son and her own desolation (*eremia*). Here we have the sole instance of the 'empty-nest-effect' which in modern times is held responsible for quite a lot of suicides among the old.

Apart from this one case the motives attributed in the historical cases are not comparable with modern motivating forces. Caligula brought the old Antonia 'to the necessity of a free death' on 1 May AD 37 (for once Cassius Dio produces a Tacitean oxymoron). Being compelled to commit suicide is not a fate reserved exclusively for old women. Also the self-killing by the elderly Christian Apollonia has nothing to do with old age as such. In AD 250, during Decius' persecution, she tore herself free from the soldiers and jumped into the fire. A woman of more than ninety on the island of Keos is said to have followed local tradition, which prescribed self-killing by the aged. She could not be dissuaded from demonstrating the island's folklore to Sextus Pompeius. Valerius Maximus describes the event as an eyewitness in his *Memorable Facts and Sayings*. She expressed her gratitude for the presence of Pompeius who permitted her to put into practice her 'last resolution' (*ultimum propositum*). She distributed her legacy, exhorted her family to unanimity, charged her oldest daughter – as she had no sons – with the care of her memory and the holy objects of the house and 'she took with a firm hand the beaker, in which the poison had been mixed'. She made libations to Mercury and invoked his divine protection for a safe passage to the best part of the underworld. Then she eagerly took a draught and described which parts were affected in turn by progressive numbness. As she said that it was nearing her belly and heart, she asked the hands of her daughters to render the last service of closing her eyes. 'She made us Romans leave, however, stunned as we were by the unprecedented spectacle, streaming with tears'[63].

The last historical and aged female self-killer is Julia Domna, a royal woman who could only conceive of living as an empress. When her son Caracalla had been deposed and killed, she could not bear to live on as a private person, although Macrinus the new emperor assured her of his respect. The Augusta made it clear even by the chosen means that she was determined to end an intolerable situation: she refused food[64]. This method of perseverance, Greek *apokarteria*, or *inedia* (Latin) is typical of aged men who deliberately seek death.

J FAILING POWERS AND RESOLUTION AMONG OLD MEN

Old men are far more frequent in the corpus of self-killings than old women. This conclusion holds not only for the sum of 74 cases, but also the hard nucleus of historic cases has some significance: 49. So they are the ones who determine the patterns of suicide among the old, regardless of sex, as shown in Appendix B 12 and Figure 1.3.

Old men are in the first place distinguished by the method of fasting to death. In 18 out of the 61 cases where a means is recorded this harsh method has been used. Metal instruments of self-destruction like sword, dagger or scalpel are in second place for this age group, whereas for the whole of the recorded cases they are by far the most popular medium in antiquity.

Inedia is a method which gives proof of determination and perseverance; it is the way of the *endura* the Cathars take in Montaillou after the sacrament of the *consolamentum*[65]. In the same vein the ancient *senes* accept the battle with their own bodily needs and the pressure of their environment. This preferred means does not only make it clear that the deed is done in full possession of the mental faculties. The motives of the old men also belong to the highest categories. With them it is not sudden despair or grief because of a lost partner that is the cause of their *ultimum propositum*. Only myth speaks of Aigeus' desperate jump into the still anonymous sea when he saw Theseus' ships returning from Crete with sinister black sails. Iphis, another mythical old man, was so shocked by his daughter's suicide that he resolved to starve himself. Historically there are only four cases at the most where grief is given as a reason. Gordianus the elder, an ephemeral emperor, is to the writer of his *vita* the opposite of a real Roman imperator. He learned of his son's death 'and because in the end the struggle had wearied him in mind and soul, he took a rope and hanged himself'. His infamous end confirmed the baseness of his character[66].

The predominating pattern of self-killing among old men is that of people who prove themselves in the end both in method and motive. The fact that aged aristocrats are relatively numerous in the sources of course has to do with the mechanisms of selection which I have already plentifully indicated. But there is also a demographic reality operative. The proles of antiquity did not grow old. The differences in expectation of life which in modern industrial society can be as high as five to ten years as compared with white-collar workers, must have been even more dramatic in antiquity.

One experience of Seneca exemplifies this disproportion: 'Wherever I turn, I see evidence of my advancing years,' such is the beginning of the twelfth letter to Lucilius. He saw signs of decay when he visited his country-place. The house which grew under his own hands was in need of repair. Plane-trees he had planted personally were in a sorry state. The bailiff excused the situation of the building and the tree as the effects of time.

> Then I turned to the door and asked: 'Who is that broken-down dotard? You have done well to place him at the entrance; for he is on his way out. Where did you get him? What pleasure did it give you to take up for burial some other man's dead?' But the slave said: 'Don't you know me, sir? I am Felicio; you used to bring me little dolls. My father was Philositus the steward, and I am your pet slave.' 'The man is clean crazy,' I remarked. 'Has my pet slave become a little boy again? But it is quite possible; his teeth are just dropping out.'
>
> Seneca, *Letters*, 12.3.

Felicio must have been a winsome toddler when he enjoyed the favour of his young master Seneca. The latter meets him again after many years when Felicio's life is nearing its end. Of course the self-centred Stoic writer has eyes only for his own sorry fate, but the difference in the pace of aging, which implicitly is brought out, is striking.

Suicides by old men from the lower orders occur in Hellenistic epigrams as part of a literary game, a playing with the possibilities of empathy. In general Hellenistic culture is characterized by a need to explore extremes of human existence, often aiming to shock by the presentation of horrible images, but sometimes there is authentic identification with individuals who are not 'our kind'. Apart from caricatures plastic art for the first time shows simple but worthy old men and women. Hellenistic poetry tries to evoke the life of plain old people. The epigram which in its form often is still an epitaph is very suitable for such a literary game. Gorgos could only exist by being supported by a stick. He asked himself what would be the sense of living on for three or four summers more – one recognizes the picture of an old Mediterranean man sitting before his cabin. Without much ado 'he kicked the old life away'. Another old man in one of the poems known as the *Greek Anthology* remains anonymous. He was without any support in his misery. He crept into a recently dug grave and had himself buried alive:

> Worn by age and poverty, no one stretching out his hand to relieve my misery, on my tottering legs I went slowly to my grave, scarce able to reach the end of my wretched life. In my case the law of death was reversed, for I did not die first to be then buried, but I died after my burial (*senex quidam*).

A. Methods used by old people in the 61 cases where these have been specified

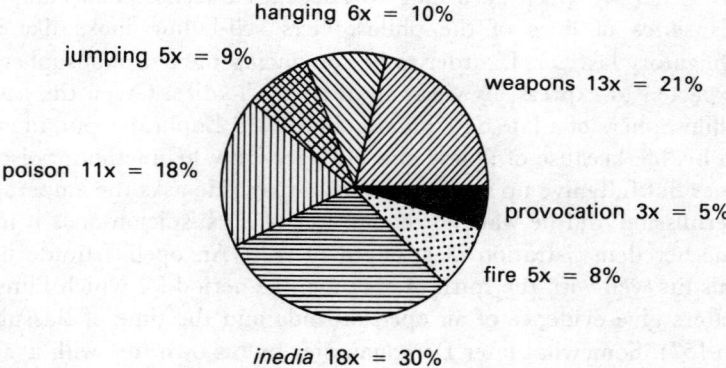

B. Motives of old people in the 87 cases where these have been specified

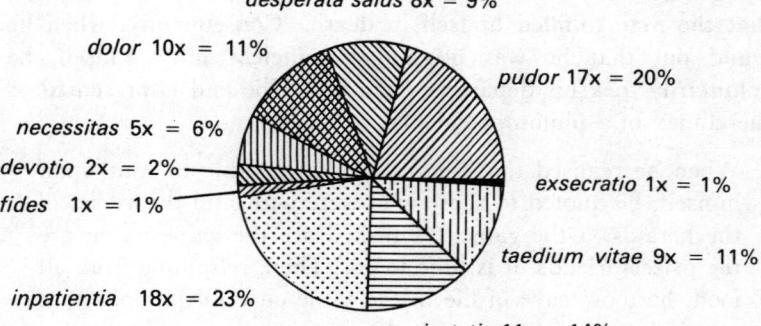

Figure 1.3 Methods and motives of the old; to be compared with Figure 2.1 (methods in general) and Figure 3.1 (motives in general)

Thus, for one moment we have a glimpse into the abyss which life for old people without means was in antiquity. Poetic imagination can feast itself on exotic customs. In one epigram the dead Philaulos is being interviewed: what was the cause of his death? 'Voluntarily I went to Hades by tasting the Cean cups'[67].

The old survivors from the elite who finally committed suicide did not have recourse to the Cean Custom (*Keion nomimon*) in their determination to put an end to their existence. As the bearers of the highest values they knew how to prove themselves to the end. For the Greek world self-killing is attributed to a series of old intellectuals: Pythagoras at the age of 82, Anaxagoras 72, Empedokles 60, Speusippos 68, Diogenes 80, Aristotle 62, Epicurus 71, Zeno the Stoic 72, Dionysios circa 80, Kleanthes 72. These ages are generally given according to Diogenes Laertios. Especially in his series of lives of the philosophers self-killing looks like an obligatory last act. In order to be convincing the old philosopher is expected to express his views by the way he dies. Given the *topos*, philosophers of a late date join in. In AD 119 Euphrates put an end to his life because of illness and old age. Only his method, poison, does not fully live up to the noble examples. He asks the emperor's permission; did he want to remain free of all suspicion or is it just another demonstration of strength of will? An open attitude like this fits well with the spirit of his time, the period for which Pliny's letters give evidence of an open attitude and the time of Bassulus (p.153). Somewhat later Demonax dies by his own free will, at the age of 100. His biography is one of the rare books by Lucian where the great mocker is completely serious. There is no trace of the usual debunking or sarcasm when the life of the beloved master is being described. Already in the introduction (4) it is made clear that the man fulfilled himself in death. 'Consequently, when he found out that he was no longer sufficient unto himself, he voluntarily took his departure from life.' The end is presented as the climax of a philosophical life.

> When he realised that he was no longer able to wait upon himself, he quoted to those who were with him the verses of the heralds at the games: 'Finished are the games; won are the prizes; friends, it is time to go.' Then, refraining from all food, he took leave of life in the same cheerful humour that people he met always saw in him[65].

Self-killings like these, committed by wise old men from the

36

upper classes, can be looked upon as cases of stylish euthanasia[68]: not much comfort could be offered by the ancient doctor if he stuck to the Hippocratic rules. The self-help of the old philosophers could be unmasked as the cowardly avoidance of pain. Here is a problem which plays its part in Seneca's writings. But there are self-killings by old people which undoubtedly demonstrate a mind philosophical till death. This pattern of suicide gets official recognition from Roman law which among other excusable grounds for self-killing mentions explicitly 'exhibition (*iactatio*) as shown by some philosophers'[69]. Empedokles made such a display of his suicide: he jumped into Etna in order not to leave any mortal remains. This is the accepted version as given by Diogenes Laertios. But he alludes to some debate about Empedokles' way of dying; thus it becomes apparent how decisive the means of suicide was. Was it certain that it was not an unfortunate fall into the crater? One reading indicated that Empedokles had fallen from a cart. Another spokesman knew for certain that he had burned himself to death ostentatiously. The extreme was Demetrios of Troizen; he cut the conceited philosopher down to size by stating that Empedokles had hanged himself on a cornel-tree, an infamous death on a sinister tree[70].

Jumping into Etna remained a unique exit. One would expect a role for self-burning in the arsenal of suicidal means in antiquity: as the most provocative method it would fit into the pattern of exhibitionism. Modern times have seen the demonstrative public self-burnings of Jan Palach in Czechoslovakia in 1968 and of Buddhist monks during the Vietnamese war. Explicit instances of such well-considered demonstrations are lacking in the Greek and Roman material. Peregrinos the pseudo-prophet is mocked by Lucian for his Heraclean death-show. Indian sages struck the Mediterranean world by their ostentatious scorn for life. Alexander's army experienced such a culture-shock when Karanos, aged seventy-three, sat down on a pyre; the pleas that he should not do it, also put forward by the conqueror of the world, were in vain. The spectators looked on the scene with different eyes: for some it was sheer madness (*mania*), for others a 'senseless show of perseverance'. But a few of those present admired the nobility of soul (*eupsychia*) and the scorn for death. Alexander bridged the gap between Greeks and Indians by holding a festival consisting of a competition in music, horsemanship and athletics. To satisfy the Indians he added also a local sport to the games: a competition in wine-drinking where a prize of one talent was put up for the winner and considerable sums of money for the second and third[71].

A similar variety of reactions was elicited by the voluntary burning to death of Zarmaros. This Indian needed a public too: he died in Athens before Augustus' eyes 'either from ambition or from ostentation'. Another source, which gives his name as Zarmanochegas, mentions his epitaph: 'Zarmanochegas the Indian from Bargysa rests here having eternalized himself in accordance with the ancestral customs of the Indians.' Athens gratefully exploited the attraction[72].

Death by fire is exotic for other age groups as well, as will become clear in the section on methods. As such death by self-burning is appreciated like other noble means such as weapons and voluntary fasting. This last method had some popularity among Roman old men. During their lives they were the representatives of *Romanitas*. They exercised their public functions in dignity and seriousness (*dignitas* and *gravitas*). The moment they realized that their present life no longer met high standards, they consciously quitted life by closing their mouths to food. This was the way out taken by Marcus Cocceius Nerva. Although he was still sound in body and mind, the moment he decided that his life had run out he refused to take food. Even Tiberius the emperor, who came to his house in person, could not change his determination.

A kind of blackmail was practised by Turannius. He made clear that public dignity was the ultimate consideration: he was more than ninety years of age when he was discharged from his office. He refused food and by this act of blackmail he was re-instated in his function. Especially for someone who had been in the centre of political life bodily and mental decay was unbearable:

> two years before his death Messala Corvinus the rhetor lost his memory and intellect to such a degree that he could hardly link one word to another. Finally a cancer grew on his sacrum. Then he put an end to his existence in the seventy-second year of his life.

A tragedy such as this refutes a modern myth that antiquity – by better conditions of life – was not familiar with phenomena like senile dementia[73].

Inedia as a protracted way of dying could even give a final glory to a life that had been worthless. Gaius Caninius Rebilus had acquired the bad reputation of a hedonist. 'He escaped the tortures of age by letting blood from his arteries; though, from the unmasculine vices for which he was infamous, he had been thought incapable of the firmness of committing suicide.' Caninius had not lived up to the rules put forward by Epicurus to shun public life; he had done his civic duty by acting as a legal expert.

In the same way a whole series of Roman political figures are said to have finished life when their bodily suffering got intolerable: general weariness of life (*taedium vitae*) or insufferable pain (*inpatientia doloris*) was the reason for suicide for Atticus, Silius Italicus, Pliny the Younger, Marcus Aurelius and Septimius Severus. Claudius contemplated self-killing when stomach-ache seemed unbearable. The old Hadrian tried several ways out of life. He complained that as an emperor he had not the means at his disposal to free himself from suffering: a slave was ordered to stab him to death with a sword and a doctor to give poison, but the latter killed himself – loyal to his Hippocratic oath or simply from fear of repercussions?

The few cases which emerge in Pliny's correspondence give the impression that at least at the end of the first century AD it was not uncommon in the upper-classes immediately beneath the elite to take one's own life after consulting one's friends and doctors[74]. The acceptance of suicide in this group is shown also by the wording of Pomponius Bassulus' epitaph which dates from the same time[75].

Even the study of numbers and groups, as we have undertaken it in this section, appears to amount to an investigation of ancient perception. It will become clear that data about the methods and motives have even been more influenced by their passage through the filters of mentality.

2

MODI MORIENDI

'Death lies near at hand,' Seneca exults.

> Whether the throat is strangled by a knot, or water stops the
> breathing, or the hard ground crushes in the skull of one
> ' falling headlong to its surface, or flame inhaled cuts off the
> course of respiration, – be it what may, the end is swift[1].

Among the instruments which ancient people had at their disposal
for executing a decision to commit suicide, drastic methods are in
the majority. Therefore on those grounds alone, modern sociological approaches which regard 'successful' attempts of suicide as
failed cries for help have little significance for the ancient world:
soporifics which enable modern people to gamble with death – in
Taylor's view to be regarded as the equivalent of an ordeal[2] – were
not available. Until recently, coal-gas was another means the use of
which often meant a calculated intervention – for instance by an
intimate friend who had been phoned shortly before the deed.
'Lethal vapours' are only attested as *exotic* means in antiquity.
Seneca alludes to them as the most recherché of means of suicide in
his praise of prompt availability of death. Quintus Lutatius
Catulus locked himself in a room with newly plastered walls. In the
centre of the chamber a fire was lit which drew the lethal vapours
from the walls which were still wet. Thus he acquired an entry
under Valerius Maximus' heading 'uncommon cases of death'[3].

The only method which was meant to provoke a reaction among
the bystanders was refusing food. In the ancient world it had as a
distinct *modus moriendi* a special name: *karteria* in Greek and *inedia* in
Latin. The typical means of suicide in our world, comparable in
drastic effect, are fire-arms, jumping under trains and provoking a

car crash. Already the differences in technical opportunities refute Grisé's assertion: 'les techniques de suicide n'ont pas beaucoup changé'[4]. Techniques have changed and, in as far as they are similar, they were used in different proportions. In Western Europe, for instance, more men than women hang themselves. As will become apparent, in the ancient world women prefer the rope.

There was little chance of survival the moment somebody in the ancient world had decided to die. A great deal of resoluteness was required in executing the decision: the means did not do the job by themselves.

> In whatever direction you may turn your eyes, there lies the means to end your woes. See you that precipice? Down that is the way to liberty. See you that sea, that well? There sits liberty – at the bottom. See you that tree, stunted, blighted, and barren? Yet from its branches hangs liberty. See you that throat of yours, your gullet, your heart? They are ways of escape from servitude. Are the ways of egress I show you too toilsome, do they require too much courage and strength? Do you ask what is the highway to liberty? Any vein in your body[5].

Among the 'chemins de la liberté' Seneca indicates, opening the veins is presented as the softest means, a judgement not many would subscribe to in modern times. What counts as hard and soft has changed completely.

In discussing ancient means of self-killing the ancient evaluation will be our rough guide-line, starting with methods which were respected till we reach the lowest ways of doing away with oneself. This order corresponds to the degree of freedom in suicidal behaviour, from a conscious choice to a panicked reaction. The selection of the right means had a greater impact on the evaluation of self-killing than it does in our world[6]; especially in the last moments it was of vital importance not to lose face.

A STARVATION: *INEDIA*

Refusing food was counted as a highly distinctive method of suicide. As we have seen, old Greek sages and Roman dignitaries have a preference for this harsh method. Why does Grisé assure us, nevertheless, that *inedia* was mainly practised by 'individus faibles et impuissants'? Her conclusion is based on two passages in ancient historiography where besieged people exhort each other to prefer death in battle above *having themselves starved to death*. In both cases the idea of suicide is lacking completely[7].

There is a marked correlation between old age and *inedia*: in the 61 cases of suicide among the old where a method is specified self-inflicted starvation was practised 18 times. These 18 cases are more than one-third of the 51 registered instances of *inedia*, regardless of age (Appendix B 6). It is not only the numbers that demonstrate that *abstinentia cibi* was regarded as showing dignity and wisdom. Philosophers recommended this exit as worthy. There was a book written by Hegesias entitled 'The Man Who Perseveres' (*Apokarteron*) in which a Greek Job confronted with the vicissitudes of life decides to starve himself to death. Impressed by this plea for a philosophical suicide many of Hegesias' students put an end to their lives. Thereupon King Ptolemy prevented the too successful 'Death-urger' (*Peisithanatos*) from teaching any longer, in order to dam the wave of suicides[8]. In demonstrating their philosophical attitude, in what Roman law calls ostentation (*iactatio*), those young Alexandrians have a high motive to which a highly

Methods in the 626 cases where the these have been specified

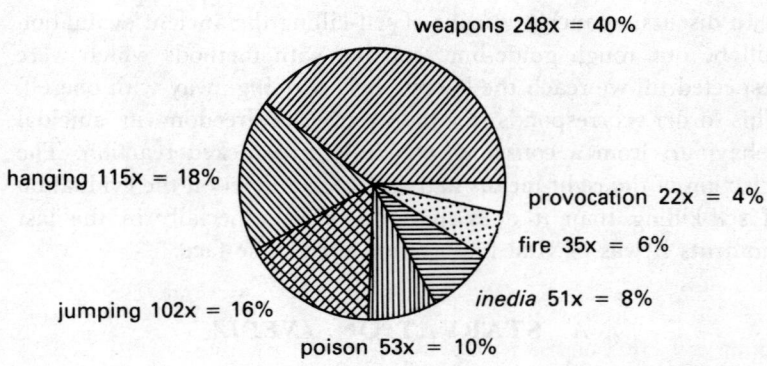

Figure 2.1 The proportions of the various methods

42

respected means corresponds. Also in the philosophical papyrus of Philodemos which has been found in Herculaneum in a carbonized form, mention is made of *apokarterein*. Because of the sorry state of the writing the place of this *persevering* in the exposition about death cannot be established, but undoubtedly it played a role in an Epicurean view of life[9].

In 161 AD Sedatius Severianus put an end to his life in order to escape the enemy. In a period which wished to regard war as the phenomenon of a mythical past his heroic deed caused much attention and writing. One historiographer was derided by Lucian for embellishing the circumstances of his death; according to that imaginative writer Sedatius had not just fallen upon his sword, but had abstained from food; undoubtedly, Lucian says ironically, the enemy had given him the time to do so[10].

The ancient world was acquainted with several aspects of voluntary starvation. It was known that drinking water kept someone who refused to take food alive for quite a long time. Seven days were needed, according to the medical doctrine of crisis, to reach the point of no return. One Hippocratic doctor asserted that anybody who does not eat or drink for seven days dies without exception. Taken on its own this communication could apply to observations made during diseases where a patient is unable to eat or drink. But the subsequent passage makes it clear that wilful starvation is meant: some were persuaded to stop 'persevering' (*apokarterein*), but then their stomach could not process anything. That medical experience, the ancient author says, underlines once more that life is 'seven daily' (*heptemeros*). This preoccupation with seven as a number, which still figures in modern medical mythology, is the subject of a special piece of writing: 'About Sevens' (*Peri hebdomadon*). In the Roman world Aulus Gellius still holds to this view, referring to the Roman polymath Varro[11].

Other, more realistic, medical experience with *apokarterein* is shown in an exposition about the workings of *melikreton*, a drink of milk and honey: general opinion had it that this mixture undermined the constitution, because some 'persevere to the end' taking only this beverage. But the nutritional value of pure honey, the Hippocratic physician affirms, is higher than that of unmixed wine; so the public conviction does not hold[12].

So at an early date, perhaps already in the fifth century BC, there existed medical experience of voluntary death by fasting. This type of death cannot have been too uncommon since it attracted the

A. Methods used by men in the 439 cases where these have been specified

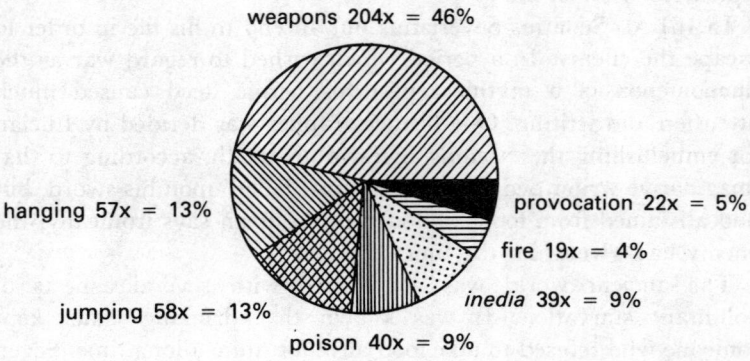

weapons 204x = 46%

provocation 22x = 5%

fire 19x = 4%

inedia 39x = 9%

poison 40x = 9%

jumping 58x = 13%

hanging 57x = 13%

B. Methods used by women in the 158 cases where these have been specified

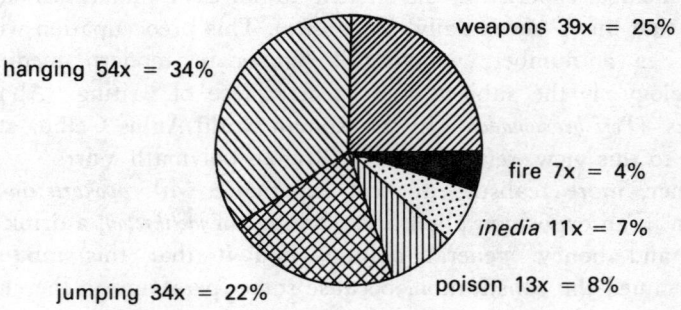

weapons 39x = 25%

hanging 54x = 34%

fire 7x = 4%

inedia 11x = 7%

poison 13x = 8%

jumping 34x = 22%

Figure 2.2 Methods of men and women compared

attention of doctors: it is not to be assumed that philosophers were a considerable part of the patients an ancient physician came across. They even felt obliged to distinguish themselves by a special technique. When Demokritos was determined 'to lead himself out of life' because of old age he did not stop eating abruptly, but diminished his ration day by day. When he was about to die during the festival of the Thesmophoria which was imminent, his female housemates, who were looking forward to the feast, beseeched him to interrupt the fasting for a while. He readily complied and prolonged his life a little by taking some honey[13].

The resoluteness required for ending one's life by abstaining from food was also found outside the circle which by its nature has attracted most attention. With those common persons *iactatio* was not the motive, but unbearable suffering or *dolor* because of irretrievable loss. In myth, the linking of grief with *inedia* is not very conspicuous: only Iphis is said to have been shocked by the self-killing of his daughter Euadne to such a degree that he intended to starve himself to death. This reading is found in Euripides who is inclined to give a 'romantic' touch to old stories[14].

Historically such excessive behaviour in mourning is found in men as well as females, for instance in Himilco the Carthaginian and the Persian queen-mother Sisyngambris. Timoleon was shunned by his mother and friends for murdering his brother Timophanes. Overwhelmed with grief he decided to fast until death, but then his friends intervened. Thus the method not only could demonstrate philosophical determination, but could also be a cry for help. An *apokarteron* does not conceal his behaviour: he wishes to elicit reactions which might turn the scale in favour of life. Exemplary women are admired for following their husband into death by refusing food, as the wives of Arruntius and Ligarius did. Petronius makes a farce out of this female pattern of mourning: in a morbid story in the *Satyricon* a widow from Ephesus has shut herself in the sepulchral chamber of her husband; her decision to starve herself to death shocked the whole community. But finally she had herself recalled to life by a soldier who was guarding some crosses on which some robbers were being executed. Having taken some food 'the woman proved no more abstinent in one part of her body than in the other'[15]. Another Roman novel remains serious in the midst of romance: in the *Metamorphoses* Charite is determined to share her husband's death by *inedia*.

Thus, *inedia* is the ancient method for attracting attention for grief, open or hidden. Phaidra could not reveal her unbecoming love for her stepson Hippolytos. 'I abstain from food' (*asiteo*); such will be 'the renouncing of life (*apostasis tou biou*)'. In this way, her old nurse discovers the awful secret of her heart. Frustration in love leading up to voluntary starvatio¬ is a theme in the ancient novel: on one occasion Chaireas is convinced that Kallirhoe is in love with Dionysios. He decides to abstain from food but on second thoughts he snatches up his sword (which is duly wrested from him by his friends). Threatening to commit suicide is a common element of the romantic armoury. But romanticism could be real: Antiochos, son of Seleukos, was enamoured of his father's young wife. He concealed his feelings and decided to die by starvation. The cause of his mysterious pining was diagnosed in time by Erasistratos, the physician who was called in. This man also furnished an effective therapy; on his bidding Seleukos readily ceded Stratonike to his son. Julian the Apostate, who is not known for his exuberant erotic life, approvingly quotes Diogenes' advice: 'Hunger frees from love; if not applicable, the rope'[16]. Rather more respect is paid to voluntary starvation than to the abrupt rope as a therapy.

The history of Antiochos' secret love makes clear that *inedia* could be used as a subtle means to communicate a message. But an unhappy person could also attract attention to his misery by starving in public. That was the way 90-year-old Turannius acted. He started, as we saw, on an outright hunger-strike to regain the political post he was deposed from. By a similar act of pressure Tiberius, the later emperor, forced Augustus to permit him to leave Rome, when he was convinced that he stood in the way of the schemes of the princeps. *Inedia* was not always a free choice: a young Spanish captive starved himself to death, having no other exit available: his determination is recorded with admiration. A person could even be compelled to commit suicide by starvation. This is said to have happened to a Roman woman who had assaulted the wine stock: 'She is forced by her relatives to die by starvation' (*bibax femina* in Appendix A). Obviously the family wished to avoid contamination by executing her actively, comparably to the mythical theme of tyrannical kings who immure princesses (Antigone). Maybe a similar striving for relative innocence accounts for the way Asinius Gallus and Agrippina maior are said to have been starved to death by the emperor, under the cover of voluntary *inedia*.

It was certainly not a matter of 'les discréditer dans l'opinion publique' as Grisé (1983 p.119) asserts, trying to establish her conviction that abstaining from food was an infamous method of self-killing. On the contrary, the Greek technical term 'perseverance' (*karteria*) and the verb 'To persevere to the end' (*apokarterein*) already bear testimony that starving oneself to death was regarded in antiquity as a method which demonstrated noble resoluteness, preferably to be used in sight of an admiring or sympathetic public.

With respect to the motives connected with this exclusive way of self-killing, Appendix B 8 shows that among the 48 cases of *inedia* where a motive can be established, in 15 instances (=31 per cent) grief was involved. Eight times starvation was practised because of unbearable disease and on 5 occasions death by *karteria* was sought as a demonstration of personal autonomy[17]. As a passive method, abstaining from food was hardly counted as an act of 'laying hands upon oneself'; rather it was the perfect way of 'leading oneself out' (*exago ek tou biou*).

B ROMANA MORTE: WEAPONS

'But oblige by taking away that knife. I can't look at the point of it. It reminds me of Roman history'. Mr Bloom readily complied with Stephen's request, understanding little of the associations[18]. The Roman world is regarded as the culture of stabbing and cutting. The cases handed down by the sources justify this image: sword, dagger, knife, razor and scalpel are by far the most common means of suicide, with 248 instances out of which Rome alone accounts for 153 (see Figure 2.1 and Appendix B 6). It will be argued that many signs indicate that in reality the proportions of the methods must have been different from the image furnished by the sources. As to weapons it is obvious that they were the means of soldiers and aristocrats, men who made and often wrote history.

In the profile of suicidal means, Greeks are outdistanced by Romans in the use of weapons: 153 Roman cases as against 66 Greek ones. Investigating the distribution over time, it becomes clear why the Roman material is so dominated by the use of weapons. In the cases of suicide committed which have been attested historically, the Romans are by far superior: 133 Roman instances to 19 Greek ones. Series of self-killings during the civil wars, pacts of mutual dispatch by troops which were in desperate situations and the ruin of the old aristocracy during the Early Empire were recorded eagerly, with horror and admiration, by ancient historians. Real cases from the Greek world lag behind the Roman 'overkill'. Dimnos 'slaughtered himself' on being unmasked as a conspirator against Alexander the Great. A cient Greek has a special verb to denote 'slaughtering oneself upon somebody': *epi(kata)sphattein heauton* – the suicide drops upon the body of the beloved one, having wounded himself fatally. In this way Straton literally made himself a sacrifice when unable to obtain Aristokleia, the bride of somebody else who had died during the kidnapping (p.27). The groom is also said to have done away with himself in his grief. A chain of self-killings is not uncommon: Euopis hanged herself when Dimoites her husband had publicised her incestuous love for her brother. At the moment of dying she cursed the man who was the cause of her death and the imprecation was fulfilled in a horrible way. It was not long before Dimoites came upon the corpse of a most beautiful woman washed ashore by the sea, and he conceived the most passionate desire for her; but soon the body, owing to the period of time since her death, began to rot, and he piled up a huge barrow for her; and then, as even so his passion was in no wise relieved, he slaughtered himself at her tomb.

This last case is told by Parthenios in his *Love Romances*, in which Greek stories appear, taken from myth and from a dim past. The Hellenic world is strikingly devoid of the martial cult of self-killing which was so prominent in Rome. Even Pantites, the Spartan who by accident had missed Thermopylae, *hanged* himself, not able to bear the shame of survival.

In his practice the ancient doctor came across suicides by cutting and stabbing: 'I saw people who intended to slaughter themselves and had already cut their throats completely; they live, but have no voice, unless somebody closes the windpipe'[19]. It would have been astonishing if the Greek world was unfamiliar with weapons as means of suicide. After all, epic furnishes the prototype of a hero who throws himself upon his sword. The much discussed and pictured case of Ajax was even staged by Sophocles 'avec une rare emphase' as de Romilly says. No messenger appears, as usually, to announce that the final act has happened behind the scenes. Contrary to all that we regard as the conventions of ancient drama, the hero throws himself on his 'benevolent' sword under the eyes of the public after having addressed the sword:

The slayer standeth where his stroke is sure – I have time to muse thus curiously – the gift of Hector, erst my foeman-friend, the man most hateful to my soul and sight, now fixed in foemen's land, the land of Troy; fresh edged upon the iron-fretting stone, here have I planted it and set it fast, a friend to help me to a speedy death.[20]

As a model of heroic self-killing Ajax plays an important part in Greek reflection on the deed. In Greek stories he is not the only one who throws himself upon his sword – or threatens to do so: Menoikeus, Achilles and Haimon are also said to have practised or considered this way of doing away with themselves. When Patroclus' death is reported, Antilochos clutches Achilles' hands 'for he feared that he might cut his throat with iron'. When Haimon finds Antigone hanged, without delay he reaches after his weapon, his 'two-edged' sword: the spheres of man and woman remain separate even in shared death. When women touch weapons, often there are special circumstances which account for this unwomanly behaviour: Thisbe uses the sword which Pyramus by a tragic misunderstanding has employed against himself: the weapon lay by the side of her dead beloved.

In myth there are some women who use the sword, whereas in recorded history they use metal only in exceptional circumstances. Of course, swords simply lie outside their reach in the same way as for slaves, but even domestic tools for stabbing and cutting are used by women only seldom: metal does not belong to the female sphere. In this respect, mythical sisters represent a higher cosmos: Althaia, Amophinome, Amphinomene, Deianeira, Eurydike, Helen (during her critical situation in Egypt), Kanake, Kyane and Polyxena live in another world. Kyane's death is the unhappy climax of a family tragedy. Her father had not honoured the god Dionysus when he made his triumphant entry in the world. In the frenzy which took possession of him by way of punishment, he raped Kyane. This violation was followed by a pestilence which came over the country. An oracle indicated sacrificing the impious man. Only Kyane understood the suggestion and cut her father's throat. Next she transfixed herself upon the corpse. By stabbing herself – or hanging (so Apollodorus) – Heracles' wife Deianeira showed herself to be a worthy daughter of Althaia. This fierce woman had thrown the log which guaranteed the life of her son

Meleager into the fire after he had killed her brothers. Then she stabbed herself to death.

Once more it has to be stressed that these mythical women represent the other world of resolute female beings. As a historical case, Pausanias tells the story of Kallirhoe: she rejected the advances of Koresos the priest. Hurt in his feelings he managed to get the girl appointed as a sacrificial victim, but at the 'moment suprême' he killed himself. At once Kallirhoe finished her life too, using the sacrificial knife, realizing that she loved Koresos after all.

Among the Romans, there is a very small number of women who achieved a manly exit by dagger or sword: seventeen as against 135 cases for men. The shining example of course is Lucretia. She belongs to the founding mothers of the Roman Republic. Her suicide, committed from pure shame, is the archetype of female ideals in Roman society, and is told as a true story by the historians, e.g. Livy: in many a way Rome's early history is its mythology. There are historically attested Lucretias in later times. Arria made herself an *exemplum* by showing Paetus the way: 'Paetus, it does not hurt'. During the persecution among the elite of the Late Republic and the Early Empire several women followed their husband in death, managing the weapon which had been used by or against the victim[21]. A Lucretia, both by means and motive, was Mallonia. When she was brought to Tiberius' bed, but refused most vigorously to submit to his lust, he turned her over to the informers, and even when she was on trial he did not cease to call out and ask her 'whether she was sorry'; so that finally she left the court and went home, where she stabbed herself, openly upbraiding the ugly old man for his obscenity.

The noble character of a weapon as a means was finally brought out by the choice made by an emperor's daughter. In AD 213 Cornificia, daughter of Marcus Aurelius, was forced by Caracalla to kill herself: only the choice of method was left free. She opened her veins.

It was only with much delay that Christianity got rid of the ancient admiration for Lucretian behaviour. Without any sign of disapproval, Eusebios tells us in his *History of the Church* that a fine lady and her daughters stabbed themselves to escape rape by the executioner[22]. Self-killing by a woman to avoid violation would become the classical case discussed by moral theologians to explore the reach of the Christian taboo on suicide.

In the classical period suicide was counted as an obligation for soldiers and politicians when confronted with the risk of losing their honour. During the Early Empire, opening the veins became the homely equivalent of old Roman *virtus* after a lost battle. A rich idiom originated, connected with the hallowed deed: incising the veins, presenting the arm, letting blood by the veins; the veins could be 'interrupted', 'cut off', 'cut through', 'furnished', 'presented in order to get undone' and 'struck'[23]. Compared to this opulent Latin vocabulary of Tacitus Dio Cassius has much less to offer; in describing the numerous tragedies in the houses of the aristocracy, he strives for some diversity with 'splitting', 'cutting', 'incising' and 'cleaving' the veins[24], but he falls short of the Tacitean *varietas*.

This richness of terminology was developed in order to come to grips verbally with the horrifying self-liquidation of the Roman aristocracy during the first century AD. Opening up the veins is stylized as a sacrificial ceremony. A doctor may be present, but most of the locutions stress that the deed was done by the suicide himself or herself. Only some terms imply medical assistance: 'presenting the veins' (*venas praebere*) is the outright expression used by Jerome in the case of Messala Corvinus. Tacitus has the more cumbersome idiom 'presenting the veins for undoing' (*venas praebere exsolvendas*). Nero sent doctors to those who hesitated to execute his order to commit suicide. He instructed them to 'treat' (*curare*) the victims, for 'thus the lethal incision of the veins was called'[25]. The pattern is reminiscent of the 'etiquette of suicide' which had been developed among the urban population of England by 1900: a young man from the middle or upper class who was in trouble because of love or money shot himself, preferably with a revolver[26].

Among the Stoic martyrs Seneca has a prominent place. His self-killing has been described with due reverence and minuteness. From the description in Tacitus, it is apparent that a great deal of medical experience had been gathered by his time. Seneca himself had recommended the opening of the veins as a worthy way to liberty: 'It is not necessary to pierce the chest with a gaping wound; a lancet will open the way to that great freedom, and tranquillity consists of a scratch'. This enthusiasm is based on the medical doctrine of *pneumatism* according to which life-giving 'bloodgas' in the veins is regarded as bearing the universal breath (*pneuma*) in a similar way, albeit on another scale, as in the earth there are streams which come to the surface in brooks and rivers[27].

The veins of Seneca and of his wife Paulina were cut by one and the same incision in their arms. Seneca, since his aged body, emaciated further by frugal living, gave slow escape to the blood, severed as well the arteries in the leg and behind the knee. Even so, the way to freedom was not opened. Next he swallowed hemlock, a holy means since Socrates had been executed in Athens by being forced to drink this poison. But Seneca took it in vain. Finally he entered a bath of heated water, sprinkling some on the slaves nearest, with the remark that he offered the liquid as a drink-offering to Jupiter the Liberator. The idea must have been to thin the blood. In Rubens' picture of 1611 this last stage was transposed to the hygienic customs of the time. In the painting, now in the Bayerische Staatsgemäldesammlung in Munich, the old Stoic stands with only his feet in a bowl (see illustration 11).

The gentleman had developed a whole ritual. In the last moments wills were made, friends were invited to share their views about the immortality of the soul. Many an aristocrat in his last hours entered the ranks of what Gourevitch calls the 'philosophes d'occasion' (1984 p.177). How firmly established the pattern was in 66 AD is shown by Petronius; he had his veins closed and undone intermittently. He wrote some invective verses addressed to Nero and enjoyed light conversation with his friends, who time and again joined in with frivolous singing. The persiflage marks what was regarded as *bon ton* in suicide during that period.

As military resistance had become impossible for the senatorial order, suicide was one way of demonstrating opposition to the emperor. Thus in AD 37 Arruntius opened his veins because he had lived out his life. However strongly his friends urged him to continue his existence, he was determined to die, not because of his conscience, but because he could no longer bear to see the shameful spectacle of Tiberius' reign. When an aristocrat had decided to kill himself, a good show was expected. Vitellius' clumsy handling of a penknife confirmed his reputation of being ridiculous.

The drawing-room lions of the Early Empire regarded themselves as the heirs of the Late Republic, when the losers attained immortality by finishing themselves off stylishly: Brutus, Cassius and above all Cato, who in Utica had linked the heroic behaviour of the defeated commander with that of the philosopher. He stabbed himself with his sword after having read *the* book of Plato, i.e. *Phaedo*, which discusses the immortality of the soul. Soon after his death, Cato became a legend. Cicero speaks about his dying as 'departing from life' and in the Aeneid he already acts as a judge in

Elysium[28]. Cato's glorification by Seneca was comfort and inspiration for Pichegru, unmasked as a conspirator against Napoleon. On 5 April 1804, Seneca's book was found next to the hanged man in his cell, open at the relevant page. In the same period Plato too played his part in encouraging self-killing. A man suffering from persecution mania was found dead in a wood with Plato's dialogue in his hand[29]; this type of classical inspiration has been lost for ever.

In Cato's suicide philosophical, political and military values went hand in hand. Afterwards, there was a progressive differentiation. The specialists who lead the armies during the Empire know on occasion what their professional ethics require: their self-destruction is an act of living up to the military code.

Military circles have always been counted as very favourably disposed towards self-killing. The generalization of Durkheim (1930 p.247) does not apply only to the officers of the French professional army whose behaviour was the ground for the statement. In Roman times whole detachments did away with themselves when the occasion required such an act of bravery. Under the heading *milites* in Appendix A a series of such collective suicides by Roman troops can be found. Among those are Crassus' soldiers who helped each other to die when the desperate situation at Carrhae had become clear to them. Crassus himself, his son and their staff joined in the wholesale *autolysis*.

This Japanese-looking glorification of martial behaviour among the Romans meets with wonderment among the Greeks. No fewer than three Hellenistic epigrams express astonishment about the extreme *virtus* of an Aelius[30]. After many military achievements a disease threatened to undermine his constitution. But 'illness overcomes the cowards, Ares the men'. Therefore he preferred to transfix himself. The reasons why Roman soldiers killed themselves with their own weapons did not always have to do with a desperate military situation. The Roman professional army of the empire was acquainted with people like Aelius. In a written answer on a legal question Hadrian among the excusable grounds for self-killing lists also 'insufferable pain' (*inpatientia doloris*)[31].

Thus, the permanent army of the Empire, a novelty in world history, developed special codes for living and dying among its members. When a man had served for so many years, military ethics became part of him to such a degree that just pining away was regarded as not befitting. In an epigram Martial (1,78) follows the literary tradition of the Aelius theme. But he is able to give a contemporary example: Gaius Calpetanus Rantius Quirinalis Valerius Festus – Festus for short – committed suicide in AD 84/85. He suffered from a tumour in his neck. He decided to pass to the lake of Styx. But 'he marred not his righteous face with secret poison, nor with slow starvation tortured his sad fate; but his sacred life he closed by a *Roman death*, and set free his soul by a nobler end'. In the context of the poem and within the Roman set of values, this only can mean: with the sword.

Tools for stabbing and cutting were in all situations decent means to bring about the desired end. The 'Profile of Self-Killing' under Appendix B 8 shows that this method was distributed evenly among all motives.

C SEEKING THE HAND OF ANOTHER: PROVOCATION

In a general sense a suicide is somebody who uses his own hand against himself. In many a modern language the astonishment about the 'alienation' of this part of the body is expressed in the idiom connected with suicide. Latin says *manus sibi in/adferre*, Greek speaks of an *autocheir* and perhaps uses *cheiras prosago* (p.156 n.51).

Sometimes a decision to die is executed by other persons. This type of elicited killing of oneself raises some questions about the definition of self-murder. Were those Christians suicides who by their behaviour provoked a martyr's death? That designation seems even more appropriate for those who gave themselves up to the authorities. In the framework of this study, they have not been counted as self-killers because they caused their own death only *indirectly*, but Durkheim's definition of suicide as 'toute mort qui résulte médiatement ou immédiatement d'un acte positif ou négatif, *accompli par la victime elle-même*'[32] leaves by its 'immédiatement' room for discussion. The general question is: to what degree should risky behaviour which plays with death be regarded as suicidal? We have been fairly restrictive in calling somebody a self-killer. Among the Christian martyrs, only those who in their fervour throw themselves upon the pyre have been counted as self-murderers. The same designation would have been attributed to any Christian jumping into a group of soldiers and thus provoking immediate death. But a case like this is unknown to me.

Such a direct invitation to be killed was present in the case of the centurion, who has already been mentioned as an instance of exemplary behaviour on the part of a humble man (p.18):

> A noble hero on that day our own age beheld in the person of Sempronius Densus. He was a centurion of a praetorian cohort whom Galba had assigned to protect Piso; he drew his dagger, rushed to meet the armed men, upbraided them for their crime, and drawing the attention of the assassins to himself by act and word, gave Piso a chance to escape, although he was wounded.

This case has been classified as a suicide, because it is said that Densus deliberately courted death in order to save someone else.

Another altruistic suicide – altruistic in the Durkheimian sense of sacrificing oneself for another - was that of Zeno of Elea. He was interrogated by Nearchos the tyrant. Zeno feared that he might be forced to betray his friends. Finally he feigned that he was willing to mention names, and asked Nearchos to come nearer, for he wanted to whisper something in his ear. Then he bit the tyrant's ear hard and provoked the murderous reaction he intended.

Among the cases of bringing death on oneself in order to safeguard others, there is a typical category, of people who 'dedicate' themselves because of an oracle. Athens has such a case of *devotio* among its mythical kings. An oracle had said that the Peloponnesians would win the war if the Athenian king stayed alive. Thereupon Kodros sought his death by plunging into the thick of the fight. In another reading he went to the enemy, disguised as a beggar. By behaving insolently he provoked his killing. In the medieval Carmina Burana 'Codrian' stands for 'poor as a beggar'[33]. Sparta too could boast of a king who dedicated himself, in spite of an oracle which promised death.

In one Roman family there was a tradition of plunging into the mêlée. Some confusion in ancient historiography, or indeed repeated behaviour, accounts for three Decii Mures mentioned as having sacrificed themselves in a succession of three generations. In BC 340 Decius Mus I dedicated himself after a 'Codrian' oracle at Veseris in Campania. Most publicized was the *devotio* of Publius on the eve of the battle of Sentinum in BC 295. He has been included in the state records: the Fasti Capitolini do not distinguish – *in bonam* or *malam partem* – between his way of falling in action and the way other commanders died. It is only said of him: 'he was killed' (*occisus est*) as if his type of seeking death was expected of any leader. One tradition has it that his son followed the paternal example in BC 279.

Ordinary soldiers did not need oracles as a stimulus to sacrifice themselves. The esprit de corps of the Roman professional army was such that individuals put the fate of the legion before their own. At the siege of Gelduba (modern Gellep near Krefeld in the German Federal Republic) Civilis, the Batavian rebel leader, sought to undermine the morale of the Roman legionaries by parading Roman standards and prisoners. 'One of these had the courage to do an heroic deed, shouting out the truth, for which he was at once run through by the Germans'. This man met Tacitus' need for examples of old Roman *virtus* among commoners, who shamed the nobility of birth[34].

More and more it was the Emperor who invited *devotio*. He was regarded as the guarantee of the well-being of society. In AD 68/69 soldiers of Galba, Otho and Vitellius showed how their fate was linked with their leader. In the light of these phenomena, reports of an acute *anomy* when an emperor or his successor designate (Germanicus) died, leading up to suicides, should not be discounted completely. Versnel has described the suicidal situation of a community from the point of view of religious history and anthropology: temples are closed, statues of the gods are violated, newly born children are abandoned[35]. When Caligula, the new hope of humanity, became seriously ill, shortly after his coming to power, some eminent Romans declared that they were willing to fight to the death in the ritual of the gladiatorial games: these *depugnaturi* wished to restore the beloved monarch to life by spilling their own blood[36]. The emperor did not show himself a good sport after his recovery. Although he recovered, he did force them to make good their promise.

Of a lower quality of motivation – but distinct from despair – are the few cases where a captive provoked his death to escape the *infamy* of his situation. Even a centurion, Pontius, of whom it is said that he was of the 'very lowest sort' (*infimae humilitatis*) demonstrated this sense of his own dignity. Crassus Mucianus, a pontifex maximus – and a proconsul at that – provoked his guard by pricking his eye with a stick. Stories like this one found their way into the collections of exempla. There was a place too for a category 'loyalty of slaves towards their masters'. Piso's slave deserved his entry by posing as his master and causing his own death during a proscription. On a rare occasion the roles were changed: the former consul Plotius provoked his own death in order to save his slaves from further torture. Somewhat misplaced, he figures in Valerius Maximus' chapter *On the loyalty of slaves* (*De fide servorum*).

Devotio, even towards community, is not unknown to women, but a provoked death as a means is not at their disposal. That way is closely linked with male self-sacrifice: among the twenty-two cases of *provocatio* where a motive can be established, *devotio* was the cause 15 times (Appendix B 8a).

D FIRE AS AN EXOTIC MEANS

Even more than self-chosen starvation or the use of weapons, self-burning is a public act, at least in the few cases which antiquity recorded. In 6 out of the 35 cases it was *suicides obsidionaux*: groups of beleaguered people threw themselves into the fire of the burning city – the means prescribed by the situation: Indians, Isaurians, Lycians, Sidonians, Victomelani and Saguntians – the last while the Senate was still deliberating. In these cases 'barbarians' were involved. Comparable to these acts was the behaviour of some Romans at the burning of their city in 64 AD: they were wholly destitute or they were desperate with grief over relations whom they had proved unable to rescue. So they chose to die, though the way of escape was open. Some Christians, mixing despair with contempt of death, threw themselves into the flames during the Great Persecution: under Diocletian the arch-persecutor Christians were accused of having set fire to the imperial palace in Nicomedia. According to Eusebios they ostentatiously jumped into the burning building[37]. In the fervour of their religious convictions, stubborn Montanists shut themselves in their churches during the persecution by the most orthodox emperor Justinian and burned themselves with the buildings.

When their beleaguered cities are captured, sometimes the commanders join in the wholesale self-burning of the population: both Boges, the Persian, and Amilcas (Hamilcar), the Carthaginian, preferred to destroy themselves in the inferno rather than to bear the disgrace of defeat and captivity. One example which is more or less historical is that of Croesus who was saved just in time by the combined efforts of Apollo and Cyrus who took his city. His attempted suicide by self-burning is one of the few which have their own iconography (see II.10). Roman generals are supposed to use their sword in such circumstances. Nevertheless one partisan of Pompey, Scapula, is said to have ascended a self-constructed pyre, when Caesar's opponents' cause was lost in Spain, and Cordoba was captured.

These self-burnings are part of a general catastrophe where the means is prescribed by the situation. The method was chosen more deliberately by two victims of the proscription during the first century BC: Cestius burned himself alive in BC 43 to escape being liquidated by the squadrons of the second triumvirate. Even more ostentatious was Statius' behaviour in the same year. He permitted anybody to take from his house what he liked. After that he set his house and himself on fire: both *familia* and *domus* were destroyed in a most spectacular way.

Scapula, Cestius and Statius are the sole historical instances of individual self-burning by Roman men. Generally speaking, the method was not often practised in the Graeco-Roman world. Pythagoras' disciples are said to have made a living ladder of themselves to save the master from a burning building. Empedokles' jump into the Etna is recorded with much scepticism. Peregrinos the philosopher was regarded as posing as a Heracles when he burned himself to death in public; this behaviour fitted well into Lucian's grim picture of the pseudo-prophet.

Self-burning was never integrated into the arsenal of ancient means of suicide. The Greeks watched the death by fire of Zarmaros and Karanos the Indian sages in astonishment (p.37). Strabo's 'Kalanos' (15,1,65) enunciates the doctrine of the so-called gymnosophists: to them disease is a most shameful condition. Whenever an ailment is suspected, such a sage is expected 'to lead himself out' by way of fire. The whole passage stresses the difference between the cultures of East and West.

The Indian habit of voluntary burning to death by widows, suttee, also caused horror among the Graeco-Macedonian soldiers. In 317 BC Keteus, commander of the Indian contingent, died. Both his oriental wives competed to be allowed to share the pyre with him. Finally the generals decided. The younger was proud of winning the honour of ascending the funeral pile. Out of respect, the army paraded three times around the fire. The scene causes Diodorus the historian to speculate about the background of this horrible custom. He holds to the view that the practice was introduced to prevent women from secretly liquidating their men; her own existence was linked with his. This rationalization made the institution to a certain degree understandable to the Greeks. In general, for ancient people suttee is something which belongs to *Varied History*, the kind of stories Aelianus and others wrote about distant people with their strange habits[38].

Under these conditions self-burning, which plays a relatively big part in myth, must be regarded as a falsification of reality: in the superhuman world the method is applied both by men and women. Heracles, who ascends the pyre, is the most heroic example. As such he is a theme for drama and painting. But self-destruction by fire occurs in the lower levels of mythical society too. This way of dying is always presented as highly admirable: Adrastos, Hipponoos, Iphias and Laodameia.

It was not only Heracles' self-burning that was the subject of paintings. Philostratos describes a picture which showed how Euadne stylized her death by ascending the pyre in full regalia. According to an older version she threw herself from the rocks, following her husband Kapaneus in death. Elsewhere Philostratos praises Euadne for the method she chose: she did not use the sword, she did not hang herself 'as women usually do with respect to (the loss of their) men', but she preferred the funeral pyre[39].

Ovid, an expert in mythology, suggests mythological behaviour on the part of his wife; she was so desperate about his banishment to the Black Sea that she contemplated burning herself to death. But in reality she did not become a Euadne or Laodameia. With respect to self-burning, myth remains the other world for the Greeks and Romans: the ancient world too would have looked with a sense of alienation upon the Indo-Chinese monks and the Jan Palachs. The profile of the methods bears out the distance: 'barbarians' account for no fewer than 15 out of the 35 cases where fire is the way of voluntary death.

E MEDICINE BY WAY OF POISON

In Aristophanes' *Frogs* the god Dionysus wishes to descend to the underworld as soon as possible. Heracles, an expert of great repute on excursions to Hades, is asked for advice. He indicates three ways, in a significant sequence: rope and ladder, a jump from a tower and finally hemlock. Because of the comic effect, the three most miserable ways of voluntary death are mentioned. Such banal methods could be expected in slaves, as Roman law proves. One law-student discusses the question of which hidden faults the seller of a slave remains accountable for: an attempted suicide is such a fault which diminishes the value of the merchandise and as such should be mentioned. Among the means which a 'bad slave' (*malus servus*) is supposed to have applied, again we have the triad hanging, jumping and 'a medicine by way of poison'[40].

Self-poisoning was not what was expected of a man like Demosthenes. Therefore some argued that he did not die in this infamous way, but that 'by the grace and the providence of the gods he was saved from the cruelty of the Macedonians with a sudden gentle death'. The banality of the exit excludes poison from philosophical reflection on a good death. Poison was used in practice, but in the profile of suicidal means it has a modest place with 53 instances out of the 626 where a method is specified. Compared to the modern situation 8 per cent must be regarded as insignificant. Death by poison was not very 'Roman': 20 times Romans took a drug as against 10 barbarian and 23 Greek cases. In the light of the overall under-representation of the Greeks, this ratio may indicate greater acceptance of self-poisoning in the Hellenic world. Certainly the expertise there was greater: people were executed by poison in Athens (Socrates). On the slopes of Mount Hymettus in the neighbourhood of the city hemlock grew in abundance; anybody could supply himself with the means[41].

By its nature the means lent itself mainly to an individual death. On only few occasions is mention made of collective consumption: when the disloyal town of Capua was regained by the Romans Vibius and 28 other members of the city council took poison. An earlier collective suicide by poisoning took place among some Roman ladies in BC 331. A number of Roman magistrates had died suddenly in quick succession. Then a loyal female slave disclosed the horrible truth: a group of poisoners was active. She brought the officials to the place where the noble witches were brewing. At first they denied that their drinks were harmful, but when challenged by the slave to prove the truth of their assertion, after a short deliberation they took a deadly dose[42]. In a comedy a group of women play with the idea of drinking hemlock. As far as Menander's story can be reconstructed from the fragments which have come to us of the *Women Who Take Hemlock* (*Koneiazomenai*), some females threaten to do away with themselves by poison, but regain a perspective on life when they have a good marriage in prospect. Hemlock was the means in the 'Cean custom' to which the 90-year-old lady held so ostentatiously (p.32). The habit was so well known that in a – fictitious – epitaph, hemlock was metonymically denoted as the 'Cean cups' (see p.36).

When somebody was *forced* to drink poison, the difference from an outright execution is marginal: Berenike, one of Mithridates' wives, had to take poison when the kingdom of Pontus collapsed. The drug however did not have the desired effect and so she was strangled by the executioner, who got impatient. Maybe the quantity was too small because she had shared the portion with her mother, to whom the dose was fatal. In general, poison is a 'risky' means and this quality does not give it the importance it has in modern times, that of enabling people to gamble with death. The overall character of self-killing in antiquity requires the use of sure and therefore hard methods. When his empire was ruined, Mithridates wanted to die, but during his life he had immunized himself against toxic assault so successfully that no drug had any effect on him. There always was uncertainty about the effectiveness of any given quantity and even the medical expert could not be trusted. He could – loyal to his Hippocratic oath? – administer a dose which was too small. This 'accident' happened to Domitius Ahenobarbus when, besieged at Corfinium, in BC 49, he called for the assistance of a doctor. This man, a slave – as Roman practitioners often were – made Ahenobarbus take too little so that the embittered follower of Pompey had to sue for the 'clementia Caesaris'.

Apart from hemlock, opium too was used as a lethal poison[43]. Pliny the Elder knew that it was not only somniferous (*somnifera*), but also death-ferous (*mortifera*). 'In this way, we are told, there died at Bavilum in Spain the father of Publius Licinius Caecina, a man of praetorian rank, when an unbearable illness had made life hateful to him, and also of several others'. Another plant which causes death is *ophiusa* (serpent's plant) 'a plant livid in colour and revolting to look at, to take which in drink causes such terrible visions of threatening serpents that fear of them causes suicide; wherefore those guilty of sacrilege are forced to drink it. An antidote is palm wine'[44].

Finally, there is the enigmatic 'bull's blood', whose effect Midas was the first to experience. Most attention has been paid to the rumour that Themistocles used it in despair. In the Athenian drama of the fifth century BC twice there is expressed the wish for death by this effective means[45]. This drink was deemed worthy of being used only once in a myth: Aison was forced by Peleus to

61

drink it. Already the 'modern' means makes clear that we have a late version of the story: in older renderings the theme of enforced suicide and the method which goes with it are missing completely.

As such, of course, bull's blood is not poisonous, in spite of what the ancients held[46]. The German pharmacologist Fühner explained the symptoms by assuming that Prussic acid was part of the brew. This could have been derived from peach-stones or bitter almonds. The Persian priests, in his view, added the poison to the blood of the sacrificial animal. Added in a moderate quantity it served as the means for an ordeal, while in an overdose it was fit for execution or self-killing. In the cases which have a bearing on the subject of this study no ordeal was involved: Midas and Themistocles were assumed to have taken the drug willingly.

Was poison in antiquity the female means it is in modern times? Apart from the lady alchemists of BC 331 Rome was acquainted with a few professional female poisoners – Canidia, Martina and Locusta – but they furnished others with means for assault, not for suicide. In the recorded cases of self-destruction, poison was used by women in proportion to their representation in the overall figures: 13 instances of female suicide by poisoning are relatively in balance with the 40 for men. Poison did not have the female signature it has in the modern world.

F   BY ALL MANNERS OF DEATH: *VARIA ET EXOTICA*

The number of cases where no method is specified is considerable: in 282 out of the 960 we are not told explicitly how individuals or groups have caused their death. Often the context gives clues to the method. Thus, in a military environment weapons must have been the favourite tools. But in order to avoid spoiling our analysis by using conclusions as data, in Appendix A question marks have been put where the sources did not mention the method. Probably the share of weapons for cutting and stabbing would be even higher than it already is in our material, if we allowed ourselves the luxury of making plausible guesses.

Sometimes, then, the method is not given in the sources, as being either self-evident or unimportant. On the other hand disproportionate attention is paid to the few instances of spectacular ways. Apart from these exotica the 'varia' will be discussed in this section.

Literally varied are the methods applied by desperate groups in 'suicides of sieges'. When Philip V conquered the city of Abydus in BC 200 the men stabbed their wives and children and after that themselves. Others burned themselves, jumped into wells or hanged themselves. Philip graciously permitted them three days 'to put an end to their lives by all manners of death' (*per omnes vias leti*)[47]. Pictures of such horrible scenes are common in ancient historiography ever since Thucydides described how the aristocrats of Corcyra did away with themselves and each other[48].

Lucan, the great epic poet of self-killing, lustily evokes the misery of the *proscripti* as a symbol of the dramatic fall of the republic:

> One put a rope round his throat and broke his neck; another hurled himself down headlong and was dashed to pieces against the hard ground; and thus they robbed the bloodstained conqueror of their deaths. Another piled up wood for his own pyre, and then, before all his blood had run out, sprang down into the flames and made haste to burn himself before he was prevented.
>
> (*Pharsalia* 2,154–9)

Gruesome self-killings fit well into Lucan's picture of the civil wars as the ruin of republican order. The author of the *Pharsalia* is totally unfamiliar with understatement. In the grimly painted scenes perhaps there is a climax in the sequence of methods, from desperate hanging (via jumping from a height) to wholesale self-burning.

The terror of a tyrant means suicides on a vast scale. The regime of Tiberius supplies examples of this *topos*: 'Of those who were cited to plead their causes some opened their veins at home, feeling sure of being condemned and wishing to avoid annoyance and humiliation, while others drank poison in full view of the senate'[49].

On a rare occasion individuals apply different methods in a row: it is not clear which means finally brought Hadrian the end he desired. Sometimes authorities are not unanimous in their opinion about the nature of an exotic means. Did Porcia, daughter of Cato Uticensis and Brutus' wife, die by poisonous gas – carbon monoxide? – or did she gulp down live coals? Servilia, Lepidus' wife, is said to have swallowed 'living fire'. Such examples found their way to the rubric 'uncommon cases of death' in Valerius

Maximus' work of compilation. In this, no distinction is made between death caused by an accident coming from the outside, or by ingenious ways to bring about a voluntary end, as long as the outcome is shocking. Three people smashed their heads – one against the wall, one against the door post, one by battering his skull with his fetters[50].

Finally there are the horrible curiosities which have been recorded to illustrate the resoluteness of ordinary people, such as the lavatory sponge used by the beast-fighter and the cart-wheel which broke the neck of the gladiator who was sent to the arena (*bestiarius* and *missus ad spectaculum* in Seneca). Some aristocrats too won for themselves a place in the collections of anecdotes by the unique means they chose: Proculus swallowed gypsum. Lutatius Catulus caused poisonous gases to escape from the newly plastered walls of a room in which he had shut himself. Kios burst the stitches of his wounds, thinking that his son had been killed. Licinius Macer thrust his sudari'm in his throat. Diogenes was said simply to have held his breath. Such will-power was not needed by the 'mouth-stinker' (*ozostomos*): according to the joke he simply shut his mouth and died from his own bad odour. Unclean breath is regarded as a sign of utmost vulgarity, as is brought out in some cruel and silly jokes which figure in an ancient collection known as *Philogelos*, the Joker's Friend.

By their nature exotic means only lend themselves to listing in a section 'de suicidiis non vulgaribus', a heading similar to Valerius Maximus' rubric of 'uncommon death'. Real significance, as far as the history of mentality is concerned, belongs to the 'vulgar' method of hanging.

G THE ROPE OF GHASTLY DEATH

In one of the readings of the Trojan War and its aftermath Helen finds herself in Egypt. All alone and pressed by the advances of Proteus' son she ponders:

> To die were best. How then with honour die?
> Unseemly is the noose 'twixt earth and heaven:
> Even of thralls 'tis held a death of shame,
> Noble the dagger is and honourable,
> And one short instant rids the flesh of life.
>
> Euripides, *Helena* 298–303

For a royal woman it is not difficult to make the choice between the two methods which have the highest scores: hanging, with 18 per cent, is easily second to weapons (40 per cent). Helen's considerations are that stabbing rapidly frees the body from life and that hanging is an unpleasant spectacle (*aschemon, ou kalon*). Hanging is an unclean death (*me katharos thanatos*), to which the female slaves were consigned by Odysseus and Telemachus, because they had neglected their duty of loyalty and had consorted with the suitors[51].

This abhorrence towards hanging is not supported by myth. In the old stories it is quite frequent. The mythical significance of hanging as a method is brought out by the proportion of historically attested cases as against the 'soft' material: in Appendix B 6a there are 38 real cases out of a total of 115. Mythical women especially are said to have used the rope. Of course Iokaste, Antigone, Arachne and – according to one reading – Ariadne were unhappy people, but in the story of their misery the means they used is not marked with misgivings. The 'unaesthetic' effect which held back Helen does not play a part. There was a connection between a goddess and hanging in a bizarre cult of *Artemis-who-hangs-herself*. The story behind the cult runs like this: one day some children during their play had thrown a rope around the neck of the statue of the goddess and said that she was hanged. The people in the neighbourhood, enraged by the blasphemy, stoned the children to death. After that the region of Kaphyai in Arcadia was struck by a curse: women fell ill and all their babies were still-born. Only when the advice of the Pythia was followed and a hero's cult for the children killed was established was the land liberated from the evil. 'The Caphyans ... call the goddess ... for they say this was part of the oracle as well ... *She-who-hangs-herself*'. Artemis was sometimes identified with Hekate and as such was supposed to drive mad people to the point of self-hanging.

Another aetiological element which has to do with hanging is present in the myth of Erigone who hanged herself in grief over the death of her father. In the historical period Athens has the festival of the Aiora, when puppets were swung on trees. In this way every year the Pythia's order was executed, according to which the city had to 'hang an effigy formked after a woman in public'[52].

Nevertheless, in real life hanging is counted as vulgar, in the double sense of the word. Especially in the Roman world there is an outspoken disgust. Even the myths were adapted to the actual taste: Seneca's Iokaste does not hang herself like Sophocles' heroine, but stabs herself to death, winning the nobility of a Lucretia. Phaidra too experienced such a Senecan adaptation[53]. In the Aeneid the malicious mother of Aeneas' bride hangs herself, assuming that the candidate of her choice has been killed in battle. Virgil speaks with abhorrence of 'the rope of ghastly death': *nodum informis leti* (12,603). An ancient commentator explains this to mean 'the most infamous death' adding some details about old Roman taboos on hanging. At the same time he mentions a more honourable version in which Amata died from *inedia*[54]. Such new renderings are the symptoms of a change in attitude towards self-hanging, which in the Greek world for the first time appears in Helen's rejection of the rope as not befitting a queen.

The frequency of hanging must have been far greater than is suggested by the data which have been creamed off. As said before, it has second place after the varied arsenal of weapons, with 115 cases. Reality glimmers through in the fact that hanging is the sole method where women almost equal men, with 54 against 57 cases. The immediate and direct evidence points to a general occurrence of the method among women. Diogenes discovered a group of women hanging on a tree (*feminae pendentes*). In the description of Euadne's voluntary death by fire, a remark in passing confirms the view that hanging was common among women: she did not use iron 'nor hang herself *as women usually do* with respect to (the loss of) men'[55]. In the Hellenic world women are in the majority as regards self-hanging: 44 against 33 male cases.

We can see only the tip of the iceberg of suicide, but this permits us to test the interesting generalization made by Aristotle: the young, he says, usually use the rope (see also p.29). With 30 per cent for the cases of hanging, this way is notably more frequent among young people than among the whole of the suicides, irrespective of age (18 per cent). Aristotle says *neoi*, but in the attested cases the *neai* are the ones who account for the high score: 26 out of the 36 of self-killing among the young by hanging are ascribed to girls or young women. The general statement about a greater tendency towards hanging among unmarried girls in *Peri parthenion* is neatly confirmed by the reality as far as we see it[56].

The Greek world does not maintain a discreet silence as Roman civilization does: there are 81 Greek cases against only 27 Roman ones. This discrepancy means that in Rome hanging was 'not done', but nevertheless many practised it. Otherwise Horatius Balbus would not have declared explicitly that the cemetery he put at the disposal of the community was forbidden to those 'who have laid hands on themselves by the rope'. They were excluded in the same way as those who had an infamous profession – gladiators, actors and the like. Voisin, who recently discussed these testamentary dispositions, is right in refuting the view that a general exclusion of suicides was meant; it was only those who have killed themselves in an abominable way who were not to share the communal graveyard[57].

There are other measures related to burials which show that hanging was regarded as an infamous death. The contractor (*manceps*) who undertook the funerals of the community had to cut down the hanged and was obliged to remove them. This was part of his job as undertaker. Voisin sees this stipulation as evidence that hanging was 'une éventualité exceptionnelle et redoutable'[58]. I agree with that 'redoutable', but the mere fact that a specific regulation was included in the contract points to a well known phenomenon. Hanging was only exceptional among the Roman male elite: Manlius Silanus was found guilty of extortion in Macedonia, whereupon his father ordered him never to darken his door again. The son was so shaken that 'he did away with himself by hanging'. Very special too was the self-hanging of the high-priest Fulvius Flaccus. As an excuse for his dying by a 'dirty death' (*foeda morte*) was brought forward the fact that he 'had lost control of himself' after suffering a catastrophe in his family. Far from pardonable but rather shameful was the death of old Gordianus. Both father and son were regarded as unfit for being emperor by the *Historia Augusta*, but 'the elder put an end to his life by hanging himself, whereas the younger was destroyed in war, and accordingly deserves greater respect because war took him'[59]. Hanging was the method which distinguished a cissy from a man: Paccius was one of the attendants of Cato the Elder. From the booty he had bought three good-looking Spanish boys, 'but finding that Cato was aware of the transaction, even before he had confronted him, went and hanged himself'.

Within the framework of Roman values only contempt for such unmanly behaviour is dominant. The Greek world too is not unacquainted with a similar disdain: the fall of Timarchos the debauchee is signalled with moral satisfaction: he succumbed under the rhetorical violence of Demosthenes and used the rope. But in the Greek world there is room for another attitude with respect to hanging as an unhappy consequence of 'l'amour Grec'. The feelings of an anonymous lover are not returned by the *ephebe*. As the last of his many presents the *erastes* brings his own rope and speaks:

> ere thou turn thee to go thy ways, cry over me three times 'Rest, my friend,' and if it seem thee good, cry also 'My fair companion's dead.' And for epitaph write the words I here inscribe upon thy wall: *Here is one that died of love; good wayfarer, stay thee and say: his was a cruel friend*[60].

So, in the Greek world too, hanging was looked upon as the death of the desperate; sometimes the observer is satisfied when the method is felt to be a justified punishment as in Timarchos' case. Such satisfaction and disdain is more prominent in the Roman world, but it does not mean that hanging was 'une éventualité exceptionnelle' as Voisin holds.

A comparison with other cultures gives strong supporting evidence that the rope must have been a common means in spite of all the public horror it caused. In all non-urban societies hanging is the normal method. This truth was established for instance in the case of the Shona in Rhodesia/Zimbabwe. At the end of the 1950s hanging accounted for half of the self-killings in Western Nigeria. In a series of studies on suicide in Africa each paper says that hanging is by far the most popular way. In Bunyoro hanging was practised in more than 90 per cent of all cases. One of those interviewed by Bohannan (1960) even mixed up hanging and suicide. With respect to method Bohannan concludes on the basis of the studies undertaken on his instigation: 'the overwhelming method of suicide in Africa is hanging'. The history of the western world too indicates that hanging was commonly chosen. It was so in 32 out of the 54 medieval cases Schmitt collected[61]. The data for Victorian England give a supplementary indication that in pre-modern society hanging was always the usual method. At that time and place hanging was practised more by men than women, more by the old than the young and above all more often by the poor. As the time goes on the proportion of hanging diminishes: in 1861 it was still practised in 48 per cent of all cases; in Edwardian England of 1911 its quota had dropped and was 29 per cent, whereas poison rose from 7 to 14 per cent. In France a third of all suicides are 'still' committed by way of hanging[62].

A priori it is to be expected that in the Roman world too hanging was the primary method, even when this way is pictured as un-Roman. Dio Cassius registers the contrast in values when he describes the end of one of the closest assistants of Gaiobomarus, king of the Quadians. He hanged himself before Caracalla could have him executed. Then the emperor had the corpse violated in order to make the barbarians believe that he had been executed after all and had not taken his fate into his own hands, 'something which was regarded as honourable with them'.

Roman law reflects the view that hanging is vulgar; several remarks in passing demonstrate this situation. The mere fact that *suspendium* is mentioned as a separate category is already an indication that it was a common method. But jurisprudence at the same time confirms the low status of this exit.

One rubric of the *Digesta* deals with the question of what is to be done with the goods of those who kill themselves during legal proceedings. Can suicide be regarded as a confession and do the possessions of the accused therefore belong to the State as if he was found guilty? Different positions were held by subsequent emperors. Antoninus Pius determined that confiscation was only appropriate if the crime was so serious that it would have been punished by death or banishment. If somebody was accused of a 'moderate' theft, his possessions were never forfeited. Therefore the goods could not be withheld from the heirs *even if the accused had ended his life by hanging*. So the particular method had the stigma of being supposed to express feelings of guilt.

Similar despicable motivation is imputed in a passage about mourning: 'usually people do not go into mourning in the case of enemies or of those who have been convicted of betrayal *nor of people who have hanged themselves and those who laid hands upon themselves, not because they were sick of life, but from consciousness of guilt'*. So mourning when somebody killed himself out of disgust with life (*taedium vitae*) was regarded as fitting, but this acceptance did not apply to people who had hanged themselves. They had chosen an infamous method which was indicative of guilt and as such brought them near to the category of enemies of society[63].

A similar linking of a low motive with a disreputable method can be found in the *Codex Justinianus* 9,50. Once again the central question is: what to do with the goods of those who kill themselves while involved in legal proceedings? The answer is clear: their goods only accrue to the State if suicide was committed because of consciousness of guilt. Then the common motives for self-destruction are named, in such a complete way that that passage will serve as a starting-point for the next section about 'causes of dying' (*causae moriendi*). No means is specified until the sinister ending: 'or if it has been established that life was ended *in another case by hanging*'.

The lawsuits mentioned in the juridical discussions in the *Digesta* and the *Codex Justinianus* imply the involvement of accused who were better off: in those the method of hanging arouses suspicion about dishonourable motives. They were disqualified in principle and only the tolerant emperor, advised by humane jurisconsults, saved them from further ignomiry. Already in Roman times hanging seems to have taken on the mark of social disrepute which it had and has in later societies: in Victorian England 55 per cent of all the self-killing among agricultural labourers was done by hanging[64].

When the Roman law-giver looks at the bottom of society his expectations are completely different. When a slave is put up for sale who has attempted suicide in the past, his owner is legally obliged to inform the would-be buyer of that 'hidden defect'. In this context three methods are mentioned which a slave is supposed to use: *rope*, poison or jumping from a height; the sequence is meaningful. In Aristophanes' triad of ways to Hades too hanging came first[65].

Again and again, hanging figures as the primary means which always comes to the mind whenever the theme of self-killing by the desperate appears. Semonides says that in many ways people die before their time, by disease and war. 'Some in their misery use the rope and leave voluntarily the light of the sun'[66].

The priority of hanging as a natural way out in cases of deep misery is brought out by such self-cursing as 'May I hang if. . .'. According to psychoanalysis these exclamations are a form of aggression directed against the self. In ancient theatre the dramatis personae regularly express themselves in this way. In one of Plautus' plays a son is helped financially by his father to maintain a *hetaera* on condition that he himself may enjoy the charms of the girl once. The young man stands before the door and expostulates:

'I'd sooner hang myself than let you get your end away without a murmur'[67].

In all kinds of situations of despair and grief in comedy hanging – and only that – is mentioned as a method to get rid of all qualms. A gastronome exclaims: 'I shall choke myself to death unless you tell where you could have found such meat as that'. There was even a comedy entitled *The Man Who Hangs Himself (Apanchomenos)*[68].

Grief – *dolor* – real or feigned, is the sole motive which is over-represented where hanging was practised, with 24 per cent, whereas the general share of sadness as a ground for suicide is 13 per cent. Whenever the self-killer anticipates the reactions of the public and cares for his reputation, he does not use the rope, especially when he sacrifices himself for the common good, when he has an incurable illness or wants to demonstrate his philosophical autonomy.

Suspendium was the only means which generated black humour. In our own times too the horror caused by suicide is neutralized by cruel jokes: a Dutch artist has produced a greetings-card to be sent in cases of failed attempts at suicide. In the epigrams of *Anthologia Palatina* and in the Joker's Friend (*Philogelos*) witticisms are made on suicide as a theme, preferably by the ridiculous method of hanging. The thin Diophantos tied himself up by means of a spider's web. Aulos the astrologer saw in the stars that he had only four hours to live; in the fifth hour he feared he would have to live on as a charlatan. He himself made the horoscope true and hanged himself. Here the method of hanging is not part of the joke as it was in the case of the spider's web. The same holds for some other funny stories: the avaricious Hermon was vexed by a terrible nightmare: he had spent too much money. When he awoke, he hanged himself out of grief. A stupid person (*stultus quidam*) had heard that in Hades the courts of justice were righteous; being involved in a law-suit, he hanged himself. In these jokes hanging merely underlines the miserable character of the ridiculous protagonists; in ancient society humour nearly always means the elite laughing at the expense of ordinary people[69].

More significance has to be attributed to medical experience. It is clear that ancient doctors were regularly confronted with people who hanged themselves. The root of the mandragora was counted as an effective medicine for those who had a propensity to hang themselves, but the dose should not be too great, otherwise they became furious. Real observation of people who hanged themselves appears in an aphorism which generalizes a medical view: if such people are not dead when they are cut down, they will not survive if there is foam around the mouth[70].

In Egypt apparently it was one of the tasks of the public doctor to report the cause of a questionable death. Such a *demosios iatros* establishes that Hierax has hanged himself. In one of the few occasions when we – by way of papyri and ostraka – are able to have a look at normal 'life' in Egypt with respect to self-killing, hanging is the method. Isidora puts pressure upon her husband by threatening to hang herself: he has to come home at once because of the serious condition of the baby. In another papyrus St John the apostle is able to bring salvation in time to Zeuxis who was about to hang himself. For Christianity hanging has a specially sinister meaning: Judas the betrayer of Jesus absolutely rejected salvation by his suicide too, whereas the robber on the cross received God's mercy. Judas becomes part of a theme. In the iconography of the Christian sarcophagi the Sinner is pictured on a side-panel in contrast with the Saviour who triumphed on the cross and who even carried the crucified bandit to Paradise. But Judas, the prototype of a man who forsakes God, had lost all hope 'und erhängete sich selbst'[71].

Conclusive evidence for the preponderance of hanging is furnished by ancient dreams. Artemidoros of Daldis collected and explained hundreds of dreams; his *Interpretations of Dreams* (*Oneirokritika*) is a priceless source for attitudes and customs in the second century AD; as such it will be the subject of a special discussion (II.5A). In the ancient nightmares which were put before Artemidoros, hanging had a prominent place: 'Dreams about being hanged and hanging oneself predict disaster'. A final confirmation of the commonness of hanging is given by an anecdote. Timon the notorious misanthrope one day ascended the speaker's tribunal in the Athenian assembly, amazing everybody by this sudden show of social behaviour. What could he have to say?

I have a small building lot, men of Athens, and a fig-tree is growing in it, from which many of my fellow citizens have already hanged themselves. Accordingly, as I intend to build a house there, I wanted to give public notice to that effect, in order that all of you who desire to do so may hang yourselves before the fig-tree is cut down[72].

H WHEREAS THE BRIDGE IS AVAILABLE: JUMPING

Postumus, are you really taking a wife? You used to be sane enough – what fur's got into you, what snake has stung you up? Why endure such bitch-tyranny when rope's available by the fathom, when all those dizzying top-floor windows are open for you, when there the Aemilian Bridge is near at hand to jump from?

(Juvenal, *Satires* 6,28-32)

Rope and jumping belong in the same category, as means for the desperate. Juvenal already sees the opportunities of the big city. What the Eiffel tower was for would-be suicides before wire-netting was installed, the apartment blocks of five or six stories were for world-weary Romans. Juvenal's Rome also had the equivalents of the bridges over the Seine.

In France drowning oneself is practised by a quarter of the suicides[73]. It is self-evident that this method is most popular in regions where substantial rivers are available. Mediterranean countries do not have broad rivers at their disposal, but still Voisin (1987 p.273) is not right in stating: 'les morts volontaires par immersion sont très rares'. A similar negative mechanism of selection to that which is operative in hanging, accounts for the fact that the number of *recorded* cases of jumping from a height or the water has little to do with what presumably was reality.

Throwing oneself – in the water or to the solid ground – is, with 102 cases, third in frequency. The method has to a certain degree been legitimized by myth. Aigeus gave his name to the sea into which he jumped. Solois baptized a river by diving into it: he had fallen in love with Antiope, queen of the Amazons, who had been won by and for Theseus. Other mythological jumpers too are driven by mourning or grief because of frustrated love. Ino had accidentally killed her own children. Selene could not bear the death of her brother. Skylla had sacrificed her purple hair to enable Minos to take her native town, Megara. Having conquered the city he did not take her with him to Crete. Thereupon she threw herself into the sea.

There is perhaps in the last story an element to which Versnel has called attention. In his article 'Self-sacrifice, Compensation and the Anonymous Gods' (1981) he has made it clear that throwing oneself into the sea or into the earth, as Curtius did in the

Roman Forum, is a way of uniting oneself with the earth. Similar self-killing in myth therefore may indicate total self-sacrifice. It can only be guessed what the impact of the mythical dimension was on the behaviour of common people.

There were in antiquity places which were preferred by the desperate for the final act. The five-hundred-metre high cliffs of Leucas, against which the waves break spectacularly, fascinated the desperate. Some undertook long travels to have this as their last prospect: Phobos from Phocaea is said to have been the first who leapt from the Leucadian rocks. Even the great poetess of love, Sappho, is supposed to have jumped into the Ionian Sea because of unfulfilled passion[74].

The Lesbian Muse, according to this reading, put an end to her life because of a desperate love *for a man*. In female homosexuality there are no equivalents of the couple Timagoras and Meles, of whom the first jumped when challenged to demonstrate his love; the latter followed from a love discovered too late. This case of *amour grec* taken together with the 'mythical' cases accounts for the preponderance of the Greeks in the harsh means of jumping: 55, as against 30 Roman instances. Throwing oneself from a height does not require any technical preparation; as a natural method it was available for Maira the dog and the Scythian stallion (pp.6 and xiii). As a primitive method it was counted as highly natural in those extraordinary cases where the community was asked by an oracle to sacrifice its highest good: the young warrior who – often mounted on a horse – jumped into a chasm, thus unifying himself with the earth[75].

The motives connected with this way out are generally of the lowest order: despair, grief, fury and shame, especially from sexual humiliation. Halia could not bear having been raped by her own sons: after her jump into the sea she became Leukotheia the sea-goddess who in Homer's epic comes to the assistance of Odysseus. The suicides committed from *pudor* are often the last episode in a story full of sex and violence. Niobe, in one of the versions of her myth, was approached by her father Assaon. When he was repulsed, he burned her children to death. Thereupon she threw herself from the rocks. 'Assaon, realizing what he had done, did away with himself'.

The combination of homicide and suicide is a well-known phenomenon in the modern world. Psychoanalytically it is explained as the turning of external into internal aggression. In the ancient world the linking of murder and self-destruction is not limited to mythology[76]. Having killed his master an anonymous slave leapt into the river Main. This *servus homicida* is known from the epitaph for his master (p.151).

This nameless slave included, there are 21 Roman *historical* examples of jumping – as said before, the Greek cases are mainly mythical. The act is always an explosion of aggression. There are no attested cases of quietly going into a river, a method which fascinated Victorian novelists. As early as the Time of the Kings many of the plebeians threw themselves in the Tiber. Under Septimius Severus the unlucky pretender Taurinus found his end in the Euphrates. The leap from the window by the young Sextus Papinius is qualified by Tacitus as a 'ghastly end' (*informis exitus*), an expression which is to be compared with *informe letum* for hanging: both methods are roughly the same in ancient appreciation. Solely in deep misery, without long consideration, are these means used, which deform people after death. Diogenes showed his disdain for all convention, even for keeping bodily integrity, by his exit.

When he had grown fatally ill, he dragged himself to a bridge near the gymnasium and threw himself from it; previously he had ordered the guard of the wrestling school to hurl him into the Ilissus once he had made sure that he had breathed his last. *For so little did death and burial bother Diogenes*[77].

When couples threw themselves from a height the disgust of the observers for the horrible method was overcome by admiration for the demonstration of loyalty. So, this respect was not reserved for those who shared death and dagger, as in the case of Arria and Paetus. A combined leap synchronized death completely. At Lake Como, a woman took the initiative in the act. During a tour on the lake Pliny's attention was drawn to a rock from which a married couple had leapt. The man was suffering from ulcerated wounds, which he tried to conceal from his wife.

She asked his leave to inspect them, protesting that no one would give him a more honest opinion whether they were curable. She looked and she despaired. She then advised him to put an end to his life; and made herself not only the companion but actually the guide, example, and instrument of his death; for, tying herself to her husband, she plunged with him into the lake.   (*Comensis uxor*, Appendix A)

A demonstration of pre-matrimonial loyalty was the subject of a painting which Philostratos admired in Naples. A boy and a girl were fellow-pupils. They were not able to satisfy their passion because the world was against them. Together they threw themselves from a rock in a first and last embrace. The god Eros, who was the cause of it all, was present on this – episodic – picture: he pointed with a hand to the scene, discreetly indicating his power. In the descriptions by Pliny and Philostratos of the two suicides by pairs disapproval is absent completely. The end of going together into death justified the means which, taken on its own, was regarded as infamous[78].

In conditions of acute distress jumping into certain death was the method prescribed and as such it is recorded without disdain. Beleaguered people threw themselves from the walls they could no longer hold. Christians escaped their persecutors by jumping from the roofs. This happened in Antioch in AD 303, during the Great Persecution. In the same centre of Christianity the young Pelagia suddenly noticed that the house was encircled, nobody being present to help her and her little sister. She encouraged her sister and thereupon they jumped into the water as in a baptismal font, for – as Ambrosius puts it – faith wipes away misdeed (*facinus fides ablevat*). With this formula the bishop of Milan soothes his own embarrassment with this act of self-killing which was hailed without reserve by Eusebios only half a century before: Christian attitudes had changed drastically in the meantime. This shift was partially caused by the behaviour of the heretic Donatists in North Africa of whom some were said to have thrown themselves from the rocks in order to reach the status of a saint (p.196)[79].

Pelagia and her sister contribute towards lowering the average age of those who jumped. Only Aigeus may be counted as an old man. Historical examples of old people who ended their life by throwing themselves are not recorded: the method required a minimum of fitness and a maximum of aggression.

Parallel to the curve of age runs the line of motives: they remain on the lower side of the spectrum. Only Kleombrotos' suicide might be regarded as a philosophical demonstration (*iactatio*): he jumped from a wall after reading *the* book of Plato. Had he ceased to be a 'vir unius libri' by reading, apart from the *Phaedo*, Plato's *Laws*, he could have reached different conclusions. Callimachus' epigram about this pointedly mocks such 'precipitate' behaviour by intellectuals who have lost common sense. In this way Kleombrotos confirms Moron's general statement (p.37): 'Historiquement, et culturellement, la mort par précipitation a toujours eu un caractère infamant'. The infamy of the method is only overcome by the high motive of devotion and matrimonial loyalty or excused by acute distress, siege or persecution.

I THE MEANING OF THE METHOD IN THE *ARS MORIENDI*

Methods such as hanging and jumping in general are looked upon as base, because they violate the integrity of the body. The well-known anxiety of ancient people about losing face is very concrete with regard to death. In modern times self-killers wish to save finder and relatives from a shocking scene. In antiquity the appearance of the mortal remains has everything to do with the way and degree in which one is supposed to live in the hereafter. The art of dying should be a worthy fulfilment of life.

That preoccupation with *dignitas* in living and dying is of course strongest in the elite which adheres to the values of manliness: only metal befits the representative of *virtus*. Even the domestic form of soldierly death, i.e. opening the veins, is superior to modern fiddling with razor blades. We saw that a full ritual was developed which aimed at creating a sphere of dignity and wisdom around the self-chosen – or forced – death. 'Going to die, a Roman senator did not call a priest, but received spiritual comfort from a philosopher'. The necessary elements of style, indicated by Atticus and Seneca, Griffin sums up as 'theatricality, social character, calmness, philosophical overtones'[80]. For an old man *inedia* is an option that bears testimony to resoluteness and dignity. Abstaining from food is a specifically Graeco-Roman way of self-killing. On the other hand ostentatious self-burning has the odour of oriental incense.

Apparently poison was far less important than in our world: the ancient medicine-cupboard did not contain many reliable means. Apart from that there was a marked aversion against the disfiguration caused by drugs. Taking poison was looked upon as an indirect, abject method in which the so much appreciated element of freedom was weakened. As to self-killing, ancient behaviour has little of the 'life-preserving and contact-seeking tendencies' which, Taylor says, are so characteristic of modern 'self-destructive acts', which leave room for intervention by another person. Ancient suicides were no 'gambles with death'. The act had a character similar to what Anderson has established for suicide in the English countryside in the last century: it was 'deliberate, direct, and resolute'[81].

At the bottom in the scale of respectability are jumping and hanging. Only in acute distress or in the case of a loyal couple was throwing oneself to be respected. Hanging underwent a change in its evaluation: mythical prototypes grant a certain hallowing to the method, especially for women. But in the recording of historical cases the method less and less befits those who care for their dignity. Here we have one of those striking pre-modern features in ancient society. In the Roman world the *image* of noble self-killing banishes hanging to the margin. Women, slaves and inferior people are expected to use that infamous means. Comparison with other cultures and data from antiquity itself indicate that in reality the 'rope of ghastly death' was most common.

The method of self-killing was very important for the quality of the death thus obtained. Still more important was the motive in the eyes of the ancient world. The sources reflect this difference in importance: whereas in 282 out of 960 cases no method is specifically mentioned – in some cases it could be guessed by deduction – only in 37 instances is it not possible to establish the motive: the style of self-killing was determined even more by the motive than by the means.

3

CAUSAE MORIENDI

Sociology and psychology can be said to owe their life to self-killing: it was in their different approaches to suicide that they each demarcated their specific domains as sciences in the nineteenth century. Psychiatrists argued that any suicide was motivated by mental disturbances. Psychoanalysis has disclosed the existence of death-desire which may lead to a voluntary end (it has been remarked that calling suicide the victory of Thanatos over Eros is just a rather complicated way of saying that someone has killed himself). Plastic and literary art of the nineteenth century, especially that of the *fin-de-siècle*, was fascinated by suicide; artistic and scientific production met with an interested general public. There is a demographic background behind these preoccupations: in the second half of the century, with the diminishing general death rate, for the first time suicide appears in the statistics[1]. 'Suicide is the most individual act committed under the pressure of social forces'[2]. The sociological approach to self-killing was initiated by Durkheim at the end of the nineteenth century. He refuted vigorously all psychological, racial and geographical explanations: on the contrary, forces operative in society were to be regarded as responsible for suicide and its growth – for all observers of the period are convinced that the rate of self-killing was increasing in urbanized Western Europe with its 'hyper-civilisation'[3]. Durkheim's view that social factors determined suicidal behaviour inspired him to formulate a programme for prevention. At the end of *Le suicide* (1897) he pleads for strengthening the integrative powers of modern society. As church, village, town and family irretrievably lose their power of linking people together, the labour community should replace them as the framework of life. In this way the classical macro-sociological study of suicide comes to a close in a plea for a corporative society.

Durkheim's faith in statistics[4], his processing of figures and his ephemeral schemes for prevention have been attacked more than once since 1897. But his theory of suicide has up to now remained virtually unchallenged, in the sense that it remained the point of reference. Gibbs' 'disruption of social relations as the etiological factor in suicide' (Gibbs 1968) is no more than a socio-psychological restating of Durkheim's concept of disintegration[5]. For the historian it is important to notice that Durkheim claims to have developed a typology which is valid for all societies, including those of the past. Anywhere where the group is involved in a process of disintegration and when excessive individualization gains ground, 'suicide égoïste' occurs. On the other hand excessive integration too may lead to suicide: in the 'altruistic' type of self-killing a person sacrifices himself because of extreme identification with the group. An 'anomic' self-murder is the reaction to a sudden change in position. Durkheim's examples are limited to capitalists who go bankrupt: this species is too closely linked with the financial scandals the nineteenth century was so full of. Finally, the great French sociologist does not observe instances of 'suicide fataliste' in his own time; in older societies it occurred as a consequence of excessive prevalence of rules ('régulation'). Self-killing by slaves is the only example of this intriguing category which is furnished in *Le suicide* (1897).

The sociological approach cannot dispense with statistics; they are gathered, grouped, explained and interpreted to support or falsify theories. The fascination of the sociologists with figures has come under attack in recent decades. Taylor's research is a specimen of this contemporary scepticism towards hard numbers (p.9). Taylor developed his own model in which special attention is paid to the numerous individuals who, having exposed themselves to high risks and having survived them, feel they have undergone an ordeal with success. In order to give this modern pattern of behaviour its due place in theory, Taylor created a new typology in which psychological and sociological dimensions are combined[6].

It is absolutely impossible to classify ancient suicides according to the categories of Durkheim, Halbwachs, Johnson, Taylor or whoever has enriched suicidological theory. The materials available do not permit the historian to make the fine analyses which are necessary to check the significance of the modern concepts. In what way could he establish the predisposition of a self-killer from the past? He is satisfied enough if his data include the circumstances of the final act itself. In general our 960 cases mention the sex, the means and the – immediate – motive, but the data of age and status are so incomplete and uncertain that only an impressionistic picture could be presented of different categories, as was done under *casus moriendi* for special groups: common people, the young and the old.

We know hardly anything about the life-history of ancient self-killers. Only the short statements by Seneca and Augustine about thoughts of suicide in their youth merit entry in a modern psychiatric report which exposes the layers of causality: the individual's origins, childhood, unique experiences, diseases, mental balance, life habits and finally the circumstance which triggered off the self-killing. Usually only the last factor in the chain of causes is known to us with respect to ancient suicide and is classified as *the* motive.

So our material remains superficial. In fact we have gathered 960 forms of which only the first questions have been filled in: man or woman; Greek, Roman or none at all; period; accomplished or only attempted; method; motive. The nature of the data does not allow us to apply the categories of Durkheim, Deshaies or Taylor.

It is not only the insufficiency of the material – the common complaint and excuse of the ancient historian – that requires restraint in processing the data. There is also the principal question whether modern theories are applicable outside their context. When surveying the theories of suicide which all originated in the last century, one becomes aware of the link between them and the specific culture the suicidologists lived in. Nineteenth-century fear of the metropolis evidently provoked sociological theories that put disintegration to the forefront. Only recently has it been realized that in spite of all its claims to be universal sociology represents an image of a specific period[7]. During the Middle Ages self-killing was ascribed to despair (*desperatio*) or anger (*ira*), states of mind which belong to people who did not comply with God's order. Does this medieval concept not make clear that every society of the past had its own paradigm of suicide?

Because of the serious doubts about the possibility of applying modern models of suicide to past societies and in the light of the limitations of the material, it seemed preferable to try to describe ancient motivation in ancient terms. In this way we would not get entangled in the discussions which go on between sociologists and psychologists: the – deficient – data are not to be laid upon the Procrustean bed of modern suicidology.

In this way, too, more justice is done to the main purpose of this study: that of examining how the ancient world saw suicide. In order to attain such a 're-enactment of the past' (Collingwood[8]) or to reconstruct the history of mentality in accordance with Vovelle's model it is essential to recreate the experience of ancient observers. No study of suicide in antiquity can claim to show 'how it really was'. Even in categorizing the 'who' and 'how', again and again we discovered that our material in many respects has already been sorted drastically. Even the 'mere' facts demonstrate aspects of attitudes towards self-killing.

Even more does this process of selection apply to motivation. The 'cause' of an (accomplished) suicide is always the explanation given by an observer: after the act he imposes a logical structure on the phenomena. If an author of a book about suicide in antiquity should ever put an end to his own life, undoubtedly that publication would be classified in hindsight as an announcement of the deed.

It has been argued that an analysis of (unsuccessful) attempted suicide is the key to a better understanding of motives for self-killing in general. But, fundamentally, an attempt is not to be compared with an accomplished act[9]. The questions asked with regard to modern analyses of motives for suicides are still more urgent in the case of the reasons which have been recorded by the survivors; poets, historians and philosophers certainly stylize the motives. What we notice are nearly always the reasons they *ascribe* to some other person. Investigating motivation means overstepping the – thin – boundary between facts and interpretations.

Was there such a thing as an ancient framework of thinking about suicide in which the attribution of causes had its place? General theories with a Durkheimian degree of generalization are lacking, of course. There are, exceptionally, certain general observations, about suicidal tendencies in young girls (p.22) and about hanging as a preferred method among the young, but that is all. Suicide is a problem often discussed in philosophy – see Part III – but there moral questions about permissibility are in the forefront. For an 'amoralistic' approach we should address Roman jurisconsults. Only marginally are they interested in suicide: Roman law does not punish (attempted) suicide, but there are situations in which a self-killing causes juridical complications. If the accused commits suicide before the court has come to a verdict, is this deed to be interpreted as a confession and – main interest of the State – may his goods be confiscated as if he had been condemned? A soldier has a special relationship with the State: may he commit suicide? It is only with respect to such limited juridical problems that jurisconsults and emperors have made known their authoritative views. These have been assembled into the late-Roman codifications: the opinions recorded in the Corpus Iuris and the codex Theodosianus reflect a long tradition of reflecting on suicide. Their representativeness is shown by the strikingly secular character in approach of the codices: they have not yet been 'infected' by the Christian condemnation of suicide as a sin, which was gaining ground in the period when the codes of law were written. The jurisconsults of the empire keep aloof from moral lessons. They only asked themselves what were the consequences of self-killing in those cases which came to court. The general line in their opinions is that self-destruction may only be seen as a confession if *no excusable motive* was apparent. Those valid grounds were listed and there was a tendency to expand the list as much as possible. In this way the Roman lawyers formulate a certain model of suicide based on legal practice. To have had enough of life, or to have conceived, as the phrase goes, 'hatred against life', was counted as an acceptable motive. This *taedium vitae* may comprise bodily or mental problems as well as a general satiety with life[10].

The general aversion to life can be more specific and the more excusable at that, when it is the consequence of bodily suffering, *inpatientia* (*doloris* or *valetudinis*)[11]. Sometimes simply the word *dolor* is used. In most cases identifiable diseases are indicated, but, as the inscription of Bassulus (p.153) shows, a distinction can be made between bodily and mental suffering (*corporis dolores* and *curae anxiae*). In this study *dolor* will be used throughout to indicate psychic pain, whereas for unbearable physical ailments *inpatientia* will act as the standard word.

Shame, *pudor*, is recognized by law as a legitimate ground for self-killing. Fear of losing face is a powerful motive for the way ancient people behave. If one feels unable to face others, self-killing is a ready solution. There are many ways in which a person may lose face. The law specifies shame because of being in debt[12].

Suicide may also legitimately be committed out of frenzy, *furor*. If this was the main factor in a self-killing, the suicide did not incriminate himself – and his possessions came into the hands of his heirs[13].

The jurisconsults go to great lengths in categorizing motives: even the quite uncommon exhibitionist suicide by philosophers was mentioned as a type in which the self-killer did not implicitly confess guilt. The law calls it self-killing from ostentation, *iactatio*[14]. Taken together these excusable grounds are a rather elaborate 'discipline of suicide'.

Taedium vitae, inpatientia, dolor, pudor, furor and *iactatio* are regarded as motives valid in law: heirs are allowed to inherit from the deceased and when soldiers have attempted a suicide for one of these reasons, they are only dismissed with ignominy, but are not otherwise severely punished. Only the soldier who had no such excuse and was not overcome with wine (*per vinum*) or wantonness (*per lasciviam*) was punished – somewhat illogically – with death[15].

Only if no valid motive could be attributed was the judge to assume that the suicide was committed because of a bad conscience (*mala conscientia*). If somebody prematurely did away with himself even before a formal charge was brought then it is assumed that he acted from fear of the imminent accusation (*metus criminis imminentis*). In our analysis of motives we will simply say *conscientia* in the – few – recorded cases where feelings of guilt lead to suicide[16].

Some motives remained unmentioned by law for obvious reasons. The Roman emperor would not have liked to see as a distinct category those suicides which were committed on his order or instigation. The historians use several words for this type of enforced self-killing; one of these is (self-murder from) necessity, *necessitas*[17].

It is not to be expected that somebody who is involved in a trial suddenly will feel the urge to sacrifice himself for the fatherland: law did not have to account for such rare motivation. Self-killings from *devotio* have such a prominent place in Greek and Roman historiography and mythology that they deserve to be reckoned as

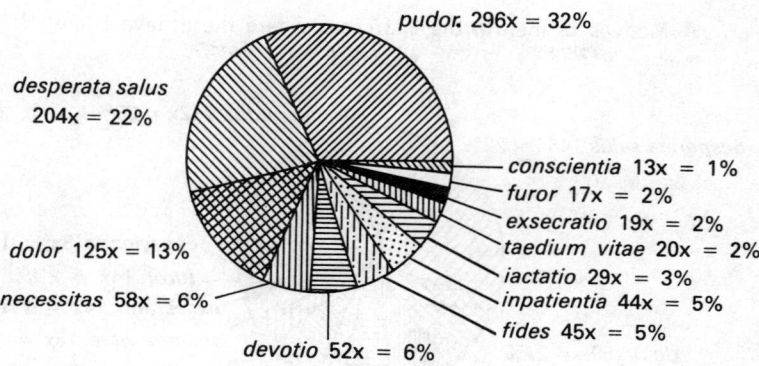

Motives in the 923 cases where these have been specified

Figure 3.1 The proportions of the various motives; motives in the 923 cases where these have been specified

a group on their own. Closely related to this is the motive of loyalty (*fides*) towards leader or husband which causes subordinates and women to die with their master[18].

Almost the opposite of fidelity is the wish to bring a curse upon a country or an individual by a suicide. For this interesting, but small, group *exsecratio* has been used to denote the motive.

Many a suicide cannot be listed under any of these twelve headings of motives. Often the texts only indicate that an individual or a group left life from despair. For this extensive, but not very specific group of cases the motive has been denoted as 'despairing of deliverance', *desperata salus*.

A   DESPAIR: *DESPERATA SALUS*

That very expression 'because deliverance was despaired of' was used by Caesar to denote the state of mind in which his soldiers, having resisted Ambiorix's attacks during the day, killed themselves to a man when night fell[19]. In general, ancient texts describing such situations are vaguer about the motive; it is only the context

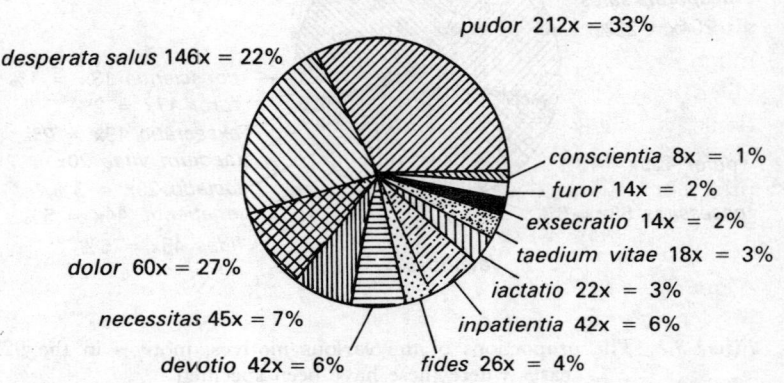

A. Motives of men in the 652 cases where these have been specified

pudor 212x = 33%

desperata salus 146x = 22%

conscientia 8x = 1%

furor 14x = 2%

exsecratio 14x = 2%

taedium vitae 18x = 3%

iactatio 22x = 3%

inpatientia 42x = 6%

dolor 60x = 27%

necessitas 45x = 7%

devotio 42x = 6%

fides 26x = 4%

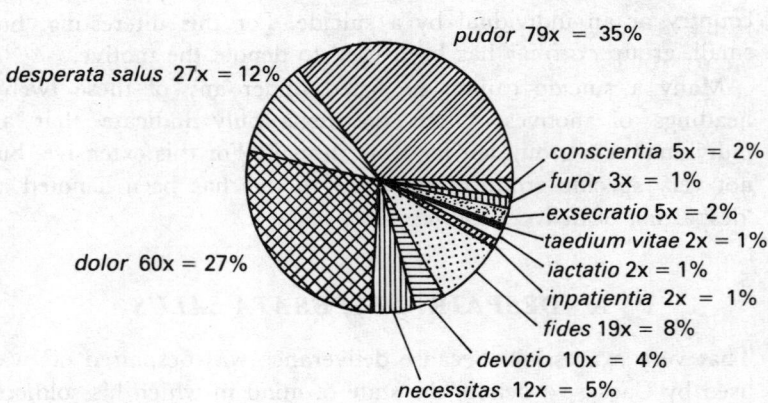

B. Motives of women in the 226 cases where these have been specified

pudor 79x = 35%

desperata salus 27x = 12%

conscientia 5x = 2%

furor 3x = 1%

exsecratio 5x = 2%

taedium vitae 2x = 1%

iactatio 2x = 1%

inpatientia 2x = 1%

fides 19x = 8%

dolor 60x = 27%

devotio 10x = 4%

necessitas 12x = 5%

Figure 3.2 Motives of men and women compared

that points at despair as the cause for suicide. Despair is hardly specific as a motive and in drawing up categories *desperata salus* is a kind of rubric for those cases where the ancient – or modern – observer 'desperately' tries to denote a cause: in the last resort all suicides are committed because hope has been lost.

In observing the causes attributed to suicides, at first in this chapter more global motives will be discussed, such as despair, and after that attention will be paid to more specific reasons in which much weight is given to the free act of will. Caesar's soldiers who killed themselves *desperata salute* did not, according to the description, act wholly out of panic: they realized that there was no alternative exit. The death of people on one's own side is not, for preference, pictured as infamous behaviour. But despair on the side of the enemy is described with satisfaction.

When cities are on the point of being taken, there are horrible scenes of self-destruction out of despair. Ancient historians wallow in picturing those orgies of desperation: all means which lead to a quick death – jumping from a height, fire, hanging – are used[20]. Leaping from the walls of the city or the citadel is a method which is especially prescribed by the situation and observed as a well-deserved fate by the historians on the winning side. The same applies to immolation in the fire of the burning city. Appendix B 8b, which concerns the relations between methods and motives, shows the link between these instant means and the motive of despair.

A certain military code of honour developed among the army gathered by Eunus, the slaves' king, in Sicily. When the end of their revolt was near, the *fugitivi* beheaded each other (BC 132). In BC 104, in Sicily again, fellow-slaves who had tried once more to rebel were suddenly surrounded, as the result of treason. The only way out was to jump from the citadel[21]. Rebels in particular deserve to expiate their infidelity by self-destruction. The leader of the Treveri, Iulius Florus, died by his own hand when the revolt in Gaul broke down in AD 21. The Dacian king Decebalus killed himself in AD 106 when Trajan's victory was inevitable.

Roman soldiers in extremis regularly used their weapons against themselves: under *milites* in Appendix A there is a series of such historical examples. Fear of losing honour (*pudor*) and loyalty to the leader (*fides*) contributed to their decision in such cases, if we are to believe the descriptions of the historians. Thus the soldiers of the legio Martia killed themselves almost ritually after the defeat of

Pompey's cause in the battle of Philippi in BC 42. In the Teutoburg forest Varus's soldiers massed about their general and killed themselves at the last moment. Their leader 'following the example of his father and grandfather ran himself through his sword'. After the downfall of the cause of the Republic at Philippi in BC 42 Varus the elder had had his throat cut by a freedman 'whom he had forced to do so . . . after having covered himself with all his decorations'. It seems that his father too had laid hands upon himself after Thapsus (BC 46). In this way he initiated an oppressive tradition in the family.

Like the battle in the Teutoburg forest the destruction of a whole army at Carrhae in BC 53 was a traumatic experience in the Roman mind. But Roman honour was saved: apart from the unhappy commander Crassus and his son, Crassus' followers Censorinus and Magabacchus, his officers and soldiers chose death when they realized that there was no escape from the revenge of the Parthians. The motive of Crassus senior is explicitly described as far above common despair. He killed himself 'in order to avoid anything which *did not befit his quality*': *pudor* was decisive in his decision according to the historian. A shameful contrast was presented by the younger Crassus: he had himself killed by his shield-bearer[22].

Roman generals decided not to survive a defeat more often than their Greek colleagues, according to ancient historiography. Perhaps Demosthenes the strategus furnishes a rare Hellenic exception: one source has it that he put an end to his life after the Sicilian disaster in BC 413 (the mainstream of the tradition says that he was killed by the victor under torture). In Hellenistic times two Greek military leaders preferred not to survive a defeat. Philoumenos had organized Hannibal's possession of Taranto. When Fabius Maximus regained the city for the Romans, he fled. His body never was found. 'He was generally thought to have thrown himself from his horse into a well'. The fall of Corinth in BC 146 was counted as symbolic of the ruin of Greek liberty. On that occasion Diaios, the leader of the last Hellenic coalition against the Romans, was overpowered by Mummius. 'He gave up (*apognous*) and killed himself'.

These last two cases were described from the Roman perspective with the satisfaction of the victor watching the enemy setting about his own destruction. The unhappy endings of sacrilegious Roman commanders were also observed with moral approbation. Iunius

Pullus, in his time the first military suicide among the Romans, had not cared for the ominous pecking of the oracle-chickens aboard his flag-ship and had kicked them into the sea: if they were unwilling to eat then let them drink. No wonder that finally he put an end to his life when he was beleaguered at Eryx.

The suicides committed during the Civil Wars of the first century BC cause controversy. Sometimes it is recorded without comment that a leader simply did what was necessary in his hopeless situation. Young Marius and Pontius Telesinus were shut in an underground corridor at Praeneste while the city was being taken. Marius gave Telesinus the wished for end and 'when he noticed that escape was impossible' he put an end to his life 'with his own hand'. More respect is paid by the sources to a contract of suicide between king Juba and Petreius. When the cause of Caesar's opponents in Africa was irretrievably lost after Thapsus in BC 46 they duelled to the death. Juba, the victor, had himself killed by a slave.

Internal wars during the Late Empire again accounted for suicides among generals: Arbogast, a Frank in Roman service, made himself virtual ruler of the West after the death of emperor Valentinianus II in May 394 AD. A few months later Arbogast was defeated near Frigidus by Theodosius' troops. On 5 or 6 September he put an end to his life.

Political and military leadership were one and the same until the Roman Principate[23]. Therefore self-killings of leaders who failed politically are in fact a variation of those by unsuccessful generals. Antalkidas had lost all credibility in Greece, being responsible for the King's Peace of 386 BC, according to which Sparta on behalf of the Persian Empire supervised the general peace. After the shocking Spartan defeat at Leuctra (BC 371) he asked the Great King for money. Artaxerxes refused and Antalkidas' world was in ruins. He feared the ephors and was oppressed by his opponents. In this situation self-killing was his desperate escape.

Gaius Gracchus 'offered his head to his slave Euporus' when his policy of radical reform had failed and the Senate's gangs were restoring the old order. Emperors and pretenders to the throne, who see the end of their cause nearing, escape from life. Nero's death was as unworthy as his life. When the horsemen came to execute the Senate's orders to kill him, Nero's hand needed the assistance of Epaphroditus to find the spot in his neck. In fact an emperor could not survive being deposed. This was so self-evident that the final victor in the troubles of AD 192–3, Septimius Severus, made use of the pattern. He had Didius Iulianus, the unsuccessful emperor, executed, pretending that he had killed himself.

Civil wars generate whole series of self-killings from despair as the result of the lost cause. Whenever a source *explicitly* states that a 'loss of face' was the main motive for suicide or that somebody was unwilling to subject himself *shamefully* to the clemency of the victor, his suicide is not counted as committed *desperata salute*, but caused by *pudor*. Such an honourable comment was not made by the historians on this case of despair: when Cassius was entering Laodikeia, Dolabella, the commander defending the city, 'offered his head to his body-guard' and urged him to go to the victor with it as a welcome gift and thereby to obtain his mercy. But the loyal servant executed only the first part of the order and then 'slaughtered himself as well', with an act of loyalty responding to a deed of despair.

What can conspirators expect of life when they have been unmasked? Dimnos was discovered planning an assault on Alexander's life; Calpurnius Piso was betrayed as the instigator of an attempt on Nero's life. Self-chosen death was the only way out of the blind alley into which the conspirators had manoeuvred themselves.

'Some have killed themselves out of fear of being killed'[24]. Has this paradox, fostered by Epicureans, been fed by the recent experience of Lucretius and his contemporaries during the terror of the proscriptions? During the Sullan persecution Mutilus discovered his name on the list of the outlawed. His wife forbade him to enter the house. Thereupon he killed himself with a sword. During a new wave of proscriptions at the time of the Second Triumvirate, horrible scenes occurred. In order to escape the assault of the 'dagger-men' (*siccarii*) Cestius and Statius burned themselves to death, the latter together with his whole house (p.58). Other *proscripti* put an end to their lives by hanging themselves in public (*en mesoi*) or by making a literal 'salto mortale'.

Some juridical forms at least were respected during the terror exercised by some *principes* of the Early Empire. There was not much hope left for those who were accused of *lèse-majesté*: most of those unlucky individuals saved their honour by dying voluntarily. There even was a premium set upon promptly fulfilling the emperor's hint: the goods of the deceased remained intact for their heirs. People who did not wait for the public disgrace of a formal hearing demonstrated some dignity; their motive can be denoted as *pudor*. But those who waited too long and only during the hearing or in jail put an end to their lives acted mainly from despair. They are to be compared with the numerous suicides in modern police-cells by people who have literally been cornered.

Even the mere possibility of being accused could cause panic. Aristomenes reacted promptly, as he tells us in Apuleius' novel *Metamorphoses*, when he found a comrade killed and all indications were against him – in reality two witches had murdered the man. 'I went to the bedroom and cast about for some rapid means of suicide (*tumultuarius mors*)'. Only the bedstead furnished him with some means. He undid the rope that corded the bed and fastened one end of it over a rafter jutting out above the window. But the rope was old, and broke.

Having been condemned Clodius Eprius seized a razor, always an important instrument for self-killing in civilized society. Nero, Germanicus' son, was in jail. The executioner pretended he had been sent by the Senate and showed ropes and pincers. 'Then the boy is said to have decided to end his life by abstaining from food'. In a grim oxymoron Suetonius puts it thus: 'one assumes that Nero was forced to a free death'. *In summa desperatione* Mela the knight 'swallowed a dose of leek-juice weighing three denarii in silver, and immediately expired without suffering any pain', when asked by Tiberius to account for his procuratorship.

Military and political careers were fundamentally closed to women. Except for their participation in *suicides obsidionaux* they have hitherto not been recorded as committing suicide from despair. In individual cases their share is only 27 as opposed to 146 male ones. The collective self-killing of the twenty women who were taken in the very act of brewing poison has the profile of a desperate suicide in a police-enquiry. Antigone herself executed the verdict of death when she was doomed by Kreon to die in an underground chamber. Seianus' wife Apicata had nothing good to expect from living on when the day of reckoning came for her husband, Tiberius' evil genius, and his clique. It is the common fate of women to share in the fall of their husband[25].

Two Vestal Virgins are said not to have waited for the punishment which followed on their loss of chastity, i.e. being buried alive[26]. Apollonia, a Christian, freed herself from the hands of the executioner and leapt into the fire; this desperate act is described without any sign of disapproval by the Church historian.

This suicide is pictured as the deed of a noble woman who acted as the situation required. As the decision was taken in a moment, the motive of despair seems dominating. But of course shame played its part in the suicidal behaviour of women. It was not only fear of being violated that dictated the course of action. Thus Hasdrubal's wife put her husband to shame during the holocaust at Carthage in BC 146. While her husband gave himself up to captivity, she seized her two children and threw herself from a roof into the blaze: she at least showed herself a worthy member of Dido's race[27].

Some women lost all hope when the man they loved died. Chilonis had left Kleonymos for Akrotatos, son of the State's ruler. When her legitimate husband was besieging the city where they were living, Chilonis held a rope against her neck, ready to end her life if she fell into the hands of Kleonymos. A similar, almost mythical, behaviour was demonstrated by Kamma, a Celtic woman. She was married to Sinatos, but was loved by Sinorix. This rogue killed Sinatos and courted Kamma. At first she renounced his advances, but suddenly she showed herself willing. She led him to the altar and made a libation, took a draught herself from the dish and had him drink the rest of the poisoned mixture.

It was not only mythical and historical Didos and Medeas that put an end to their life when they had lost all hope. Among humble women we can assume many suicides. An anonymous Greek maidservant (*ancilla Graeca* in Appendix A) got into a desperate situation. She had money deposited with her by two gentlemen which she was only allowed to restore to both at the same time. But the one appeared and told her that the other had died. Thereupon he got the money. When the second turned up 'she was petrified from misery . . . she considered rope and hanging'. But then Demosthenes' genius came to her rescue: he demanded that the second creditor appear with the other to receive his money back, in accordance with the contract. Of course, Demosthenes is the central figure of the story; it is a neat example of the way in which sometimes common people come to our attention as minor players in the stories of gentlemen. Behind the old female slave Staphyla we may suspect the presence of a mass of old women who also made themselves 'a long letter' when they could see no escape from misery. For the desperate old of humble rank may stand Aristeides, the man who lost his only sheep and cow, Menophanes who even had to use another man's tree and the anonymous old man who according to the epigram usurped the grave-pit of somebody else. Generally, historical men from the lower classes who commit suicide from despair remain nameless, as the slave (*servus homicida*; p.151) who threw himself into the Main after killing his master, the barbarian before the naumachia and the gladiator who was on his way to the arena (*missus ad spectaculum*).

As a type suicide from despair was well known. It lent itself to rhetorical exercises: during his schooling the would-be public speaker had to be able to plead for both sides in the case of:

The Cut Noose[28]

A man who had been shipwrecked, and had lost three children and his wife in a fire at his house, hanged himself. A passer-by cut the noose. He is accused of an offence (*maleficium*) by the man he saved.

To the Christian, despair implied renouncing God's mercy. Judas was the example of the man who despaired of salvation: his self-hanging is the climax of his sin. In the iconography of Christian sarcophagi his deed is pictured in the margin of the crucifixion by way of contrast. Various notorious sinners were said to have destroyed themselves in hopelessness. Thus Pontius Pilate became an *autophontes* and punisher and *autocheir* of himself. In his *Chronicle of the World* Jerome notes down for the third year of the 203rd Olympiad (= 39 AD): 'Pontius Pilate finding himself in numerous disasters kills himself by his own hand, as Roman historians have it'. He had seen the Light, but had renounced it. In medieval legend, his body is said to have been thrown into the Tiber, but it had to be pulled up, because the river protested against this defilement by flooding its banks. The Rhône too refused to accept him in its waters. Finally a well in the Alps brought him the eternal rest of hell. In the Middle Ages *desperatio* is the key-word for interpreting suicide. Despair then becomes one of the capital sins – and is depicted by Giotto in Padua as a woman in a noose. It is no longer considered as merely a state of mind of groups or of individuals in a hopeless situation[29].

In the last resort, any self-killing is an act of despair. In the pattern of suicide presented to us by ancient observers loss of perspective on life is not an important issue. They prefer to attribute despair to the losers, those who do not write history.

Their sorry but deserved end is described with satisfaction: besieged people, unsuccessful generals and politicians, conspirators, pretenders and sinners. More sympathy is shown to soldiers of one's own side who in some way save their honour. It is to be assumed on the basis of indirect evidence, mainly light literature, that hanging was the common method in individual cases. Epigram and comedy play with the noose as the appropriate means to end all misery. Even the rich man who feels strangled by public duties and taxes is supposed in comedy to entertain the idea of hanging himself from despair[30].

B FORCED INTO A FREE DEATH: *NECESSITAS*

Can suicide committed on orders be regarded as a *mors voluntaria*? Ancient authors play with oxymoron to give relief to the paradox[31]. The margin for freedom is not over-large if the emperor commands someone to put an end to his existence. In this chapter only self-killings on explicit orders and under duress are discussed; suicides before an imminent hearing have generally been categorized as done out of shame, *pudor*. In the cases of ordered suicide, nobody is ever said to have refused by fleeing after having received the final and fatal written order. Banishment is pictured by Dio – in general not an admirer of suicide – as something that makes suicide obligatory. In cases of enforced suicide the 'freedom to choose death' (*liberum mortis arbitrium*) only means the liberty to choose the method. Domitianus acted as a humane prince asking the Senate to permit at least this freedom to the doomed[32].

Messalina was assisted by her mother in her last moments: Claudius' ministers had finally succeeded in persuading the lethargic emperor to issue the order to his degenerate wife to die. Messalina hesitated but her mother insisted, saying that her life was over and that no other honour was available than through death. She handed over the dagger to her daughter, obviously in an attempt to make her daughter a Lucretia at least in death.

Whenever the means of self-killing is recorded, in the cases of enforced suicide the common and noble means is a weapon, 18 out of the 27 times when a method is specified[33]; more often – 31 out of a total 58 cases of *necessitas* – the instrument is not mentioned at all, presumably as being too self-evident.

94

Roman examples come automatically to the mind. But the Greeks are not completely lacking under this rubric of motivation which consists of 58 cases. Seven instances of enforced suicide belong to the Hellenic sphere. There is no mythical legitimization for this type: the case of Aison who was forced by Pelias to drink bull's blood is an outright execution – and it is a late version of the story of the Argonauts at that[34]. Two Greek members of king Mithridates' harem were ordered to kill themselves; Monime hanged herself with the diadem which had proved fatal, but it proved to be of no use even for this purpose: it broke. Then she offered her neck to the eunuch who had brought the order to die. Berenike chose poison, but she too was unsuccessful (p.61). Thereupon the eunuch, who was in a hurry, strangled her. Eurydike, the unlucky wife of Alexander's half-witted half-brother, made use of the only freedom which was left to her: she renounced the means – sword, noose and poison – sent to her by the demonic Olympias and hanged herself with the help of her own girdle.

It is not always the will of a prince which forces somebody to commit suicide: Nikokles killed himself on the orders of the soldiers who encircled his palace. Thereupon his wife Axiothea stabbed their daughters to death and urged her husband's sisters 'to choose death with her'. In the Roman world we have the curious example of an enforced suicide in the private sphere in the drinking woman (*bibax femina*) who was forced to abstain from food. Tertullianus describes it as an outright execution, saying: they killed a respectable woman by *inedia*.

Apart from this one family drama the female cases in Rome are public ones: an emperor's daughter, three unchaste Vestal Virgins, the wife of a fallen praefectus praetorio and a repudiated wife of an emperor are the eight Roman women who on explicit orders – and not out of loyalty to a husband – put an end to their lives[35].

Among the 41 *viri boni* who commit suicide under constraint are Lucan the poet who in his *Pharsalia* showed himself fascinated by suicide – and by other macabre phenomena – and the Stoic martyr Thrasea Paetus. Not everybody met this standard. Ostorius Scapula caused compassion by his clumsiness. At first he took poison, next he opened his veins and then he used the sword. Neither did Silanus impress people by using a razor. Also Tigellinus seized the *novacula* 'when he received the message of ultimate necessity' (*accepto supremae necessitatis nuntio*). Roman men who deserved the name took up the sword and added a fine saying to the deed. Corbulo exclaimed 'deserved', because he had not assembled an army against Nero.

The anger of a tyrant could be roused by trivialities. Iulius Montanus had defended himself when attacked by Nero – in disguise – and his clique who molested passers-by during the night. Seleucus, the grammarian, had dared to inquire which authors Tiberius was reading at the moment in order to prepare himself adequately for the dinner-table conversation. The emperor was enraged. At first he removed him from his company; 'afterwards he even forced him into death'. Hadrian compelled his brother-in-law to die to make sure that he would not survive him: the man was ninety years of age. Such behaviour contributed to the hesitation in the Senate over whether to regard Hadrian after his death as a good princeps. Only with much effort could Antoninus Pius obtain permission for Hadrian's deification from a Senate which itself had suffered from his tyrannical behaviour[36]. More and more, the emperors learned that issuing orders for suicide was bad behaviour which damaged their reputation. And in the Late Empire there was no need to coerce the senatorial aristocracy in this way. The last of the rare cases of enforced suicide is attested in AD 353[37].

C A PROOF OF MADNESS: *FUROR*

In one of the rhetorical mock-battles which the Elder Seneca had his students give, a slave refused to administer poison to his master in spite of his explicit orders. Arguments are adduced on both sides. On behalf of the slave who was to be crucified by the heirs, but appealed to the tribunes, the defender says: 'You require a proof of his insanity (*insania*)? He wanted to kill himself[38]. Establishing that a suicide was not accountable at the moment of his deed was a common practice in nineteenth-century England to spare the relatives much trouble with the authorities and their own conscience. Nowadays, the first person to appear at the bedside of the failed suicide is the psychiatrist. It is reassuring in a way for the survivors that the 'only' ground for the attempt was psychic imbalance. According to Taylor (1982) modern statistics are biased towards psychological problems as the motivation for suicides. Even Meerloo, who gives much room to well considered self-killing and mentions a percentage of 25 per cent for this type, says that psychological problems account for the same share[39]. In the ancient paradigm as it appears in generalizations and recorded cases, such a bias is not present: only 17 cases can be explained by mental troubles.

Roman law sees only *acute* madness (*furor*) as a possible cause for self-killing and as the appropriate method it mentions throwing oneself from a height. In some of the concrete cases the mental problems may have deeper roots; theoretically antiquity recognized the category of pathological insanity (Latin: *insania*) but in practice ancient doctors only came across cases of acute *mania*, which in their view was caused either by physiological factors – a disturbed balance of the fluids of the body – or by an acute affect (*pathos*). *Mania* was subdivided: Aretaios distinguished a good-natured form from a violent one in which patients become 'furious from anger'. They tear their clothes, kill the servants and *lay hands upon themselves*. In general, ancient people hardly noticed inherent mental imbalance. Sometimes they speak about a depression, *athumia*, in which somebody may consider self-killing. But cases of suicide committed for this reason have not been recorded[40]. Porphyrios, the philosopher of late antiquity, came close to self-destruction from psychological troubles. He is said to have suffered from melancholy and to have fostered thoughts about suicide. His ailment was discovered by his master Plotinos – by way of telepathy! Plotinos also recommended a therapy: a stay in Sicily restored Porphyrios' mental balance.

In cases of accomplished suicide attention is only drawn by spectacular fits of madness. An instance of acute insanity – or pathological religious mania? – occurred in Rome in AD 38. A slave named Machaon astounded the whole city by climbing up onto the altar of Jupiter Capitolinus. There he slaughtered himself – as a sacrifice? Outright insanity may be surmised in king Kleomenes of Sparta. He was put in the stocks, for he endangered both himself and his environment. The moment he could get his hands on a sword, he cut himself to pieces. The Greeks were not sure whether his state of mind was caused by drinking unmixed wine or by violating sanctuaries[41]. The gods are often said to have caused madness in a person who sins against the divine. In the series of myths about the triumphant entry of Dionysus, the obstinate who do not give the god his due are often struck with insanity. Bytes had violated Koronis, a follower of the god. She called in the god to take revenge. Madness overpowered Bytes and 'thereby enraged, he threw himself in the well'.

In the nineteenth century psychic imbalance is discovered as an important cause of self-killing among women. In antiquity this ground is hardly mentioned. But there is one curious case in Miletus. In BC 277 some girls were infected by a collective urge to kill themselves, one of the rare instances of a suicide epidemic attested in antiquity. Words did not dissuade them, 'for the disease had a divine origin'. In spite of all efforts, one girl after the other hanged herself. Finally a prudent man proposed bringing the corpse of the hanged naked to the burial place. This shock-therapy restored the mental balance of the Milesian *parthenoi*. Apart from the reference to the gods a rational explanation was also put forward: a change in the air was said to have played a part. One could speculate about a föhn (a dry wind blowing from the mountains) – but why did it only affect girls? That *mania* could have anything to do with the vulnerable position of young females in ancient society, lies outside the scope of ancient observation and speculation. But for the rest madness resulting in suicide was preferably seen as the reaction of a tormented mind.

> To many there doth come because of grief
> Insanity and ills incurable,
> And some for grief have ended their own life[42].

In this way, *furor* overpowered Heracles because of the agony which was caused by Nessos' tunic. In this rage he burned himself to death. Rome saw the breakdown of a high-priest with horror: Fulvius Flaccus lost his mental faculties after various disasters in his family. In a fit of madness he hanged himself and thus died a ghastly death (*foeda morte*). Dion's son literally went mad from grief and threw himself from the roof. Finally one Marius threw himself from a height, mad from love. In these cases madness is the reaction to some pain and as such the last but one stage on the way to self-destruction.

Lunacy could even be the consequence of adhering to the wrong philosophical school, as opponents held. The Academy in its extremely sceptical Pyrrhonian form stressed the inadequacy of all sensory perception. One *academicus* was taught a lesson by his slaves, according to a polemical anecdote: when he ordered something they deliberately brought the wrong items, mocking his view that his senses deceived him one way or the other. Thus he went out of his mind and committed suicide.

From a Christian point of view it was very satisfactory to know that Lucretius had gone mad because of a love-potion. He was said to have written the epicurean poem *De rerum natura* during intervals of lucidity. Finally the despicable materialist and atheist committed suicide. In the Christian view which was developed by Augustine, a human being is not the will-less victim of madness. By consciously choosing Satan, as the heretical Donatists did, people invoked *furor* which made them kill themselves. The high percentage – 30 – of *furor* in medieval suicide has to be interpreted in the light of this Christian line of thinking. Schmitt's somewhat pedantic attempts to apply the 'critères modernes de la psychiatrie' are completely wrong, in my view: even the paradigm of madness is dictated by the time[43].

In the 17 ancient cases where madness is the cause, it is the last link in a chain of factors which lead up to suicide. The development of the story about Ajax's suicide shows how the ancients wanted to see the role of insanity. In the Heroic Age Ajax's deed could be seen as the wholly understandable, introverted rage of a superman who had fatally lost face, through not being accorded his due respect. In process of time, new elements were added to the theme. His anger had darkened his mind to such a degree that he slaughtered a herd of sheep, believing he was taking his revenge on a mass of Greeks. When he regained his senses he realized that he had become ridiculous. In Sophocles' play that is the ultimate reason for his final act. But even the rage was explained by the playwright: it was sent by Athena by way of punishment for an act of blasphemous self-confidence (*hybris*)[44]. After many ages, his suicide is even denied. Heroic madness does not fit in the picture of internal virtue of late antiquity. Heracles too is modernized: he had not burned himself through frenzy, but had died a natural death brought about by old age and disease[45].

Griffin (1986 p.70) is right in stating that suicide committed from madness is rare in ancient times. But there is more to the role of mental disturbance than ancient observation allows. Antiquity is unacquainted with the psychotic personality who is predisposed to suicide. Only acute frenzy in consequence of punishment by the gods or as a reaction to severe grief has a place – and that a small one – in the experience of self-killing in the ancient world.

D GRIEF: *DOLOR*

Grieving for the dead is the task of a woman in antiquity: mourning befits Elektra. She represents the values of the *oikos* and as such is expected to experience most poignantly the loss of relatives. In tragedy the women are the ones who raise the 'aiaiai'. Female relatives are responsible for the lamentations during the burial service. There are women for hire for this task. Knowing that these special domains were attributed to women, one is not very astonished that self-killings from grief were ascribed to women in a disproportionate way . In 60 female cases grief, *dolor*, causes suicide (or attempts or wishes) against 63 times for male instances. This is a high score for women in the light of their general under-representation. In this chapter *dolor* is taken in a narrow sense; the Latin word may also signify bodily pain[46]. In our classification of motives the mourning must take some time to deserve being seen as *dolor* which led to self-murder: an acute suicidal reaction to a (sudden) loss of the beloved is regarded as a suicide from despair.

An example taken from an ancient novel, where (attempted) suicide plays its romantic part, may clarify these distinctions. In Achilles Tatios' history of Kleitophon and Leukippe the 'jeune premier' is made to believe that his girl is dead. Thereupon the young man gives himself up to the authorities with a false self-accusation in order to bring death upon himself by way of a judicial verdict: 'Then I can leave this cursed life'. This ingenious scheme is taken as resulting from *dolor*. A different situation arises when Kleitophon 'sees' pirates aboard another ship slaughter Leukippe. Without much ado he jumps into the sea. This prompt 'anomic' reaction, which of course was premature – the slaughter had been staged – is more an act of despair than of mature mourning.

On the other hand *dolor*-suicides are to be distinguished from the – rare – occasions where a woman joins her husband in seeking a free death or even shows him the way, as was the case with the wife from Lake Como and with Arria. Their suicides have been regarded as prompted by loyalty, *fides*.

In the domain of *dolor*-suicides two types of grief are predominant: grief for a dead beloved and distress because of a lost or unfulfilled love. With regard to pangs of love all female cases belong to the sphere of fiction[47]. 'If he is unwilling to marry me I will embrace his knees and beseech him. If I do not succeed, I will lay hands upon myself. For I know that I cannot live without him', Acroteleutium exclaims in a comedy. In the charming pastorale of Longus, on one occasion Chloe thinks that Daphnis has broken his vows: 'I will not live on' is her reaction. Phaidra is determined to starve herself to death when she realizes the impossibility of her love for her stepson. In the world of fiction there are not only thoughts of suicide. According to an apocryphal version of the story of Theseus and Ariadne, the Cretan princess hanged herself when abandoned on Naxos. Byblis was said to have ended her life which was desperate because of her passion for her brother. Calypso too, disappointed in her love for the Wanderer, was said to have hanged herself. This reading must have caused some problems to pagan theologians: nymphs were regarded as immortal. How came Calypso into the possession of that human omnipotence? Even if the passion was mutual, a malevolent environment could stand in the way of love. Philostratos admired a picture of the suicidal end of such a situation (p.175).

Among men there are some historical cases, apart from the fictitious ones which are not quite lacking: no fewer than 5 times Chaireas is about to kill himself in Chariton's novel when Kallirhoe seemingly does not wish to become his[48]. As a real story of true love Plutarch tells us about Phobos who was the first to throw himself from the Leucadian rocks. Undoubtedly historical at least is Antiochos who decided to starve himself to death because of his hopeless love for his father's wife. Of course a Hellenistic prince is far above gallivanting with choir-girls. It is with such unmanly behaviour, leading up to suicide, that the Alexandrians are reproached by Dio Chrysostomos in a speech in which he criticizes their effeminacy[49]. The means Antiochos uses, *inedia*, is not only much nobler than hanging, it also implies some communication with other people; relatives and friends have the opportunity to recall to life the one who is determined to die. Especially in mourning the would-be self-killer may find out what bonds there are still with life.

Grief over an unhappy love can be mingled with an element of revenge when the disappointed or frustrated lover wants to curse the cause of his death. That is what the *erastes* does who hangs himself in the porch of the house of the boy who does not reciprocate his love. This fictitious case has also an ingredient of suicide which is well known in the modern world, but that is strikingly lacking in antiquity: the message to the survivor who may feel responsible. This homo-erotic case presents us with a text full of reproof against the harsh friend (p.68). I have only found five instances of farewell letters, but they do not aim – as is usual in contemporary ones – at absolving others from guilty feelings. On the contrary, they put the whole blame on the addressee[50].

The case of the depressed *erastes* shows that suicide could be caused by an unhappy love between man and man as well as by a tragic passion between man and woman. But there is no equivalent in lesbian love; in general the passion between women is hardly spoken of in ancient literature. Women had little chance to develop mutual emotional ties. In a Hellenistic poem girls complain that their life is so much harder than for boys who have their network of friendship outside home, whereas they are always confined by the four walls[51].

In the man's world friendship plays an important role, whether with homo-erotic undertones or not. Having discussed instances of remarkable matrimonial love Valerius Maximus lists striking cases of *amicitia*. Under the protection of Publius Caelius, Lucius Petronius had reached the status of knight. When his *patronus*, old and ill, was about to be arrested by Cinna he implored him to lend his hand. At first Petronius tried to dissuade his friend from his intention to kill himself. Finally he gave in, but 'he linked to his death his own; he could not live on while the source of his promotion died'. Especially in the schools of the philosophers friendship is the substitute for the links of family and State: Pythagoras did not think life worth living after losing Pherekydes and other friends. This behaviour runs counter to the doctrine: Pythagoreanism is the first philosophical sect to forbid self-killing in principle.

Friendship is also stressed as the main factor which led to Cornelius Sabinus' self-killing. His *amicus* Charea, who had prepared the way for Claudius' emperorship, had been executed by this new *princeps* because after all the killing of any emperor set a bad precedent. Sabinus was so struck by this fate that he dispatched himself. According to the ancient text his self-killing was prompted by friendship. A modern observer may surmise that he feared having to share the fate of the tyrannicide, but this supposition is irrelevant for our purpose of disclosing the ancient paradigm of suicide, in which self-killing as a reaction to the loss of a friend was conceivable and respectable.

Roman *amicitia* should not be regarded as a highly emotional affair: Lucius Petronius anticipated being reproved for living on while his *amicus* to whom he was linked by the ties of public life had passed away. Public opinion and formal loyalty played their part.

There is a purely emotional case in the young Augustine who considered suicide on losing 'his soul's half'. More diverse were the motives of Timoleon. He was shunned by his friends and mother after having murdered his brother. 'Depressed and disturbed' he was about to starve himself to death, but that was the signal for his friends to rush to his side.

The most specific form of grief is grief over the death of a relative. The degree to which *dolor* caused by the loss of the partner provokes self-killing in Roman culture is strikingly different for men and women. Under his rubric 'About conjugal love' (*De amore coniugali*) Valerius Maximus has only two memorable suicides committed by men. They also shared their family-name. When Gaius Plautius Numida, a senator, heard about the death of his wife, he pierced his breast with a sword, 'unable to bear the grief' (*doloris inpotens*). His servants intervened, but on the first occasion he tore his bandages and kept the wound open. 'Of the same name and love was Marcus Plautius.' His task was to lead a flotilla to Asia. His wife accompanied him as far as Taranto – in itself a touching proof of attachment. There she fell ill and died. During the obsequies he drew his sword and threw himself on it. His friends laid him in his toga and his senator's shoes next to his spouse. When Valerius was writing his work their tomb was still to be seen in Taranto with the epitaph written in Greek: OF TWO LOVERS. It was quite uncommon for a Roman man to link his existence to such a degree to that of his wife. In the Greek sphere the instances are more numerous. Two cases are presented as historical ones by Plutarch[52]. Five times in the Greek novel men are about to end their lives firmly convinced that the beloved is no more[53]. Habrokomes starts on a search for the body of his beloved one whom he believes to be dead. He announces that he will do away with himself when he has paid her his last respects. Should his quest prove unsuccessful, he promises to return to Ephesus and having constructed there a cenotaph for Anthia to kill himself.

In the mythical sphere there is only one successful male suicide in the course of a very morbid process of mourning, that of Dimoites (p.48). But in myth woman is expected to link her own fate to that of the beloved man. Kleite hanged herself, Phyllis thought her husband (or affianced) dead and did likewise. Euadne threw herself from the rocks into the flames which devoured the mortal remains of her Kapaneus. Especially in the picture

Philostratos describes she did not act in panic: she strode to the pyre in full pontifical regalia[54]. It is a general characteristic of later versions of myths that they dwell at length on the emotional side: bizarre, cruel stories from the past are adapted to the new taste. According to the old myth Priam's daughter Polyxena was sacrificed without much ado at Achilles' grave to elicit a favourable wind for the fleet which was waiting for its return to Greece. In his *Heroikos* Philostratos constructs a complete love-suicide from the old material: Polyxena threw herself on the sword next to the tomb of the man she loved in vain[55]. The mythical *ménage-à-trois* of Euphron resulted in a double suicide when the master of the house succumbed to the consequences of Bacchic rapture. His two wives Demo and Methymna killed themselves from grief.

This is the ideal which myth preaches to women. Ancient humour exploits the familiar theme of the wife whose existence has lost all meaning after the death of her husband. A misogynist – who nevertheless was married – was dying. His wife cried in despair: if anything happens to you (euphemism for dying), I will hang myself. The dying man opened his eyes and said: please do me that pleasure while I am still alive (uxor mulierum osuris).

In the light of this diverse material which legitimizes female self-killing in mourning, it is curious that there are no historical Greek examples of this type. In the Roman sources there are some clear-cut cases: Agrippina starved herself to death. Ligarius' wife too, who remains nameless in the sources, followed her husband. A wife in mourning always finds a way to kill herself. This is the message of a poem by Martial (1, 42) which describes how Porcia, daughter of Cato Uticensis and wife of Brutus, furnishes herself with the means for dying in spite of the vigilance of those around her. Most common is the reading that she swallowed live coals. This household remedy was also used by Servilia, Lepidus' wife, for similar reasons, a mixture of mourning and loyalty.

Much greater still is the discrepancy between the sexes when children have died. Both fathers and mothers dispatch themselves when a *son* has passed away[56]. Only on rare occasions are daughters the cause of a suicide, in spite of all the expressions of deep grief in epitaphs. The death of Anthia's parents in the love novel is clearly a case of a burden fairly shared. The writer sacrifices the parents of the male Habrokomes as well: all four are convinced of the death of their children. In myth we have the exceptional instance of Iphis who wishes to do away with himself after the tragic death of his daughter Euadne. But for the rest, both in myth and reality, it is the loss of a son which is the cause of self-killing. The sex of Isidora's baby is not explicitly mentioned in her letter to her husband-brother in which she threatens to hang herself if the child dies. Here self-killing is used as a means to force the man to come home. The death of a brother too may be reason to destroy oneself: a sister does not seem worthy of such excessive grief[57]. As symbolic for the curse of civil war, on two occasions the story is told of a soldier killing his brother who fought on the opposite side and putting an end to his life when he discovered the awful truth[58].

A mother's death alone is no reason for children to kill themselves – in the case of Ilione both parents were dead. The mythical example of a daughter who follows her father in death is Erigone. Historical instances of sons wanting to die after losing their father are Aquilius Florus and Kleomenes' son, who unexpectedly threw himself from a roof; he may be the sole attempted suicide by a *child* recorded in antiquity[59].

Dolor clearly is a motive for self-killing in antiquity, but it has far less significance than in the modern world with its stress on social deprivation and personal well-being. The percentage of cases which can be attributed to grief as a motive is a modest 13 per cent. The pattern of self-killing which appears confirms the picture of sexual asymmetry which is prevalent in antiquity[60]. The exercises in the rhetor's school assume the existence of the discrepancy between the sexes. One of the fictitious but conceivable situations goes like this: a woman wished to die. At first she hanged herself, but her son undid her in time. Then she gave herself up to the authorities as having committed sacrilege. She longed for a death sentence in order to have the end she yearned for. The son opposes her in the hearing and explains why she is so desperate as to desire death: she had lost her husband and two children[61].

Hanging oneself and refusing food are the means which correlate with the motive of *dolor*. The first method has all the marks of resoluteness in misery, whereas the latter leaves room for intervention. In this way it has the function which poison has in our time: drugs are completely lacking in those ancient cases where grief was the main motive for suicide.

E THE CURSE OF THE SUICIDE: *EXSECRATIO*

'To me death, to you mourning': such an element of revenge can
sometimes be demonstrated as being present in contemporary
suicide. Such *psychological punishing* of those held responsible for
misery cannot be discovered in ancient self-killing. Of quite
another order is the group of 'Samsonic' suicides in which the self-
killer wants to bring down a curse on the head of a person or a
group. This *exsecratio* is sometimes contributory to a motivation of
which the primary ground is different. In his monologue on the
beach Ajax invokes the Furies to take revenge on his enemies. The
place where the deed was done was significant. One hanged oneself
in the porch of the cruel beloved. That was done by the *erastes* who
was rejected, and by the woman who during the Civil War chose
for her husband against her father. When her husband's party was
defeated, she humbly returned to the paternal home. But it
remained closed. She exclaimed: 'How can I make it up to you?'
'Die'. So she hanged herself in front of the door. An essential pre-
condition for an element of revenge to appear is a firmly
established identification of the suicide with the person who
is hated. Psycho-analysis says that an enormous amount of
psychic energy is needed in which a desire to kill and an urge for
self-punishment (for unjustified trust) find an outlet in self-
destruction[62].

Cicero entertained the idea of taking revenge when he had been
betrayed by Octavian by killing himself in BC 43. He had plans to
stab himself to death next to the hearth of that unreliable young
man and in this way send a revenging demon into the house. These
were very primitive instincts which emerged in the civilized
politician and philosopher. About 1900 among the 'Ishi-speaking
people' of the Gold Coast there was, according to Westermarck,
this institution:

> should a person commit suicide and before doing so attribute
> the act to the conduct of another person, that other person is
> required by native law to undergo a like fate. The practice is
> termed 'killing oneself upon tl.e head of another'.

In some African cultures threatening to commit suicide can be a
very effective means of putting pressure on a person. In China,
which in Westermarck's classification was just above primitive

society, suicide before the door of one's tormentor was the characteristic revenge of the powerless[63].

Revenge may be invoked as well against the whole community. Melissos' son had many lovers: one of these tried to kidnap him. In the struggle which ensued the boy died. The fellow-townsmen left the injury unpunished in spite of Melissos' pleas for satisfaction. Finally he leapt from the platform of an elevated temple, having invoked the gods. The result is easy to predict: a pestilence occurred, an oracle spoke, etc. Skedasos did away with himself when no attention was paid by the Spartans to his appeal against the violation of his daughters by their country-men. At his self-killing he invoked the Furies. In cases like these, suicide is the weapon of the weak which may even be used against the gods. Orestes was about to starve himself to death in front of Apollo's temple. In this way he forced the god to assist in freeing him from the curse which lay on him as the murderer of his mother[64].

There is a wide-spread belief that a guilty community or an unjust individual can be afflicted by a suicide which is carried out with that intention. This conviction about the effectiveness of *exsecratio* is connected with a general idea that magic forces were raised by the audacious deed (see II.5.B). In fact the number of 19 cases of Samsonic suicide is less than one would expect in a society which was very sensitive to ghosts. In recording and interpreting the concrete cases, ancient culture did not stress the element of revenge.

F NO LONGER BEING WHO YOU USED TO BE: *PUDOR*

On three occasions during his career Cicero toyed with the idea of self-killing. The second time was after the battle of Pharsalus when a series of republican leaders killed themselves. Cicero shows himself in all his – annoying and disarming – indecision in the letter he addressed to Marcus Marius two years after the events. After the defeat

> I withdrew from a war where there was nothing left but either to die in battle, or fall into some ambush, or pass into the conqueror's hands, or to take refuge with Juba, or to find a spot for what could be practically exile, or *deliberately to die by one's own hand.*

The various options are rejected one after the other, including suicide, although there was an old saying 'if one is no more who one used to be, there is nothing to live for'[65]. But the opportunity had passed for doing what could have saved his reputation, Cicero says.

Cicero reproaches himself for not maintaining his honour. The anxiety of losing face is one of the strongest motives among ancient people. In the modern western world keeping one's honour is a value which is only strong in certain closed domains of society, like the military. There one finds 'individuals with a high commitment to a particular self image'. They possess a rigid personality and are highly sensitive to failure. Then they are overtaken by 'great shame'[66]. Ancient society was oriented to the heroic ideal and as a whole can be regarded as a 'shame-society'. Beattie (1960), referring to African cultures, explains how shame differs from guilt in this way: 'it implies rather the suffering of what is felt as a grave and perhaps irremediable indignity'. The students of African suicide say that the significance of 'shame' as a factor varies from culture to culture. Graeco-Roman civilization is marked by *pudor*. It shows almost Japanese traits: status defines dignity. It is said that 'many Japanese tend to become excessively involved with their social role. . . . Such individuals are often vulnerable to social disturbances or personal mistakes'[67].

In the earliest Greek cases *aidos* is the predominant factor in self-killing. The syndrome of shame remains strong during the history of ancient society – shame is still more important in the Mediterranean world than in North-West Europe. It stretches from Ajax to Maximus, who, in AD 389, is scoffed at for not having shown the courage which even slaves demonstrate in desperate situations[68]. In the public debate between Demosthenes and Aeschines the latter mocks: Demosthenes will never kill himself, insensitive as he is to civil honour[69].

An ancient leader is expected to end his life if he has been defeated or for some other reason can no longer face his people. An individual with Ajax's personality had to commit suicide when he had experienced the deadly disgrace of not receiving Achilles' weapons. Ajax remained one of the models of heroism. He was the only non-Athenian who lent his name to one of the new districts that Cleisthenes instituted. The *phyle* of his name was exhorted by Demosthenes to act like the man 'who thought life unlivable when the reward for courage was withheld from him'. A Hellenistic poem says: 'Among mortals the goddess of Fate could find no other killer for Ajax than himself'. A whole iconography originated from Ajax's suicide and contrary to ancient conventions he plays his final act in the presence of the audience, all alone on the stage[70].

Perseus, last king of Macedonia, is counted as the classic example of shamelessness: after the ruin of his and his country's fortunes he did not act in accordance with his royal honour, but adhered to life 'in vain hope'. 'Nothing, however, seems so sweet to those who have suffered misfortune as life itself, even when their sufferings would warrant death. That is what happened to Perseus king of the Macedonians'. He was ridiculed by Aemilius Paullus, his victor, who held him in captivity, keeping him for his triumph. But one source has it that under pressure of that imminent disgrace he finally put an end to his shameful life by *inedia*[71].

The stage of history is full of princes and generals who fall on their sword: Amilcas (Hamilcar), Andromachos, Boges (Bytes), Brutus, Caecilius Metellus, Caelius, Carnulus and Cato Uticensis, who did not wish to have to depend on the *clementia Caesaris*. His self-killing brought him the reputation of acting as a perfect politician, general and philosopher – during his last night he had read Plato's *Phaedo* – and in this way he became an object of identification for the intellectual opposition during the Early Empire.

On their side Caesar's soldiers did not wish to rely on the mercy of the enemy, as Granius Petronius declares before his suicide. One Carthaginian fleet-commander slaughtered himself 'because he preferred death to captivity'[72]. Often the shining example of the leader is followed by those immediately around him. That is what happened in the cases of Crassus and Kleomenes. In saving their own faces they did everything to avoid the impression that they were acting in panic. After the defeat at Philippi Labeo dug a pit in his tent, made arrangements, gave a loyal slave his freedom and only then held out his neck to receive the liberating blow. Apart from the long list of Greek, Roman and barbarian leaders who actually committed suicide from *pudor*, there are many generals who made arrangements not to survive a defeat. Mark Antony, who was later to sacrifice himself in loyalty to Cleopatra, earlier during the dangerous campaign against the Parthians in AD 36, told his freedman Rhamnus to kill him immediately if he was ordered to do so. At three decisive battles Caesar is said to have been determined not to survive an eventual defeat: he, dignity incarnate, under no circumstance could tolerate being the loser. Sometimes the execution of a suicide-plan was thwarted by chance; when the unlucky king Croesus was seated on his self-chosen pyre the flames were extinguished by the intervention of Apollo the god or – as another tradition has it – by king Cyrus, the victor. Only with much exertion could friends withhold Demetrios from suicide when he had to give himself up to the mercy of Seleukos. Domitius Ahenobarbus missed his honourable death when he was treacherously given too little poison by his doctor at Corfinium (p.61).

For the sole survivor of a battle it was hardly possible to face his people. For Othryades life became impossible when the other Argives had perished in the struggle for Thyreatis. By accident Pantites the Spartan missed the battle of Thermopylae; he put an end to his unenviable situation by hanging himself, a method very uncommon for a soldier. In general, hanging is not a fitting means for men in the case of *pudor*. Although there are 3 times as many male cases of *pudor*-suicide (212 against 79) women surpass men with regard to hanging as the method connected with this motivation, 18:14.

Captivity makes the loser a plaything in the hands of the victor. Should he wait for some of his relatives to pay the ransom or should he face slavery? The distinguished captive would have to bear the disgrace of marching in the triumph or in some other way functioning as the symbol of a crushing defeat. He could be disfigured by torture, which especially in ancient eyes meant a fatal loss of dignity. Therefore in most cases of suicide of people confronted with captivity it was not anguish or despair that were regarded as the main motives, but shame.

Often it is stressed by the historians that the ground for self-killing was to avoid dishonour. When Alketas was about to be handed over, he laid hands on himself first in order not to come into the hands of his enemies (the original Greek plays with the word 'hand'). When Aquilius was to be delivered up to Mithridates, the hater of all things Roman, 'he had the courage to perform an heroic deed. Forestalling the men who were about to arrest him, he chose death in preference to ill-usage (*hybris*) and a shameful execution'. In this description full weight is given to preserving dignity; this is brought out in the words 'had the courage to', which are meant to render the Greek *tolmao*, which means to endure, to venture. Words like these are often used with regard to heroic suicide.

Sometimes ingenious ways were found to escape the disgrace of captivity. Mucianus Crassus surprised his guard with a jab to his eye and in this way provoked the deadly blow he sought. It is not only people on one's own side who are said to have preferred dignity to captivity. It is recorded with due respect that barbarians were often not willing to pass under the yoke. Spaniards especially were regarded as a proud and stubborn people. In BC 195 and again in BC 133 groups of Hispani dispatched themselves. In the year first mentioned they acted this way because they had been disarmed by the Romans. 'This action they took so hard that many committed suicide, a high-spirited people, who thought that life without arms was not worth living'. Some generations later the same Iberian spirit prevailed: in BC 133 Spanish prisoners of war could not endure the *hybris* of slavery. A boy is mentioned as a shining example of Spanish pride. First he had cut the throats of his sisters, for their life had lost all dignity. 'He himself, by refusing to eat, ended his life by starvation'. Stories of horror and honour like this can be presented from all periods and corners of the ancient world. Krinippos, a Spartan, was captured. 'He died from grief by a self-inflicted death' before he could be ransomed or sold into slavery. Again and again it is stressed that the people concerned acted primarily from motives of honour[73].

One of the functions of the Roman gladiatorial games was to make the City's public aware of Rome's might by having the captives kill each other. On some occasions the prisoners of war refuse to play the game: they kill each other before the show or they look privately for other, ingenious ways out of an unbearable life. When Romans on rare occasions find themselves in the same situation, sometimes they too are said to have refused to perform. In that way they withheld from the Sicilian slave-rebels the satisfaction of a perfect reversal of roles[74].

A slave is counted as a creature that reacts with suicide to all kinds of situations. Generally, his motivation is looked on as just despair. But the Spartan who had become a slave stood upon his dignity. He refused to bring the chamber-pot to his new master (p.28). This story has a counterpart in a similar anecdote about a female Spartan slave. When she was ordered to do 'something that is not fitting to free woman, she led herself out of life'. The expression 'to lead oneself out of life' (in Greek: *exago heauton tou biou*) is, as we shall see, a highly philosophical and euphemistic way of putting things.

111

One specific type of ancient self-killing has always enjoyed much attention. The stylistic qualities of Tacitus – and of Robert Graves – made suicide among the nobility the focus of reflections on self-murder in antiquity. Tacitus' circle was deeply shocked to see the senatorial order being smashed by the imperial autocracy. What was left of aristocratic pride was shown in the face of the inevitable end. Several factors contributed to dramatizing: the tradition of the last of the republicans was revived. Thus the ultimate deed could be stylized as a protest against tyranny. Stoic philosophy added an aura to the protagonist. A complete set of effects was developed amongst an elite that was fully aware of what was expected by fellow-aristocrats and by the general public. It was better to die heroically on the eve of a hearing than to wait for the degradation that went with it.

Legal processes were always seen as potentially dangerous for one's reputation in antiquity. They were said to be risky (cf. *kindunos* in Greek, *crimen* in Latin). In BC 427 the Athenian *strategus* Paches stabbed himself to death on the speaker's tribunal, on hearing himself convicted of the violation of two women from Lesbos. The earliest Roman case where an individual, Quintus Fabius, is mentioned as killing himself during a hearing happened in BC 389[75]. In principle, in all cases where people withdrew from a trial or conviction by self-killing shame is regarded as the primary motive. Those who made away with themselves during Seianus' persecution did so, according to Dio Cassius, in order not to have to endure dishonour and disgrace (*hybris* and *aikia*)[76]. That was the way the general public regarded such dramas: the aristocrat involved maintained his honour. Iulius Priscus was explicitly said to have ended his life 'rather from shame than from necessity' (*pudore magis quam necessitate*).

In this way the representatives of the Roman nobility disappeared from the scene: Aemilius avoided being convicted in order to maintain the dignity of his family. His wife Sextia exhorted him to do so. She was 'stimulus and participant in death'. Usually the malicious emperor was the instigator, but some non-political cases occurred: Plautius Silvanus 'in a fit of insanity' (*mente turbata*) had thrown his wife out of the window. To forestall a conviction he 'had his veins opened'. It is exceptional for such private instances to have been recorded by historiography. Attention was centred on the members of the senatorial order who were forced to liquidate themselves when accused of *lèse-majesté*. The absolute number of individuals who can definitely be traced is not so enormous as the historians suggest in their generalizing pictures[77]: 'Of those who were summoned to answer charges (*citati ad causam dicendam*) some wounded themselves at home, sure as they were of a conviction and in order to avoid the distress and *ignominy*, while some swallowed poison in the very Senate-chamber'. For those accused the way to save both *dignitas* and family property was to dispatch themselves. But the emperor could also be annoyed if he was frustrated by too prompt a reaction: when Carnulus forestalled conviction by laying hands upon himself, Tiberius exclaimed: 'Carnulus escaped me' (a similar exclamation was made by a minister of the German Federal Republic when some members of the Red Army Fraction had committed suicide in jail).

For some time the Roman senate had cherished the illusion of sharing the administration of the *res publica* with the princeps. In what was styled a dyarchy by Mommsen, the friendship of the emperor was sought along the lines *amicitia* was practised in high society. But already at an early date losing the favour of this high 'friend' meant a deadly loss of status. Between *amicitia* and hatred there was no room; when a nobleman was removed from the inner circle of political confidants, he had to fear the imperial anger[78]. Thus it was not clear whether Cornelius Gallus put an end to his life out of fear of being convicted – thus Suetonius – or only because he was removed from Augustus' circle. Fulvius immediately realized he had fallen from grace when the emperor said to him 'vale' instead of 'salve'. This greeting with 'goodbye' caused him to say farewell to life. His life had lost all dignity since he had violated Augustus' trust. The latter had confidentially told him that he intended to call back Postumus Agrippa from the island to which he was banished. Fulvius broke his promise of secrecy by informing his wife of the great news that the grandson and stepson of Augustus would soon return to the City. In no time the whole of Rome knew of this sensational development.

Losing the emperor's favour was a prelude to the formal trials which under Tiberius became the odious means by which the princeps made his power felt. Theoretically 'those who were summoned to plead their cause' could have fled to a place where they were safe from the whims of the emperor. But outside Rome they had no life. They were, as is said of the Japanese, 'excessively involved in their social role'.

Over-identification with an established role was not limited to the political sphere. The epigram that mocks Aulos for fulfilling his astrological prophesy by killing himself demonstrates that in principle the loss of a professional reputation could be fatal. One tradition has it that Anaxagoras did away with himself because the Athenians did not accept his doctrine about the solar system – in other readings being in jail proved too much for him. When Septimius Severus disbanded the praetorian guard one member killed both himself and his horse, which 'looked glad to die'. The Iunii Blaesii could not bear being passed over for priesthoods to which they thought themselves entitled. Various forms of damage to personal reputation drove people to suicide: not being entrusted with the administration of a province, banishment, not being able to fulfil a promise[79]. Caesellius Bassus could not find the treasure he had promised to the emperor and he 'avoided disgrace and danger by a voluntary death'. Labienus' books were burnt in public because of their Pompeian bias. In his frustration the author had himself transported to the ancestral tomb and shut himself in. An athlete discovered he could not stretch the bow any more. He threw first the weapon and then himself into the fire. 'I am not sure,' Pausanias comments on this story of Timanthes, 'whether this was an act of *mania* more than *arete*': the author of the second century AD distances himself from the traditional values.

The *pudor* the Roman law-giver alludes to as a potential cause for suicide is not the shame felt before or during a trial, nor are the curious cases of losing one's professional status meant. When the jurisprudent specifies, he speaks of shame caused by being in debt[80]. It is not only in capitalist society that insolvency can deal a deadly blow to one's social position; Durkheim apparently took suicide by businessmen and bankers as wholly typical for his own age. He illustrated his idea of 'anomy' by the ruin of a personal world through bankruptcy. But already in Alexander's army a financial problem made a soldier, Antigenes, kill himself. The notorious gourmand Apicius drew up his balance-sheet and discovered that he was unable to live on the same scale as before: suicide solved his problem. The Sicilians Diokles and Tyrakinos were so hard pressed by Verres' taxes that they hanged themselves. Such self-killings must have been quite common if jurisprudence made explicit provision for that category.

Dreams of ancient people confirm this view. A man of reputation dreamt that he 'used himself sexually' – the act is not specified. Soon he committed suicide. No wonder, Artemidoros the interpreter of dreams says: he was precluded from intercourse with others (because of his debt) and moreover he had so little money that he had to help himself. In the case of another dream in the *Oneirokritika*, Artemidoros is more outspoken. A man dreamt that an evil smell came from the region of his navel. Later he committed suicide pressed by debts. It was not so much the loss of money that was fatal as the consequent loss of status. 'Poverty oppresses a gentleman above all else . . . one has to flee that situation and throw oneself into the depths of the sea and from the steepest rocks'[81].

As the spheres of army, politics, profession and money are closed to ancient women, their vulnerability to a deadly *pudor* lies in other fields. Indirectly women could lose their status by the ruin of their husband; their position is dependent on his. Thus Axiothea, wife of the ruler of Paphos, put an end to her life after the – enforced – suicide of her husband, and she exhorted her sisters-in-law 'to choose death with her'. The world was in ruins for both Fulvius and his wife when Augustus said 'goodbye' to him. The wife who, by her indiscretion, was the cause of the tragedy, ended her life together with Fulvius. When Demetrios lost his royal power, Phila could not bear seeing the former king reduced to a wretched commoner and she took poison.

The position of a queen-mother too is derived from that of a man, i.e. her son. After the fall of Periander the tyrant's mother did away with herself 'lamenting her miserable fate'. For Julia Domna existence lost all meaning when her son Caracalla was deposed (p.32). The only exception in a way to this general rule of linked status and fall is Cleopatra. By her planned death she showed herself even steelier than before (*deliberata morte ferocior*)[82].

But most of the female suicides from shame are the result of private disgrace. Mothers collapse under the shame caused by the behaviour of their children: Leda was mortally ashamed by Helen's infidelity. Themistocles' mother – a historical figure – could no longer bear the disgraceful conduct of her son. One father, Iulius Fabius, could not acquiesce in his son's frivolity (*malakia*) and he wanted to throw himself in the river.

Women may feel shame or guilt – in this subcategory it is very difficult to draw the line – about their responsibility for the fall of their man. Deianeira mythically points the way. She killed herself –

according to Sophocles with a sword, whereas Hyginus says by hanging – after her son called her the murderess of Heracles: she reacted with suicide only after somebody else had blamed her. Therefore her motivation lies more in the sphere of *pudor* than of *mala conscientia*. Shame and guilt are inextricably combined in the case of Pantheia. This Persian lady had exhorted her husband to join Cyrus's campaign to Egypt. Thus, she was responsible for his premature death. She made her death a public event. By her ostentatious suicide she in a way saved her reputation. Around her tomb her faithful eunuchs stabbed themselves.

Even an orphan showed self-respect: Charilla had been struck in the face by the king with a sandal. Thus humiliated, she hanged herself – using the weapon of the weak? The oracle commanded purification. Each year an image of the girl was brought to the remote place where her mortal remains lay. There a rope was put around the neck of the effigy; in this way it was buried.

Women seldom incurred the risk of losing face in a legal trial. Once – in the case of Mutilia Prisca – the loss of political favour was the cause. On the two other occasions, the ladies Albucilla and Aemilia Lepida were tried for dishonouring themselves by having relations with a slave.

In the case of female *pudor*-suicide sexual humiliation was the common cause. A poignant instance is furnished by Orosius in his *Anti-pagan History*. In this work he dwells at length on suicides from the past as models of the misery which dominated history in pre-Christian times: thus he effectively undermined the position of those pagan opponents who held the *christiana tempora* responsible for contemporary catastrophes, preferring the situation of the empire when the old gods protected the Romans. During the Revolt of Spartacus (BC 73–1), Orosius tells us, the fugitive slaves indulged in grim jokes: one time they held gladiatorial games using Roman captives at the burial of their leader Crixus and on one occasion they paid, in cruel mockery, the last honours to a lady who had killed herself from grief after being raped (*matrona violata*).

When women were taken captive, the menace of violation was added to the loss of status and freedom. When the Romans took Corinth, in BC 146, Boiska killed first her daughter and then herself, because to her only a 'free lot' (*potmos eleutheros*) was livable. 'I prefer a free death', Kallirhoe exclaimed when she was sold as a slave, 'if I may not live nobly (*eugenes*)'. Prokopios includes in his history as a true story the fate of a Byzantine woman. The capital of the Eastern Empire was ravaged by the blue circus-party. She and her husband fled overseas to their country seat. En route, they were attacked by pirates who took only her aboard their ship. From there she cried to her husband that he ought not to fear any disgrace as far as she was concerned. She threw herself into the sea in full regalia (*matrona ornata*): in a way she wanted to protect *him* from being 'dishonoured'. In this 'altruistic' *pudor* she used the despicable, but only, means that was available, jumping in the deep (p.9).

The most clear-cut *pudor*-suicides among women took place after, or in a case of imminent, rape. Many dishonoured women put an end to their lives, according to the sources: the Teutonic women, Dionysios' wife who had been violated during a rebellion, Hippo, Mallonia, Phegeus' daughter, Spartan girls and the maid from Tegea. The model of a shame-suicide following on violation is Lucretia's: her story was, in Donaldson's words, 'fashioned into a powerful aetiological myth'. Only St Augustine casts doubt on the sincerity of her motivation. In Roman pagan literature she is the example of a noble lady who, although herself blameless, knows what honour requires of her[83].

The chastity of women is linked to the welfare of the community. Skedasos' daughters had been raped by some Spartans. Killing themselves afterwards, the girls cursed the country of their violators. It took some time before the malediction was effected, in spite of the prayers of Skedasos to the Furies; he could not wait for them to avenge the crime, but committed suicide. Much later, on the eve of the battle of Leuctra, the Thebans realized what ominous meaning the place had. They sacrificed a foal and then saw to the implementation of the curse which had been over Sparta for such a long time.

The Vestal Virgins are looked upon as the guardians of the harmony between god and man. In Rome's darkest hour, in the time of the battle of Cannae, all sorts of magic means were used in an attempt to restore the good relationship with the gods which had obviously been disturbed. On behalf of the *pax deorum* gladiatorial fights were held and outright human sacrifices were made. Only afterwards through the suicide of a Vestal Virgin did it come out that she, by her immoral behaviour, was responsible for the anger of the gods. Concepts similar to this were noted by Bohannan in Africa. With respect to a case of incest upon which a suicide followed, he says that there was more involved than just

117

shame: 'it is connected with notions of ritual impurity (luswa) which are thought to affect the entire community'[84].

Women who kill themselves after being violated win respect. Three Milesian girls were hailed in an epigram because they preferred death above being subjected to *hybris* by Gauls. An authentic epitaph is the one for Domitilla, who maintained her purity when the Goths invaded (p.24). She belongs to the much-discussed group of Christian women who committed suicide and were honoured, at least at the time of their deed.

In female *pudor*-suicide the theme of incest is predominant: Euopis, Halia, Harpalyke, Kanake, Kyane, Niobe, Pelopeia and Phaidra. In the sources there is no interest in the possible guilt-feelings of the girls. Generally, the girls are the involuntary victim of the lust of a father or brother, but the *shame* is theirs. The blame is less deadly for the male party: only two fathers and one brother do not survive the disgrace (Kinyras, Klymenes and Makareus).

Being dishonoured is in itself a curse which a woman cannot get rid of. What was the 'sin' Iokaste committed? She had no real reason to blame herself, any more than Lucretia had. Personal guilt is explicitly denied by Artemidoros in a case from his dream-practice. A woman dreamt that ears grew from her breast and bent downwards into her vagina. Later *by accident* she had intercourse with her son. This dreaming woman (*femina somniens* in Appendix A) could not bear the shame and killed herself.

Almost exclusively it is the female victims of incest who are the ones that have to pay with their lives. The sole boy to become the victim of his mother's passion was Sextus Papinius, who ended his shame by throwing himself from a window in an ugly death (p.27). According to one text Iokaste was not the only one who put an end to her shameful existence; this source says that Oidipous too killed himself on discovering the disgusting relationship. In the classical treatment of the myth by Sophocles the question of guilt is not raised: the tragedy is only about shame. At the end of the drama, when Oidipous is about to leave Thebes, broken by the destruction of his house, the chorus asks – to modern taste impudently: Why did you not end your life, just as Iokaste did? Then Oidipous gives an answer which to our ears sounds burlesque, but which makes clear the concrete significance of shame: because if I did I should have to *face* my parents in Hades[85].

With respect to moral codes too, antiquity is a face-to-face culture; guilt in which the reactions of the outside world are anticipated internally does not play an important role in the system of values. There are situations in which a human being is expected to show shame. Many may have dreamt about sleeping with their mother[86], but sexuality between mother and son is taboo, as is brought out even in the natural world – always an important argument in Greek discussion: the Scythian stallion threw himself into a ravine when he discovered that he had been deceived by his master into mating with his own mother (p.xiii).

Bestiality also could cause (attempted) suicide. We have the unique opportunity to see the animal side of the situation in Lucius, the main figure of Apuleius' novel, who has become an ass. At one point, he is about to become the executioner of a horrible punishment: a woman is to be sexually subjected to him in the middle of an arena. Desperately he looks for means to kill himself, but for an ass there are no ways open. Finally, the omnipotent novelist saves the criminal woman and the noble Lucius from unbearable shame.

To a man the danger of *pudor* in sexual matters occurs mainly in homosexual relations. One rhetorical exercise concerns the following case: a man sexually assaulted a freeborn citizen; the latter hanged himself. However, that is no reason for the author of the assault to suffer capital punishment for having caused the death; he will instead pay 10,000 sesterces, the fine imposed by law for such a crime[87]. A historical case concerns one Demokles; he refused all advances whether accompanied by presents or menaces. In order to avoid importunement he visited only private bath-houses. Once he was nevertheless surprised by King Demetrios. Demokles at once jumped into boiling water.

A freak of nature put one man into an embarrassing position: Samiades' wife Herais became a man and as such took the name Diophantos. The husband was so ashamed about his now unnatural marriage that he 'removed himself from life'.

Various anecdotes which end in suicide illustrate how ancient man was what was thought of him. The mocking verses of Hipponax drove Boupalos and Athenis to death. They had made a caricature statue of the poet Archilochos, who himself could boast professional success similar to Hipponax's when he took revenge for a broken engagement. By his satires he made life impossible for his former fiancée Neoboule, her sisters and their father Lykambes. Of course, such apocryphal stories are told to demonstrate the power of art. But scorn could be deadly indeed. Two men, both named Pausanias, competed for the erotic favours of king Philip II. When one was relegated in favour of the other as an *eromenos*, the repudiated beloved abused the new favourite so effectively that he 'voluntarily and unexpectedly (*paradoxôs*) removed himself out of life'. In a letter – one of the few in antiquity written by suicides[88] – addressed to the royal *erastes* he explained his action.

The sheer number of 296 cases of *pudor*-suicides, i.e. one-third of all instances where motives can be established, show how highly the ancient world valued this type of self-killing. Where modern observers would rather assume despair or grief as the predominant motive the ancient reporter was inclined to put shame in the forefront. The predominance of shame as a motive is the most important difference from the modern paradigm of suicide, which concentrates on internal motives like depression and feelings of guilt.

G   GUILT: *MALA CONSCIENTIA*

In many cases that ancient literature attributed to shame, a modern suicidologist would rather assume feelings of guilt as the driving force. Did Alexander suffer from shame or from guilt when he was about to cut his own throat before his friends with the dagger with which he had stabbed Kleitos in passion? One could argue that their presence was calculated, for Alexander did not withdraw himself from company to do away with himself. In a way he confirmed the significance of his existence by eliciting their intervention. We do not know whether soldiers who were said to have killed brothers unwittingly during the Civil War and who afterwards committed suicide on realizing the atrocity of their deed, could not face the world or were haunted by their conscience.

Mala conscientia is only assumed by the Roman law-giver when other, excusable motives have to be excluded. For the jurists of course bad feelings were only relevant in so far as they pertained to the cause of the legal proceedings; they were not interested in feelings of guilt connected with facts which lay outside the lawsuit[89].

What an individual feels, receives more and more attention in the course of antiquity. The egocentric Stoics and Cynics focus on the inner life just as the ancient novelists do for their main characters. In accordance with this line of development, more attention was paid to motives which lie inside man, like grief and guilt.

On the whole a bad conscience is not readily assumed as the explanation for self-killing. As the driving force behind a suicide, guilt-feelings are preferably suspected in an opponent: it is very satisfactory to be sure that *others* killed themselves on realizing the awfulness of their own crimes. Had Rome been a ruthless leader of its allies? No, says Furius Purpurio in BC 200 to the hesitating Aetolians. During the Hannibalic War that had just ended when he delivered his speech, more Italian allies had done away with themselves 'conscious of their crimes' (*conscientia scelerum*) than had been punished with death by the Romans for their perfidy.

Cases where feelings of guilt are unequivocally presented as the cause scarcely exist. In some passages in drama where persons reproach themselves, they entertain the idea of self-killing because of their responsibility, like Helen who caused a war. In myth, Assaon, who had desired his own daughter, is said to have committed suicide because he perceived his sin. He fits well into the psycho-analytic model of explanation in which a suicide often executes himself in order to prevent a more humiliating punishment by others. Such a self-execution is explicitly ascribed to a criminal in a novel: Thrasyllus had cunningly murdered Charite's husband. But then remorse came over him. He thought that a sword wielded with his own hands was not enough in the light of his wrongdoing and he resolved to destroy his soul, 'condemned by his own sentence' (*sua sententia damnatum*) by starvation[90]. Alkinoe too felt obliged to expiate her sin. She had left her husband. Aboard the ship of her lover she was pained by her conscience and threw herself in the sea before the eyes of the crew: her self-inflicted punishment had to be public.

Grisé also ascribes to Gavius Silvanus 'sentiments de culpabilité' and 'remords'; the reference in Tacitus is too brief to allow for such an interpretation. As one of the officers of the praetorian guard he was acquitted of being involved in the conspiracy against Nero. Nevertheless, 'he fell by his own hand'. Grief because of lost friends, shame for having been disgraced or loyalty can account for this behaviour as well as guilt.

Unless modern motivation is forced upon ancient cases, guilt is a very under-developed category in the motives *attributed*: with 13 cases *conscientia* is the smallest group. Ancient observers always preferred to see self-killing as the reaction to the – assumed –

opinion of the world. In explaining suicide they chose shame where possible.

H OLD AND FULL OF YEARS: *TAEDIUM VITAE*

'But vexed by anxieties of a hard-pressed mind as well as by numerous pains of the body, so that both were extremely disgusting, I procured for myself the death I wished for'. In this way Marcus Pomponius Bassulus expounds to passers-by why his remains lie in the tomb: mental and bodily suffering had exasperated him to such a degree that he had had enough of life. This *taedium vitae* was acknowledged by Roman law as a sufficient ground to leave life. The motive comprises, as Bassulus' text explains, pain both of the soul and of the body. Even disgust with the political situation – the imperial regime – could be a part of the *taedium*.

The inclusion of this category in the codes of law suggests frequent occurence, but there are remarkably few concrete cases in our material that can be recorded under that heading, namely 20. The discrepancy between the explicit distinction as a motive and the small number of historical cases can be attributed to the fact that such suicides in general had no public significance and therefore did not gain entry into the official records. Of course *taedium*-suicide shocked the narrow circle of friends and relatives. We feel the impact in some of Pliny's letters. Typical for this kind of self-killing is the high degree of forethought. The individual draws up the balance-sheet of his existence. This type of suicide comes close to what in modern time is styled 'balance-suicide' or 'autolysis'[91].

Sometimes the *taediosus* consults his friends before acting. When the decision has been made, nothing can deter him from his resolve. Arruntius' friends advised him to wait for some time. He replied that the same things were not becoming to all men, trying to reprove them. His life had been long enough; 'not from feelings of guilt, but because he could no longer endure, seeing the outrageous deeds of Tiberius, he cut his veins'. More often the cause is less public. Bodily pain is generally the factor which makes a person decide for death at last. Often the ailment has manifested itself for a long time, but finally the patient is weary of it. Thus, eventually Latro was tired of his 'double fourth-day-fever' (*duplex quartana*)[92].

What made life unlivable for Cocceius Nerva? His position was secure and his health was unimpaired. Nevertheless he decided to die. When Tiberius got wind of this decision, he sat down by his side, inquired after his reasons, proceeded to entreaties, and in the last resort confessed that it would be a serious matter both for his conscience and for his reputation if the nearest of his friends were to flee from life with no motive for dying. Declining all conversation, Nerva continued his abstention from food till the end. His decision simply was made and no force on earth was able to change his mind.

There is only one historical woman to whom the motive of *taedium vitae* may be ascribed, Vipsania Agrippina[93]. This grand old lady had seen enough misery during her long life under the empire. Things came to a head when even after Sejanus' fall the terror did not stop. She too chose the ostentatious way of the *endura*: she abstained from food, the preferred method in the case of *taedium vitae*. The dignity of the means well befitted this very Roman death of a noble woman.

I UNBEARABLE SUFFERING: *INPATIENTIA*

Mainly because the cases of Cocceius Nerva and Vipsania Agrippina occurred in Rome's high society and political motives were suspected, they attracted special attention. In the layers under the top of society such conscious self-killings probably were a common phenomenon. Only in this way does it become explicable why Roman law reacted to this type of suicide in the way it did. In Pliny the Younger's correspondence we meet nobility in the Italian countryside. Pliny reports this remarkable case:

> a short while ago Titius Aristo invited me and some other people as well whom he likes most, and asked us to consult the doctors about the general state of his health (*summa valetudinis*). If his disease was incurable, he would leave life voluntarily, but if it was only painful and long-lasting, he would endure it and stay alive for the sake of his wife, daughters and friends.

The scale dipped on the side of life. In another case, that of Silius Italicus, death's arguments weighed more.

Seneca had recommended suicide when old age threatened to

bring undignifying decay: did he give his philosophical blessing to – what is essentially – atavistic behaviour? In African suicide incurable disease is an important motive. Beattie comments on his conclusion that 19 out of the 28 male cases where he could establish a cause were to be attributed to that motive, in this way: 'It is hard for anyone who has not lived in a primitive community to conceive of the despair which painful or chronic illness can induce where medical facilities are few and little used'. Self-killing for this reason is not regarded as sinister. An old woman whose husband pre-deceased her, so that she was dependent on her children, contracted leprosy on top of all her other misery. For this reason her house was destroyed by her son and she had to move into a hut outside the community. Thereupon she hanged herself, but 'her ghost was not considered to be any more dangerous than that of a person who died a normal death because she was old and her suicide was from old age and weariness. She held no grudge against anyone'[94].

The way the people who live in Pliny's world handle suicide has much in common with the world of Bassulus' epitaph. It seems that at the turn of the first century it was accepted behaviour to draw up the balance-sheet of life and to decide for death. Maybe the Roman aristocracy of the imperial terror paved the way for a more general openness towards suicide in the next epoch.

With respect to suicide due to unbearable bodily suffering Atticus is the bridge between Roman political nobility and Greek philosophers, such as Kleanthes and Speusippos, who already had the habit of taking their own life in such cases. Under the Roman regime Greek thinkers continued to act in this way: in the second century AD Demonax compared the ending of his life to the final act of the Olympic Games (p.36). The last words of such thinking men's suicides were kept for posterity. On the lips of the Epicurean Diodoros it was Dido's goodbye: 'I have lived my life and finished the course which Fortune allotted me'[95].

In the 19 Greek cases of suicide from *inpatientia* heroes of the mind acted in the way of Heracles. The Greek world reacted with some astonishment to the willingness of *common* Romans to put an end to their lives: the epigrams on Aelius demonstrate the respectful surprise at the Roman habit: 'I, whom war dreaded and slew not, am now afflicted by disease, and waste away by intestine warfare. Pierce my heart then, sword, for I will die like a valiant soldier, beating off disease even as I did war'[96].

Mostly the reason for voluntary death is furnished by tumours and other ailments of old age; people do not hesitate to share their bodily sufferings with the public. 'Albucius Silus returned to Novaria because of an evil tumour; he called the people together and artfully dwelt at length on the reasons why he had decided to die, before he finally abstained from food'. The husband of the resolute woman at Lake Como had to show his ulcers. In younger persons other problems of health may awaken the desire to die: in his youth Seneca considered putting an end to his life because of his bronchial troubles (p.28). In Seneca's Stoicism bodily suffering could be a sufficient ground for a wise man to give up life, where the quality of his existence was in danger of deteriorating; suicide never was allowed to be a mere cowardly flight. This higher code of behaviour had already been established by the Cynics. When Diogenes suffered from pain in his shoulder, someone who was vexed by his demeanour, mocked: 'Why don't you die and free yourself from evil?' But he said to this Pharisee: 'For those who know what to do and say in life, it is fitting to live'. He made it clear that he belonged to this class himself. 'But for you', he said, 'who do not know what to say or do dying is fine'[97].

Losing one's eyesight of course was a great disaster, which happened many a time in antiquity. Decius Vibellius was made blind. He was the leader of a gang of Campanians that had taken possession of Rhegium. When he suffered from an eye-disease, he was 'treated' by one of the expelled Rhegians who posed as a physician. This pseudo-doctor deprived him of his eyesight. At last Roman order was restored and Decius was held in captivity, but because of his condition he was guarded negligently. He seized an opportunity and killed himself with a sword. Blindness occurring naturally was a terrible catastrophe: only with much difficulty could Terrinius Gallus be prevented from suicide by Augustus himself 'when his eyes were suddenly afflicted and he therefore decided to die by starvation'.

The elder Pliny sums up some diseases which are known to lead to suicide because of the unbearable pains which are linked with them: stones in the bladder, stomach-ache and headache[98]. According to a Christian writer, worms ate Maximianus who had persecuted his co-religionists. The doctor who was consulted added insult to injury by diagnosing the ailment as God's punishment. To the great satisfaction of Orosius, the Christian writer who wrote such fierce anti-pagan history, the emperor put an end to his life.

This venomous story raises questions about the scope of the Christian taboo on suicide: at least the disgraceful suicide of a hated enemy was greeted with enthusiasm by Christian historiography. But was a person with a bodily handicap allowed to put an end to his life? On the isle of Arados St Peter met a woman begging (*mendicans mulier* in Appendix A): 'Why don't you work?' Her hands were paralysed. 'If only I had a manly (*sic*) spirit, there would be a precipice or a deep sea that would bring me deliverance'. The dialogue is continued in this vein: do you believe that those who destroy themselves will be free from punishment? Or will they be punished more severely? The moral of this story is in line with the changing attitude of the fourth century when Christianity started to express disapproval of all and every suicide.

In the literature of the Later Roman Empire sympathetic descriptions of self-killing because of unbearable suffering do not occur any more: the climate of complete tolerance which existed in Pliny's times was apparently over.

J DEVOTIO AND FIDES

Ancient assessment of suicide does not leave much room for mental imbalance as an important factor. Antiquity preferred to see the deed as done after some deliberation. Therefore there is a marked tendency to ascribe self-killing to ostentation (*iactatio*), shame (*pudor*), unbearable suffering (*inpatientia*) or *taedium vitae*. Durkheim saw the predominance of 'egoistic' suicide as characteristic of his own age, in which social links had been weakened. In a way different from his interpretation, the pattern of suicide in antiquity is marked by egoism: in the descriptions it is stressed that an individual took a final decision in relative freedom.

Altruism in a Durkheimian sense was less frequent than one would expect in such an integrated society. But in the 52 cases in all much attention is paid to the exemplary value of *devotio*. In the fullest sense individuals 'devote themselves' (*se devovere*), sacrificing their lives for the well-being of the whole. Oracles ask leaders to free the community from a curse by giving up their own life or they promise military victory if they have themselves killed. Adrastos and Hipponoos, father and son, jumped willingly into the fire. Chasms received Anchouros and Curtius when the god had announced that only sacrificing the highest good could bring salvation. Kings and generals made their way to the thick of the fight to ensure by their voluntary death the victory of their own side. In those cases, as Versnel has made clear, the victim is the most valued possession of the State: not only the king or leader himself, but also his daughter or son, the young warrior or the chaste virgin. Soldiers, even those of the lowest ranks, killed themselves to underline the truth of the message they brought and to serve in this way the great cause or rather the great leader (p.18): the Year of the Four Emperors showed us some striking examples. The military environment according to Durkheim is favourable towards 'suicide altruiste'. The professional army especially develops a code which obliges suicide in certain well-defined circumstances[99].

The Greek world is acquainted with the hero who gives himself up for the community practically only in the mythical sphere: for example, Kodros. The sole more or less historical case is that of the Athenian *strategi* who began the battle of Arginusae in spite of Thrasyboulos' dream that had predicted their death. The community was not always the polis: the philosophical school in many ways was a substitute for the political community. It could ask for *devotio*: when Pythagoras was encircled by fire his students saved him by forming a living bridge (p.58).

Devotio is a man's duty. The means reflect the *virtus*: provocation (41 per cent) is the predominant method which goes with this motive. In the rare cases where women sacrifice themselves for the sake of the community, they do so to put to shame their men who did not live up to the standards set for them. According to an oracle the most noble Theban citizen had to give himself up. Antipoinos refused the honour, but then his daughters took his place voluntarily. Heracles' daughter was the type of woman to make a king ashamed: the king of Athens refused to hand over his daughter to ensure victory in the war with Argos, but Makaria offered herself as a substitute.

Devotion can have its place in personal relationships too: the common soldier of Otho (*miles Othonis gregarius*) sacrificed himself for the common good and his leader. Among the examples of moving loyalty of slaves there are some cases where a slave poses as his master, thus provoking an attack on his own person. The striking exception in the one-way traffic was Plotius Plancus. As a master he provoked his own death to free his slaves from further torture (p.57).

In this personal type of devotion females are not wholly absent:

Epicharis, freed slave and a woman at that, by her behaviour put the weak partisans of Piso to shame (p.19).

This last case already contains some features of loyalty. *Fides* is a virtue of slaves, women and other 'low-ranking friends' towards their master. Japanese culture has this type as 'junshi'. The Gauls/Celts had the *soldurii* who had pledged their life and soul to a leader to such a degree that they shared death with him. Among them, according to some ethnographic reports, a person could sacrifice himself for the material well-being of his relatives. The public put silver, gold and jars of wine together; strong oaths were sworn that the collected goods would become the property of the family. After this ceremony this actor in his own death-scene lay down on the back of his shield and a bystander cut his throat. A similar primitive spectacle is reported for early Rome. In his *Historical memoranda* Ephorion of Chalcis told that twenty pounds of gold were offered to the person who was willing to have his head cut off with an axe. Often, as the astounded Greek reported, there were several applicants to compete for the honour of being beheaded[100].

Pantheia's eunuchs and Cleopatra's female slaves are the exceptional instances of *fides*-suicides committed for a woman. Valerius Maximus has striking examples of loyalty shown by women to their husbands, never the other way round[101]. Wives accompany their men in death because they are nothing without them: thus there is a small difference in motivation from mourning *simpliciter*. Arria 'was not willing to live on when he (Paetus) was no more'. Among the Greeks historical examples of such matrimonial loyalty are lacking. With bewilderment they look at the competition between the two Indian wives of Keteus over the honour of accompanying their husband on the pyre (p.58). Greek myth and novel do present models of female loyalty which does not shrink away from suicide: Anthia faithful to her beloved, Helen to Menelaus who was her legal husband after all, and as the most exemplary case Alcestis who by her death saved the life and the *oikos* of her Admetus. She and Euadne are so well known as prototypes that a rhetor can dispense with naming them: alluding suffices[102].

Only in the Late Republic and the Early Principate do we hear about real Roman women who accompany their husband on his last journey. Sometimes they even show the way. In BC 82 Calpurnia took the initiative in demonstrating loyalty all the way to voluntary death. She stabbed herself – in a manly way with a sword – when her husband had been executed. She won by her strong *fides* both *gloria* and *fama*. Sextia inspired and shared the death of her Scaurus[103]. Ovid makes his readers believe that his wife wished to throw herself into a fire when he was forced into exile: in *fides* too sexual asymmetry predominated.

K SHOWING OFF: *IACTATIO*

In *To himself* (11,3) Marcus Aurelius glorifies the soul that is prepared to leave the body at the moment decreed by Fate. 'Such preparedness, however, must be the outcome of its own decision; a decision *not prompted by mere contumacy, as with the Christians*, but formed with deliberation and gravity and, if it is to be convincing to others, with an absence of all heroics'. Fundamental disapproval and mockery accompany the suicides meant as a demonstration of a philosophical attitude: You, Decianus, are a Stoic. 'I do not like the hero who buys his reputation with blood easily shed. I prefer someone who deserves praise without having to die to gain it'[104].

Exhibitionist suicide is acknowledged by Roman jurisprudence with the words 'from ostentation as some philosophers do'[105]. Looking to public reaction in general is the mark of ancient behaviour in suicide. Relatively rare are the cases where somebody withdraws to his attic or to the mountains to commit the deed. One prefers to kill oneself in front of an audience or at least in the company of some good friends. This need for publicity is characteristic of a world in which the private sphere is under-developed. Also the upper layer of society, which could afford a private domain, clung to the principle of life and death as public events.

In suicide *iactatione ut quidam philosophi* purpose and staging are a whole: the freedom attained by philosophical insight is demon-strated in a final show. As a stimulus for ostentatious suicide in Ptolemaic Egypt Hegesias' *Apokarteron* played a role (p.42).

The biographies of philosophers written by Diogenes Laertios as a rule end with suicide or at least rumours about voluntary death. Most of those cases were discussed earlier in the course of describing self-killing among old men. The last deed had to set a seal on a life of firm principles: a charlatan like Peregrinos was as unauthentic in his suicide as he had been in life according to Lucian. In the full moon he went to his pyre to complete the show of life in full regalia, like his illustrious model Heracles. Freely chosen death was not allowed to be a game. Only barbarians are said to have played a kind of Russian roulette. During their drinking-bouts the Thracians set up a noose at a certain height, directly under which they placed a stone which could easily be rolled by any who stepped upon it. Then they drew lots, and the one who received the lot mounted the stone, holding a pruning-knife, and placed his neck in the noose; another came by and pushed the stone, and while it was rolling from under him, the man hanging there, if he did not quickly loose himself with the knife before it was too late, was dead, and the others laughed, holding the poor devil's death a great joke[106].

Ancient epigrams mingle admiration and mockery in their lines on philosophical suicides. Pheidon says: flee the storms of life and head for the safe haven of death. In an epitaph in the form of a dialogue Philaulos justifies his voluntary journey into Hades. These, of course, are only literary games – played with common themes. A real case happened in BC 43. In that troubled year in Rome a soothsayer declared that royal power would return and that all would be slaves except for him. Thereupon he closed his mouth and held his breath till death came (*divinus* in Appendix A).

What is strikingly lacking in ancient suicide is the element of protest: there are no aims involved lying outside the individual. It is simply his liberty that is underlined by the final act. This presupposes the presence of a public that gapes in admiration at the philosophical artist or at the believers who demonstrate their contempt of death. During the Great Persecution in the imperial residence of Nicomedia Christians leapt into the fire which destroyed the imperial palace. The methods which go with the motive of *iactatio* are spectacular indeed: fire and *inedia* (Appendix B 8 a and c).

L THE ANCIENT PARADIGM OF SELF-KILLING

In attributing motives the ancient world demonstrates its doctrine of suicide. No historical study can disclose the real causes of self-killing. What appears is – in Baechler's terminology – not the *étiologie*, but the *sens* and this only in the eyes of the survivors. The autobiographical documents of ancient (would-be) self-killers are sparse: Augustine, Cicero, Isidora, Seneca. In the ancient world, as Bayet says, there was 'une morale nuancée jugeant les suicides sur leurs motifs': only when Cato had a *causa moriendi* and a just one (*iusta*) at that, was he glad to say goodbye to life[107]. Ancient interpretation is biased towards stressing freedom and consciousness in motivation. Therefore hardly any attention is paid to mental imbalance, although Roman law mentions *furor* as a ground for suicide. But it had to be the heroic fury of a Heracles to gain an entry in the literature.

Self-killing is preferably understood as the deed of someone who hopes to preserve his honour. The strong presence of the complex of *pudor* in the material is to be explained in this way. Despair is mainly ascribed to a defeated enemy and as such is noted with satisfaction by the observer, who can dwell at some length on horrible scenes of self-destruction. *Dolor* and *fides* reflect the sexual asymmetry of the ancient world: it is only these motives that are often ascribed to women. In general, the driving forces attributed to the cases of suicide lie in the sphere of male virtue, literally *virtus*.

This stressing of the element of dignity makes ancient suicide fundamentally differ from 'le suicide égoïste', which is the focus of Durkheim's theory. The main integrative factor to which Durkheim ascribed such an anti-suicidal power, the family, was the corner-stone of ancient society. But being married and having children did not prevent people from committing suicide. Maybe religion in its ancient form could not have the integrative effect of the religious communities of the nineteenth century[108], but in general there was a strong interaction between the community and the individual: even in a suicide from *dolor* a public audience was often sought. Porterfield was right in calling Graeco-Roman suicide 'semi-institutional'[109]. The 'individuation démésurée' which in Durkheim's 'egoistic' type causes self-killing is not characteristic of the ancient world. With regard to the significance of Durkheim's theory for antiquity the same problems arise which Bohannan met when he tried to use the concept on African suicide. Finally, he had to conclude that Durkheim's model did not have much explanatory value for his material. 'Secret, personal suicide' in his judgment is fundamentally linked with the 'open society', from which the ancient world was as far distant as the African communities which were studied by Bohannan[110].

On the other side, the ancient idea of suicide can only partly be described in terms of altruism in the Durkheimian sense. Among primitives the 'individuation insuffisante' according to Durkheim (p.233) causes old people to say goodbye to life; women accompany their husband in death and servants their master, because the individual is 'totalement absorbé dans le groupe'. But that is not the behaviour we see among Greeks and Romans, in spite of some atavism in *devotio*. What they strongly need is a public: they wish to be seen when they think themselves unable to face people.

Part II

EXPERIENCE OF SELF-KILLING

4

SUICIDE IN WORDS
AND TEXTS

Every aspect of ancient self-killing has gone through filters. On any level, studying Graeco-Roman suicide means looking through the eyes of ancient observers and investigating their perspective. This problem of perception came out clearly in the first part: the numbering and categorizing of groups, methods and motives demonstrated the schemes of thinking in which the ancient world wished to comprehend suicide. Once this framework of – interpreted – facts is established we have the basis for a 'history of mentality' for ancient suicide. Above the bottom layer where concrete cases were studied comes the level of experience; in the second part of this study different kinds of material that show popular attitudes will be discussed. After that, in part three, reflection on suicide or what Vovelle styled the *discours* is treated.

Thus, in between the levels of reflection and phenomena there is the rich vein of popular material. In the first place, the language tells a story: the terms in which the Greeks and Romans spoke about self-killing are revealing of their attitudes. The highly developed culture of the word is a second important source: how did ancient orators exploit the theme? They are crucial as spokesmen, because in their speeches they play upon the opinions they assume in their public. Another communication of a different order and complexity took place between the ancient dramatist and the audience: tragedy and comedy, each in their own way, disclose many of the values which the public was expected to hold. Not only on the stage could suicide arouse laughter. Jokes were made and epigrams were written; some of them have already been discussed as 'cases'. This light-hearted material too must not be left out. Special attention has to be paid to *direct* material:

135

inscriptions and papyri did not pass through the filter of literary tradition. Is the way they look upon self-killing different from the stylized representation of ancient literature? It is also important to know whether people in their epitaphs broadcast the fact that suicide was the cause of death.

It is not only words, rhetoric, drama and other texts that reveal ancient attitudes. Medical men in their practice were confronted with cases which encouraged them to formulate some generalizations on several occasions. As experts in applied science they competed with other consultants; astrologers and an interpreter of dreams came across suicide in their branch as well. Artemidoros comments on a dream that there exists a taboo on paying tribute to a self-killer. A number of burial customs seem to confirm his remark: a suicide was not regarded as an ordinary deceased. Does the evident repugnance result in legal measures to dam or to stigmatize self-killing? Apart from some varied evidence for different ancient cultures we have the Roman jurisconsults who developed a practical philosophy and thus add to our understanding. Finally there is the language of pictures: was suicide represented and, if so, with what intentions?

A *SUICIDIUM*, A NON-WORD

In his *L'Age d'homme* Michel Leiris describes how he tasted the word suicide in all its elements; every sound and syllable evoked the image of self-burning and an Indian dagger: the S had the form of the kris and made him think of the rotary motion of the body in falling. The U crackled like fire and CIDE finished off the scene[1].

Latin and Greek did not have words with the sinister sound and the pregnant meaning of our 'suicide' and 'self-murder'. *Suicidium* looks like an ancient word, but it did not exist in classical Latin. Neither could it have found a place in the vocabulary of the Romans, not only because the idea it carried was far from their mind, but also because it is bad Latin. The word was only coined in the seventeenth century. Commonly, Caramuel the theologian is named as the creator of this Latin neologism[2]. In the second edition of his monumental *Theologia moralis fundamentalis,* which came out in Rome in AD 1656, he uses the terms *suicidium* and *suicida* without claiming originality. *Fundamentum* 55 discusses homicide which is forbidden in the fifth command (*De Homicidio, quod in quinto praecepto interdicitur*). There Caramuel argues that *any*

killing of a human being is prohibited by God's order and 'you
are no less forbidden to kill yourself than your fellow-man'[3]. Is
there really no case for self-killing? 'I will discuss one which needs
a closer investigation. On purpose I present this controversial case
of *Suicidium*'. In n.1628 we find the promised *Quaestio de Suicidio*.
The only signal that the words were uncommon is a small sentence
in the margin: '*Suicida* means the one who kills himself'. Clear signs
of satisfaction about coining a new word are lacking. Griffin says
that the word appears for the first time in AD 1643 in the *Religio
Medici* written by Sir Thomas Browne. The least one could say, is
that the word was in the air in the middle of the century, that is to
say among experts who were in need of an inclusive technical
term[4].

In the same period Comenius was composing his Latin
dictionary with pictures for children. The *Orbis Sensualium Pictus*
started on its triumphant career in Nuremberg in AD 1643. Under
the heading *Patientia* the sorry consequences of not possessing this
Christian virtue are described: 'On the contrary, the *impatient person*
(*impatiens*) waileth, lamenteth, *rageth against himself* (*debacchatur in
seipsum*), grumbleth like a Dog and yet doth no good; at the last he
despaireth, and becometh *his own murderer* (*Autochir*)'. All the words
in italics are followed by figures which refer to details of the
drawing which accompanies this rubric. Thus, *Autochir* is explained
by a moving picture of a man who throws himself on his sword
(See Ill.13). Comenius still makes use of the Greek *autocheir*, the
'own-handed', i.e. the one who lays hands upon himself. When
Donne, having become a Roman Catholic, tried to argue that self-
killing was not a sin under all circumstances, he employed as the
title for his writing the Greekish *Biathanatos*, i.e. the one who is
killed violently. Even when *suicidium* came into use, the more
flexible Greek was called in for variation with its *autophonos*,
autophonia, *autothanatos*, *biaiothanatos* and the like[5].

Did those who wrote Neo-Latin realize that *suicidium* was not a
well-formed word? In the modern languages *suicidium* was accepted
by way of the French rendering that abbé Desfontaines introduced
in 1737. The *Académie* gave its blessing to the word by including it
in the *Dictionnaire* in AD 1762. There is no reason to share Grisé's
astonishment that the Romans did not invent this handy word.
Unlike Greek, which had the flexibility of German, Latin could not
make words that had a pronoun as a prefix[6]. In Cicero's ears
suicidium would have sounded as 'swine-slaying' (*sus* = swine).

Latin was not in need of such a term. Moreover, it could dispense with a coined word for self-killing altogether.

Only in Christian times was there a market for a general Latin word, although the Greek expressions long survived. At first in late and medieval Latin such circumscriptions are in use as *homicida sui/suipsius* (man-killer of oneself) and *assasinium sui/suipsius* (of Islamic origin). Nearest to the Christian usage is the Elder Seneca when he uses as a title for one case *homicida in se* (man-killer with respect to oneself). But in general, the Roman was well-equipped with effective *circumscriptions*.

The presence of a rich circumlocutory vocabulary is not a unique feature of the classical languages; writing a book on suicide one becomes aware of the potential of modern usage. But modern ways of putting things are always orientated to the central concept of self-murderer/suicide, especially when new words are tried.

The rigidity of Latin in forming words is not the main reason for the absence of a distinctive word. The flexible Greek has at its disposal various striking words for self-killer – *autophonos*, *authentes*, *autocheir*, but none of these terms obtained the exclusive rights of modern 'suicide'. Nor do the words solely stand for 'killer of oneself'. They may mean 'someone who kills his own kin'. If an enemy slays a relative, he may indignantly be called an *authentes*. Thus is Neoptolemos denoted to Andromache, because he slew her family in Troy[7]. An 'own-handed', *autocheir*, may be the one 'who kills his own blood', especially his father or mother, but other relations are also possible in 'authentic' (*authentes*) killing. When the messenger reports on the stage that Haimon lies in his own blood as an *autocheir*, the chorus curiously asks: by the paternal hand or his own? The idea behind these terms obviously is much broader and more diffuse than just 'suicide'[8].

In the vocabulary present in the two classical languages more than three hundred words and expressions have been gathered (Appendix C). At first sight this seems quite a number, but one has to realize that the majority of the words refer to specific ways of doing away with oneself. Most interesting are the general words and phrases. Both the diffuseness of the concept and the rhetorical requirements of *variatio* forced the ancient author to look for diversity.

What are the ideas that come to the fore in the ways self-killing was denoted? The Greek neutral terminology comprises all kinds of expressions: 'to kill oneself', 'to do away with oneself', 'to destroy

oneself', 'to bereave oneself of life' and 'to put an end to one's life'[9].
Of course, the English translations do not fully cover the terms of
the original language, but the general sense is clear: Greek is quite
capable of denoting the deed in various neutral terms. Euphemisms
of the kind modern languages are so full of are also present in
Greek usage; as 'taming' (*damnemi*) is poetically said for killing, an
epigram discreetly using 'taming oneself'. In the sphere of
euphemistic speech there figure expressions like 'giving a turn
(*katastrophe*) to life' or 'turning life upside down'[10]. These
expressions are as circumlocutory as the equivalent Latin idiom.
By its prefixes Greek is capable of adding nuances to a standard
word. With *pro* some of the words already mentioned can acquire
the supplementary meaning of killing oneself *before* being accused
or condemned.

A self-killer may be included among those who died by an
external cause. Such a person, unnaturally and violently killed, is
called a *biaiothanatos*. The word is even used in a specific sense for a
suicide, *the* violently killed. Even Latin makes use of the exotic
word. With derivations and its shortening to the strange *biothanatos*,
which at first sight looks like meaning life-death, it remains in use
for a long time in Christian Latin literature, which, as we saw, did
not have a pointed, sinister word before *suicidium* appeared.

As one might expect, Latin has also general expressions
equivalent to 'killing oneself', 'destroying oneself', 'putting an end
to one's life' and the like[11]. Common Latin usage for 'to bring
death upon oneself' is *adsciscere/consciscere sibi mortem*. With respect
to general and euphemistic ways of speech, there is a striking
richness of subtle expressions: 'to take away oneself', 'to strive after
death', 'to finish oneself off', 'to take the last measure', 'to decease
from life', 'to emit the soul', 'to emit oneself', 'to exanimate
oneself', 'to suppress the soul', 'to withdraw from human affairs',
'to hasten death with respect to oneself', 'to take refuge in death',
'to impose death upon oneself', 'to offer oneself to death', 'to
bereave oneself of soul/life', 'to seek death' and 'to rage against
oneself': these renderings are simply meant to evoke the tone of the
original phrases[12]. As in Greek, the idea that violence is done to
one's own life, is expressed in words and phrases[13]. Exquisite ways
of putting things were in use in epitaphs. There we read of
'abhorring life' (*abominare vivere*) which obviously was chosen to
avoid the common *taedium vitae*. Pomponius Bassulus addresses us
in person in his epitaph (p.153). This is a well-known device in

texts that ask for attention from the passer-by: stop, traveller, and read (*siste, viator, et lege*). In the text Pomponius glories in his literary achievements; it has to be assumed that he composed his own epitaph in which he uses the very special expression 'to appropriate death' (*potiri mortem*)[14].

Many are the words and phrases the ancients had available to express the horror, the astonishment and the respect for the hand that was directed against the body it was part of. How could it come about that a part acted 'autonomously', in obedience to the will of the mind? There are numerous variations on 'laying hands on oneself' (*cheiras heautoi epi/prosphero*, maybe – see p.156 n.51 – *cheiras prosago, manus ad/inferre*); many Latin expressions for suicide were strengthened by adding *manu*, with one's own hand.

The rich rhetorical usage is dominated by the mixture of bewilderment, approval and admiration. Greek coins terms with the prefix *auto-*, without making any one the key-word: 'self-seizing (*autagretos*) I leave the sun's light', 'self-chosen death' (*authairetos thanatos*), 'self-willing (*autothelei*) I go to Hades'. Latin expresses the same syndrome with *sponte*, 'on one's own initiative' in connection with 'leaving, quitting and taking death' (*decedere, exire, mortem sumere*). More simply somebody can be said to die by way of himself (*huph' heautou apothneisko*).

There is a complex of terms which express the act of will. Self-killing is described as a 'free fate' (*eleutheros potmos*), 'voluntary death' (*hekousios thanatos*). Latin has *mors voluntaria* as a phrase that dominates the scene without ever becoming *the* technical term. It has some variations with *exitus* and *finis*. It was exquisite to say 'to exanimate oneself voluntarily' (*voluntate se exanimare*). Volition is also stressed in Greek phrases like 'I die/finish off/destroy myself voluntarily' (*ethelontedon, ethelontes, ethelonti, hekontos, hekon, hekousios*).

Parting from life is another central idea. It is called 'loosening from life' (*apallage tou biou*). One can 'undo oneself from life' with all kinds of variations on the verb *apallatto* or 'distance oneself from existence' (*aphistamai tou biou*); there is the noun-phrase *apostasis tou biou*. 'To place oneself out of life' (*methistemi heauton ek tou zen*) uses the same verbal root of *histemi*.

Self-killers are those 'who leave life' (*leipo, ekleipo, kataleipo ton bion/to zen*). Greeks may cast away or reject life (*aphiemi . . . . proiemi . . .*). One can 'thrust away' life (*apotheo zoen*) or more expressively 'crush it under the heel' (*pateo lax zoen*). Philosophical usage came into being with 'to lead oneself out' (*exago*), culminating in the exulting euphemism 'rational leading out' (*exagoge eulogos*). Antisthenes, one of Socrates' followers, is mentioned as the creator of this concept[15]. The Latin equivalent is *excessus e vita rationalis*.

Some verbal and nominal expressions are meant to exclude all doubt concerning the degree of consciousness of the suicide. One speaks of 'taking death' (*lambano thanaton*), 'inviting death' (*arcessere mortem*), 'seeking death' (*mortem quaerere*), 'considered death' (*deliberata mors*), 'destined death' (*destinata mors* with the verbal phrase *destinare mori*), 'free disposal of death' (*liberum mortis arbitrium*), 'deciding about oneself' (*statuere de se*), 'condemning oneself' (*iudicare de semetipso)* and 'the ultimate plan' (*ultimum consilium*). Some of these sayings are personal adaptations on the part of authors who wish to embellish a special case. A certain popularity was enjoyed by the simile of a shipwreck: if all is in ruins one 'swims away from the body' (*aponechomai tou somatos*) and hopes to land in the safe haven of death.

These translations have been designed to convey the atmosphere in which the ancient world spoke of suicide. The general characteristic of classical vocabulary is the absence of a completely hostile usage. St Augustine tries the Neo-Platonic 'wringer-out of one's own soul', *extortor animae suae*. On the negative side one mainly finds horror which is not far away from respect. The numerous euphemisms are sometimes meant to express the unspeakable, but often they only denote the admiration of the observer for such a show of personal autonomy and free will. Greek and Latin do more than just softening a hard edge in their many circumlocutions.

B RHETORICAL, DRAMATIC AND HUMOROUS EXPLOITATION

Suicide and rhetoric

An ancient rhetor's success is dependent on his capacity to titillate the sensibilities of his public. Since Socrates and Plato, philosophy has despised the prostitution of the word by the art of speech which 'makes the worse *logos* better'. The wise man keeps to the truth, while the orator is led by an ethic of success. The aim of his art is merely to convince. The successful public speaker is the central ancient communicator; ancient speeches are most valuable as a source for prevailing values, as Dover has shown in his book on popular morality. The speaker does not strive after elevating his public morally or subjecting it to a purification (*katharsis*) as the dramatist does. Nor does he, as the comedy-writer, try to reconcile his audience with the existing order by his humour. The rhetor wishes to score. He appeals to the instincts which he thinks present in the mass of the Assembly or the Court.

Some examples of rhetorical exploitation have been discussed before under means and motives; we saw that Aeschines tried to denigrate his opponent Demosthenes by suggesting that he did not possess the sense of honour to commit suicide on the proper occasion. Cicero adheres to the same idea that a man of moral nobility knows when his moment has come, but he uses it in the opposite direction while defending his client Cluentius from the accusation of murder by poison. He wishes to establish that the defendant was a weak figure who lacked the courage for audacious deeds. Cluentius, he argues, had suffered much distress and was oppressed by sorrows. 'If he had had some spirit and manliness (*animus* and *virtus*) he would, like many men in similar *dolor*, have brought about his own death'[16].

In rhetorical practice the syndrome of values was exploited which said that a man of honour knew when his time had come. Already during his training the would-be public speaker was confronted with cases of suicide. He had to take both sides in debatable cases (*controversiae*). In attempting to produce a well-balanced case some rhetorical pedagogues invented very artificial situations: a woman after an unsuccessful attempted suicide accuses herself of sacrilege in order to attain her aim. A suicide charges his Samaritan with injustice. The lawful authority of the master and the equally binding obligation to abstain from killing clash in the case of the sick master (*aeger dominus*). A slave had refused to present his master with the poison he requested. When the latter finally succeeded in dying, his will said that the stubborn slave must be crucified. The slave appeals to the Tribunes of the People – an unreal element in this made-up case. But the young rhetor could argue for maintaining the old Roman idea of a master's right to dispose of his slave how he chose and also side with the Cornelian Law against assassination and murder by poison, which the slave would have infringed if he obeyed his master.

Quintilian, a man of subtle pedagogical views, remonstrates against these alienating practices in his *Rhetorical Instruction*. One case that amused him looked like this: a father asked to be exempted from military service, but his son managed to get him into the ranks. After some time, the father deserted, but was arrested. In battle the son showed himself a hero and he was entitled to a reward. He asked for his father's release. His father pleaded against being given mercy. The two sides in the controversy were set up in this way, but Quintilian thinks the whole situation unimaginable. Rhetors who invent such cases have 'forgotten the many examples of voluntary death', i.e. in such a situation the father had no need of rhetorical advice, as long as he had his sword at his disposal[17].

It was not only the artificiality of the cases for exercise that aroused Quintilian's reproof. In elaborating on a theme too, rhetoric often missed the mark. 'Take, for instance, the exclamation from the classroom theme, where a man, after being ruined by the barrenness of his land, is shipwrecked and hangs himself: "Let him whom neither earth nor sea receives, hang in mid air".' Quintilian also mocks the theme of the luxurious man (*luxuriosus*) who is alleged to have pretended to starve himself to death – the Greek *apokarteresin* is used – 'Tie a noose for yourself: you have good reason to be angry with your throat. Take poison: it is fit that a luxurious man should die of drink!' The art of rhetoric does not remain insensitive to the change in attitude that is noticeable in the second century AD. Dio of Prusa, the highly successful rhetor of the time, is not prepared to acknowledge a superhuman element in the way Ajax and Heracles died. By him suicide is condemned as a degenerate form of behaviour[18].

Suicide in drama

Like rhetoric, ancient drama presupposes a mass public whose ideas and sentiments are exploited. The playwright also wants to win success; to win the tangible prize at the festivals of Dionysus. The process of communication between the dramatist and his public is more complex than that between the public speaker and the audience in court or in the assembly. Firstly, there is the context of a religious festival which lends a ceremonial background to the plays. Further, the subject-matter of tragedy is dictated by tradition. Also the conventions of the stage cause the author and his public to enter together a self-contained world. The special atmosphere of the play is of course not completely separated from the every-day world, but myth and epic, which almost exclusively furnish drama with themes, are of a higher order than ordinary existence. On one side, the world of the heroes has to be comprehensible to common man, but on the other hand it is distant and strange: the events happened in a remote and dim past. The persons involved are of a superhuman order both in their admirable and their evil qualities.

So, only with much reservation may ancient drama be used as evidence for 'public opinion'. The forces which drive people to self-killing on the stage are in quantity and intensity different from the general picture. The bodily suffering of a Philoktetes or Heracles is of another order from normal human pain: Philoktetes' festering wound was so unbearable to the other Greeks that they left him behind on the isle of Lemnos on their way to Troy. After many years a Greek delegation visits him to try to carry him off to the army at Troy, as his presence was necessary for victory according to the oracle. At several moments in Sophocles' play Philoktetes announces his resolution to put an end to suffering. He plans to throw himself from the rocks – the means characteristic of acute despair – or use his weapons against his own person[19]. Finally, he agrees to go to Troy. In most of the 37 cases of suicide we have counted in ancient drama, it is only intentions to kill oneself that are expressed[20]; 11 times the deed is actually accomplished, most often in the margin of the main events on the stage. Solely in the cases of Heracles and Ajax is suicide the central theme of a play[21]. In Sophocles' *Aias* the changing sentiments of the hero are spun out to such a degree that a modern observer – mistakenly – took them for the moods which modern suicidology describes in a would-be self-killer. According to Seidensticker it is 'erstaunlich in welchem Masse die . . . zusammengefassten Ergebnisse der modernen Suizidologie auf den sophokleïschen Aias zutreffen'[22]. In principle, the motives of the suicides in drama are the same as on the human level, only they have been intensified: the *inpatientia* of Philoktetes and Heracles, the fierce mourning (*dolor*) felt by Admetus for his wife Alcestis or by Euadne for Kapaneus, have their human equivalents in ancient society. The demonic Klytaimnestra assures Agamemnon on his return that she has been loyal to him all the time up to the point of wanting to hang herself when she thought her husband was dead or had suffered serious injuries. Phaidra's pangs of love have tragic proportions: she wants to starve herself. At another moment she aims at taking revenge (*exsecratio*) by means of suicide[23]. Euripides' heroines are also less one-dimensional in their suicidal motivation than the Sophoclean females: the latter's Iokaste and Deianeira kill themselves when unable to face people. Deianeira only decides to do away with herself after her son calls her the murderess of his father. Iokaste is the purest example of female shame-suicide in tragedy, the female counterpart of Ajax.

Among the motives that do not lend themselves to dramatic exploitation is *taedium vitae*: only in a bourgeois play, which antiquity never developed in its real sense, could it have found a place. Nearest to it comes the New Comedy with the type of the morose old man in Menander's *Dyskolos*, but his peevish behaviour is directed against others. Having enough of life makes its appearance as a plausible motive for self-killing in the early Roman empire. Nor do philosophers with their ostentation (*iactatio*) fit in tragic theatre. Madness does play its part: whenever the heroes are insane, they are really out of their mind. But the *furor* of Heracles and Ajax is never presented as the primary motive, but as the reaction to insufferable pain or loss of honour.

On the stage altruism (*devotio*) was represented by Menoikeus and by Makaria, Heracles' daughter. They sacrifice themselves on behalf of, respectively, Thebes and Athens. Makaria gives herself to death in order to save the city and – again the motive of *pudor* – to save her face as well[24]. In drama women in particular have a grand manner that is unattainable in normal life. In the fierce shame, *aidos/pudor*, felt by Ajax there is an element of revenge. When he has come to the conclusion that his life has become impossible, he rejects the idea of seeking death by throwing himself into the ranks of the Trojans: in that case the hated Atreids would profit from his death. Only a self-chosen death can save his ego. After the deed his wife Tekmessa reproaches him for a certain egotism: 'To me his death is bitter, but for him a relief'. This saying is that of a sad woman: ancient epitaphs contain similar gentle reproof in which those left behind complain about the mourning that is their share[25]. Nobody in the *Aias* expresses a principled rejection of heroic suicide as such. Ajax's resoluteness contrasts with the endless discussions about his burial: the other Greeks are weak souls. In the tragedy there is nobody who raises the question whether a suicide is entitled to a ceremonial burial, although there was an old tradition that Kalchas the priest opposed giving those who had killed themselves to the 'holy fire'[26]. Sophocles' text and staging was aimed at confirming Ajax' virtue, *arete*. He was an *agathos* in every respect, his brother Teucer says at the end[27].

Ajax long remained the model of an heroic self-killer. Augustus himself tried to win a literary reputation along with his other glory by composing a tragedy on the theme, but he could not manage it. When his friends asked him how his Ajax was doing, the amateur-writer answered: 'He has fallen on his sponge'. Augustus' successor Tiberius was thoroughly versed in Greek classics. He gave proof of this when Mamercus Aemilius Scaurus had written a tragedy on Atreus. In the same way as in Euripides' original the subjects had to endure the irrationality, *aboulia*, of the monarch. Tiberius saw the play as indirect criticism and made a menacing remark aimed at the author: 'I shall make him an Ajax'[28].

Ajax lived on as an inspiring figure, mainly in his Sophoclean form. He was appropriated by Athens, just as it had annexed his island Salamis; the Athenian tribe called after him, the *Aiantis*, was never put in last place in any institutional procedure, in order to keep the hero from being harsh and implacable[29]. On the other side was Heracles, regarded as a Spartan blockhead – in Euripides' *Alcestis* he even has burlesque traits. In Sophocles' *Trachinian Women* his suicide takes place at the end of the play, but it lacks the character of a heroic finale. Tormented by Nessos' coat he decides to die, realizing that the oracles are to be fulfilled: one had said that he would be killed by a dead creature (Nessos). When Heracles' hour came, he had great difficulties in forcing his son to assist him in his voluntary death by fire.

In many respects, Euripides' *Enraged Heracles* is the counterpart of Sophocles' *Aias*. In Euripides' play Theseus represents Athenian values. He tries to prevent the hero from suicide, which he is determined to commit because, in the fury sent by Hera, he had slaughtered his own children. Heracles himself is in doubt whether suicide is the right solution: in this way he would be opposing the will of the gods, depriving them of a servant. This last consideration reminds us of the Platonic idea that a human being is the property (*ktema*) of the gods: by committing suicide he would be robbing his own masters. Theseus plays upon Heracles' own doubts and calls a suicide an act of unwisdom (*amathia*). On his side Heracles wonders whether he would be demonstrating cowardliness (*deilia*): *arete* in this Heracles already stands for more than just fear of losing face[30]. We see here how the process of internalizing values which Adkins has observed in general for Athens towards the end of the fifth century, also has its impact on the stage. At least the playwright expects a certain sensibility on the part of his public to these shifts of values. In this way the tragedy no longer represents the level of Homeric heroism. It refines the traditional themes and makes them digestible for the public of the polis[31]. New attitudes too were registered by Euripides. He closes the development of the suicide-theme in tragedy. Aeschylus has only wishes and threats of self-killing in the matter-of-fact Homeric vein, whereas Sophocles includes 6 accomplished suicides in his plays. In 4 cases self-killing may be a personal addition to the mythical data by the author[32]. His suicides still represent the higher order of superhuman beings, while Euripides' drama has figures with an almost bourgeois sensibility. Does this evolution reflect a change of attitudes in Athens during the fifth century?

Public interest in suicide appears also in comedy. It gets no subtle treatment in Old Comedy. The audience is expected to laugh when an admirer of Euripides says: 'If it were true what some hold, that a dead person has eyesight, I should have hanged myself to see Euripides'. And Aristophanes' Heracles gives his blunt advice to Dionysus to arrange the meeting with Euripides he wishes for, by means of hanging, poison or jumping. In the humane comedy of Menander and in Plautus' more hilarious adaptations, from time to time the lovers are tempted to kill themselves when their passion is hopeless. In desperate situations, the slaves immediately set their thoughts on poison and noose. Making oneself a long letter acts, as we have seen (p.31), as a comic metonymy for hanging and Lysidamos, an Athenian citizen, says in despair: 'I will make my sword a pillow and lay myself on it'[33].

The sphere of the ancient novel bears close resemblance to that of Attic New Comedy. The lovers who get involved in complicated adventures in the books of Achilles Tatios, Chariton, Xenophon Heliodoros and Longos, cannot exist without each other. The – supposed – loss of the partner's love or life leads the thoughts rapidly towards suicide. The author himself is quite aware that self-killing is one of the ingredients of the genre. He can even address his reader in this way: 'I am sure my readers will much

147

enjoy this last book, because it will break with the grim content of the previous ones. Nothing more about piracy or slavery or trials or battles or *suicide* or war or imprisonment'[34].

Light-heartedness towards self-killing

Self-killing can elicit black humour. This is one of the possible reactions by which man frees himself from anxiety. Whenever ancient jokes and light verse specify the method, it is mainly hanging as in the satirical poem in the *Anthologia Palatina* on the blockhead (*stultus quidam*; p.71). He had heard that in Hades there were fair law-courts. As soon as he had a law-suit, he hanged himself. A miserable person was about to hang himself, but at the final moment he discovered a pot full of gold. The unlucky owner who afterwards arrived on the spot found only the rope and used it in despair. The *Anthology* twice chuckles about the same theme. Hanging as a method is prescribed by the situation: the gold had to be hidden in a remote place, the same loneliness the would-be suicide looked for. One of the pleasantries in the *Joker's Friend* mocks the stupidity of the Abderite who attempted suicide by hanging. The rope broke and he was injured by the fall. Thereupon he went to the doctor and then he hanged himself with plaster and all.

Handicaps of mind, character or body were mercilessly exploited by ancient humorists. The avaricious Hermon dreamt that he had spent too much money. He hanged himself 'from excessive grief'. The stingy Deinarchos was about to hang himself, but he changed his mind on discovering that a rope cost six copper pieces. Diophantos was so thin that he could use a spider's web to hang himself. People with bodily infirmities are the object of relentless mockery. Many people must have had bad teeth and because of that have smelled ill. It was a sensitive issue, as Plutarch assures us, for 'men get angry when they are teased about a bad-smelling nose or mouth'[35]. Such a 'mouth-stinker', *ozostomos*, according to the *Philogelos*, only needed to close his mouth with a cloth to attain the end he wanted. People with pretensions are another object of ridicule. Apart from the absent-minded scholar the would-be philosopher figures in ancient humour, e.g. Kleombrotos who had read Plato's book on the soul and leapt from a wall (p.76). As we saw earlier, Aulos the astrologer saved his professional honour by hanging himself at the hour that was written in the stars (p.114).

The humour of Old Comedy, the jokes and light verse, is the

counterpart of the deadly seriousness that grand literature shows towards suicide. But epigram also has some traits which show that ancient mentality had more nuances than outright respect or scorn. The poor devil who commits suicide is not only seen as ridiculous. In the empathy which Hellenism is capable of, occasionally one could look with compassion on those who did not meet the standards of the *kalokagathia,* like Aristeides who, having lost his sole sheep and sole cow, came to hate life and hanged himself with the strap of his knapsack on the pear-tree, or on the beam of the desolate shed in another of the three versions in the *Anthologia Palatina* (p.92). Another miserable person did not even possess a tree to hang himself on: Menophanes' land was so small that he had to resort to his neighbour's tree when he 'hanged himself from hunger'. The 'thrice unhappy' (*trisdystenos*) Anaxis had had a life that could not be called a life. In the wording of the epigram 'he trampled life under his heel'. On the day of her brother's burial Basilo died by her own hand (*autocheri*). The same sexual asymmetry that we became aware of when discussing suicide in mourning, is shown in the story that after Euphron's death, carried away by Bacchic rapture, both his wives, Demo and Methymna, hanged themselves (see p.104).

Old age too becomes visible to the Hellenistic poet, just as the sculptor of the period discovers the wrinkled, drunken crone and the old fisherman who has lived out his life. A certain old man (*senex quidam* in Appendix A) could find no help to free him from his misery (*dystychia*). He crept into a recently dug grave and had himself buried (see p.35). For an elderly person the cup simply could be full, i.e. the poet clearly distinguishes the motive of *taedium vitae*. Thus Gorgos wondered why he should bother to warm himself in the sun for three or four summers more. He was only supported by his stick — he really was 'three-legged', *tripous*. Without more ado 'he kicked away his old life'.

The epigrams cover the whole spectrum of attitudes. Respect for heroic suicide is represented by poems on Ajax's suicide, for whom Fate could find no other killer than himself (p.109), and by the Roman soldiers Aelius and Festus who put an end to unbearable suffering by *Romana morte* (p.53). But heroism could also be criticized by the poet: 'I do not like the hero who buys a reputation by blood easily spilt', Martial exclaims in epigram 1,8. But on the other hand the Romans who saved their honour during the imperial persecutions did receive respectful mention: Fannius

149

Caepio, Lucanus, Paetus and Arria Prisca. Boiska, the woman who killed herself in order to escape slavery, gained herself a glorifying epigram in the Greek Anthology (p.116).

Philosophers are hailed in poems on account of their honourable life's end[36]. At the level beneath this gallery of official heroes there are the common followers of the great, who did not find an entry in the biographies of the philosophers. But they are important because they show that some of the philosophical ideas about self-killing had their impact, although the fact remains that the mere existence of a poem proves the exceptionality of the deed. Many epigrams of the *Anthologia* remain close to the origin of the genre; in form they are still an epitaph. Thus Pheidon the suicide addresses the passer-by as on a real grave-stone: 'flee the storms of life and enter the safe port of death'. Even the dialogue between the *viator* and the dead is recorded in a poem. In this way Philaulos presents himself and makes it known that 'of his own will' (*autothelei*) he went to Hades 'having tasted the Cean cups' (p.36). There is some authentic epigraphic material that demonstrates the link between the fictitious epitaphs and the real speaking stones of antiquity.

C DIRECT EVIDENCE FOR SELF-KILLING ON STONES AND PAPER

Epigraphical sources

Nearly all our sources are literary, in the broad sense. Is the one-sidedness of this material corrected in some way by direct evidence, like that of the speaking stones of the inscriptions? Of course, both those who ordered an epitaph and those who made it were led by all kinds of conventions, but tracing those conventions may contribute to a study of mentality with regard to suicide. Some reservations must be made: we do not come across the common people. They could not afford to order a tomb and have it inscribed. But in principle, a broad upper-class is audible, a group that lived over a vast area and over a long period of time. Among the several hundred thousands of inscriptions epitaphs are by far in the majority, with some eighty per cent. So the conditions do not seem too unfavourable to get a glimpse of prevailing attitudes towards self-killing, as ancient people were not reticent about the cause of death[37]. However, the harvest of epitaphs in which mention is made of suicide is far from impressive, far less than one would expect in a society where openness is supposed to exist.

I know of about 12 inscriptions in which self-killing is mentioned or is alluded to. The whole-hearted wish addressed to Atimetus the freedman has already been discussed (p.5). Clearly the most miserable death possible was desired. So this case does not support the view that self-killing was regarded as a respected end without qualification. A similar tone is noticeable in an inscription of Mayence where a slave is mentioned who had killed his master (*servus homicida*). The latter is speaking in the epitaph:

> I could not live longer than thirty years, for a slave robbed me of life. He threw himself into the river afterwards.

With undisguised satisfaction the text establishes the fully deserved, disgraceful end of the criminal slave.[38] Also this record of a jump into the river cannot be counted as proof of an ancient tolerance of suicide. The way in which the method – the desperate leap – is marked, demonstrates all the more the moral satisfaction felt by the relatives of the murdered man. In the same vein hanging is wished for as a despicable end for an enemy: in the graffiti that Samius wrote in the basilica at Pompeii, he expressed a desire that one Cornelius should make use of the noose[39].

One suicide was regarded as important enough to be recorded on stone in a calendar: for the year 31 AD, when Tiberius' evil genius Sejanus was overthrown, it is mentioned as a memorable fact that his wife Apicata destroyed herself. The style of the communication is sober, as befits a list of data: 'October 25th: Apicata, Seianus' wife, killed herself'. The context shows marks of satisfaction, to be compared with the reaction to the death of the slave in the river: first the liquidation of Sejanus himself is recorded, then the miserable death of his wife and finally the murder of their children. Thus the whole viperous brood was exterminated[40].

In other cases of known suicide the calendars do not specify that the death was sought. In the *Fasti Capitolini* the simple entry for the year 82 BC is: 'Gaius Marius, Gaius' son, Gaius' grandson, was killed during his magistracy'. The same word *occisus* was used for Brutus, Caesar's hated murderer. The Fasti say that he was killed at Philippi by Augustus. According to Voisin (1987 p.269) these neutral announcements make it clear 'que le suicide du consul vaincu est considéré comme un événement normal, non pas banal, mais faisant partie des risques du métier'. Nor is there any tendency to chisel away the names of self-murderers. This only happens if they are subjected to a general *damnatio memoriae* because of a bad reputation[41].

Those who become the victims of the imperial terror, like Vipsania Agrippina and Germanicus' son Nero, were not disgraced in the *Fasti*: their sorry end is not mentioned. In the case of Antonia a general euphemistic phrase was used: 'she met her final day' (*diem suum obit*) at the Calends of May.

These last inscriptions do not mark self-killing as a noteworthy occurrence. Some others do pay attention to suicide. The first one is a dubious case. The inscription was found on the island of Thasos and was devoted to a gladiator called Ajax. This is an ominous name in view of his predecessor in heroic suicide. This Ajax proudly announces that he always spared his opponents. As for himself, he died 'on his own', *idio* in Greek. The first editor of the inscription was sure that self-killing was indicated. And, without further qualification, *idios thanatos*, the more complete expression, might mean voluntary death, so that the inscription would have a verbal phrase derived from the nominal expression 'own death': the affecting attempt to compose a verse could account for the clumsy wording. But the context points to a different interpretation. Epitaphs on gladiators usually glorify their successes. So it is more plausible that the Ajax of Thasos announces that he was not killed by any opponent, but died a *natural* death[42].

Do not mourn the man who has taken leave of life. After having died on earth no further pain follows.

This poem was made as a (fictitious) epitaph, i.e. an epigram in the proper sense[43]. Such a *jeu d'esprit* suggests that a certain experience existed in making such texts for tombs, but in reality we have only 6 authentic epitaphs which mention suicide as the cause of death in a non-derogatory way. We have already discussed the case of young Domitilla; her suicide fitted well into the important category of female shame-suicide (p.24). Here it suffices to notice that this is one of the few texts that acclaim a self-killing.

In the case of Oppia the self-killing is indicated discreetly:

Receive this soul and add it to the holy number,
You Arria on the Roman and you Laodamia on the Greek side[44]

So on behalf of the woman buried in the tomb the wish is expressed that she will be received in the underworld by the Greek and Roman prototypes of female matrimonial loyalty till death. The invocation of these two saints of female suicide causes Voisin to suppose that Oppia too has ended her life in *devotio*.

One wonders how Oppia could have sacrificed herself. Did she take a vow, like a historical Alcestis, to pay with her life for that of her husband? Did she, having made the vow, actively take her own life? Maybe she simply died away on account of her strong conviction that she had saved another's life. Something like this must have happened in 3 other cases of women who were acclaimed for their devotion and who were explicitly compared to Alcestis. The first remained nameless. Her stone was found at Odessos in Thracia. Her husband praises her because she gave life and freedom to him.

> Now she is dead instead of me and has fame and praise like Alcestis.

(*Alkestis in Odessos* in Appendix A). Another second Alcestis is known by name: Kallikrateia. She herself says: 'I am a new Alcestis. I died for my noble husband Zeno'. And a whole series of Greek and Latin texts glorifies one Atilia Pomptilla who, in the second century AD, devoted herself to her husband Philippos. In this case too the way of dying remains obscure.

What we still lack is a defiant and positive indication of a suicide in an epitaph. Much more explicit about the way of dying is the text about one Telesinia Crispinilla. She is said to have passed away after 15 days, grieving over the death of 'her most pious son'. One could wonder whether this is just a case of pining away or one of wilful suicide, by refusing food.

Two male cases are more outspoken, both with respect to motive and method. One Roman soldier sacrificed himself in Mauretania, in the second century AD. The 'fury of the battle' sent Ulpius Optatus into the midst of the enemy's arms and there he 'did away with himself by his own arms', preferring to dispense with his life (*vitae dispendia praefert*) rather than be defeated.

Finally, we come across a pure instance where we are not left in doubt about the fact and the motivation of suicide. In an epitaph which has been dated to AD 120–6, Marcus Pomponius Bassulus himself speaks openly about his life and death. First, he speaks of his literary activities. He had translated some of Menander's plays into Latin. He himself too had written comedies. At local level, he had attained the highest political position, that of mayor, *duovir*. But after all these successes came decay:

> but, vexed by anxieties of an oppressed mind as well as by numerous ailments of the body so that both were extremely repulsive, I appropriated the death I longed for.

Some uncertainty about the exact reading of the text does not affect the interpretation of this case as an open confession of suicide. The motives mentioned are the ones acknowledged by Roman law. The expression 'repulsive', *taediosum*, or, in a different reading, repugnance, *taedium*, does reflect general Latin usage: as we saw, *taedium vitae* or *taedium vivendi* is a common formula. The text excels in literary, archaic vocabulary and a Stoic pose[45]. In his rhetorical need for variation Bassulus chooses the exquisite phrase 'to appropriate the death I longed for', a very special expression as we discovered when discussing suicidal terminology. As a type Bassulus' suicide fits well into the series of self-killings Pliny mentions in his letters[46].

Maybe the meagre harvest will be supplemented by another suicide, recorded on stone; Voisin has announced an article about the inscription of P. Atilius Septicianus. At first glance his text reads like the message of a suicide: there is the theme of *taedium vitae* as the consequence of illness and other 'mighty evils of life' (*vitae mala maxima*). The deed itself is not so unambiguously indicated as by Bassulus' 'I appropriated death'. This dead man says: 'Now I am free of punishments and enjoy a serene peace'[47].

Self-killing in papyri

After all, only in the epitaphs of this Atilius and Bassulus do we find something of the openness which marks some modern death notices; in the rest of the sparse epigraphic material other mechanisms account for the advertising of a case of suicide: respect for devotion, admiration for Christian heroism in the face of rape or satisfaction about a deservedly disgraceful end. There is another category of material that is worthy to be reviewed on account of its directness: the papyri of Greek and Roman Egypt. Especially in private documents one would expect occasional family tragedies.

There is one such private letter which contains a threat of suicide. Isidora wrote it to her 'master-brother' Hermias, who was obviously her husband, according to common practice in Egypt:

> Do anything, postpone everything, and come, preferably tomorrow. The baby is ill. It has become thin. It is already two hundred days [since you went away?]. I fear it will die in your absence. Know for sure: if it dies in your absence, be prepared that you do not find me hanged.

In the staccato phrases and the change from one syntactic structure to another ('know for sure', 'be prepared that') the anguish of this mother is evident. As a climax she exerts pressure upon her brother-husband, threatening to hang herself. In a similar way the young Theon puts pressure upon his absent father to give him permission to join him in Alexandria: 'If you do not send for me, I will not eat and will not drink either'. In Egypt there was a tradition of using suicide as a threat to have one's way: Thrasyllos, a medical student, cried and said he would kill himself in order to force an old priest to make a private contact with Asclepius[48].

Of special interest as a source for early Christian attitudes towards suicide is a fragmentary papyrus from the fourth century containing the *Acts of St John*: the original was probably written in the second century. In this apocryphal text St John is preaching in Asia Minor. On one of his travels he saves one Zeuxis 'who was about to hang himself'. After a prayer by John, Zeuxis duly takes part in holy communion[49]. In this text Zeuxis is the model of a miserable person who is saved just in time for eternal life. His attempted suicide simply underlines the degree of his misery: as such it does not cause aversion. Had Zeuxis been a robber, he could equally have acted as a fitting object for an act of conversion.

Was it a natural death or suicide? On this question in Roman Egypt a correspondence was conducted on potsherds. On one such ostracon that has been found, a leading resident of Upper Egypt responds to a request from the Roman curator Bassus to give details about a death. The correspondent says that he made inquiries among the elders of the village. They answered that the person involved had died an *idios thanatos*, namely by lack of food. There is little reason to surmise suicide. The death is not specified as brought about by 'starvation' (*apokarteria*), the technical term, and 'own death' most probably means here a natural end[50].

There is one piece of papyrological evidence which stands the most severe test: somebody was forced into suicide by financial pressure. The papyrus contains a complaint addressed to Apollonios, strategus of Arsinoitis, probably in 47–8 AD. A local informer, Orses, had got many people into trouble. The victims of his blackmail had complained, but the financial pressure had been so great that 'because of the insolvency with regard to Kronion he (i.e. Kronion) laid hands upon himself and died'[51].

Finally, there is an intriguing medical report that may touch on a case of self-killing. In AD 173, the public doctor Dionysios reports to Claudianus the strategus:

> Today I was ordered by your servant Herakleides to inspect the dead, hanged body of Hierax and to inform you about the conclusion I would come to with respect to it. Therefore I inspected the body in the personal presence of the servant in the home of Epagathos, son of . . ymeros, son of Sarapion, in the Broad Street and I found it hanged with a noose. Thus I report[52].

The public doctor, *demosios iatros*, was regularly called in by the authorities to establish the cause of a death. The interest of the State is limited: was a crime committed? Was the person really dead and had he to be removed from the list of tax-payers? It is quite imaginable that the relations asked for a report to prevent being made accountable for Hierax's tax.

5

EXPERTS, LAW-GIVERS AND ARTISTS

A EXPERTS: DOCTORS, ASTROLOGERS AND AN INTERPRETER OF DREAMS

Medical expertise

So there was a task for the public doctor to establish the cause of a death; in exercising this duty he might come across a suicide. Obviously ancient physicians were regularly confronted with self-killing, as became clear when we discussed the different methods and quoted from medical writings. One doctor established that those who had cut their throat only retained their voice if the wound was closed (p.48). Large-scale experience with hanging comes to the surface in the aphorism: 'Those who have hanged themselves and are cut down when still alive, will not survive when there is foam around the mouth'[1]. Hanging and cutting one's throat were not the most noble ways out. Once an ancient doctor generalized about the cause of the phenomenon that young girls remarkably often felt tempted to hang themselves (p.22). Basing himself on a purely physiological explanation the Hippocratic practitioner advised a simple but efficient therapy: having sexual intercourse would end all problems.

But in some situations medicine was used: the root of mandragora, taken in the morning, was counted as a tried and tested remedy for 'people who are sombre, suffer from disease and wish to hang themselves'[2]. In this case of complete bodily and mental depression the use of that psychiatric drug is recommended; it has to be assumed that the three forms of sufferings in the statement are complementary. Are the people who are depressed (*aniomenoi*) suffering from *taedium vitae*?

157

So some therapy was available to the doctor who by his Hippocratic oath was forbidden to assist in self-killing: 'I shall not give a lethal poison to anybody, *even if asked to do so*, nor will I give advice'[3]. Maybe Hadrian's personal doctor remembered his vows when he refused to lend his hand for the emperor's intended suicide. However, in the first century AD, medical expertise was available for those who were in need of it: doctors were experts in opening the veins. One of the Latin expressions is 'offering the veins *to the doctor* to cut'. Nero sent medical experts to his victims to give 'assistance'. He called it *curare*.

The changing attitude of late antiquity is reflected in medical practice: then doctors describe therapies for those 'who took lethal poison deliberately to lead themselves out'[4]. But in general ancient medical men acted pragmatically. Self-killing occurred and the doctor – certainly in Rome – was willing to assist with his medical skill. As psychiatry was hardly developed – Godderis has shown this in a recent book on Galen's attitude to psychic diseases – it did not help him to see the background of the concrete cases he came across. Only Aretaios distinguished a malicious form of insanity which sometimes caused the patient to use violence against himself (p.97).

Suicide in astrology

One of the terms in use for a suicide was, as we discovered, 'the one violently killed', *biothanatos*, in a bizarre oxymoronic shortening of *biaiothanatos*. That Greek word occurs in one of the Latin biographies of the emperors, the *Historia Augusta*. It survives antiquity as a scholarly word. The inclusive meaning was derived from the general notion that something was wrong with a premature death. Astrologers saw the stars announcing an abrupt end to life. According to Paulus Alexandrinus a certain constellation made those who were born under it 'short-lived or doomed to die by violence' (*oligochronous e biaiothanatous*). In a specific configuration Mars had the same effect, but 'if it is in conjunction with Jupiter and Venus those (who are born then) will have a pleasant old age and will escape the risk of a violent death' (*biaiothanasia*)[5].

Mars as the symbol of aggression was especially sinister.

When Mars stands in a quarter or in opposition to sun or

moon . . . stands in a sign of human nature' it causes those who fall under this constellation to be slaughtered in civil wars or by the enemy or 'by laying hands upon themselves'[6].

Even the methods were prescribed by the stars. One constellation brought hanging. Mars was 'the destroyer of oneself' (*heautou anairetes*). Therefore he made people *autocheires*, i.e. people who throw themselves from heights and people who are prepared to die (*hetoimothanatous*). Self-murderers are put on a par with audacious people by the astrologers. They lay hands upon themselves or make a fatal leap. Poison was indicated by a celestial configuration with Venus: 'therefore they become *autocheires* by drinking poison'[7].

Artemidoros on suicide

People who did not spend the night observing the stars could be confronted with suicide in their dreams. If one dreams of being hanged or of hanging oneself, disasters are bound to happen, Artemidoros knows from his rich experience. Obviously there is no difference whether life's breath is cut short by someone else or by the dreamer himself. In a similar way it does not matter whether one cuts the throat oneself or it is cut for one: both alternatives announce misery that will arrive sooner than in the nightmare of hanging[8].

The expert of Daldis did not only know of dreams in which suicide occurred: there were also visions that symbolically indicated a self-killing. This was the experience of the man who dreamt about an evil smell coming from the region of his navel: heavily in debt he later put an end to his life. For the same reason in another case which has already been discussed, a man committed suicide after dreaming that he used himself sexually – Artemidoros is not explicit about how the act is to be imagined. Here the interpreter has a double explanation to offer. Dreaming that he had to 'use himself' was a sign that his debts caused him to remain outside human communication. Moreover, he possessed so little money that he could not pay for his sexual enjoyment. Here we have one of the attractive sides of Artemidoros: he is very commonsensical in his explanations, rational in his obscurantism.

The woman who saw ears growing from her breast into her vagina was also doomed to die by her own hand. She has already been discussed as a fine example of a pure shame-suicide, for it was explicitly stated that she had sexual intercourse with her son *by accident*. But she put an end to her life[9].

Astrologers and the only dreambook that remains show ancient self-killing, without heroic glory, as a fate written in the stars. or as a misfortune that is announced in dreams. This attitude of horror is more representative than the respect for noble, exemplary cases which dominate the scene.

B   A LAST TRIBUTE TO A SUICIDE?

Also in his casual remarks Artemidoros is valuable as a source for our knowledge of ancient customs. As an example of a type of dream in which 'much may be forecast by little' he presents this one:

> Someone dreamt that he lost his name. That came to pass: first, he lost his son (the outcome was in accordance with the vision, for he lost what he loved most and the son had the same name as his father). Moreover he forfeited his whole fortune, for actions were brought against him in which he was accused of political mistakes and convicted. When he had lost honour and land, he ended his life by the rope, so that even after his death he did not have a name. *For those are the only ones among the dead who are not named by their relatives at the death-meals*[10].

The interpreter of dreams refers to a custom that was known to his readers: when the members of the family gathered on memorial days to make ritual contact with their dead, they excluded suicides. About the geographical span of the taboo one can only speculate: Ionia, Artemidoros' homeland, Asia Minor in general, the whole of the Greek East or all the territory of the Roman Empire, including Italy and the West? In any case, this information of Artemidoros's has more value than the many vague communications about taboos on paying the last tribute to self-killers supposed to have existed in remote and past societies. Dio Chrysostomos, first/second century AD, knows of a Cypriot female law-giver, Demonassa, who had laid it down 'that the one who had killed himself was thrown away without burial'. In accordance with the topos of the loyal law-giver who conforms to his own laws, she left the son who had destroyed himself to nature. But when she saw a cow grieving over a dying calf, her motherly instinct got the upper hand. She killed herself, and in an exotic way at that: she had bronze melted and threw herself into the hot burning mass. A similar habit of abandoning a suicide to nature existed in Thebes, according to Zenobios[11].

Such occasional glimpses do not prove that classical civilization as a whole was accustomed to a drastic 'rejection' of suicides. Ancient authors liked to dwell at length on the *unusual* habits of other peoples, contrasting them with civilized customs. The distance in both time and geography have a utopian function when such usages are presented as exemplary. But on the other hand by their horrible nature they might confirm the values of civilization[12]. But Artemidoros' evidence cannot be discounted in that way. Time and again he claims extensive experience (*peira*) and extensive contacts with the world around him. There are many reasons to regard him as a reliable source for the existence of specific phenomena and values: his readers knew that families distanced themselves from the member who had determined his own fate.

In the mixture of feelings that was aroused by self-killing horror had its place. In various – mainly literary – cases the would-be suicide wishes to curse those whom he holds responsible for his misery. Thus, Dido threatens Aeneas with an *exsecratio* and asks the perfidious man to go away: 'Though far, yet I shall be near, haunting you with flames of blackest pitch. And when death's chill has parted my body from its breath, wherever you go my spectre will be there'[13].

The ancient world shared the fear that is attested for many peoples, that those who died prematurely, especially by suicide, do not find rest. In general, Cumont states, cultures may assume different attitudes towards suicide – or a mixture of these four:

1 no distinction is made between a natural and a violent death
2 suicide is posthumously honoured as an heroic deed
3 the suicide is assumed not to find rest, going to and fro from the world of the dead to that of the living
4 the self-killer is posthumously 'punished' by being denied the normal rituals or by being subjected to ritual that separates him from the community both of the living and the dead[14].

In ancient behaviour the distinction between a natural and a violent death was always felt. When life is cut short, the natural order is disturbed. Greek has a special compound verb for 'dying before one's time' (*proapothneisko*[15]). Violent death (*biaiothanasia*) could be brought about by a falling object, by murder or by suicide. The souls of those who had died an unnatural death were believed to remain near to the body. A Neo-Platonist says of them:

'They roam for a long time in the neighbourhood of the corpse and the grave or the place where one laid hands upon oneself'. Neo-Platonic philosophy appeals to popular beliefs as a source of eternal wisdom, whereas the great master Plato himself did not refer specifically to existing practices, intending to free his ideal society of the evil of self-killing[16].

The place where the violent end took place was regarded as defiled: the fear of this *miasma* distinguishes between premeditated murder and accidental manslaughter only after much time. But even this last type, the *akousios thanatos*, required purification by means of a special procedure. In the speeches that Antiphon made up as models of forensic practice, the Tetralogies, time and again the theme of defilement is exploited. So there was a general ambiguity, which only in the case of a hero was overcome by outright respect.

The hero who buys his glory by self-spilt blood is, as the Greek language says, *deinos*: grand, audacious, formidable. In the case of an Ajax the balance of the ambiguous feelings is on the positive side of the *deinotes*. The same nuances are present in the Latin *audax* and the verb *audere*. An evil slave, who got his bad reputation by attempting suicide, is said to be able to attempt other audacious deeds, having ventured (*ausus*) such a thing as self-killing. So, overstepping the limits of human existence is not always looked on as a positive act. Where no noblemen from honourable motives 'lead themselves out of life', mechanisms are operative which make the suicide the prey of nature and exclude him from communication with the world of the living.

As Artemidoros disclosed, at least in his time and his world taboos were present, but already in the fourth century BC in Athens self-killers received a sinister treatment. Aeschines the rhetor says: 'For if somebody kills himself, we bury the hand separate from the body'. The special revulsion for the hand that turned against its own body was not only conveyed in expressions like *autocheir* and *manus sibi inferre*, but was neutralized by separating the 'autonomous' part from the rest of the corpse. Probably Flavius Josephus had this Athenian practice in mind when he said that there 'are even people where the right hand is cut off as an enemy who marched against the self'.

Perhaps there is a primitive relation between this violation of the self-killer and the way in which in olden days a murderer deprived his victim of the possibility of revenge. He cut off parts of the slaughtered body and strung them on a thread. From the sparse information about this *maschalismos* it is not clear whether this string of parts was worn by the murderer or was put around the dead.

The corpse of a suicide as a whole was also handled in a special way by the Athenians. The *biothanatoi* - including others who died unnaturally? – were thrown into the Kynegeion. It remains unclear if this was a habit during the whole history of Athens. Plutarch reports as a contemporary habit that bodies, clothes and nooses of those who had hanged themselves were thrown away by officials in Melite: so towards the end of the first century a taboo was operative in Attica. It seems that in Rome there was the idea that those who died prematurely – children and self-murderers – together with criminals were denied the community of the shades[17].

Virgil, for instance, reserves in the underworld which Aeneas visits a special place for babies, for those who have been executed on a false accusation and for those who

> though without guilt, gained death for themselves by their own hand, flinging their lives away in utter loathing for the light. How willingly they would now endure all the poverty, and every harsh tribulation, in the bright air above.

Not far from there Aeneas finds in the Fields of Mourning those who died because of a *durus amor*; among them, remarkably enough, is Dido, who apparently was not reckoned to be a suicide by Virgil. The self-killers were in the company of miserable people, not of sinners as in Dante's hell. In the speech of Flavius Josephus which was referred to in the introduction to this study, mention was made of specific measures among the Jews with respect to suicides. They waited for the sunset to bury those sinister dead. Probably in Josephus' days the *Semahot* was written which laid down rules for mourning and burial ceremonies. It stressed that only where there can be no doubt about the volition in the deed of self-killing may the last tribute be denied. It was not enough that someone had climbed a tree or a roof: his death could be an accident. Only if he said in advance that he wanted to throw himself off, or if there was an eye-witness to a deliberate jump, did the leaper have to be counted as a suicide. In that case he was denied any attention: he should not be bewailed and people should not speak good or evil of him. Children were ritually buried all the same, for instance if they killed themselves from fear of punishment[18].

Anthropological data about Africa make it clear that separate burial places for self-killers are not meant as a kind of posthumous punishment: they are a remedy for the feelings of fear among those who are left behind. The ghosts of those who died in war, by accident or by suicide, may become malicious. There are numerous reports of special measures aimed at neutralizing the menace: bodies of the hanged are burnt, along with the hut or the tree that was instrumental in the self-killing. Elsewhere, among the Gisu, the hut is defiled with the contents of a sheep's stomach, a normal practice for purification. The body of the dead is buried without much ado. Characteristically, the removal of the tree is rationalized as well: in this way nobody else can be inspired to follow the example. The evil spirit of a suicide may be appeased by giving his name to the first son born to the brother: he is then supposed to continue the family line. The Western Middle Ages had practices that were comparable: the house of the self-murderer was destroyed or remained closed as an 'espace maudit'. Pictures illustrating the legend of Pontius Pilate show how his doomed soul could not find a way out as long as he floated in a horizontal position in the river. Only when he was thrown headlong down a well could the soul escape via the anus[19].

The ancient habits do fit to a general pattern of reactions to self-killing. But they were not accepted without controversy, for the taboos were used for rhetorical exercises. Quintilian wants students to elaborate their points of view on the problem 'should a self-killer remain unburied? Is a self-killer a homicide (*homicida*)? The matter is clear, that is to say that killing oneself is not the same as killing another'. The suicide does not deserve the infamous treatment that the murderer gets: for instance bandits were crucified close to the city and their corpses decayed on the cross. Quintilian's rational point of view was not generally shared. There are indications that suicides were kept apart not only in the Virgilian world of fiction, but that there were special practices for self-killers. The old books of the priests are said to have ordered that anyone who hanged himself 'was thrown away unburied'. For the Roman abhorrence against 'the noose of ghastly death' (*nodum informis leti*) Pliny makes reference to a historical 'charter-myth': when Tarquinius Priscus forced people to work on the sewers, many killed themselves. The tyrant then ordered the corpses of such people to be fixed to crosses. 'Then for the first time it was regarded as shameful to do away with oneself'. Was the disgrace felt for all suicides or only for hanging? We already discovered that this exit had a sinister meaning. Popular belief confirmed this attitude. It was not allowed to pour out to the gods wine which was made of grapes coming from a vine that had been struck by lightning *or in the neighbourhood of which a noose has hung*. Neglecting the taboo was blasphemous, for life and religion were linked. Such fears confirm the image which we derived from looking at hanging as a method: the *suspendiosi* formed a separate, infamous group among the self-killers. Varro the encyclopaedist said that 'it was not *iustum* that *iusta*' were paid to those[20].

Having a decent burial was 'vital' for ancient people; the condition in which they expected to exist after death depended on the *iusta* paid to them, i.e. on the way in which their body was carried out for burial, cremated and got a last, permanent dwelling in a tomb that was visited by the relatives who on solemn occasions recalled their dead to life.

People with a limited family and means joined one of the associations that guaranteed a ceremonial burial. The regulations of some of these *collegia funeraticia* have been laid down in inscriptions. The one from Sarsina, in Umbria, excluded three categories from enjoying its services: first, gladiators; second *those who had laid hands upon themselves by hanging*; and third people with an immoral profession. At first sight all seems clear: the collegium wanted to protect itself from misuse of the funds. In this primary interpretation gladiators were excluded as belonging to a risky sort of profession. Self-murderers could be regarded as people who enjoyed the fruits of their contributions prematurely. But the mention of the last category, those with an immoral profession, shows that it was the infamy that united the three kinds. Therefore, not all self-murderers were excluded without qualification, but only those who had put an end to their lives in an utterly disgraceful way. We met the same 'distinction' of *suspendiosi* in a legal text where it was said that enemies, traitors and those who had hanged themselves did not deserve to be mourned (p.69). The same special treatment of the hanged appeared in the regulations governing the contracts between an undertaker and a community: the funeral society was obliged to remove the hanged (p.67)[21]. These indications about funeral habits do not treat self-murderers as a special category: sometimes only the sub-category of the hanged is specified. On other occasions they were part of a general abhorrence of infamous people. Thus it is said that the Roman executioner, another man of violence, was buried at a distance from the city just like the suicide[22].

But the rules of the funeral association of Lanuvium were radical: 'whoever for whatever reason shall have laid hands upon himself is not entitled to the *ratio funebris*'. Some ingenious but unconvincing attempts have been made to interpret the regulation differently from what it explicitly says: no motive, no personal quality is excluded as excusable and no special method is highlighted. In a rational explanation the Lanuvian collegium simply wants to protect itself against improper use of its provisions. But taboos too will have played their part: audacious dead disturbed the rest of the grave-yard[23].

The regulation of the Lanuvian burial club is one of the many indications of an ambiguity that prevailed in ancient society with respect to 'common' suicide. So there were elements which the later Christian taboo on suicide could make use of. How deep and general the abhorrence was cannot be established, but indications of its existence come from all corners and all periods of antiquity. According to some sources a few communities even legally sanctioned existing taboos. These indications are disparate and could be discarded as noticeable exceptions to an attitude which generally did not find much worth saying. In fact, it is only the legal system of the Roman Empire that is known to a high degree; therefore it is worth while to turn to its approach to suicide.

C *SUICIDIUM* AS AN INSTITUTION AND A CONFESSION

In finding an answer to the question whether and to what degree communities saw it as their task to fight self-killing, philosophers are about the least authoritative sources. There is a large distance between 'wie es eigentlich gewesen' and 'how it ought to be'. Nevertheless, ancient thinkers are often used as spokesmen for the reaction of the community to suicide. But when Plato in the *Laws* says that a self-murderer is buried in disgrace without ritual, stone, inscription or company, it is to be regarded as a utopian statement: the *Nomoi* advocate a better society than the existing one[24]. For a Popperian it is a lucky fact that philosophers only seldom get the chance to organize an ideal society. When Philolaos the Pythagorean once got the opportunity in South Italy, he is said to have issued laws against self-killing. Even before Plato the Pythagoreans posited a dualism of body and soul and they had a strong sense of community in their own fraternity. It is a general rule that wherever a strong distinction is made between soul and body and a totalitarian conception of society prevails, the individual is denied the right to take his own life. Dualism and totalitarianism are the two constant elements in the undercurrent of philosophical disapproval of *mors voluntaria* in the ancient world.

Ancient ethnography is often mere utopianism: exotic habits are reported with eagerness, with respect to suicide as with everything else. Among the Ethiopian Trogodyts (*sic*) those who because of age could no longer keep up with the herds tied an ox's tail around their neck and thus voluntarily put an end to their life. Among the Heruli when someone was old or ill, they had him take his place on a pyre. Somebody, but not a relative, killed him with a dagger. A wife who cared for her reputation was expected to hang herself next to her husband's tomb. In the ancient bewilderment over the Indian custom of widow's burning – in spite of Euadne – there is an attempt to rationalize the practice, as we saw. It was said to have been introduced because once a woman had poisoned her husband. Suttee made it unattractive for a woman to kill her husband, even if no one suspected her of murder[25].

Even some central areas of the *oikoumene* are reported to have practised connivance if not encouragement of suicide. Some ancient authors describe with fitting perplexity the *Custom of Ceos*: on this island in the Aegean Sea old people – of sixty according to Strabo – were expected to end their lives. Some writers even state that suicide was prescribed for that age. Valerius Maximus reports on the basis of autopsy that a 90-year-old woman remained faithful to the old tradition: this high age proves that there was no fixed limit nor a legal obligation, 'only' an established habit (p.32). The *Varied History* of Aelianus confirms this interpretation:

> This is the custom (*nomos*) among the Ceans: those among them who are very old summon each other as it were for an interchange of presents or some ceremonial sacrifice. Having gathered together, they drink hemlock with a wreath on their head, having realized that they have become useless for the activities that serve the fatherland when their mental faculties already are in decline.

In ancient Marseilles, those who wanted to take leave of life had to ask for permission from the authorities. Having been given permission they were allowed to make use of the poison kept at the town hall. The information on this institution does not specify the period. The lack of clearness in the information is a strong indication that the customs of Ceos and Massilia were exaggerated to meet the taste of a public that enjoyed hearing of strange situations 'abroad'. People's own past had a similar function of presenting a different world: the Latin proverb 'the sixty-years of age from the bridge' according to some ancient scholars went back to an annual sacrifice in Rome to Father Dis, the god of the underworld, when a man of sixty was thrown into the river. When Hercules undertook his civilizing mission in Italy he abolished the practice and established a substitute: annually an effigy was thrown into the Tiber from then on[26].

Ancient rhetoric created its own fictitious world out of authentic elements. Thus Quintilian makes up a case starting from the regulation 'whoever has not declared the reason of his voluntary death to the senate, has to be thrown away unburied'. It is not to be assumed that a specific law in a real country, Rome or Marseilles, is meant: we are in the land of rhetoric. The significance of such an example is that it was imaginable to ancient people for a polis to have such regulations. Actually, sometimes people of distinction felt obliged to report their intention of self-killing to the authorities: responsibility towards the community, ostentation and the wish to free the relatives of any suspicion were mingled in such behaviour. When Euphrates the philosopher asked for Hadrian's approval to kill himself that looks largely like an instance of *iactatio ut philosophi*[27].

Apart from Ceos and Marseilles, Athens may have been the source for the idea that sometimes and in some places a State had the right in the most personal decision. At least in Late Antiquity Libanios knew for sure that there permission of the Council was required. Under the entry 'Selbstmord' in Pauly-Wissowa's encyclopaedia Thalheim says that this statement was 'natürlich Erfindung'. But the possibility cannot fully be ruled out that Athens had some regulations. Not only do we meet there special habits in throwing away the bodies of self-killers, but according to Aristotle there existed sanctions against attempted suicide: fines and loss of political rights. Such an attempt in the eyes of the Stagirite was rightly punished as an instance of anti-social behaviour[28].

So far we have only pieces of evidence for some interference by certain states. For Rome the regulations of the law are known directly. We do not have to resort to the rhetorical fiction of Seneca the Elder who projected an action of *maleficium* brought against his saviour by the man who had tried to hang himself. In the first place it has to be established that only a few types of suicide attract the interest of the Roman State. It could be a bad example if occurring among the patrons of traditional values. For this reason Claudius the emperor tried to remove from the senatorial role 'someone who was suspected of having used iron against himself'. This attempt failed when the man involved threw off his garment and showed his body unharmed. In order to maintain order it was in the interest of the community that a person arrested on a charge of taking part in disgraceful orgies remained alive to stand trial. For this reason Minius Cerrinus was kept in custody to prevent him from killing himself before the case of the Bacchanalia came before the court. In general the guardian was held responsible if the accused did away with himself when waiting for his trial[29].

The main worry for the Roman authorities was the question whether suicide committed during (or shortly before) a trial could be counted as a confession. In Early Rome self-killing seemed to have been regarded as such: the goods of Appius Claudius and Spurius Oppius were confiscated by the tribunes of the people. 'Is it allowable to stop someone who wants to die in order to escape lawsuits' after having given a 'reason for dying' (*rationem mortis*)? In the Early Empire there was rather a premium on such behaviour: the goods of those who anticipated a trial of *lèse-majesté*, were not confiscated and a ritual burial was not denied. Cassius Dio qualifies Tacitus' grim comment on 'the premium on making haste' (*pretium festinandi*) which was set under Tiberius: he says that very *few* fortunes were confiscated from those who died voluntarily before their trial. In order to profit from the favourable settlement, it was probably necessary to kill oneself before the formal accusation, *nominis receptio*, was lodged[30].

In the first century AD the principle had obviously been established that, without qualification, suicide was counted as a confession if it was committed during the trial in serious cases where a conviction led to capital punishment and confiscation. This is the starting-point for the clarifications and modifications which the 'good' emperors of the second century made. In an important paper Wacke has demonstrated that suicide was of interest to the State only in these serious cases: it could profit from a verdict by the confiscation that was the corollary of any condemnation. It is hardly necessary to add that the jurisconsults' discussions assume that only wealthy defendants found themselves on trial: it was only then that the avaricious state stood to profit.

The emperors of the second century and their legal advisers narrow down the conditions under which the suicide of the defendant can be regarded as a *confessio*. Marcianus had specified the situation in which self-killing amounted to a confession: 'those who have been accused or were taken in the act and then from fear of an imminent verdict laid hands upon themselves, do not have an heir', that is to say: the State gets the goods after a fitting reward has been given to the denouncer. Papianus went somewhat further. He declared that there had to be a formal accusation or at least the evidence had to be overwhelming, e.g. if the accused was taken in the act, for 'not the acceleration of fate' (*celeritas fati*) as such was incriminating, but the 'fear for the conscience in the accused had to be similar to someone who confesses'[31].

Further limits were set to the greediness of the State by Antoninus Pius. He declared in a rescript that the treasury could only claim the goods of an accused who committed suicide if the legal sanction for the crime was capital punishment or deportation. To clarify his point the emperor mentioned parricide: if someone accused of this serious crime lays hands upon himself, the treasury is the heir. If he dies a natural death during the trial, the heir mentioned in the will gets possession. Even if there is no will, the treasury has no claim. Then the normal rules apply which regulate the shares each member of the family receives. In a case of 'moderate' theft death was not the penalty, the emperor said in another legal response. So *even* if the defendant hanged himself in that case, no confiscation followed. Once more we see that hanging is placed in a special category: someone who destroys himself in such a miserable way exposes himself in the highest degree to the suspicion of having no clear conscience[32].

The law-giving emperor specifies even more exactly when a suicide may be a confession of guilt. If the accused has put an end to his life from *taedium vitae* or because of *unbearable pain* or *otherwise*, 'he has an heir' (*successorem habet*). A test-case occurred under Hadrian: a father was said to have killed his son and under these circumstances he committed suicide. When the emperor was asked for advice he declared that the father had laid hands upon himself in the first place because of grief in consequence of having lost his son. This case has several interesting aspects: in the first place we see that the notorious right of life and death of the *pater familias* no longer existed in the second century AD. Otherwise, the emperor could simply have answered that a complaint – if there was one – was inadmissible. If I am right, Hadrian could have taken three lines of defence to motivate a decision which favoured the father. He could have argued that a rumour was not a formal complaint. Maybe he could have appealed to the old right of life and death (*ius vitae necisque*) that was the prerogative of a head of the family. But the emperor chooses humanitarian arguments and thereby poses in his favourite role of benefactor[33].

The series of valid motives for suicide continues to be expanded. Shame is acknowledged as a legitimate ground for suicide. This *pudor* is specified as 'shame in consequence of debt'. The philosophy of *in dubio pro reo suicida* is taken to extremes. Even the exotic ostentatious suicide of philosophers is added to the list of self-killings which are not to be regarded as committed *ob conscientiam criminis*: the will remains valid and the goods do not become the possession of the treasury. This last curious refinement demonstrates once again that the room for assuming confession on the part of the accused who commits suicide is limited to the utmost degree[34].

In order to avoid any risk of perpetrating an injustice against the heirs Antoninus Pius gave them a last chance. If no valid cause (*iusta causa*) for the suicide of the defendant could be put forward, the heirs had the right to prove the innocence of the dead. Until the case was decided, the treasury had no claim on the goods of the deceased. This regulation meant a reversal of the *onus probandi*: the relatives had to give evidence posthumously of innocence and they had to do so with 'crystal-clear proofs' (*liquidis probationibus*). All these rules, that obviously were the result of long consideration, show a spirit of extreme tolerance with respect to the (wealthy) suicide and his heirs. So many were the legitimate grounds for self-killing that only in the last resort did the State have the right to assume that a guilty conscience had led to a voluntary death[35].

The Roman State as seen by the jurists is no moralist. Even slaves were allowed the natural right 'to rage against their own body' (*licet etiam servis naturaliter in suum corpus saevire*). This phrase occurs in a passage about the tricky problem of how the buyer may be protected against the hidden defect of a propensity to suicide. A slave who has once attempted to kill himself has less market-value, not so much because he might give it another try, but 'as someone who, having ventured this against himself (*qui hoc adversus se ausus est*), might venture (*ausurus*) something also against another person'. The future buyer therefore has to be informed by the seller; if the latter was negligent on this point, the purchase could be annulled afterwards[36].

More than marginal is the State's concern about suicide among soldiers. They have a close relation with the State. A self-killing by a member of the armed forces in principle is regarded as a form of desertion that is to be punished with death. But the emperors and their juridical advisers are alert to mitigating circumstances in these cases too. 'A soldier who has laid hands upon himself, but did not complete the deed' only then is to be punished – with death! – 'if he did not act from unbearable suffering, disease or mourning or for other (excusable) reasons'. The *aliae causae* are specified by Hadrian as *taedium vitae, furor* and *pudor*. In all these cases the soldier is only dismissed with ignominy. If he attempted to kill himself 'because of wine' (*per vinum*) or 'in wantonness' (*per lasciviam*), a lighter penalty is fitting: a demotion. The regulations for the will of a soldier who has killed himself are similar to those for civilians who stand in court accused of a capital crime. The only peculiar clause is that if there are no relatives, the goods go to the legion[37].

So Roman law shows some interest in the phenomenon of self-killing in specific circumstances. On rare occasions it even uses suicide as an example to illustrate a point about the scope of laws about wilful manslaughter: 'if somebody throws himself from a height and falls on someone else and kills this person' the law of murder does not apply. In general the conclusion must be that self-killing is not totally neglected by the Roman jurists, but that the attention they pay to it is very limited. The regulations about suicide during a legal trial, among slaves offered for sale and in the army may be assessed under no circumstance as a general attempt by the Roman State to discourage self-murder. On the contrary, the attitude manifest in the rules is one of minimal attention and of connivance. It is therefore striking that European legal systems appealed to Roman law to justify the idea that the state was entitled to confiscate the goods of *any* suicide. While canonical law punished the self-murderer with a 'dog's burial', the civilian authorities saw an opportunity for profit. In the 54 medieval cases that Schmitt traced by means of legal sources, it is always citizens of some wealth that were involved (noblemen were outside the reach of the law and humble people had nothing to offer). The French Revolution laid down the principle that suicide was not punishable any more. In England the official legal sanctions on suicide(-attempts) were only abolished in 1961. As we saw, even Durkheim, with his sociological interest, held the view that 'homicide de soi-même' (a characteristic circumlocution) should be subjected to official disapproval. In this context he speaks of the 'immoralité du suicide'. The methods by which he wants to dam the stream of suicide are of a naive simplicity: marriage should be made 'plus indissoluble' and professional organizations should integrate people once more. This approach has more of the Platonic totalitarianism than the matter-of-fact attitude of the ancient world reflected in Roman law[38].

D THE IMAGE OF SELF-KILLING

Caesar's triumph of 46 BC celebrated the victories in the Civil War which had just ended. Captives and booty were led through the streets of Rome. 'Veni, vidi, vici', Caesar's famous slogan, was displayed on a board that was carried through the Urbs: so far the people of the eternal city reacted with enthusiasm to this show, but there were mixed feelings about the novelty: Caesar not only triumphed over the barbarian enemies, he was also unconcerned to hide the ways in which he had finished off his direct opponents in the Civil War, that is to say Roman citizens. On panels that were carried in the triumph he showed his enemies in their deepest humiliation, which signified his greatest glory: one could see in the pictures how the last of the Pompeians killed themselves in Africa when they realized that their cause was lost[39].

There was no general taboo on picturing self-killing. Therefore a more direct answer can be given to the central question of this study: how did suicide look in antiquity? The iconography of self-murder, however, is not extensive. The views we came across when discussing other kinds of material are also present in the plastic arts[40].

In the first place the despair of defeated enemies could be pictured: Cato and the other suicides had lost all hope of escaping total destruction. Their alternative was having to appeal to the mercy of the hated victor Caesar. Their *desperata salus* gave an extra dimension to the victory. The paintings Caesar had made are of the same nature as the pictures of ancient historiographers when describing the despair of the beleaguered: women killed their children before throwing themselves in the fire. The ancient writer in his imagination is present at the scene and observes the misery with the complacency of the victor, but in order to strengthen the effect he has to show some compassion for the victims.

Such ambiguous empathy was also present in the famous monument by which Attalus I celebrated his victory over the Celts in Asia Minor. In Athens he erected symbolic allusions to his triumph over barbarism: scenes from the battles with the Amazons and from the Athenian victory at Marathon. In his own capital, Pergamum, the battle between the gods and the giants was used as a parallel in the baroque reliefs of the altar of Zeus. But here the references were more concrete: dying enemies were pictured. In the centre stood the Gaul who had just killed his wife and was about to push the sword in his own body. The central couple (Ill.1) was encircled by four recumbent figures: one of them is the famous dying Gaul who is represented in his last moments having pierced himself. The whole group is marked by a subtle play of humiliation and compassion.

Fewer niceties are demonstrated in the way Trajan's victory over the Dacians is celebrated. The comic strip that winds around the column shows the Romans in all their confidence. Their campaign is completely finished when king Decebalus kills himself in despair (Ill.2). This final act had a great impact in that age. Not only is the soldier who brought the head of the king to the emperor known by name – and he was promoted in consequence – but a potter in Gaul stamped his earthenware with the historic scene of Decebalus about to stab himself. This is a very rare specimen of an historical theme in pottery (Ill.3)[41].

Outside the iconography of power there was a place for suicide in pictures of love. The tone is similar to that of novel and erotic anecdote. Scenes of exemplary loyalty or mourning up to the point of suicide were the subjects of paintings, but hardly any of them are preserved. They are mainly known by the descriptions that Philostratos gives in his *Eikones*. In this work he tells us about a visit to a collection of paintings in the neighbourhood of Naples. In a painting of Menoikeus' act of devotion he praises the artistic value and the deed itself. The young man obeyed the warning of Teiresias that Thebes would be freed of its siege if he died at the cave of the dragon:

See what the painter has achieved. He pictures a lad, not pale
and effeminate, but robust and breathing the spirit of the
wrestling-ring (. . .). He stands near the dragon's cave and
draws the sword from the loins which it has penetrated. Let
us, boy, catch the blood by putting our garments under it.
For it pours forth and the soul is already leaving – in a
moment one will even hear it sing like a bird; for souls too
cherish love for beautiful bodies and take their leave
reluctantly[42].

Two other paintings Philostratos saw had female mythical
suicides as their theme: Euadne and Laodameia (p.59). A semi-
historical self-killing is that of Pantheia, described by Xenophon:
she killed herself out of a feeling of responsibility for the death of
her husband. In the painting Pantheia pushed the sword so deep in
her so that no sigh arose[43].

A boy and a girl concluded a pact of suicide and jumped
together into the water. Their deed was part of a panorama of the
Bosporus also on display in the gallery (see also p.76). There were
various scenes gathered in the painting that Philostratos admired.

The coast is rugged and it preserves traces of the following
story: a boy and a girl, both handsome, were pupils of the
same teacher. They fell in love and when there appeared no
opportunity to embrace each other, they decided to die by
throwing themselves from that rock. Thus they flew into the
sea in a last and first embrace. And Eros on the rock stretches
his hand to the sea; in this way the painter alludes to the
story.

This self-killing has been classified as a *dolor*-suicide, for the
dominating motive was the grief arising from an unrealizable love.
The way in which the self-killing was perpetrated is similar to the
Japanese 'shinju': in that pattern two lovers tie themselves together
and throw themselves from a height[44].

So far we have only been able to report the descriptions of
paintings which are lost to us. One fresco that depicts a couple's
sentimental suicide has survived: in the house of Octavius Quartio
in Pompeii a – rather clumsy – painting has been found which
shows the moment when Thisbe throws herself on the sword of the
beloved Pyramus, who killed himself in a fatal misunderstanding
(Ill.4).

At least one statue of Iokaste existed, sculpted by Silanion in the fourth century BC. It depicted the wife-mother of Oidipous on the verge of death. We do not know whether the sculptor followed Sophocles in having Iokaste hang herself or preferred Euripides who said that she stabbed herself. In any case the statue must have been ghastly, for Plutarch uses it as an argument against the Epicureans when proving that there may be pleasure in looking at pictures of suffering.

Apart from the desperate and romantic suicide, the mythical and heroic self-killing too left its traces in the plastic arts. Dido's self-murder lies somewhat in between. In the codex of the *Virgilius Vaticanus*, which was made in Late Antiquity, she lies on a sofa which is placed on top of a pyre (Ill.5 and 6). Dido had needed a stepladder to get so high. In deviation from Virgil's text the scene is set inside the palace. The embittered queen of Carthage has exposed her right breast and has drawn out the sword ready for thrusting. As so often in classical art the moment just before the decisive action has been chosen to heighten the dramatic tension. A similar choice of moment was made on a Greek vase where we see Croesus on his pyre (Ill.7). A third ancient self-burning which we can still see is Heracles' apotheosis in a small two-dimensional picture[45].

It has been shown that Ajax was a prototype of a complete hero. The significance of his suicide is brought to the fore by the quite numerous depictions which still survive[46]. In her entry in the *Lexicon Iconographicum Mythologiae Classicae* Odette Touchefen has 38 items in various genres of art: vases, gems, little bronze statues and reliefs. The iconography is also extensive in the sense that various moments of Ajax's *moment suprême* are chosen. The vase in Boulogne painted by Exekias is unique: Ajax is giving the finishing touch to the little mound in which the sword has been fixed (Ill.8). On a *lecythus* in Basle he is kneeling in front of the erected sword. He has lifted his hands as in a last prayer to the gods.

Etruscan art has a general preference for the morbid moments from Greek mythology. In the light of this taste it is not astonishing that most of the pictorial evidence for Ajax comes from Etruscan graves. From Vulci comes a *stamnus* on which Ajax is staring thoughtfully at the sword in his right hand. The woman who stands nearby may be Tekmessa. From the earth beneath the sword a plant has sprouted, which bears on its stem the letters AIVAS. This is an allusion to a version of the story according to which at Ajax's death a flower sprang up with the Greek cry of distress, AIAI, on it.

The next episode is mainly depicted on gems. The round or oval form was well adapted to an Ajax bending over his sword. In the next stage Ajax is jumping; he is caught in the moment he is in the air, his hands and feet free from the earth. Some of these depictions make the hero of Salamis almost an athlete. A vase in the British Museum shows the next moment. The sword has gone right through Ajax's body: the point appears at the left shoulder. In a different view the sword penetrates his body, fully bent over the erect weapon. Thus a well-balanced composition originates which has been sculpted on a metope on display in the museum of Paestum (Ill.9).

The last scene is when Ajax lies on the earth, face to the ground, while the sword has gone right through him. This is the moment chosen in most (remaining) depictions. Some images suggest that there was a deviant version according to which the hero did not throw himself on his sword, but pushed it in. A servant may give him assistance. The full range of pictures devoted to Ajax's suicide is completed with the painting in which a woman, presumably Tekmessa, covers the naked body through which the sword has passed from breast to back.

So we see that in depiction too Ajax is the model. Number and variety surpass the image of any other famous suicide. One should expect pictures of other notorious or exemplary self-destructions, that of Cleopatra and especially Lucretia. But I only know of the existence of three depictions of Lucretia's deed on Etruscan funerary urns of the first century BC. As I said before the Etruscans had a taste for the more lurid aspects of the ancient stories. There is some reason to suppose that one of their depictions shows a hostile version: the Roman lady is shown naked from the waist up. That is the way she is commonly depicted in early modern times when she became a popular subject (Ill.10). She then appears in the company of various ancient suicides: Saul, Hannibal, Mark Antony and Cleopatra[47]. At an early date Pyramus and Thisbe were allegorized. They were depicted on a capital of the choir gallery in the monastery of Basle.

Early Christianity developed a certain imagery of its own with respect to suicide which is continued in the Middle Ages. In Christian eyes the self-murderer is in the first place the sinner who rejects God's grace completely. That is the reason why Judas' hanging is depicted on ivory diptychs and on sarcophagi beside the central crucifixion: he who brought salvation is contrasted with the man who absolutely despaired of *Salus*. The *Desperatio* painted by Giotto in the Arena Chapel in Padua is a woman who hanged herself (Ill.12).

Despair is also depicted as a man who throws himself onto his sword or spear. In the porch of Amiens cathedral four pairs of figures exemplify the opposition sin–virtue. Hope is opposed to Despair; the latter throws himself backwards on the sword. Despair may come in the hour of death when Satan makes a final attack. The *Artes moriendi* warn against the 'fünf Anfechtungen' (five temptations). The devil tempts the dying person with 'do kill yourself' (*interficias te ipsum*). If one listens to his suggestion, one chooses for Despair and forfeits Salvation. This medieval view is still present in Comenius' pictorial Latin dictionary in which a desperate man throws himself on a sword (Ill.13)[48].

1. A Gaul kills himself having slayed his wife first; Roman copy in the Museo delle Therme in Rome of a Hellenistic original which was part of a monument erected by King Attalos I celebrating his victory over the Gauls in Asia Minor.

2. The Dacian king Decebalus stabs himself when the victorious Romans approach his hiding place. On segment 145 of Trajan's column in Rome (drawing from S. Reinach, *Répertoire de reliefs Grecs et Romains I*, Paris 1909, p. 367.

3. The Dacian king Decebalus stabs himself when the victorious Romans approach his hiding place. On an earthenware cup from southern Gaul signed by Lucius Cosius (detail of a drawing in A. Vernhet, 'Un four de la Granfesengue', 1981, *Gallia* 39:33).

4. Thisbe throws herself on the sword with which Pyramus has stabbed himself shortly before: fresco in the house of Octavius Quartio in Pompeii (photograph by Alinari).

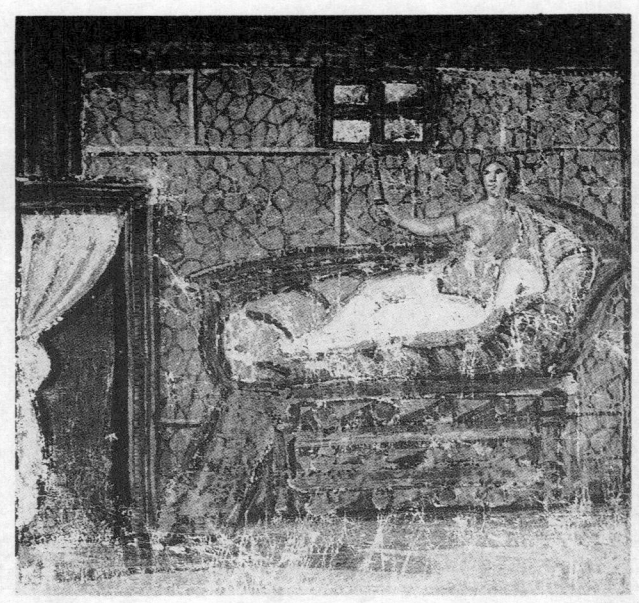

5. Dido stabs herself on top of the pyre; from the *Virgilius Vaticanus* (photograph by Sansoni).

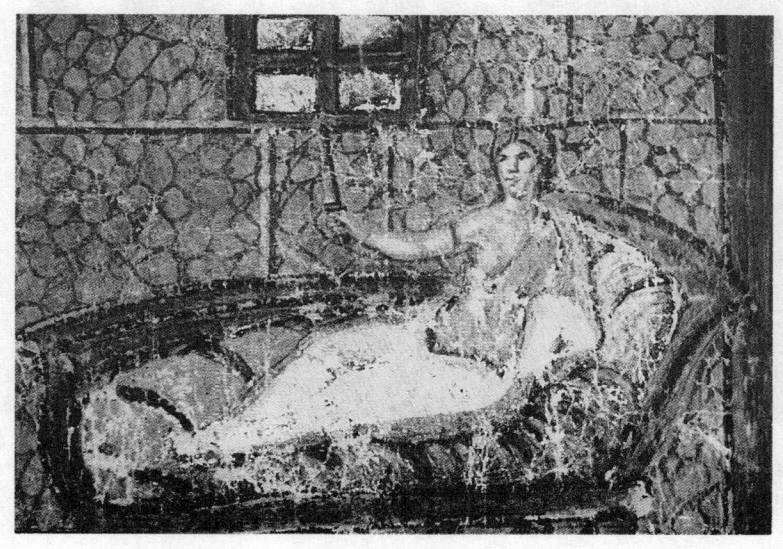

6. A detail of Dido's suicide (see illustration 5).

7.   Croesus attempting to burn himself on the pyre. Drawing after a vase painting in the Louvre Museum, Paris. Taken from Furtwängler-Reichhold, *Griechische Vasenmalerei*, Munich 1909, second series, illustration 132.

8. Ajax fixes his sword in preparation for his suicide. Vase painted by Exekias, reproduced with kind permission of the Musée Communal in Boulogne-sur-Mer.

9. Ajax on his sword. An unfinished metope of the Hera temple at the mouth of the Sele, now in the Museum of Paestum (photograph by the author).

10. Lucretia as a Christian heroine of chastity. Painting by 'The Master of the Holy Blood', reproduced with kind permission of the Szépmüvészeti Museum, Budapest.

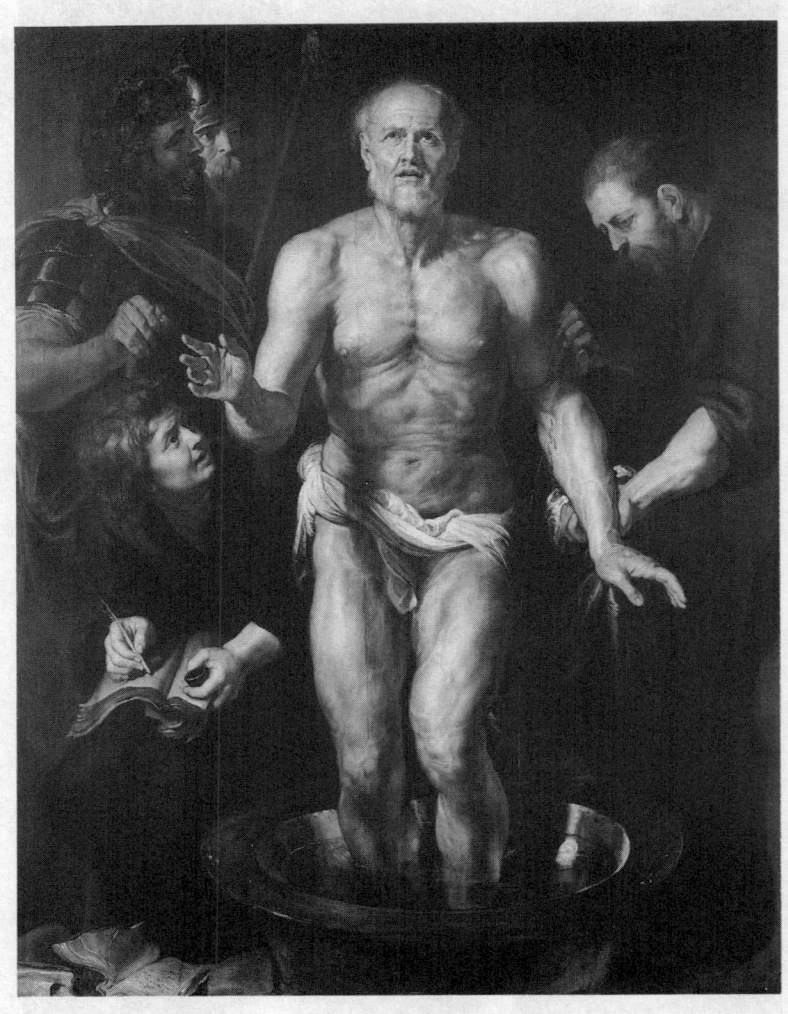

11. Seneca dying in a bath; painting by P. P. Rubens, reproduced with
     kind permission of the Alte Pinakothek, Munich.

12. Despair depicted as a hanged individual. Fresco by Giotto in the
Arena Chapel, Padua (photograph by Scala).

13. The impatient man throws himself on his sword. Detail of the illustration for the rubric *Patientia* in the *Orbis Sensualium Pictus* by Comenius. Reproduced with kind permission of Harenberg.

Part III

REFLECTIONS ON SELF-KILLING

6

PHILOSOPHERS AND THEOLOGIANS

In Jotapata Flavius Josephus mobilized all his anthropological, philosophical and theological knowledge to convince himself and his people that self-killing in their situation was fundamentally reprehensible. In the face of God suicide was wrong, because man was not entitled to dispose freely of the soul that was poured by Jahweh into the body. The soul that prematurely left the body acted like the steersman who during a storm had his ship go down by his own hand. Animals did not kill themselves; that is to say, self-killing was against nature. No honour was to be gained by destroying oneself: it was an act of cowardliness (*deilia*). Moreover, the community was damaged by the exit of its members. The dishonouring treatment certain states gave to suicides further proved the point Josephus wanted to make. Also in other episodes of the Jewish War Josephus shows that self-killing was a vital question for him. His description of the mass suicide of the Jews at Massada demonstrates the ambiguity of his feelings: admiration for heroism, but serious doubts about the sense of such a sacrifice. His own escape in Jotapata is reflected in the survival of some who had hidden themselves in a water conduit in Massada: an old woman, five children and a female relative of Eleazar, an educated person, as Josephus adds (like himself?). He shows himself an advocate of survival under the walls of Jerusalem during the fatal siege, when he tries to prevent his fellow-Jews from collective suicide[1].

Josephus' *apologia pro vita* (*sua*) in Jotapata is a reservoir into which the undercurrents of ancient disapproval of suicide come together. The arguments are on various levels: the customs of a foreign people and animal behaviour are treated together with the nature of God and the soul. Such a mixing of different orders often

181

occurs when the permissibility of suicide is discussed, and also when the circumstances are less pressing than in a cave during a siege. In order to justify his rejection of suicide, the Neo-Platonic philosopher Porphyrios first argues for the dualism of body and soul. Only by wisdom may the soul free itself from the flesh. Self-killing is anything but a rational act. The soul that, in passion, is forced to leave the body, remains in the neighbourhood of the body. Therefore – an argument of quite a different order – magicians like to use a bit of such a corpse in their black arts (one is reminded of the habit of not mentioning the names of suicides at feasts for the departed). The distance from philosophy to folklore is often not very large[2].

The relation between ancient ideas about self-killing on the one hand and reality and mentality on the other, is better not reviewed as the autonomous development of philosophical concepts. Doxographic publications of this kind are not rare. By their approach they suggest, in spite of all noble protestations, that the ideas jump like Athenas from the heads of divine thinkers. An existential problem like suicide in the first place is not an autonomous theoretical problem discussed in the philosophic schools. As we see, on many occasions philosophers resort to arguments and emotions of a less than theoretical order. For instance, when the Ephesians drove Herakleitos' friend Hermodoros into exile, the sage declared: 'The Ephesians had better put an end to their lives'[3].

The final section of this study is the last and smallest part of a three-stage rocket: we look at philosophical and religious reflections in connection with the phenomena (quotas, means, motives) of part I and at their relations with the popular morality as shown in part II. Often existing situations were only legitimated and wrapped in a philosophical-theological attire. Sometimes there is a conscious attempt to distance oneself from existing values. The thinker or church-man then advocates a change. A chronological framework would present the least attractive approach. Moreover, it would do no justice to the dialectical process between reflection and reality. The reality of self-killing does not show a linear development and thinking about suicide is not a simple set of continuities.

Self-killing is the most individual death, but it is always connected with the surrounding world. This world is very small if personal reasons like despair, grief and pain are involved. Much wider is the circle when suicide is placed in the perspective of the community: to sacrifice oneself for the well-being of the whole was always held as an exemplary deed, but how should a polis react to suicides committed for personal reasons? Finally, the self-killer is part of a cosmos: do nature, the gods and God allow self-destruction? These three circles of *oikos*, *polis* and *cosmos* form the perspectives for the reflections on suicide in this section.

A   SELF-KILLING AS A PRIVATE ACT

Mourning befitted the ancient female. Her world was that of the household, the *oikos*. If she does away with herself when husband or son dies, no questions are raised. The wise man, however, has to avoid 'effeminate' behaviour. For the Stoa losing one's wife or child is a test-case of wisdom: the philosopher should realize that such a death is part of the great order of things (*logos*). Immoderate sorrow, not to mention suicide, is a foolish protest against the great scheme that rules the cosmos. The consolatory addresses, *Consolationes*, become a genre of their own, in which such points of view are developed to comfort a Marcia or Helvia.

In principle, the philosopher shrugs off female suicide. Occasionally it gives him the opportunity to utter a *bon mot*, like Diogenes' reaction to the sight of a bunch of hanging women on an olive-tree: would that every tree had such fruits (p.20). Early Christianity did not pay much attention to suicide from despair either. It did not yet see it as a sin, but as an act born of utmost human misery: it reacts pastorally rather than morally. When Paul and Silas were held in custody in Philippi, suddenly the doors burst open in consequence of an earthquake. The guardian thought that his captives had flown, and was about to use his sword against himself, as he was legally responsible (p.169), but Paul said: 'Don't do yourself any harm'[4].

So Paul felt compassion for an unhappy individual and he did not address him as a (potential) sinner. In the first centuries Christian doctrine has no special interest for the ethical side of suicide. Less pastoral is St Peter in a Christian novel, written some centuries after the Acts of the Apostles. On one of his missionary travels Peter comes across a begging woman; we have already discussed the case under the heading *inpatientia*, for she answers his question why she did not work by indicating her crippled hands (p.126): 'If I had a manly spirit (*andreion phronema*), there would be a precipice, the deep sea; by throwing myself I would put an end to my misery'. Peter: 'Do you think that those who do away with themselves will be free from punishment? Will not the souls of those who die that way be punished with a worse penalty because of the self-killing (*autoktonia*)?' The woman sighs: 'If only I could believe that the souls live on in the underworld.' Thereupon she tells a story of her life that would do well in an ancient comedy or novel. During her husband's long absence she was hard pressed by the advances of her brother-in-law. She fled, together with her sons, but suffered shipwreck. She stayed on the island of Arados, hoping to find her sons again. 'If I had not cherished that hope', she says, 'I would already have jumped into the deep.' After some time she found corpses which she assumed to be her sons. She was admitted into the house of some compassionate people and made a decent living by working with her hands. But to add to the misfortune, these were paralysed by 'bites' (*degamata*), probably rheumatism. The story, which emphasizes Peter's preaching, has a happy ending: she finds one son again and her hands are miraculously healed[5].

The reflections do not discuss unbearable mental suffering as a ground for suicide in a man: in this way the silence of the concrete evidence is confirmed. But bodily pain as a cause for self-killing is at the centre of a philosophical debate. The founder of the Stoa was said to have done away with himself for that reason. Diogenes Laertios, who tells the story of Zeno's death, says that among the Stoics it is generally held that the sage 'leads himself rationally (*eulogos*) out of life, namely on behalf of fatherland and friends, and also when he suffers from *pain which is too fierce, mutilations or incurable diseases*'. As we saw, Seneca himself while young seriously thought about putting an end to his life and his chronic infliction of the chest. In his writings he does not approve *inpatientia* without qualification as a sufficient ground for suicide. For instance, he, a Stoic, has praise for Aufidius Bassus, an Epicurean who endured bodily decay. Perhaps the latter was keeping to Epicurus' directive that the sage was not permitted to conclude rashly that well-being (*hedone*), the central idea of Epicureanism, had irretrievably been lost: 'Even if he has lost his eye-sight, he will not withdraw from life'. Seneca, the – eclectic – Stoic, requires withdrawal to be fully rational: fear of misery or death are affective motives, as well as a fit of anger. Frivolous reasons (*frivolae causae*) run counter to the 'high standard of ratiocination' that the Stoa asks of its adherents. It is silly to hang oneself in front of the door of a girl-friend or to throw oneself from a roof to escape a morose master or to 'thrust iron through the bowels' in order to avoid being brought back from running away. Suicides like these are to be regarded as caused not by *virtus* but by excessive fear (*nimia formido*)[6].

Sacrificing oneself on behalf of friends is already more than an individual suicide; here one thinks in the first place of avoiding being forced by a tyrant to betray one's friends: a self-sacrifice, as the Stoa put it, had to be dignified and really unselfish. Life and discipline were not always in harmony: Pythagoreanism with its dualistic conception of body and soul is very outspoken in its taboo on suicide. On the other hand Pythagoras' circle was seen as an ideal community of friends. To underline the affection felt by the disciples for the master Porphyrios in his *Life of Pythagoras* tells the story that once when the master was shut up in a burning house, the students made themselves a living fire-ladder (p.58). Also Pythagoras himself is praised for his strong feelings of friendship; he is said to have died from voluntary starvation after Pherekydes' death[7].

So the various philosophical schools offer a qualified legitimation for withdrawing from life from private reasons, but the risk of losing one's dignity is always stressed: suicide could easily be a perverted form of self-love. This is an Aristotelian argument. A self-murderer trespasses against himself. Like habitual criminals self-killers have a depraved form of self-love. In fact, both categories of evil-doers seek to escape from life. The perversion could grow side by side with the virtue of *amour-propre*. The Epicureans, who were always suspected of only aiming at short-term enjoyment, do warn against acting prematurely. Cicero is absolutely wrong when summarizing their point of view as 'one should drink or die'. In *About Death* Philodemos qualifies the Epicurean attitude: it is preferable not to seek death before the best of life has been enjoyed (and one never is sure whether the best is not still ahead). The founder of his philosophical school himself had explicitly stated in his *On Life* that the wise man, even when he has lost his sight, will not withdraw himself from life[8].

B SELF-KILLING IN THE POLIS-COMMUNITY

With regard to the polis, suicide is laudable as long as it happens on behalf of (*hyper*) the fatherland. This view is attacked by no philosophical school; it is regarded as self-evident. More attention is paid to the place of institutionalized self-destruction in utopian societies.

In the State of the Sun (*Heliopolis*), devised by the Stoic Iamboulos, certain harmful elements are forced to suicide. 'Anyone among them who has become crippled or suffers in general from any physical infirmity is forced by them, in accordance with an inexorable law, to remove himself from life'. The regulation that one is only permitted to live for a stipulated number of years appears modelled on the Cean Custom. At the completion of this period they have to make away with themselves not by drinking hemlock, but by lying down on a plant of a particular kind and finding eternal rest. Similar stories are told about the Ethiopians who since Homer have the role of exotic people living at the edge of the world. Anecdotes about them are not based on direct observation: they project ideas on a far-away situation which cannot be verified. In that 'teletopian' world of the Ethiopians there is no formal capital punishment. The man found guilty receives a message containing the sign of death. Thereupon he withdraws to his home and 'removes himself from life'. The loyalty of the king's vassals is also exemplary: if the monarch is maimed in some part of his body, all his companions suffer the same loss of their own choice. They are also said to die with their kings of their own accord[9].

In Plato's Utopia the doctrine of the soul and a totalitarian idea of the State forbid suicide. In the *Laws* self-killing is the climax in a triplet of direct homicide against one's own people. In the first place someone might kill a fellow-tribesman with his own hands. This deed is unheard of, as is brought out by the appropriate term for this type of man-killer: *autocheir*, the word that later receives the narrow meaning of self-killer. More serious still is to slaughter one's relatives: this deed is unimaginable and the defilement – *miasma* – is punished by the gods, but the mortal law-giver adds to the disgrace: the offender is executed and his naked body is carried outside the city to a three-forked road and in the name of the State all the magistrates stand near, stone in hand, and 'throw them on the head of the corpse to cleanse the whole state'. After that ceremony the corpse is brought outside the borders of the polis and left unburied. Finally, the case is discussed of the man who kills what is most private, who violently robs fate of its disposal – at least when not killing himself on the explicit orders of the state or because of painful and inescapable misery or by unavoidable, unbearable shame. This despicable person is buried on his own, without a grave-stone to mark the place[10] (immediately after suicides in this passage of the *Laws* are mentioned other persons who have been dealt a violent death by animals or inanimate objects, the *biaiothanatoi*).

The idea of self-killing as murder remains outside the scope of Platonic thought. But it means overstepping the limits set to a human being. 'Suppose', Socrates says in the *Phaedo*, 'that one of your domestic animals should kill itself without having been given permission. Wouldn't you be angry and willing to punish the animal, if possible?' The man who kills himself does not know his place. Like a fugitive slave he steals himself[11].

To Aristotle the reasons for disapproval do not lie in the high spheres of the soul or relations with the gods. His arguments are, in line with the whole of his philosophy, down-to-earth and remain within the horizon of the human community. He also keeps closer to existing prejudices and measures. In the first place he adheres to the criticisms expressed, for instance, by Tekmessa and Theseus in tragedy: self-killing is a deed of cowardliness (*deilia*). Taken on its own, braving death is noble in Aristotle's eyes, but a suicide does not have a noble motive. He is only seeking to escape one evil or another.

In another context Aristotle wonders whether someone can do injustice to himself. As an example he mentions suicide. Contrary to other brave acts self-killing is not prescribed by the law – law taken in the sense of the unwritten *nomos*. In a rather exaggerated argument the philosopher declares: 'what law does not prescribe, it forbids'. Killing someone on purpose is doing injustice. The man who kills himself in a fit of rage similarly commits an act of injustice. But who is damaged? Rather the State than the man himself. For this reason a suicide suffers a certain disgrace (*atimia*). On this point Aristotle explains existing taboos as conscious sanctions by the community. As far as I know the potential damage to the community was never an important argument in European laws against suicide. Only in those philosophers of later ages who have a concept of a strong State do we find a similar aversion. To Rousseau suicide is 'une mort furtive et honteuse'[12].

The ideologies developed by Plato and Aristotle do not find a clear echo in later rejection of suicide. Only in the cumulated arguments put by Flavius Josephus into his own mouth are there allusions. Their disapproval of suicide was based on thinking in terms of the polis. That framework loses its significance in the world-wide culture that originated with Alexander: in the cosmopolis man faces mainly himself and god.

C SELF-KILLING AND THE COSMOPOLIS

When man is seen as an autonomous individual with the immense cosmos far away as his background, there is in principle much room for 'leading oneself out' (Epicureanism and Cynicism). This permissiveness is also present if the relations are reversed: in Stoicism man is a minuscule particle in the vast world. In such a system self-killing may be prescribed if the sage can be sure that it lies in the order of things. But in Neo-Platonic, Jewish and Christian dualistic concepts of body and soul a fundamental right to suicide is denied.

The founder of the Cynics' school, Antisthenes, is held to be the inventor of the euphemism 'leading oneself out of life'. He was also credited with writing a book on Ajax. His even more cynical disciple Diogenes showed himself a model student: 'When Antisthenes was fatally ill, he handed him a dagger saying: in case you need help. So little did the philosopher regard death as something painful or terrible'. Not much was needed to make Diogenes mention suicide. Once he asked a gruff person for alms. The man said: 'All right, if you can persuade me'. Diogenes reacted: 'If I could have persuaded you, I should have persuaded you to hang yourself'. The Cynics do not trouble what happens to their little body, their *somation*, as Diogenes himself made clear by his own death (p.75). Antisthenes relentlessly mocked those who believed in a soul and survival after death, like the Eleusinians did. He asked the priest: 'Why don't you die?' (if you really are convinced of a better existence in the hereafter). The Cynics are the philosophers of ostentation. They admired the Indian sages, the gymnosophists who renounced everything. They did not even have a place for love: it could tie a philosopher to the world. But Diogenes and Krates have a remedy: 'From love hunger frees: if this is not applicable, the noose'. Death is under no circumstances abhorrent to a Cynic. He amuses himself with the paradoxical behaviour of the stupid man who kills himself from fear of death, for instance having been shipwrecked or being encircled by enemies[13].

The attitude of the 'Doggish' philosophers is essentially provocative and tries to question established behaviour; in fact it does not aim at changing existing attitudes. Also the Cynics are part of public life. They are even acknowledged by Roman law as extravagant people in their last moments; it is to be assumed that philosophers of their kind are meant when the jurisconsults distinguish as one of the excusable motives for self-killing the ostentation of philosophers. To their sect belonged the 'death-urger' Hegesias who pointed his disciples the way to a voluntary exit. The death of Demonax, a Cynic as well, is described with due reverence by his student Lucian, whereas the same author fiercely derides Peregrinos as a pseudo-prophet who even makes his death a show[14] (pp.36 and 58).

Unlike the Cynics, the Epicureans were not too ostentatious with their wisdom. Their rule 'live in hiding' runs counter to demonstrative behaviour. They shared the Cynics' contempt for the stupid fear of death which drove some to suicide: 'And often it goes so far, that for fear of death men are seized by hatred of life and of seeing the light, so that with sorrowing heart they devise their own death, forgetting that this fear is the fountain of all their care'[15]. Having attained the insight of Epicureanism that the gods have nothing to do with human existence and that death has no significance, as it only exists when man is no more, in principle the ground is prepared for a great permissiveness, especially with regard to *inpatientia doloris*. But as we saw, the school of Epicurus warns its followers against deciding too rashly that the quality of life has been lost. But when the sage has come to the conclusion that his well-being is damaged, he must go without giving airs to his dying. The Epicurean despises death. 'Let us go out of life unconcerned, when it does not please us, as out of a theatre'[16].

The world as a stage on which everybody has to play his role is a metaphor with which the Stoics are familiar. To any man the *logos* has attributed his specific place and it is his task to fulfil well the task given to him. A good actor plays the role, a slave with as much conviction as a king. In the same fashion, a sage has to strive after a dignified life in the function and under the circumstances disposed by the great order. Pain, mutilation and incurable diseases may harm the quality of the performance, according to Diogenes Laertios' description of the Stoic doctrine. Probably he has the Stoicism of his own age in mind, for the founders of the movement were of a somewhat different opinion. Zeno considered disease and health as indifferent things which ought not to have impact on the freedom of affections (*apatheia*) that the sage was after. He himself put an end to his life when, as a curious anecdote tells, he got a sign that he had lived out his term: he hurt his toe and exclaimed: 'I am coming, why do you call me?' and thereupon, according to one story, he immediately died by holding his breath[17]. For Poseidonios, of the Middle Stoa, sanity had some significance, as bad health could put pressure on the spirit. An individual who meets various setbacks (*contraria*) or has to expect them, is obliged to retire from life (*e vita excedere*). Chrysippos had said that a wise man is not inferior to Zeus in beatitude if he leads himself out of life because of diseases and mutilations[18].

Usurping god's power is the reproach made to suicides by the movements that have an elaborated concept of the soul. But the Roman Stoics did not look upon suicide as an offence against the higher order, as long as it really is an act of freedom and reason. Whenever the divine *logos* orders death 'you must dissolve yourselves'. Cato Uticensis and Socrates are above any suspicion of frivolous motives. They both received a godly order to migrate from 'these darknesses to yonder light'. Cato, the republican as well as the Stoic hero, was called away and dismissed as it were by a magistrate or by legal authority. The free disposition of death for Seneca is the symbol of liberty: 'We are in no one's power as long as death is in our power'. Seneca stresses less than Epictetus the need to receive a sign from the *logos*. When the body is no longer able to exercise its functions, it is allowable to set the soul free. 'And maybe this should be done somewhat earlier than strictly is necessary to prevent you from being unable to do it when it has to be done'. For Seneca self-killing was more than just a theoretical problem: his weak constitution had made him familiar with mortality from his youth up. Apart from his personal disposition the climate of his age also made him the pre-eminent philosopher of suicide; the terror exercised by Tiberius, Caligula and Nero gives the philosopher the role of the advocate of free death[19].

Stoic and Roman aristocrat come together in the 'stiff upper lip attitude'. *Dignitas* is irretrievably forfeited if life is ended for frivolous reasons. The sage always asks 'how life is, not how much'. When numerous misfortunes, *contraria*, or burdens, *molesta*, occur and his peace of mind (*tranquillitas*) is in danger of being disturbed 'he emits himself' (*emittit se*) or 'he swims away from the body as if from a small boat that takes in water'. The quality of life may be damaged by bodily pain, but the Stoic has to wonder whether under those circumstances he 'bursts the chains of slavery' in a really dignified way. Praise is to be given to a man who braves his bodily suffering. Seneca's friend Lucilius had not withdrawn from the 'fury of the potentates' by committing suicide. Seneca assured him that he need not reproach himself with cowardliness for not 'in an acute urge' (*praecipiti impetu*) having taken the 'ultimate decision' (*ultimum consilium*). He had preferred a higher value than his personal *dignitas*, i.e. loyalty to his friends. But in general, suicide to escape the tyrant's craving for power is the highest example of permitted suicide the Stoa puts forward. In such a case the 'high standard of ratiocination' is met that Seneca required for the deed to be philosophical. In such a way the Stoa furnished the elite with 'the etiquette and style for suicide' which Rome needed in the first century AD. The Stoa gave to the motive of shame a philosophical backing that has such an importance in the ancient paradigm of suicide[20].

In the art of *bene mori* that the Stoa preaches, its specific idea of the soul does not play a major part in formulating the attitude towards suicide. The soul is regarded as the element in each individual that is part of the great *logos*. Some Stoics hold that the soul irretrievably disappears when the body dies, others say that it takes part in a cosmic process of recycling in which all individuality is lost. Neither opinion has any specific bearing on the Stoic doctrine on self-killing. The Epicureans' soul consists of minuscule atoms which are distributed over all parts of the body. When the body disintegrates, the soul-atoms lose their function and disperse. There is no life for a soul apart from the body. When Epicureanism and Stoicism occasionally warn against taking one's own life, the soul is not an argument.

Naive or malicious observers wondered why those who believed in the individual existence of the soul outside the body did not at once commit suicide to reach that pure state. This is at the back of the question which the Cynic Antisthenes put to the priest of Eleusis: why do you not thrust that sacrificial knife into your own body? Wilful or stupid misrepresentation also leads to the mocking epigram on Kleombrotos who killed himself having read Plato's book on the soul (p.148). Someone really acquainted with the doctrine of the Academy would have known that the Platonic ideas on the soul were anything but a licence for suicide. For the argument of an individual soul strengthened the Platonic rejection of self-killing as an antisocial deed.

Plato's conception of the soul is rooted in dualistic views on the relation between body and soul that had been in circulation since Orphism and Pythagoras. In the *Phaedo* Socrates appeals to a part of the secret doctrine: the soul is the divine element in man that has been enclosed in a body by the Master. Freeing the soul from this jail has to be attained in a spiritual way, not by means of a violent death. It does not befit the sage to leave the position in which the god placed him. As one form of a violent death, *biaiothanasia*, suicide is classified lowest. Dying a natural death is at the top, because the time measured out is fulfilled. Disease is inferior as a cause of death, because it does not comply fully with nature, *physis*. In one violently killed, a *biaiothanatos*, a separation of body and soul is forced. Least blamable is death brought about by an inanimate object. It is worse to die as the victim of a murder, but – as said – lowest of all is a self-chosen death. In consequence of telescopic effects in which various periods have been blurred in the tradition, it is unclear which ideas are originally Orphic or Pythagorean and which are later interpretations. Euxitheos, a Pythagorean, declared 'that the souls of all were imprisoned in the body and in this life by way of a punishment and that the god had ruled that, if they did not stay there until he was willing to free them, they would be exposed to more and heavier penalties'. The Orphics based their interdiction of suicide on a myth: in consequence of the Titans' rebellion the soul had been poured into the body. Only when a person initiated in the Orphic mysteries became Dionysic would the soul be set free. For his part Plato justified his rejection of suicide with rational arguments, but atavistic abhorrence. Orphism and Pythagoreanism gave his ideas the air of old wisdom. The sages who figure in Plato's philosophy and mysticism often use tradition as an argument[21].

Even suicides held in honour by tradition are questioned by the Academics: Brutus' self-destruction according to them was 'not holy' (*ouch hosion*). The most forceful motive for suicide, shame (*pudor*), is rejected by the followers of Plato: even if the sage has lost face he will not withdraw from life. This opinion, at least according to Diogenes Laertios, prevailed among those who continued the Academic tradition[22].

In the course of the third century AD New Platonism establishes itself as the dominant philosophical school. Its rejection of suicide becomes a commonplace in philosophical as well as in religious reflection. The views of Neo-Platonism were put forward by Plotinos in his *About removing oneself rationally*. This monograph has been lost, but its content is summarized by a later author as: it is out of order (*atopon*) to lead oneself out in advance of the time determined, before the binder unties. In Plotinos' *Enneads* these views are related in a special chapter about leading out (*exagoge*) formulated in the style of commandments: 'Thou shalt not lead out, in order not to go outside thyself'. By an enforced separation of body and soul, the harmony between them is disturbed and one does violence to the time predisposed, the *heimarmenos chronos*. Views like this are not the exclusive possession of the narrow circle of the professional sages. When Julian the Apostate was dying, he thanked the gods for freeing his soul from his body. He added to this statement that it was absurd and undignified to invite death when the time had not come, or to reject it when the moment was there. In that age the Christian rejection is based on these Neo-Platonic views; only later are biblical justifications added to the argument. Prudentius' *Battle of the Soul*, for instance, takes the Neo-Platonic line: suicide is disapproved of, while in it *Patientia* is beaten by *Ira*. Anger in its rage breaks its sword into pieces, but stabs itself with the stump left. The scene is depicted in medieval manuscripts[23].

So the Christian interdiction of suicide is formulated only late and at first in Neo-Platonic terms. As we saw, in the first centuries suicides were regarded as unhappy persons who in due time could be converted by apostles. About 200 AD Tertullian does not hesitate to use freely ancient examples of self-killing to argue his plea for a change in the legal regulations on being a Christian. The law forbidding people to be Christian does not have to be valid for all time. Even the Spartans have improved Lycurgus' laws, 'although he disposed of himself by *inedia*'. In a different context the Spartan law-giver is the standard for equanimity (*animi aequitas*); he demonstrated this quality by *apokarteresis* when the Spartans corrected his laws. But the Christians possess that virtue to a still higher degree, for they express their thanks even when having been condemned. As regards torture, they are not inferior to Mucius Scaevola who had his right hand burned. They have the mental force, *vigor mentis*, of an Empedokles, who gave himself completely to the fires of Etna. Christians have the chastity of the foundress of Carthage, Dido, who made use of the pyre to escape a second marriage. Even Lucretia is put forward as a prefiguration of Christian virtue in *On exhortation to chastity*. Many centuries later, when the influence of St Augustine's condemnation had abated, Lucretia would become one of the 'good heathens' once more. According to Tertullian the Christian martyrs are in their ways of dying superior to 'those who earned praise by means of their own sword or by a similar rather mild death'. Of course, these examples are referred to in a rhetorical context by an author who was well versed in the ancient traditions. And it is evident that the apologist tries to beat the (supposed) opponent with his own weapons, but if in Tertullian's environment suicide was out of the question, he certainly would have omitted these arguments as apologetic texts were intended to be read by the Christian rank and file as well as by the pagan authorities that were formally addressed[24].

Martyrdom forces the Christian to take a moral position. In the end the orthodox standpoint is established that it is not permitted to seek death, that one is not allowed to expose oneself to excessive risks of temptation and finally that self-killing is the worst sin imaginable. Cyprianus' reaction to the problems of avoiding martyrdom or subjecting oneself to it, is still dictated by a pastoral approach. He himself fled the city of Carthage, because he thought it his duty to assist his brethren in their desolation. While defending his behaviour he says that the Christian doctrine forbids giving oneself up to the authorities. This interdiction is not prescribed by a general taboo on suicide, but by the anguish of the shepherd who fears that his sheep will falter when put to the test. In a letter he exhorts his flock to keep calm and not to be infected by an irresponsible urge to seek martyrdom: 'let nobody give himself up to the pagans on his own initiative'. Clemens of Alexandria has a more formal argument against provoking one's own death: a Christian who gives himself up causes another to sin. He makes his executioner a murderer. In general, the Egyptian theologian sees Christians who precipitate their death as self-killers, not as martyrs:

> Nor do we approve those who jump to their death. For there are those, only in name our people, who hurry to give themselves up from hatred against the Creator [*demiourgos*], they who die a sorry death. We say that they lead themselves out without giving evidence [of their faith: *martyrion*], even if they are punished by the state . . . . They give themselves up to a senseless death, like the Indian gymnosophists to the fire[25].

Christian doctrine and practice do not always go hand in hand. Cyprianus does discourage giving oneself up to the persecuting authorities, but he does not disapprove of such behaviour in principle. Tertullian in his writing *On the crown* is so carried away by his own enthusiasm for the soldier who refused to wear the wreath which had a pagan background, that his text almost becomes a plea for provoking martyrdom. The shifts and doubts in the Christian attitude emerge in the revisions of the stories about martyrs. In the Greek tale about Karpos, Papylos and Agathonike the latter *spontaneously* leapt on the pyre on which Karpos had just met his death. To her Karpos' fate sounded like a divine call and she exclaimed: 'This meal is prepared for me. I have to join in and eat of this glorious meal'. The bystanders shouted: 'Think of your son', but she told them that he had God. She put off her clothes – in the later Latin version the public is moved by the spectacle of such a beautiful body given to the flames. Thereupon she threw herself on the pyre, jubilating. But the later Latin Acts of the Martyrs tell a different story: she *was* arrested and *was* executed. When Christian ethics with respect to suicide were established, around 400 AD, Ambrose and Augustine struggle to find an excuse for the self-killings of Christian females done in order to escape being violated by the executioner. In the same period Jerome has unreserved praise for the Milesian girls who killed themselves in order to experience 'nothing indecent' from the Gauls. His opinion does not differ from the way in which Eusebios the church-historian in the first half of the fourth century had described various self-killings by Christian women and girls without any sign of disapproval[26].

Quintilian had presented as rather ridiculous the position that somebody who killed himself was a murderer. In principle, killing oneself differed from killing another person. But Lactantius roundly says that the philosophers who laid hands upon themselves were murderers. The divine law defines them as *homicidae*. Lactantius' argument is Neo-Platonic in character: God has given the soul the temporal abode of the body (*temporale corporis habitaculum*). It is not for a human being to migrate without an explicit order from him who assigns residences to souls. Supplementary to this is the command: 'One should not do violence to nature'[27].

These are still motives borrowed from Neo-Platonism. No arguments were derived from Scripture. Finally, Augustine appeals

to the Bible as an authority for condemnation of suicide. He needs
the backing of the Holy Word because he is fighting the heretical
Donatists who acknowledged as martyrs people whom Augustine
saw as suicides. They appealed to the Old Testament in which
Saul and Samson gave legitimation to self-killing. If the Donatists
had been acquainted with the Jewish interpretation of the biblical
doctrine, they would have found some support there: 'Better it is to
kill or to have killed oneself than to commit adultery, incest or
murder or be forced to do so'. For the Donatists who actually
followed these Maccabean lines of thinking those who provoked
their own death or killed themselves, were also martyrs. Under a
rock at Ain M'lila, 43 kilometres south of Cirta in Algeria, rough
stones have been found, inscribed with a name, month and the
Latin word *redditum*, which must mean here something like
'compensated, settled'. There the Circumcellions, the activists
among the Donatists, are said to have committed their ritual self-
destruction. In order to differentiate between authentic, orthodox
martyrs and false Donatist suicides Augustine looks in their
common authority the Bible for arguments against a self-chosen
death. Jesus' refusal to obey Satan's request to throw himself
from the Temple's pinnacles is seen by the father of the church as
the rejection of self-killing as an act of the devil. But the ten
commandments furnish him with his key argument. What for
Quintilian had been a shaky position in a faked controversy, is
actually held by the bishop of Hippo: 'Whoever kills himself, is a
murderer' (*qui se ipsum occidit, homicida est*), for the commandment
'Thou shalt not kill' implies a general prohibition of killing human
beings – 'neither another, nor yourself'. Starting from this biblical
position Augustine reviews the classical examples: Regulus is
superior to Cato, for the former *had* himself killed by the
Carthaginians, whereas the sage of Utica laid hands upon himself.
Kleombrotos was far from ridiculous for jumping into eternity: at
least he was after a better life. Everything is judged by Augustine
in terms of sin: the Christian women who killed themselves to
escape rape deserve human compassion, but not approval, because
in cases of violation it was not they but their persecutors who were
the sinners (as we saw Jerome found chastity worth the sacrifice).
In this reversal of traditional values even Lucretia is dethroned.
What was it that she could reprove herself for, Augustine asks,
fully disregarding the argument of objective *pudor*. The mere fact
that she killed herself points to some feeling of guilt. Augustine's

infamous suggestion is: maybe she had felt sinful pleasure while being raped.[28]

So it was Augustine who defined the Christian doctrine that would find its way into the regulations of canonical law. In the centuries that followed Augustine, Church councils would make his theological and moral views the rules for the practical behaviour of the church: attempted suicide was punished by ecclesiastical sanctions and suicides were only accorded a 'dog's burial'. Judas became popular in the iconography as the model sinner who lost all hope, up to the point of doing away with himself. By taking his life into his own hands, the Christian usurps the place of God. So he is even denied Pliny's comfort that at least in being able to end his life man is superior to almighty, but horribly ever-lasting god[29].

APPENDIX A:
960 CASES OF SELF-KILLING

name[1]	sex[2]	culture[3]	method	motive	accomplishment[4]	reality[5]	source[6]
Abderites	m	G	hanging	?	+	–	Philogelos 112
abdicatus venenum terens	m	R	poison	taedium vitae	–	–	Sen. Rhet. Contr. 7,3
Abydeni	?	G	various means	desperata salus	+	+	Pol. 16,34, 9–12
academicus	m	G	hanging	furor	+	–	Epikt. Diatr. 2,20,31
Achaios	m	G	weapons	desperata salus	–	+	Pol. 8,20,6
Achilles	m	G	weapons	dolor	–	?	Hom. Il.18, 34
Acroteleutium	f	R	?	dolor	–	?	Plaut. Mil. 1239–41
Admetos	m	G	various means	dolor	–	?	Eur. Alk. 897
Adrastos	m	n	weapons	pudor	+	+	Her. 1, 45
Adrastos	m	G	fire	devotio	+	?	Hyg. Fab. 242
aeger dominus	m	R	poison	inpatientia	?	–	Sen. Rhet. Contr. 3,9

1 The Greek names are given in a transcription which keeps as close as possible to the ancient spelling. When no name is given in the source, a Latin circumscription has been used, e.g. *academicus* for a follower of the Academy, *aeger dominus* for 'the ill master'; this pseudonym always is indicated in the text of the book, often between brackets.

2 m=male, f=female, n=non-human, ?=groups of both sexes.

3 G=Greek, R=Roman, n=neither Greek nor Roman (barbarian).

4 +=suicide committed, –=suicide not committed (attempt, consideration, wish, curse), ?=result unknown.

5 +=true (i.e. by the source presented as historically true), –= unreal, ?= unknown or dubious.

6 Here the primary source is given, i.e. the source which is the first attestation of a case, or – in a few instances – which is the most important documentation.

aeger medicum consulens	m	G	hanging	inpatientia	–	–	Philogelos 183
Aeginetae	?	G	hanging	desperata salus	+	?	Ov. Met. 7,604
Aelius	m	R	weapons	inpatientia	+	?	A.P. 7,233+234
Aemilia Lepida	f	R	?	pudor	+	+	Tac. An. 6,40, 4 (6,46,4)
Aemilius Scaurus	m	R	weapons	pudor	+	+	Val. Max. 5, 8, 4
Aemilius Scaurus, Mam.	m	R	?	pudor	+	?	Tac. An. 6,29, 7(6,35,7)
Aemilius Sybaritis	m	G	weapons	desperata salus	+	+	Plout. Mor. 310F
Afranius Dexter	m	R	?	?	+	?	Plin. Ep. 8,14,12
Afranius Potitus, P.	m	R	?	necessitas	+	+	Cass. Dio. 59, 8,3
Afranius Quintianus	m	R	?	necessitas	+	+	Tac. An. 15,70, 2
Agathokles	m	G	weapons	exsecratio	+	+	Diod. 20, 21,4
Agathonike	f	G	fire	iactatio	–	+	Acta SS.Mart. :Karpos e.a.
Aglauros et Herse	f	G	jumping	furor	+	?	Paus.1,18,2
Agrigentini multi	?	G	?	desperata salus	+	+	Diod.13, 89,2
Agrios	m	G	?	pudor	+	?	Hyg.Fab.242,1
Agrippina maior	f	R	inedia	dolor	+	+	Suet.Tib.53,2
Agrippina minor	f	R	?	pudor	+	–	Cass.Dio 61(62),14,3
Aiax	m	G	weapons	pudor	+	–	Hom.Od.11,541–567
Aigeus	m	G	jumping	desperata salus	+	?	Plout.Thes.22
Aithra	f	G	?	dolor	+	?	Hyg.Fab.243,2
Albucilla	f	R	weapons	pudor	–	+	Tac.An. 6,48, 6(6,54,6)
Albucius Silus	m	R	inedia	inpatientia	+	+	Suet.Rhet.6
Alexander	m	G	weapons	pudor	+	–	Plout.Alex.51
Alkestis	f	G	?	devotio	+	+	Hyg.Fab.243,4
Alkestis in Odessos	f	G	?	devotio	+	+	Peek,Gr.Versinschr.I2088a
Alketas	m	G	?	pudor	+	?	Diod.18, 46,7
Alkinoe	f	G	jumping	mala conscientia	+	?	Parthenios Er.Path.27,2
Althaia	f	G	weapons	dolor	+	?	Ov.Her. 9,157
Althaimenes	m	G	jumping	pudor	+	+	Apoll.3,2,2,3

APPENDIX A

name	sex	culture	method	motive	accomplishment	reality	source
Amata	f	n	hanging	dolor	+	?	Verg.Aen.12,603
Ameinas	m	G	weapons	exsecratio	+	?	Konon,frg.24(FGrH I 197)
Amilkas (Hamilkar)	m	n	fire	pudor	+	+	Her.7,167
Amophinome	f	G	weapons	exsecratio	–	?	Diod. 4, 52,5
Amphikrates	m	G	inedia	desperata salus	+	+	Plout.Luc.22,5
Amphinomene	f	G	weapons	pudor	+	?	Diod. 4, 50,2
Anaxagoras	m	G	?	pudor	+	+	Diog.Laert.2, 13
Anaxis	m	G	?	taedium vitae	+	?	A.P. 9,574
Anchouros	m	n	jumping	devotio	+	+	Plout.Mor.306F
ancilla Graeca	f	G	hanging	desperata salus	–	+	Val.Max.7, 3 ext.5
Andromachos	m	G	?	pudor	+	+	Xen.Hell.7,4,19
Anicius Cerialis	m	R	?	pudor	+	+	Tac.An.16,17, 9
Annius	m	n	jumping	pudor	+	?	Plout.Mor.315F
Antalkidas	m	G	inedia	desperata salus	+	+	Plout.Artox.22,7
Anteius Rufus	m	R	weapons	necessitas	+	+	Tac.An.16,14, 6
Anthia 1	f	G	?	desperata salus	–	–	Xenoph.Eph.2, 1, 4 sqq
Anthia 2	f	G	?	devotio	–	–	Xenoph.Eph.2, 4, 5 sqq
Anthia 3	f	G	poison	desperata salus	–	–	Xenoph.Eph.3, 5, 7 sqq
Anthia 4	f	G	?	dolor	–	–	Xenoph.Eph.4, 5, 6
Anthia 5	f	G	?	desperata salus	–	–	Xenoph.Eph.5, 8
Antigenes	m	G	weapons	pudor	–	+	Plout.Alex.70
Antigone	f	G	hanging	desperata salus	+	?	Soph.Ant.1221
Antikleia	f	G	?	dolor	+	?	Hyg.Fab.243,1
Antilochos	m	G	provocation	devotio	+	?	Pind.Pyth.6,28
Antinoos	m	R	jumping	devotio	+	?	Cass.Dio 69,11,2–4
Antiochos	m	G	inedia	dolor	–	+	Plout.Demetr.38,2
Antipatros	m	G	?	dolor	+	?	Philostr.Bioi Soph.2,24

Name			Means	Motive			Reference
Antipatros Tarsensis	m	G	poison	*inpatientia*	+	+	Diog.Laert.4, 64
Antipoini filiae	f	G	?	*devotio*	?	+	Paus.9,17,1
Antisthenes	m	G	weapons	*inpatientia*	?	–	Julian.Apaid.kun.181B
Antistia Pollita	f	R	weapons	*fides*	+	+	Tac.An.16,11, 4
Antistius Vetus	m	R	weapons	*necessitas*	+	+	Tac.An.16,11, 4
Antonia	f	R	?	*necessitas*	+	+	Cass.Dio 59, 3,6
anus Cea	f	G	poison	*iactatio*	+	+	Val.Max.2, 6,8
anus quaedam	f	R	hanging	*taedium vitae*	–	+	Apul.Met. 6,30
Anytos et Meletos	m	G	hanging	*desperata salus*	?	+	Plout.Mor.538A
Apicata	f	R	?	*desperata salus*	+	+	CIL XIV,4533cII,r.17/18
Apicius (Gavius)	m	R	poison	*pudor*	+	+	Sen.Helv.10, 8–19
Apokarteron	m	G	*inedia*	*iactatio*	–	–	Cic.Tusc.1,34,84
Apollonia	f	R	fire	*desperata salus*	+	+	Eus.H.E. 6,41
Appius Claudius	m	R	?	*pudor*	+	+	Liv. 3,58, 6
Apriate	f	G	jumping	*pudor*	?	+	Parthenios Er.Path.26,2
Aquilius Florus	m	R	weapons	*dolor*	+	+	Cass.Dio 51, 2,6
Aquillius	m	R	weapons	*pudor*	?	+	Diod.37, 27,2
Arachne	f	G	hanging	*pudor*	+	+	Ov.Met. 6,134
Arbogast	m	R	?	*desperata salus*	+	+	Oros.7,35,19
Archelaos	m	G	?	*exsecratio*	–	–	Plout.Sulla 23,9
Ardiaii	?	n	jumping	*dolor*	+	+	Athen.10,443C
Arganthone	f	G	*inedia*	*dolor*	+	+	Parthenios Er.Path.36,5
Argi pater	m	R	various means	*dolor*	?	+	Luc.Phars.3,748
Argivi nobiles	m	G	?	*pudor*	+	+	Diod.15, 58,2
Ariadne	f	G	hanging	*dolor*	?	+	Plout.Thes.20
Aristagoras	m	G	provocation	*pudor*	+	+	A.P. 7,231
Aristeides	m	G	hanging	*desperata salus*	?	+	A.P. 9,149 + 150 + 255
Aristodemos	m	G	?	*desperata salus*	?	+	Paus.4,13,4
Aristodemos erastes	m	G	?	*fides*	?	+	Athen.13,602D
Aristomenes	m	R	hanging	*desperata salus*	–	–	Apul.Met. 1,16
Aristoteles	m	G	poison	*pudor*	+	+	A.P. 7,107
Aristotimi uxor	f	G	hanging	*desperata salus*	+	+	Plout.Mor.253B
Arria Prisca 1	f	R	various means	*fides*	+	–	Plin.Ep.3,16,12

name	sex	culture	method	motive	accomplishment	reality	source
Arria Prisca 2	f	R	weapons	fides	+	+	Mart.1,13
Arruntii uxor	f	R	inedia	dolor	+	+	App.Emph.4, 4,21
Arruntius Furius	m	R	?	desperata salus	+	?	Cass.Dio 60,15,3
Arruntius, Lucius	m	R	weapons	taedium vitae	+	?	Tac.An. 6,48, 3(6,54,3)
Artapates	m	n	weapons	fides	+	?	Xen.Anab.1,8,29
Asinius Gallus	m	R	inedia	?	+	?	Tac.An. 6,23, 1(6,29,1)
Assaon	m	G	?	mala conscientia	+	?	Parthenios Er.Path.33,3
Astyanax	m	G	jumping	necessitas	+	+	Sen.Troades 1102
Atanius Secundus	m	R	?	necessitas	+	+	Cass.Dio 59, 8,3
Athenienses multi	?	G	hanging	?	+	+	Plout.Ant.70
Atheniensis iuvenis	m	G	?	dolor	+	+	Aelianus,Poik.hist. 9,39
athleta aeger	m	G	various means	inpatientia	+	+	Epikt.Diatr.1,2,25–26
Atilius Septicianus, P.	m	R	?	inpatientia	+	?	CIL V 5278
Atimetus libertus	m	R	hanging	mala conscientia	–	+	CIL VI, 12649, r.14/15
Atratinus	m	R	?	taedium vitae	+	+	Hier. Chron. 189,4
Atticus	m	R	inedia	inpatientia	+	+	Nep. Att. 21–22
Atticus Vestinus	m	R	weapons	necessitas	+	+	Tac. An. 15,69,3
Aufidius Victorinus	m	R	?	desperata salus	+	+	Cass. Dio 72 (73), 11,2
Augustinus	m	R	?	dolor	–	+	Aug. Conf. 4,6,11
Aulos	m	G	hanging	pudor	+	+	A.P. 11, 164
Autokles et Epikles	m	G	poison	iactatio	+	+	Athen. 12,537C
Axiothea et affines	f	G	?	pudor	+	+	Diod. 20,21,2
Bacchantes quidam	?	R	?	desperata salus	+	?	Liv. 39,17,5
Bagoas	m	n	poison	necessitas	+	+	Diod. 17,5,6
barbarus in naumachia	m	R	weapons	desperata salus	+	+	Sen. Ep. 70,26
Barea Soranus	m	R	?	necessitas	+	+	Tac. An. 16,33,2
Basilida filia	f	G	hanging	desperata salus	+	+	Suidas s.v. Pythagoras Eph

Basilo	f	G	?	dolor	?	+	A.P. 7,517
Bassulus, Pomponius	m	R	?	taedium vitae	+	+	CIL IX,1164
Berenike	f	G	poison	necessitas	+	–	Plout. Luc.18,6–7
Berenikes mater	f	G	poison	fides	+	+	Plout. Luc.18,6–7
bestiarius germanus	m	R	various means	pudor	+	+	Sen. Ep. 70,20
bibax femina	f	R	inedia	necessitas	+	+	Plin. N.H. 14,89
Bisaltia	f	n	weapons	dolor	+	+	Plout. Mor. 311D
Blossius	m	R	?	desperata salus	+	+	Plout. T. Gracch. 20,7
Boges/Bytes	m	n	fire	pudor	?	+	Her. 7,107
Boiska	f	G	hanging	pudor	+	+	A.P. 7,493
Boudicca	f	n	poison	pudor	?	+	Tac. An. 14,37,2
Boupalos et Athenis	m	G	hanging	pudor	?	+	Hor. Epod. 6,14
Brennos	m	n	weapons	devotio	?	+	Diod. 22,9,2
Britomartis-Diktynna	f	G	jumping	pudor	?	+	Kallim.Hymn.in Artem.195
Brutulus Papius	m	n	?	pudor	+	+	Liv. 8,39,14
Brutus	m	R	weapons	pudor	+	+	Vell. 2,70,5
Brutus, Decimus	m	R	weapons	desperata salus	+	+	Cass. Dio 46,54,1
Byblis	f	G	hanging	dolor	?	+	Ov. Ars am. 1,283
Bytes	m	G	jumping	furor	?	–	Diod. 5,50,5
Caecilius Agricola	m	R	weapons	pudor	+	+	Cass. Dio 76 (77), 5,6
Caecilius Classicus	m	R	?	pudor	?	+	Plin. Ep. 3,9,5
Caecilius Classicus, C.	m	R	?	pudor	?	+	Plin. Ep. 3,9,5
Caecilius Cornutus	m	R	?	taedium vitae	?	?	Tac. An. 4,28,2
Caecilius Metellus	m	R	weapons	pudor	+	+	Val. Max. 3,2,13
Caecilius, P. Metellus	m	R	weapons	pudor	+	+	Liv. Per. 114
Caelius	m	R	weapons	pudor	+	+	Val. Max. 4,7,5
Caesar apud Dyrrhachium	m	R	?	pudor	+	–	Suet. Caes. 36
Caesar apud Mundam	m	R	?	pudor	+	–	Suet. Caes. 36
Caesar apud Pharsalum	m	R	weapons	pudor	+	–	Luc. Phars. 7,309

name	sex	culture	method	motive	accomplish-ment	reality	source
Caesellius Bassus	m	R	?	pudor	+	+	Tac. An. 16,3,2
Caldus Caelius	m	R	various means	pudor	+	+	Vell. 2,120,6
Calpurnia, Antistii	f	R	weapons	fides	+	+	Vell. 2,26,3
Calpurnius Piso, C.	m	R	weapons	desperata salus	+	+	Tac. An. 15,59,7
Calpurnius Piso, Cn.	m	R	weapons	pudor	+	?	Tac. An. 3,15,6
Calpurnius Piso, L.	m	R	?	desperata salus	+	+	Tac. An. 4,21,5
Calvisius Sabinus	m	R	?	pudor	+	+	Cass. Dio 59,18,4
Campani	m	n	?	desperata salus	+	+	Diod. 19,76,5
Caninius Rebilus	m	R	weapons	inpatientia	+	+	Tac. An. 13,30,2
Cannutia Crescentina	f	R	jumping	desperata salus	+	+	Cass. Dio 77 (78), 16,3
Canulia	f	R	weapons	pudor	+	?	Plout. Mor. 312D
Caparronia Vestalis	f	R	hanging	pudor	+	+	Oros. 4,5,9
captivus Romanus	m	R	provocation	devotio	+	+	Tac. Hist. 4,34,4
Carmulus	m	R	?	pudor	+	+	Suet. Tib. 61
Cascae fratres	m	R	weapons	desperata salus	+	?	Anth. Lat. 1,338, nr.457
Cassius	m	R	weapons	pudor	+	+	Vell. 2,70,2
Cato Uticensis	m	R	weapons	pudor	+	+	Cic. Phil. 2,6,12
Catuvolcus	m	n	hanging	taedium vitae	+	+	Caes. B.G. 6,31,5
Censorinus	m	R	weapons	pudor	+	+	Plout. Crass. 25
Cestius	m	R	fire	desperata salus	+	+	App. Emph. 4,4,26
Cestius Macedonicus	m	R	weapons	desperata salus	+	+	Vell. 2,74,4
Chaireas 1	m	G	?	dolor	−	−	Chariton 3, 3, 1
Chaireas 2	m	G	jumping	desperata salus	−	−	Chariton 3, 5, 6
Chaireas 3	m	G	?	dolor	−	−	Chariton 5, 2, 5
Chaireas 4	m	G	hanging	dolor	−	−	Chariton 5, 10, 6
Chaireas 5	m	G	inedia	dolor	−	−	Chariton 6, 2, 8
Chaireas 6	m	G	weapons	dolor	−	−	Chariton 6, 2, 11

Charilla	f	G	hanging	*pudor*	+	+	Plout. Mor. 293D
Charite 1	f	G	*inedia*	*dolor*	–	–	Ap. Met. 8,7,4
Charite 2	f	G	weapons	*pudor*	+	–	Ap. Met. 8,14
Charmion	f	G	poison	*fides*	+	+	Plout. Ant. 85
Charondas	m	G	weapons	*iactatio*	+	+	Diod. 12,19,2
Chilonis	f	G	hanging	*desperata salus*	–	+	Plout. Pyr. 27,9
Chloe 1	f	G	?	*dolor*	–	–	Longos 4,18,2
Chloe 2	f	G	?	*dolor*	–	–	Longos 4,27,2
christiani Antiocheni	?	R	jumping	*desperata salus*	+	+	Eus. H.E. 8,12
christiani Nicomedenses	?	R	fire	*iactatio*	+	+	Eus. H.E. 8,6
Cicero in exilio	m	R	?	*pudor*	–	+	Cic. Fam. 7,3,3/4
Cicero post Pharsalum	m	R	?	*pudor*	–	+	Cic. Att. 3,7,2
Cicero proscriptus	m	R	weapons	*exsecratio*	–	+	Plout. Cic. 47
Cimbrorum principes	m	n	weapons	*pudor*	+	+	Oros. Hist. 5,16,19
Circumcelliones	?	R	jumping	*iactatio*	+	+	MacKendrick, p.263
citati ad causam	m	R	various means	*pudor*	+	+	Suet. Tib. 61
cives divites	?	R	?	*desperata salus*	+	+	Cass. Dio 59,18,3
cives divites quidam	?	R	?	*desperata salus*	+	+	Cass. Dio 63 (62), 17,1
cives divites quidam	?	R	weapons	*pudor*	+	+	Suet. Cal. 39
Claudius	m	R	?	*inpatientia*	–	?	Suet. Claud. 31
Claudius Senecio	m	R	?	*necessitas*	+	+	Tac. An. 15,70,2
Clodius Albinus	m	R	?	*necessitas*	+	+	Aur. Vict. Caes. 20,8
Clodius Eprius	m	R	weapons	*desperata salus*	+	+	Cass. Dio 66 (65), 16,4
Clodius Quirinalis	m	R	poison	*pudor*	+	+	Tac. An. 13,30,1
Clusia	f	R	jumping	*pudor*	–	?	Plout. Mor. 308F
Coma	m	G	various means	*devotio*	+	+	Val. Max. 9,12 ext.1
Comensis maritus	m	R	jumping	*inpatientia*	+	+	Plin. Ep. 6,24, 2–5
Comensis uxor	f	R	jumping	*dolor*	+	+	Plin. Ep. 6,24, 2–5
coniurati contra Galbam	m	R	?	*desperata salus*	+	+	Plout. Galba 15

name	sex	culture	method	motive	accomplish-ment	reality	source
coniurati multi	m	R	?	desperata salus	+	+	Cass. Dio 60,15,5
conspirata	f	R	weapons	pudor	+	+	Cass. Dio 58,27,4
consul alter AD 39	m	R	weapons	pudor	+	+	Cass. Dio 59,20,3
consulares et praetorii	m	R	?	pudor	+	+	Plout. Caes. 53
Corbulo, Domitius	m	R	weapons	necessitas	+	+	Tac. Hist. 2,76,3
Corellius Rufus	m	R	inedia	inpatientia	+	+	Plin. Ep. 1,12, 1–11
Coriolanus	m	R	poison	pudor	+	?	Cic. Brut. 10,42
Cornelia, Calvisii uxor	f	R	?	pudor	+	+	Cass. Dio 59,18,4
Cornelia, Pompeii uxor	f	R	various means	dolor	–	+	Luc. Phars. 654–661
Cornelius Gallus	m	R	weapons	pudor	+	+	Suet. Aug. 66
Cornelius Longus	m	R	weapons	pudor	+	+	Josephus Pol. Ioud. 6,188
Cornelius Merula	m	R	weapons	exsecratio	+	+	Vell. 2,22,2
Cornelius Scipio	m	R	poison	pudor	+	?	App. Emph. 1,3,20
Cornificia	f	R	weapons	necessitas	+	+	Cass. Dio 77 (78), 16,6a
Cornutus	m	R	?	desperata salus	+	+	App. Emph. 3,13,92
Crassi tribuni militum	m	R	weapons	pudor	+	+	Plout. Crass. 25
Crassus	m	R	weapons	pudor	+	+	Liv. Per. 80
Crassus filius	m	R	weapons	desperata salus	+	+	Plout. Crass. 25
Crassus Mucianus	m	R	provocation	pudor	+	+	Val. Max. 3,2,12
Cremutius Cordus	m	R	inedia	pudor	+	+	Sen. Marc. 22, 6–7
Curtius	m	R	jumping	devotio	+	+	Liv. 7,6,4
custos Pauli et Silae	m	G	weapons	desperata salus	–	+	Praxeis Apostolon 16,27
Damokrita	f	G	weapons	pudor	+	+	Plout. Mor. 775E
Damon	m	R	hanging	exsecratio	?	–	Verg. Ecl. 8,60
Danae	f	G	hanging	pudor	–	?	Aisch. Diktuoulkoi frg. 168
Daphnis 1	m	G	?	pudor	–	–	Longos 4,18
Daphnis 2	m	G	jumping	pudor	–	–	Longos 4,22

Darii frater	m	n	weapons	*exsecratio*	+	+	Aelianus, Poik. hist. 9,42
Decebalus	m	n	?	*desperata salus*	+	+	Cass. Dio 68,14,3
Decentius	m	R	?	*necessitas*	+	–	Aur. Vict. Caes. 42,10
Decius Mundus	m	R	*inedia*	*dolor*	+	+	Josephus Ioud. Arch. 18,69
Decius Mus I	m	R	provocation	*devotio*	+	+	Liv. 8, 6+9
Decius Mus II	m	R	provocation	*devotio*	?	+	Liv.10,26,13–18
Decius Mus III	m	R	provocation	*devotio*	?	+	Cic.Tusc.1,89
Decius Vibellius	m	n	?	*inpatientia*	?	+	App.Samn.9,3
Deianeira	f	G	weapons	*pudor*	?	–	Soph.Trach. 881
Deinarchos	m	G	hanging	?	–	+	A.P.11,169
Deinokrates	m	G	?	*desperata salus*	+	+	Paus.8,51,8
delatores Thurini	m	G	?	*pudor*	+	+	Diod.12, 11,2
demens uxorem cedens	m	R	weapons	*dolor*	–	–	Sen.Rhet.Contr.6,7
Demetrios	m	G	weapons	*pudor*	–	+	Plout.Demet.49,9
Demo	f	G	hanging	*dolor*	?	+	A.P. 7,473
Demochares	m	R	weapons	*desperata salus*	+	+	Cass.Dio 49,10,3
Demokles	m	G	various means	*pudor*	+	+	Plout.Demetr.24,5
Demokritos	m	G	*inedia*	*inpatientia*	+	+	Louk.Makr.18
Demonassa	f	G	various means	*dolor*	+	+	Dio Chrys.Or.64,4
Demonassae filius	m	G	?	?	+	+	Dio Chrys.Or.64,3
Demonax	m	G	*inedia*	*inpatientia*	+	+	Louk.Dem.65
Demosthenes	m	G	poison	*pudor*	+	+	Plout.Dem.29
Demosthenes strategos	m	G	?	*pudor*	?	+	Plout.Nik.38
depugnaturi pro Calig.	m	R	provocation	*devotio*	–	–	Suet.Cal.14
Diaios	m	G	poison	*desperata salus*	+	+	Cass.Dio 21 (Zon.9,31)
Didius Iulianus	m	R	poison	*desperata salus*	+	–	SHA Did.Iul.8,7
Dido	f	n	weapons	*dolor*	?	+	Verg.Aen. 4,642–692
dikaios logos	n	G	hanging	?	?	?	Aristoph.Neph. 988
Dimnos	m	G	weapons	*desperata salus*	+	+	Diod.17, 79,6

name	sex	culture	method	motive	accomplishment	reality	source
Dimoites	m	G	weapons	dolor	+	+	Parthenios Er.Path.31
Diocletianus	m	R	poison	pudor	+	?	Aur.Vict.Epit.39,7
Diodoros Epicurius	m	G	weapons	inpatientia	+	+	Sen.Vit.19,1
Diodoros Kronos	m	G	?	pudor	+	+	Diog.Laert.2,112
Diogenes	m	G	various means	iactatio	+	?	Diog.Laert.6, 76
Diokles	m	G	weapons	iactatio	+	+	Diod.13, 33,3
Diokles Centurinus	m	G	hanging	pudor	+	+	Cic.Verr.2,3,56,129
Dionis filius	m	G	jumping	furor	+	+	Plout.Dio 55
Dionysii uxor	f	G	?	pudor	+	?	Plout.Dioon 3,1
Dionysios	m	G	?	dolor	-	-	Charitoon 3, 1
Dionysios epicurius	m	G	inedia	iactatio	+	+	Diog.Laert.7,167
Dionysios Metathemenos	m	G	inedia	inpatientia	+	+	Diog.Laert.7,167
Dionysos	m	G	various means	?	-	-	Aristoph.Batr.120 sqq.
Diophantos	m	G	hanging	?	-	?	A.P.11,111
Dioxippos	m	G	?	pudor	+	+	Diod.17,101,4
divinus	m	R	various means	iactatio	+	+	App.Emph.4, 1, 4
Dolabella	m	R	weapons	desperata salus	+	+	App.Emph.4, 8,62
Dolabellae satelles	m	R	weapons	fides	+	+	App.Emph.4, 8,62
Domitilla	f	R	?	pudor	+	+	Lebek ZPE 59 (1985) 7–8
Domitius Ahenobarbus, Cn	m	R	poison	pudor	-	+	Sen.Ben.3,24,1
Domitius Ahenobarbus, L.	m	R	poison	pudor	-	+	Plin.Nat.Hist. 7.186
Donatistae AD 347	?	R	various means	iactatio	+	+	Aug.Ep.185,12
Donatistae AD 410	?	R	?	desperata salus	+	+	Aug.Ep.185 III 12
Drusus Libo	m	R	?	pudor	+	+	Sen.Ep.70,10
dux Carthageniensium	m	n	weapons	pudor	+	+	Diod.20, 61,8
dux Romanus	m	R	?	?	+	+	Eus.H.E. 9, 6
Eiras	f	G	poison	fides	+	+	Plout.Ant.86

Eleazar Auran	m	n	various means	*devotio*	+	+	Josephus Ioud.Arch.12,374
Elektra	f	G	weapons	*fides*	?	−	Eur.El.688
Eleusinius sacerdos	m	G	weapons	*?*	+	−	Diog.Laert.6,4
Empedokles	m	G	fire	*iactatio*	?	+	Diog.Laert.8, 74
Ennia, Macronis uxor	f	R	?	*necessitas*	+	+	Cass.Dio 59,10,6
Epicharis	f	R	hanging	*devotio*	+	+	Tac.An.15,57, 2
Epikouros	m	G	various means	*iactatio*	+	+	A.P. 7,106
equus Scythicus	n	n	jumping	*pudor*	+	+	Arist.Hist.zoion 9,47
Erasistratos	m	G	poison	*inpatientia*	+	+	Stob.Anthol.3,7,5
erastes	m	G	hanging	*dolor*	−	+	Theokr.Id.23,36 sqq.
Erechthei filiae	f	G	weapons	*fides*	?	+	Apoll.3,15,4,5
Erigone	f	G	hanging	*dolor*	?	+	Apoll.3,14,7,3
eromenos	m	G	weapons	*dolor*	?	+	Konon Fl.16 (FGrH.26)
Eros	m	R	weapons	*fides*	+	+	Plout.Ant.76
Euadne Kapanei uxor	f	G	fire	*dolor*	?	+	Eur.Hik.1016
Euadne Peliae filia	f	G	?	*pudor*	?	−	Diod. 4, 52,5
Euenos	m	G	jumping	*pudor*	?	+	Hom.Il.Schol. 9,557–8
Eumenes	m	G	weapons	*pudor*	?	−	Plout.Eum.17
Euni socii	m	R	weapons	*desperata salus*	+	+	Diod.34/35,2,22
Euopis	f	G	hanging	*pudor*	+	+	Parthenios Er.Path.31
Euphraios	m	G	weapons	*pudor*	+	+	Dem.Phil.3,62
Euphrates	m	G	poison	*inpatientia*	+	+	Cass.Dio 69, 8,3
Euporus	m	R	weapons	*fides*	+	+	Vell.2,6,6
Euripidis admirator	m	G	hanging	*?*	+	−	Philemon frg.130
Europa	f	G	hanging	*desperata salus*	−	?	Hor.Od.3,27,57
Eurydike Arrhidaei uxor	f	G	hanging	*necessitas*	?	+	Diod.19, 11,7
Eurydike Kreontis uxor	f	G	weapons	*dolor*	+	+	Soph.Ant.1282;1315
Eurylochus	m	G	?	*?*	?	+	Liv.36,33, 6
exules multi	?	R	?	*necessitas*	+	+	Cass.Dio 67, 3,4 (2)

name	sex	culture	method	motive	accomplishment	reality	source
Fabius Maximus	m	R	?	pudor	+	?	Tac.An. 1, 5, 4
Fabius, Quintus	m	R	?	pudor	+	?	Liv. 6, 1, 7
Fannius Caepio	m	R	?	desperata salus	+	?	Mart.2,80
favens Felicis aurigae	m	R	jumping	fides	+	+	Plin.Nat.Hist. 7,186
femina se iugulans	f	G	hanging	?	+	+	Hipp.Ep.5,33 (L.5,230)
femina somniens	?	G	?	pudor	?	+	Artem.Oneir.5,63
feminae pendentes	f	G	hanging	?	+	+	Diog.Laert.6, 52
feminae quaedam	f	R	?	pudor	+	+	Aug.Civ.1,17
Festus	m	R	weapons	inpatientia	+	+	Mart.1,78
filia patris dementis	f	R	hanging	exsecratio	+	–	Sen.Rhet.Contr.10,3
filius caedere nolens	m	G	jumping	desperata salus	+	–	Sen.Rhet.Contr.9,4
filius quidam	m	R	?	fides	+	+	Suet.Aug.13
Firmus	m	R	?	necessitas	+	+	Oros.Hist.7,33, 6
Flavianus, Nicomachus	m	R	?	?	+	+	Rufinus Hist.eccl.11,33
Flavius Fimbria	m	R	weapons	desperata salus	+	+	Vell.2, 24,1
Flavius Scaevinus	m	R	?	necessitas	+	+	Tac.An.15,70, 3
Florianus	m	R	weapons	?	+	+	Aur.Vict.Epit.36,2
Floronia	f	R	?	desperata salus	+	+	Liv.22,57, 2
Fuficius Phango	m	R	?	desperata salus	+	+	App.Emph.5, 3,26
fugitivi Sicilienses	m	G	jumping	desperata salus	+	+	Diod.36,3,6
Fulcinius Trio	m	R	?	pudor	+	+	Tac.An. 6,38, 2 (6,44,2)
Fulvii uxor	f	R	weapons	pudor	+	+	Plout.Mor.508B
Fulvius	m	R	weapons	pudor	+	+	Plout.Mor.508B
Fulvius Flaccus M.f.	m	R	?	necessitas	+	+	App.Emph.1, 3,26
Fulvius Flaccus p.m.	m	R	hanging	furor	+	+	Liv.42,28,10–12
Furius Camillus, Marcus	m	R	?	pudor	+	+	Cass.Dio 60,15,3
Gadareni	m	n	various means	pudor	+	+	Josephus Ioud.Arch.15,358

Name			Means	Motive			Source
Gaiobomari socius	m	n	hanging	*pudor*	+	+	Cass.Dio 77 (78), 20,4
Gallaeci	?	n	various means	*desperata salus*	+	+	Oros.Hist.6,21, 8/9
Galli	m	n	provocation	*devotio*	+	+	Pol. 2,30, 4
Galli morientes	?	n	weapons	*desperata salus*	+	+	statue in Pergamon
Galli, Sabini socii	m	n	?	*desperata salus*	+	+	Plout.Mor.770D
Gamalani 5000	?	R	jumping	*desperata salus*	+	+	Josephus Pol.Ioud.4, 79
Gavius Silvanus	m	R	?	*mala conscientia*	+	+	Tac.An.15,71, 4
Geminus Fufius, C.	m	R	weapons	*pudor*	+	+	Cass.Dio 58, 4,6
Germanicus	m	R	?	*fides*	?	−	Tac.An. 1,35, 5–7
Gidica	f	R	hanging	*dolor*	?	+	Plout.Mor.314C
Glaukos	m	G	jumping	*furor*	−	+	Athen. 7,297A
Gnathon	m	G	weapons	*exsecratio*	+	−	Longos 4,16,4
Gobryas	m	n	weapons	*devotio*	−	−	Her.3, 78
Gordianus senior	m	R	hanging	*dolor*	+	+	SHA Gord.16,3
Gorgias	m	G	?	*inpatientia*	+	+	Louk.Makrobioi 23
Gorgos	m	G	?	*taedium vitae*	+	+	A.P. 7,731
Gracchus	m	R	weapons	*desperata salus*	+	+	Vell.2,6,6
Granius Marcianus	m	R	?	*pudor*	+	+	Tac.An. 6,38, 4 (6,44,4)
Granius Petronius	m	R	weapons	*pudor*	+	+	Plout.Caes.16
Gylippos	m	G	*inedia*	*pudor*	?	?	Athen. 6,234A
Habrok.& Anthiae matres	f	G	?	*dolor*	−	−	Xenoph.Eph.5, 6, 3
Habrok.& Anthiae patres	m	G	?	*dolor*	−	−	Xenoph.Eph.5, 6, 3
Habrokomes 1	m	G	?	*desperata salus*	−	−	Xenoph.Eph.2, 1, 4 sqq
Habrokomes 2	m	G	?	*desperata salus*	−	−	Xenoph.Eph.2, 7, 1
Habrokomes 3	m	G	?	*dolor*	−	−	Xenoph.Eph.3,10
Habrokomes 4	m	G	?	*dolor*	−	−	Xenoph.Eph.5,10, 5
Hadriani medicus	m	R	?	*fides*	+	+	SHA Hadr.24,13
Hadrianus	m	R	various means	*taedium vitae*	−	−	SHA Hadr.24, 8
haeretici multi	?	R	?	*iactatio*	+	+	Prok.Anekd.11

name	sex	culture	method	motive	accomplish-ment	reality	source
Haimon	m	G	weapons	desperata salus	+	?	Soph.Ant.1234–1239
Halia	f	G	jumping	pudor	+	?	Diod. 5, 55,7
Hampsicora	m	n	?	dolor	+	+	Liv.23,41, 4
Hannibal	m	n	poison	pudor	+	+	Diod.25, 19
Harpalyke	f	G	?	pudor	+	?	Parthenios Er.Path.13
Hasdrubal Gisconis	m	n	poison	desperata salus	+	+	Ap.Lib.38
Hasdrubalis uxor	f	n	jumping	pudor	+	+	Flor.1,21,17
Hegesiae discipuli	?	G	inedia	iactatio	+	?	Cic.Tusc.1,34,83
Hekabe	f	G	jumping	desperata salus	+	?	Hyg.Fab.111
Helena dolens	f	G	weapons	mala conscientia	–	?	Eur.Hel.298+355
Helena in Troia	f	G	?	pudor	–	?	Hom.II. 3,173
Helena petita	f	G	weapons	fides	–	?	Eur.Hel.839
Helena repetita	f	G	poison	desperata salus	–	?	Soph.frg.Radt 178
Helvius Blasio	m	R	weapons	fides	+	+	Cass.Dio 46,53,3
Herakles	m	G	fire	inpatientia	+	?	Soph.Trach.1252 sqq.
Herakles furens	m	G	?	dolor	–	?	Eur.Her.1246
Herennius Siculus	m	R	various means	desperata salus	+	+	Vell.2, 7,2
Hermione	f	G	hanging	mala conscientia	–	?	Eur.Andr.811
Hermon	m	G	hanging	dolor	+	?	A.P.11,264
Hero	f	G	jumping	desperata salus	+	?	Musaios 341
Herodes 1	m	n	weapons	desperata salus	–	+	Josephus Ioud.Arch.14,356
Herodes 2	m	n	weapons	inpatientia	–	+	Josephus Pol.Ioud.1,662
Hierax	m	G	hanging	?	+	+	P.Oxy.I, 51
Hierosolymitae a.Chr.63	?	n	jumping	desperata salus	+	+	Josephus Pol.Ioud.1,150
Hiketides	f	G	hanging	pudor	+	?	Aisch.Hik.465+787+803
Himilco	m	n	inedia	mala conscientia	–	+	Diod.14, 76,4
Hipparchia	f	G	?	exsecratio	–	+	Diog.Laert.6, 96

Name	sex	cat	means	motive			source
Hippitas	m	G	?	*desperata salus*	+	+	Plout.Kleom.37,13
Hippo	f	G	jumping	*pudor*	+	+	Val.Max.6, 1 ext.1
Hippodameia	f	G	?	*desperata salus*	?	+	Hyg.Fab.85
Hipponoos	m	G	fire	*devotio*	?	+	Hyg.Fab. 2
Hispani captivi	m	n	?	*pudor*	+	+	Diod.34/35,4,1
Hispani multi	m	n	?	*pudor*	+	+	Liv.34,17, 6
Hispanus puer captivus	m	n	*inedia*	*pudor*	+	+	Diod.34/35,4,1
homicida in se	m	R	weapons	*desperata salus*	−	−	Sen.Rhet.Contr.8,4
homines se iugulantes	m	G	weapons	?	+	+	Hipp.Sark.18(L,8,608)
Hostilius	m	R	poison	*pudor*	+	+	Cic.Att.12, 5, 3
Hyrkanos Josephi filius	m	n	?	?	+	+	Josephus Ioud.Arch.12,236
Ianus et fratres	m	R	hanging	*desperata salus*	?	+	Plout.Mor.307F
Iason	m	G	?	*dolor*	?	+	Diod. 4, 55,1
Ilione	f	G	?	*dolor*	?	+	Hyg.Fab.243,4
Indi obsessi	?	n	fire	*desperata salus*	?	+	Curt.9,4,7
Ino	f	G	jumping	*dolor*	?	+	Hyg.Fab. 2,5
Ioessa	f	G	various means	*dolor*	−	−	Louk.Hetair.Logoi 12,2
Iokaste (Hom:Epikaste)	f	G	hanging	*pudor*		−	Hom.Od.11,278−280
Iole	f	G	jumping	*pudor*	?	+	Plout.Mor.308F
Iotapatae superstites	m	n	weapons	*desperata salus*	?	+	Josephus Pol.Ioud.3,391
Iphias	m	G	fire	*fides*	?	−	Ov.Pont.3,1,111
Iphikrates	m	G	weapons	*pudor*	?	+	Sen.Rhet.Contr.6,5
Iphis	m	G	*inedia*	*dolor*	?	+	Eur.Hik.1104−1108
Isauri	?	n	fire	*desperata salus*	?	+	Diod.18, 22,4−7
Ischomachi filia	f	G	hanging	*pudor*	+	+	Andokides 1,125
Isidora	f	G	hanging	*exsecratio*	−	−	P.S.I.177
Isokrates	m	G	*inedia*	*taedium vitae*	+	+	Plout.Mor.837E
Iuba rex	m	n	weapons	*desperata salus*	+	+	Caes.B.Afr.94,2
Iubelius Taurea	m	n	weapons	*dolor*	+	+	Liv.26,15,15

name	sex	culture	method	motive	accomplishment	reality	source
Iudaei	m	n	various means	desperata salus	+	+	Cass.Dio 66(65), 6,3
Iulia Domna	f	R	inedia	pudor	+	+	Cass.Dio 78(79),23,1
Iulius Agrestis	m	R	weapons	devotio	+	+	Tac.Hist.3,54, 8/9
Iulius Alexander	m	R	weapons	desperata salus	+	+	Cass.Dio 72(73),14,3
Iulius Celsus	m	R	various means	desperata salus	+	+	Tac.An. 6,14, 2(6,20,2)
Iulius Fabius	m	R	jumping	pudor	?	+	Cass.Dio 69,19,4
Iulius Florus	m	n	weapons	desperata salus	+	+	Tac.An. 3,42, 4
Iulius Marinus	m	R	?	necessitas	+	+	Tac.An. 6,10, 2(6,16,2)
Iulius Montanus	m	R	?	necessitas	+	+	Tac.An.13,25, 2
Iulius Priscus	m	R	?	pudor	+	+	Tac.Hist.4,11, 8
Iulius Vindex	m	R	?	pudor	+	?	Plout.Galba 6
Iulius Antonius	m	R	?	necessitas	+	+	Vell.2,100
Iunii Blaesii	m	R	?	pudor	+	+	Tac.An. 6,40, 3(6,46,3)
Iunius Pullus	m	R	?	desperata salus	+	+	Cic.N.D.2,3,7
iuvenes Terracinenses	m	R	jumping	devotio	+	+	Acta S.S.Nov.1
Iuventius, M.Laterensis	m	R	weapons	devotio	+	+	Vell.2, 63
Judas	m	n	hanging	desperata salus	+	+	Matth.27:5
Kaineus	m	G	?	?	+	?	Hyg.Fab.242
Kalchas	m	G	?	pudor	+	?	Strabo 14,1,27
Kallikrateia	f	G	?	devotio	+	+	Peek,Gr.Versinschr.I1738
Kallikratidas	m	G	provocation	pudor	+	+	Diod.13, 97,4/5;13,98,1
Kallirhoe	f	G	?	pudor	-	-	Chariton 2, 5,12
Kallirhoe Calydonia	f	G	weapons	pudor	+	+	Paus.7,21,1
Kallirhoe Lyci filia	f	G	hanging	dolor	+	?	Plout.Mor.311C
Kallisthenes	m	G	?	dolor	?	+	Plout.Mor.772C
Kalyke	f	G	jumping	dolor	+	?	Athen.14,619E

214

Kalypso	f	G	?	*dolor*	+	?	Hyg.Fab.243,7
Kambles	m	n	weapons	*pudor*	+	?	Athen.10,415C
Kamma	f	n	poison	*desperata salus*	+	+	Plout.Mor.258B
Kanake	f	G	weapons	*pudor*	+	?	Eur.Aiolos
Karanos	m	n	fire	*iactatio*	+	+	Diod.17,107,4
Karneades	m	G	?	*inpatientia*	−	+	Diog.Laert.4, 64
Kastor et Pollyx	m	G	weapons	*pudor*	+	?	Eur.Hel.142
Kerkyraioi 1	?	G	various means	*desperata salus*	+	+	Thouk.3,81, 3
Kerkyraioi 2	?	G	various means	*desperata salus*	+	+	Thouk.4,48, 3
Kinyras	m	n	?	*pudor*	+	?	Hyg.Fab.242,4
Kios	m	n	various means	*dolor*	+	+	Diod.22, 13,6
Kleanthes	m	G	*inedia*	*inpatientia*	+	?	Diog.Laert.7,176
Kleite	f	G	hanging	*dolor*	+	?	Parthenios Er.Path.28,2
Kleitophon 1	m	G	weapons	*dolor*	−	−	Ach.Tat.3,16/17
Kleitophon 2	m	G	jumping	*desperata salus*	−	−	Ach.Tat.5,7
Kleitophon 3	m	G	?	*dolor*	−	−	Ach.Tat.7,6
Kleoboia	f	G	hanging	*mala conscientia*	+	?	Parthenios Er.Path.14,4
Kleombrotos	m	G	jumping	*iactatio*	+	?	A.P. 7,471
Kleomenes	m	G	weapons	*furor*	+	+	Her.6, 75
Kleomenes III	m	G	weapons	*pudor*	+	+	Plout.Kleom.37,14−16
Kleomenis amici	m	G	weapons	*pudor*	+	+	Plout.Kleom.37,13
Kleomenis filius	m	G	jumping	*dolor*	−	+	Plout.Kleom.38,3
Kleopatra	f	G	poison	*pudor*	+	+	Vell.2, 87,2
Kleopatrae eunuchus	m	n	poison	*fides*	+	+	Cass.Dio 51,14,3
Klymenos	m	G	?	*pudor*	+	?	Hyg.Fab.242,4
Klytaimnestra	f	G	hanging	*dolor*	−	?	Aisch.Agam.875/6
Kodros	m	G	provocation	*devotio*	+	?	Lykourgos, Kata Leokratous
Komasdo	m	G	hanging	*exsecratio*	−	−	Theokr.Id. 3,9+25
Koneiazomenai	f	G	poison	*desperata salus*	−	−	Men.Koneiazomenai

215

name	sex	culture	method	motive	accomplishment	reality	source
Koresos	m	G	weapons	dolor	+	+	Paus.7,21,1
Kratinos	m	G	?	devotio	+	?	Athen.13,602D
Kreusa	f	G	various means	pudor	−	?	Eur.Ion 1065
Krinippos	m	G	?	pudor	+	+	Xen.Hell.6,2,36
Kroisi uxor	f	n	jumping	desperata salus	−	+	Ktesias Pers.4
Kroisos	m	n	fire	pudor	−	+	Bakch.Epin.3,48/49
Kronion	m	G	?	pudor	+	+	P.Mich.5.231
Kyane	f	G	weapons	pudor	+	?	Plout.Mor.310C
Kyanippos	m	G	?	desperata salus	−	+	Parthenios Er.Path.10,4
Kyklops	m	G	jumping	desperata salus	−	−	Eur.Kykl.166
Labeo, Pac. Antistius	m	R	weapons	pudor	+	+	App.Emph.4,17,135
Labienus, Titus	m	R	various means	pudor	+	+	Sen.Contr.10 praef.7
Lactorius	m	R	jumping	devotio	+	+	Val.Max.4, 7, 2
Laelius	m	R	weapons	desperata salus	+	+	App.Emph.4, 7,56
Laetorius Mergus	m	R	?	pudor	+	+	Val.Max 6, 1,11
Laetus	m	R	poison	necessitas	+	+	SHA Car.3,4
laktistes Sokratis	m	G	hanging	pudor	+	+	Plout.Mor. 10C
Laodameia	f	G	fire.	fides	+	?	Hyg.Fab. 94,3
Latro	m	R	?	taedium vitae	+	+	Hier.Chron.194,1
latro senex	m	n	jumping	desperata salus	+	?	Josephus Pol.Ioud.1,313
Leda	f	G	hanging	pudor	+	+	Eur.Hel.200/1
legionarii Legionis Martiae	m	R	weapons	desperata salus	+	+	App.Emph.4,15,116
Lentulus	m	R	?	taedium vitae	+	?	Suet.Tib.49
Leokorides	f	G	?	devotio	+	?	Versnel, self-sacrifice p. 142
Leukippe	f	G	hanging	exsecratio	−	−	Ach.Tat.2,30,2
Leukippos	m	G	weapons	dolor	−	−	Parthenios Er.Path. 5,2
Libanios	m	G	?	dolor	−	+	Lib.Or.1,135

Licinii pater	m	R	poison	*inpatientia*	+	+	Plin.N.H.20,199
Licinius Macer	m	R	various means	*pudor*	+	?	Val.Max.9,12, 7
Ligarii uxor	f	R	*inedia*	*dolor*	+	+	App.Emph.4, 4,23
Ligarius	m	R	jumping	*dolor*	-	+	App.Emph.4, 4,22
Livius Drusus	m	R	weapons	?	+	+	Sen.Brev. 6,2
Livius Drusus, Liviae pater	m	R	weapons	*pudor*	+	+	Vell.2, 71,2
Lollius	m	R	poison	*pudor*	+	+	Vell.2,102
Longinus	m	R	poison	*devotio*	+	+	Cass.Dio 68,12,4
Lucanus	m	R	weapons	*necessitas*	+	+	Mart.7,21
Lucius asinus	m	R	?	*pudor*	-	-	Apul.Met.10,29
Lucius, Quintus	m	R	jumping	*inpatientia*	+	+	App.Emph.4, 4,27
Lucretia	f	R	weapons	*pudor*	+	+	Liv. 1,58,11
Lucretius	m	R	?	*furor*	-	?	Hier.Add.Chron.659 A.U.C.
Lupicini servus	m	R	hanging	?	+	+	Sulp.Sev.Vita Martini 9
Lutatius Catulus	m	R	various means	*pudor*	+	+	Diod.38,4,2/3
Lycidas	m	R	hanging	*dolor*	-	+	Calpurnius 3,87
Lycii	?	n	fire	*furor*	+	+	Plout.Brut.31
Lykambes	m	G	hanging	*pudor*	+	+	A.P. 7, 69+70+71
Lykourgos	m	G	*inedia*	*iactatio*	-	?	Plout.Lyk.29
Lykourgos Dryantis	m	G	?	*furor*	+	+	Hyg.Fab.242,2
Lysidamos	m	G	weapons	*dolor*	+	-	Plaut.Cas.307/8
Machaon	m	R	weapons	*furor*	+	+	Cass.Dio 59, 9,3
Macro	m	R	?	*necessitas*	+	+	Cass.Dio 59,10,6
magistratus curules	m	R	provocation	*devotio*	+	+	Liv. 5,41, 3
Magius, P. Magius Cilo	m	R	weapons	*furor*	+	?	Cic.Fam.4,12,2
Magnentius	m	R	?	*necessitas*	+	+	Aur.Vict.Caes.42,10
Mago	m	n	?	?	+	?	Plout.Tim.22
Maion	m	G	weapons	*pudor*	?	?	Stat.Theb.3,87-91
Maira, Erigones canis	n	G	jumping	*dolor*	+	+	Amp.2,6

name	sex	culture	method	motive	accomplish-ment	reality	source
Makareus	m	G	?	pudor	+	?	Eur.Aiolos
Makaria	f	G	?	devotio	+	?	Eur.Herakleid. 530 sqq.
Mallonia	f	R	weapons	pudor	+	+	Suet.Tib.45
Mamerkos	m	G	various means	desperata salus	–	+	Plout.Tim.34
Manlius Silanus	m	R	hanging	pudor	+	+	Val.Max.5, 8, 3
Marcellus	m	R	?	necessitas	+	+	SHA Hadr.15, 4
Marculus	m	R	jumping	iactatio	+	?	Frend p.179 n.5
Marcus Antonius in Parthia	m	R	weapons	pudor	–	+	Plout.Ant.48
Marcus Antonius in Alexandria	m	R	weapons	desperata salus	+	+	Vell.2, 87,2
Marcus Aurelius	m	R	inedia	taedium vitae	+	+	SHA Marcus 28,1
maritus reversus	m	R	hanging	desperata salus	+	–	Sen.Rhet.Contr.8,3
Marius	m	R	weapons	pudor	+	?	Diod.37, 29,4
Marius filius	m	R	?	desperata salus	+	+	Liv.Per. 88
Marius quidam	m	R	jumping	furor	+	+	Hor.Sat.2,3,276–80
Marsus	m	R	weapons	desperata salus	+	+	App.Emph.4, 8,62
Masadani	?	n	weapons	desperata salus	+	+	Josephus Pol.Ioud.7,400
matrona et filiae	f	R	weapons	pudor	+	+	Eus.H.E. 8,14
matrona ornata	f	R	jumping	pudor	+	+	Prok.Anekd. 7
matrona violata	f	R	?	pudor	+	+	Oros.5,24,3
matronae venenum terentes	f	R	poison	desperata salus	+	+	Liv.8,18, 8
Maximianus, Galerius	m	R	?	inpatientia	+	?	Oros.Hist.7,28,13
Maximinianus, Herculius	m	R	hanging	necessitas	+	+	Lact.Mort.persec.30,5
Maximinus Daia	m	R	poison	desperata salus	+	+	Lact.Mort.persec.49,3–7
Medea	f	G	hanging	dolor	–	?	Apoll.Rhod.3,789
Megabacchus	m	R	weapons	pudor	+	+	Plout.Crass.25
Meiros et Joseph	m	n	fire	pudor	+	+	Josephus Pol.Ioud.6,280

Mela eques	m	R	poison	*desperata salus*	+	+	Plin.N.H.19,110
Mela, Lucani pater	m	R	weapons	*necessitas*	+	+	Tac.An.16,17, 6
Meles	m	G	jumping	*desperata salus*	+	+	Paus.1,30,1
Melikertes	m	G	jumping	?	?	+	Hyg.Fab.243,1
Melissos	m	G	jumping	*exsecratio*	+	+	Plout.Mor.773A
mendicans mulier	f	G	various means	*inpatientia*	−	−	Clem.12,13/14 (PG2,312B)
Menedemos	m	G	*inedia*	*pudor*	?	+	Diog.Laert.2,143
Menekrates	m	R	jumping	*desperata salus*	+	+	App.Emph.5, 9,82
Menelaos ob fratrem	m	G	?	*desperata salus*	?	−	Hom.Od. 4,538–540
Menelaos ob Helenam	m	G	weapons	*pudor*	?	−	Eur.Hel.843
Menenius Agrippa, T.	m	R	*inedia*	*pudor*	+	+	Dion.Hal.Rom.Arch.9,27,5
Menestratos	m	G	provocation	*devotio*	?	+	Paus. 9,26,7–8
Menippe et Metioche	f	G	weapons	*devotio*	?	+	Ov.Met.13,692
Menippos	m	G	hanging	*desperata salus*	+	+	Diog.Laert.6,100
Menoikeus	m	G	weapons	*devotio*	+	+	Eur.Phoin.331
Menophanes	m	G	hanging	*desperata salus*	+	+	A.P.11,249
Messala Corvinus	m	R	?	*inpatientia*	+	+	Hier.Chron.197
Messalina	f	R	weapons	*necessitas*	?	+	Tac.An.11,38, 1
Methymna	f	G	hanging	*dolor*	?	+	A.P. 7,473
Metrokles	m	G	various means	*inpatientia*	+	+	Diog.Laert.6, 94/5
Midas	m	n	poison	*furor*	−	−	Plout.Mor.168F
miles cruces asservans	m	R	weapons	*desperata salus*	+	+	Petr.Sat.112,6
miles nuntius quidam	m	R	weapons	*devotio*	+	+	Suet.Otho 10
miles Othonis gregarius	m	R	weapons	*devotio*	+	+	Plout.Otho 15
miles Pompeii Strabonis	m	R	weapons	*dolor*	+	+	Oros.Hist.5,19,13/14
miles qui fratrem occ.	m	R	weapons	*pudor*	+	+	Liv.Per. 79
Milesiae puellae	f	G	hanging	*furor*	+	+	Plout.Mor.249B–D
Milesiae puellae tres	f	G	?	*pudor*	+	+	A.P. 7,492
milites Antonii	m	R	?	*desperata salus*	?	?	App.Emph.5,10,90

name	sex	culture	method	motive	accomplishment	reality	source
milites Caesaris	m	R	?	desperata salus	+	+	Caes.B.G.5,37,6
milites Crassi	m	R	weapons	desperata salus	+	+	Cass.Dio 40,25,2
milites esurientes	m	R	jumping	desperata salus	+	+	Liv.23,19, 6
milites ex Venetis	m	R	weapons	desperata salus	+	+	Cass.Dio 39,43,3
milites Gaii Antonii	m	R	?	desperata salus	+	+	Cass.Dio 41,40,2
milites Iotapatae	m	n	weapons	desperata salus	+	+	Josephus Pol.Ioud.3,331
milites Opitergini	m	R	weapons	desperata salus	+	+	Liv.Per.110
milites Othonis	m	R	weapons	fides	+	+	Tac.Hist.2,49
milites Pompeii	m	R	weapons	desperata salus	+	+	Caes.Civ.1,22,6
milites post Trasymenum	m	R	weapons	desperata salus	+	+	Pol. 3,84,10
milites Romani captivi	m	R	?	pudor	+	+	Liv.22,61, 9
milites Romani CCCC	m	R	weapons	desperata salus	+	+	Tac.An. 4,73, 7
milites Romani pauci	m	R	?	pudor	−	+	Cass.Dio 54, 8,1
Minius Cerrinius	m	n	?	pudor	+	+	Liv.39,19, 2
missus ad spectaculum	m	R	various means	desperata salus	+	+	Sen.Ep.70,23
Mithridates	m	n	weapons	pudor	+	+	Cass.Dio 37,13
Mnester	m	R	weapons	fides	+	+	Tac.An.14, 9, 4
Molpadia et Parthenos	f	G	jumping	pudor	−	?	Diod. 5, 62,3
Monime	f	G	weapons	necessitas	+	+	Plout.Luc.18,6
Montani	?	R	fire	desperata salus	+	+	Prok.Anekd.11
morosus	m	G	hanging	desperata salus	−	+	Diog.Laert.6, 59
mulieres Ardubenses	f	n	jumping	pudor	+	+	Cass.Dio 56,14,5
multi ex plebe	?	R	jumping	desperata salus	+	+	Liv. 4,12,11
Munatia Plancina	f	R	?	pudor	+	+	Tac.An. 6,26, 5 (6,33,5)
Mutilia Prisca	f	R	weapons	pudor	+	+	Cass.Dio 58, 4,6
Mutilus	m	R	weapons	desperata salus	+	+	Liv.Per. 89
Mycerini filia	f	n	hanging	pudor	+	?	Her.2,131

Myro et soror	f	G	hanging	necessitas	+	+	Plout.Mor.253D
Myrrha (Smyrna)	f	G	hanging	pudor	–	?	Ov.Met.10,378
Myrtion	f	G	hanging	dolor	–	–	Louk.Hetair.logoi 2,4
Narcissus libertus	m	R	?	necessitas	+	+	Tac.An.13, 1, 4
Narkissos	m	G	weapons	dolor	+	?	Konon.frg.24 (FGrH I 197)
naufragus	m	R	hanging	desperata salus	+	–	Quint.8,5,22
nautae Ioppae	m	n	weapons	desperata salus	+	+	Josephus Pol.Ioud.3,425
Neaira	f	G	?	dolor	+	?	Hyg.Fab.243,4
Neoboule	f	G	hanging	pudor	+	?	A.P. 7, 69+70+71
Nero	m	R	weapons	desperata salus	+	+	Suet.Nero 49
Nero Germanici filius	m	R	inedia	desperata salus	+	+	Suet.Tib.54
Nerva, Cocceius M.	m	R	inedia	taedium vitae	+	+	Tac.An. 6,26, 1 (6,32,1)
Nikerati uxor	f	R	?	pudor	+	+	Hieron.adv.Iov.1,44
Nikias	m	G	?	desperata salus	+	?	Plout.Nik.38
Nikokles	m	G	?	necessitas	+	?	Diod.20, 21,2
Niobe	f	G	jumping	pudor	+	?	Parthenios Er.Path.33,3
Nisos	m	G	?	desperata salus	+	?	Hyg.Fab.242,3
Norbanus	m	R	weapons	desperata salus	+	+	Liv.Per. 89
Novius Calavius	m	n	?	pudor	+	+	Liv. 9,26, 7
Numantini	?	n	weapons	desperata salus	+	+	Liv.Per.59
Ocellatae sorores	f	R	?	necessitas	+	+	Suet.Dom.8
Ochne	f	G	jumping	mala conscientia	+	?	Plout.Mor.300F
Odysseus	m	C	jumping	desperata salus	–	?	Hom.Od.10,49–53
Oidipous	m	G	?	pudor	+	?	Hyg.Fab.242,4
Oinokles	m	G	?	devotio	?	?	Versnel, self-sacrifice p. 72
Oinomaos	m	G	?	dolor	+	?	Diod. 4, 73,6
Oinone	f	G	hanging	dolor	+	+	Apoll.3.12,6
Onnes	m	n	hanging	dolor	+	+	Diod. 2, 6,10
Oppia	f	R	?	?	+	+	CIL X 5920

name	sex	culture	method	motive	accomplishment	reality	source
Oppianus	m	R	?	*dolor*	−	+	Cic.Cluent.61,171
Oppius	m	R	?	?	−	?	Quint.5,10,69
oppressi a S.Petronio Probo	m	R	hanging	*taedium vitae*	+	+	Amm.Marc.30,5,6
orbata sacrilega	f	R	hanging	*dolor*	−	−	Sen.Rhet.Contr.8,1
Orestes 1	m	G	?	*mala conscientia*	−	?	Eur.Or. 415
Orestes 2	m	G	weapons	*necessitas*	−	?	Eur.Or. 947
Orestes 3	m	G	*inedia*	*desperata salus*	−	?	Eur.Iph.Taur.973
Orgetorix	m	n	?	*pudor*	+	?	Caes.B.G.1, 4, 4
Ostorius Scapula	m	R	weapons	*necessitas*	+	+	Tac.An.16,15, 4
Otho	m	R	weapons	*desperata salus*	+	+	Tac.Hist.2,49
Othonis amici	m	R	?	*fides*	+	+	Tac.Hist.2,49
Othonis eques	m	R	weapons	*devotio*	+	+	Cass.Dio 64 (63),11,2
Othryades	m	G	?	*pudor*	+	+	Her.1, 82
Ovidii uxor 1	f	R	?	*desperata salus*	−	+	Ov.Trist.1,3,99
Ovidii uxor 2	f	R	fire	*fides*	−	+	Ov.Pont.3,1,111/2
Ovidius	m	R	weapons	*desperata salus*	−	+	Ov.Pont.1,6,39–44
Ovius Calavius	m	n	?	*pudor*	+	+	Liv. 9,26, 7
ozostomos	m	G	various means	?	+	−	Philogelos 231
Paccius	m	R	hanging	*pudor*	+	+	Plout.Cato Maior 10,6
Paches	m	G	weapons	*pudor*	+	+	Plout.Arist.26
Paetus	m	R	weapons	*pudor*	+	+	Mart.1,13
Panteus	m	G	?	*pudor*	+	+	Plout.Kleom.37,16
Pantheia	f	n	weapons	*pudor*	+	+	Xen.Kyr.7,3,14
Pantheiae eunuchi	m	n	weapons	*fides*	+	+	Xen.Kyr.7,3,15
Pantites	m	G	hanging	*pudor*	+	+	Her.7,232
Papirius Carbo	m	R	poison	*pudor*	+	+	Cic.Brut.27,103
Papirius Romanus	m	R	weapons	*pudor*	+	?	Plout.Mor.312D

Name	sex	type	method	motive			source
Parmenionis cognati	m	G	?	desperata salus	+	+	Curt.6,11,20
Parmeniskos	m	G	?	taedium vitae	−	+	Hipp.Ep.7,89 (L.5,446)
Parthenope	f	G	jumping	dolor	+	−	Dionysios Periegetes 359
pater filicida	m	R	?	dolor	+	+	Dig.48,21,3,5
pater quidam	m	R	?	fides	+	+	Cass.Dio 51, 2,6
Patrenses	?	G	?	desperata salus	+	+	Pol.38,16, 5
Paulina, Senecae uxor	f	R	weapons	fides	+	+	Tac.An.15,63
Pausanias I	m	G	provocation	exseratio	−	+	Diod.19, 93,6
Pausanias II	m	G	?	pudor	+	+	Diod.16, 93,5
Paxaea, Labeonis uxor	f	R	weapons	fides	+	+	Tac.An. 6,29, 1 (6,35,1)
Pelagia & soror (& mater)	f	R	jumping	pudor	+	+	Ambros.Virg.3,33–36
Pelopeia	f	G	?	pudor	+	?	Hyg.Fab. 87;243,8
Peregrinos	m	G	fire	iactatio	+	+	Louk.Per.40
perfugae	m	n	jumping	desperata salus	+	+	Oros.Hist.4,23,4
perfugae ad Hannibalem	m	n	?	mala conscientia	+	+	Liv.31,31,14
Periandri mater	f	G	?	dolor	+	?	Plout.Mor.146D
Periandros	m	G	provocation	taedium vitae	+	?	Diog.Laert.1, 96
Perikles, Kallias, Nikias	m	G	poison	iactatio	+	+	Aelianus,Poik.hist. 4,23
periturus pro Caligula	m	R	?	devotio	−	+	Suet.Cal.27
Persae	m	n	jumping	devotio	+	+	Her.8,118
Perseus	m	G	inedia	pudor	+	+	Plout.Aem.37,2
Pescennius Niger	m	R	?	necessitas	+	?	Aur.Vict.Caes.20,8
Petreius	m	R	weapons	desperata salus	+	+	Caes.Bell.Afr.94,2
Petronius	m	R	weapons	dolor	+	+	Val.Max.4, 7, 5
Petronius arbiter	m	R	weapons	iactatio	+	+	Tac.An.16,19, 2
Petronius, M., centurio	m	R	battle	devotio	+	+	Caes.B.G.7,50,6
Petronius Turpilianus	m	R	?	necessitas	+	+	Plout.Galba 15
Phaedrae nutrix	f	G	jumping	dolor	−	?	Eur.Hip.356
Phaidra 1	f	G	inedia	dolor	−	?	Eur.Hip.277

name	sex	culture	method	motive	accomplishment	reality	source
Phaidra 2	f	G	hanging	pudor	+	?	Eur.Hip.726
Phasael, Herodis frater	m	n	various means	desperata salus	+	+	Josephus Pol.Ioud.1,271
Phegei filia	f	G	hanging	pudor	+	?	Cert.Hom.et Hes.245
Pheidon	m	G	?	iactatio	+	?	A.P. 7,472b
Pheidonis filiae	f	G	jumping	pudor	+	?	Hieron.ad.Iov.1,41
Pherekydes	m	G	jumping	inpatientia	+	?	Diog.Laert.1,118
Pherorae uxor	f	n	jumping	pudor	–	+	Josephus Pol.Ioud.1,594
Phila	f	G	poison	pudor	+	+	Plout.Demet.45,1
Philaulos	m	G	poison	iactatio	+	?	A.P. 7,470
Philemon	m	G	hanging	iactatio	–	?	A.P. 9,450
Philistios	m	G	?	pudor	+	?	Plout.Dio 35
Philistios	m	G	weapons	pudor	+	+	Diod.16, 16,3
Philokleon	m	G	weapons	pudor	–	–	Aristoph.Spekes 522
Philokrates	m	R	weapons	fides	+	+	Val.Max.6, 8, 3
Philoktetes	m	G	jumping	inpatientia	–	?	Soph.Phil.819,999,1081
Philomelos	m	G	jumping	pudor	+	+	Diod.16, 31,4
Philoumenos	m	G	jumping	desperata salus	?	+	Liv.27,16,4
Phobos	m	G	jumping	dolor	+	+	Plout.Mor.255A
Phoebe	f	R	hanging	pudor	+	+	Suet.Aug.65
Phyllis	f	G	hanging	dolor	+	?	Hyg.Fab.243,6
Pindarus	m	R	weapons	fides	+	+	Val.Max.6, 8, 4
Plautius Numida, C.	m	R	weapons	dolor	+	+	Val.Max.4, 6, 2
Plautius Numida, M.	m	R	weapons	dolor	+	+	Val.Max.4, 6, 3
Plautius Silvanus	m	R	weapons	pudor	+	+	Tac.An. 4,22, 3
Plinius Secundus	m	R	weapons	inpatientia	+	?	Suet.Vit.Plin.
Plotius Plancus	m	R	provocation	devotio	+	+	Val.Max.6, 8, 5
Poeni obsessi	m	n	jumping	desperata salus	+	+	Liv.23,37, 5

224

Poenius Postumus	m	R	weapons	*pudor*	+	+	Tac.An.14,37, 3
Polemon	m	G	?	*dolor*	−	−	Men.Perikeiromene 869/70
Poliagros	m	G	hanging	*pudor*	+	+	Aelianus,Poik.hist. 6,8
Polyaenus	m	R	?	*exsecratio*	+	+	SHA Hadr.15, 4
Polyxena	f	G	weapons	*dolor*	−	?	Philostr.Her.51,2–6
Pompeia Paulina	f	R	weapons	*fides*	+	+	Tac.An.15,63, 1
Pompeius	m	R	?	*desperata salus*	+	+	Sen.Brev.13,7
Pompeius Macer filius	m	R	?	*pudor*	+	+	Tac.An. 6,18, 4 (6,24,4)
Pompeius Macer pater	m	R	?	*pudor*	+	+	Tac.An. 6,18, 4 (6,24,4)
Pomponius	m	R	provocation	*devotio*	+	+	Val.Max.4, 7, 2
Pomponius Labeo	m	R	weapons	*pudor*	+	+	Tac.An. 6,29, 1 (6,35,1)
Pomptilla, Atilia L.f.	f	R	?	*devotio*	+	?	CIL X 7563–7578
Pontius centurio	m	R	provocation	*pudor*	+	+	Val.Max.3, 8, 7
Pontius Pilatus	m	R	?	*desperata salus*	?	?	Eus.H.E. 2,7
Pontius Telesinus	m	R	weapons	*desperata salus*	+	+	Liv.Per. 88
Poppaea Sabina	f	R	?	*desperata salus*	+	+	Tac.An.11, 2, 5
Poppaeus Sabinus, C.	m	R	?	*pudor*	+	+	Cass.Dio 58,25,4
Porcia Catonis filia 1	f	R	?	*inpatientia*	−	−	Plout.Brut.53,5
Porcia Catonis filia 2	f	R	various means	*dolor*	+	+	Val.Max.4, 6, 5
Porphyrios	m	G	?	*furor*	−	−	Porph.Bios Plot.11
Postumus	m	R	various means	*desperata salus*	−	?	Iuven.Sat.6,28–31
praetorianus	m	n	jumping	*pudor*	+	+	Cass.Dio 74 (75), 1,2
Prexaspes	m	R	?	*devotio*	+	+	Her.3, 75
Priscianus	m	R	various means	*pudor*	+	+	SHA Anton.7,4
Proculeius	m	R	various means	*inpatientia*	+	+	Plin.N.H.36,183
Propertius	m	R	various means	*dolor*	−	?	Prop.2,17,13/14
proscripti	?	R	various means	*desperata salus*	+	+	Luc.Phars.2,154–59
proscriptus quidam I	m	R	jumping	*desperata salus*	+	+	App.Emph.4, 4,22
proscriptus quidam II	m	R	hanging	*desperata salus*	+	+	App.Emph.4, 4,26

name	sex	culture	method	motive	accomplishment	reality	source
Psammenitos	m	n	poison	desperata salus	+	+	Her.3, 15
Psyches sorores	f	G	hanging	dolor	−	−	Apul.Met. 5,16
Ptolemaios rex Cypri	m	G	poison	pudor	+	+	Plout.Cato Minor 36,1
puella in pictura	f	G	jumping	dolor	+	?	Philostr.Eik.1,12
puellae ingenuae	f	R	?	pudor	+	+	Lact.Mort.persec.38,5
puer in pictura	m	G	jumping	dolor	+	?	Philostr.Eik.1,12
Pylades	m	G	weapons	fides	−	?	Eur.Or.1091
Pyramus	m	n	weapons	desperata salus	+	?	Ov.Met. 4,119 sqq.
Pythagorae discipuli	m	G	fire	devotio	+	?	Porp.Vit.Pyth.57
Pythagorae discipulus	m	G	hanging	pudor	+	?	Plout.Mor. 70F
Pythagoras	m	G	inedia	dolor	+	?	Diog.Laert.8, 40
Pythia pressa	f	G	jumping	furor	+	+	Plout.Mor.438B
quaestor Ferentinus	m	n	jumping	pudor	+	+	Gell.10, 3, 3
rex Gallorum	m	n	weapons	pudor	+	+	Diod.25, 13
Rhodii	?	G	various means	desperata salus	+	+	Aristeides (ps) Or.25,23
Rhodii quidam	?	G	?	desperata salus	+	+	Liv.45,10,15
Romani quidam	?	R	fire	desperata salus	+	+	Tac.An.15,38, 7
Roscius	m	R	weapons	desperata salus	+	+	App.Emph.4, 7,56
Rufrius Crispinus	m	R	?	necessitas	+	+	Tac.An.16,17, 2
Sabinus,Cornelius	m	R	?	dolor	+	+	Cass.Dio 60, 3,5
Saevius Plautius	m	R	?	pudor	+	+	Hier.Chron.200
Saguntini	?	n	fire	desperata salus	+	+	Liv.21,14, 2
Samiades	m	n	?	pudor	+	+	Diod.32, 10,9
Samius	m	R	weapons	pudor	+	+	Tac.An.11, 5, 2
Sappho	f	G	jumping	dolor	+	?	Amp.8,4
Sardanapal	m	n	fire	pudor	+	?	Athen. 9,529B-D
Satyri socii	m	G	weapons	pudor	+	?	Diod.36,10,3

Satyrus	m	G	weapons	*pudor*	+	?	Diod.36,10,3
Saxones gladiatores	m	n	?	*pudor*	+	+	Symmachus Ep.2,46,2
Scapula	m	R	fire	*desperata salus*	+	+	App.Emph.2,15,105
Scribonius Curio	m	R	provocation	*pudor*	+	+	Caes.Civ.2,42,4
Scribonius Libo Drusus	m	R	weapons	*pudor*	+	+	Tac.An. 2,31, 2
Scribonius Proculus	m	R	weapons	*pudor*	+	+	Cass.Dio 63 (62), 17,4
Scribonius Rufus	m	R	weapons	*pudor*	+	+	Cass.Dio 63 (62), 17,4
Sedatius Severianus	m	R	weapons	*pudor*	+	+	Louk.Hist.Scrib.21
Segestani	m	G	various means	*desperata salus*	+	+	Diod.20, 71,4
Seiani amicus	m	R	weapons	*pudor*	+	+	Tac.An. 5, 7, 1 (6,2.1)
Seiani familiares	?	R	?	*pudor*	+	?	Cass.Dio 58,15, 2
Selene	f	G	jumping	*dolor*	+	+	Diod. 3, 57,5
Seleucus	m	R	?	*necessitas*	+	?	Suet.Tib.56
Semiramis	f	n	fire	*dolor*	+	?	Hyg.Fab.242,4
Sempronius Densus	m	R	provocation	*devotio*	+	+	Tac.Hist.1,43, 1
senatores negligentes	m	R	?	*pudor*	+	+	Cass.Dio 60,11, 8
Seneca	m	R	weapons	*necessitas*	+	+	Tac.An.15,63, 4
Seneca adulescens	m	R	?	*inpatientia*	-	+	Sen.Ep.78,2
Senecae fratres	m	R	?	*desperata salus*	+	?	Cass.Dio 62,25,3
senes Athenienses	m	G	jumping	*desperata salus*	+	+	Her.8, 53
senes Trinacienses	m	n	?	*pudor*	+	+	Diod.12, 29,4
senex quidam	m	G	various means	*desperata salus*	+	?	A.P. 7,336
Septimius Severus	m	R	various means	*inpatientia*	+	+	Aur.Vict.Epit.20,9–10
servi duo	m	G	poison	*desperata salus*	-	-	Aristoph.Hip.83
servi multi	?	n	weapons	*desperata salus*	+	+	Flor.2,7,11
Servianus	m	R	?	*necessitas*	+	+	SHA Hadr.15, 8
Servilia, Bareae filia	f	R	?	*necessitas*	+	+	Tac.An.16,33, 2
Servilia, Lepidi uxor	f	R	various means	*dolor*	+	+	Vell.2, 88,3
servus homicida	m	R	jumping	*desperata salus*	+	+	CIL XIII,7070

name	sex	culture	method	motive	accomplish-ment	reality	source
servus Pisonis	m	R	provocation	devotio	+	+	Tac.Hist.4,50, 4
servus proscripti	m	R	weapons	fides	+	+	App.Emph.4, 4,26
Sextia	f	R	weapons	fides	+	+	Tac.An.16,11, 4
Sextia, Scauri uxor	f	R	?	fides	+	+	Tac.An. 6,29, 7 (6,35,7)
Sextius, Q.	m	R	jumping	desperata salus	−	+	Plout.Mor. 77F
Sextus Papinius	m	R	jumping	pudor	+	+	Tac.An. 6,49, 1 (6,55,1)
Sidones	?	n	fire	desperata salus	+	+	Diod.16, 45,4
Silanus, Appius Iunius	m	R	weapons	necessitas	+	+	Suet.Claud.29
Silanus, L.Iunius	m	R	?	pudor	+	?	Tac.An.12, 8, 1
Silanus, Marcus	m	R	weapons	necessitas	+	+	Suet.Cal.23
Silius	m	R	?	pudor	+	+	Tac.An. 4,19, 7
Silius Italicus	m	R	inedia	inpatientia	+	+	Plin.Ep.3,7,1
Simike	f	G	jumping	desperata salus	−	−	Menander Dyskolos 583
Simon Scythopolitanus	m	n	weapons	mala conscientia	+	+	Josephus Pol.Ioud.2,476
simulator luxuriosus	m	R	inedia	?	−	−	Quint.8,5,23
Sisyngambris	f	n	inedia	dolor	+	+	Diod.17,118,3
Skedasi & Leuctri filiae	f	G	hanging	pudor	+	+	Diod.15, 53,3
Skedasos	m	G	?	exsecratio	+	+	Plout.Mor.774B
Skylla	f	G	jumping	dolor	+	?	Hyg.Fab.197,3
Solois	m	G	jumping	dolor	+	?	Plout.Thes.26,3–5
soror sponsae corrupta	f	G	hanging	pudor	+	+	Canon.Conc.Ancyrae 25
Sosipatros	m	G	?	dolor	+	−	Anth.Pal.5,52
Spargapises	m	n	?	pudor	+	+	Her.1,213
Spartana serva	f	G	?	pudor	+	+	Plout.Mor.242D
Spartanae puellae	f	G	?	pudor	+	?	Paus.4, 4,2
Spartanus puer	m	G	jumping	pudor	+	+	Plout.Mor.234C
Spartanus quidam	m	G	jumping	?	−	+	Plout.Mor.236D/E

Speusippos	m	G	?	*inpatientia*	+	+	Diog.Laert.4,3
Sphinx	n	G	jumping	*pudor*	+	?	Diod. 4, 64,4
Sporus	m	R	weapons	*pudor*	+	+	Cass.Dio 65 (64), 10,1
Spurius Oppius	m	R	?	*pudor*	+	+	Liv. 3,58, 9
Staphyla	f	R	hanging	*desperata salus*	–	–	Plaut.Aul. 77
Statilius Taurus	m	R	?	*pudor*	+	+	Tac.An.12,59, 3
Statius	m	R	fire	*desperata salus*	+	+	App.Emph.4, 4,25
Statius Proxumus	m	R	?	?	+	+	Tac.An.15,71, 4
Statyllius	m	R	?	*desperata salus*	–	?	Plout.Cato Minor 73,7
Stheneboia	f	G	?	*dolor*	+	+	Hyg.Fab. 57,5
Stilpon	m	G	poison	*taedium vitae*	+	+	Diog.Laert.2,120
Stoeni	?	n	various means	*desperata salus*	+	+	Oros.Hist.5,14, 5/6
strategi Athenienses	m	G	?	*devotio*	+	+	Diod.13, 97,6/7
Straton	m	G	weapons	*dolor*	+	+	Plout.Mor.772C
stultus quidam	m	G	hanging	*furor*	+	–	Philogelos 109
stupratus	m	R	hanging	*pudor*	+	–	Quint.4,2,69
Sugambrorum legati	m	n	?	*desperata salus*	+	+	Cass.Dio 55, 6,3
Sulla	m	R	?	*pudor*	+	+	Cass.Dio 52,17,4
Sulpicius Galba	m	R	?	*pudor*	+	?	Tac.An. 6,40, 3 (6,46,3)
Taochi	?	n	jumping	*desperata salus*	+	+	Xen.Anab.4,7,13
Tarquinii plebeii	?	R	hanging	*pudor*	+	+	Plin.N.H.36,107
Tarrias	m	G	?	*pudor*	+	–	Plout.Mor.339C
Taurinus	m	R	jumping	*desperata salus*	+	+	Aur.Vict.Epit.24,2
Tedius Afer	m	R	jumping	*necessitas*	+	+	Suet.Aug.27
Tegaea puella	f	G	?	*pudor*	+	+	Paus.8,47,6
Telesinia Crispinilla	f	R	*inedia*	*dolor*	+	+	CIL IX 2229
Telesinus	m	R	weapons	*pudor*	+	+	Oros.Hist.5,21, 8
Tellias	m	G	fire	*pudor*	+	+	Diod.13, 90,2
Terrinius Gallus	m	R	?	*inpatientia*	–	+	Suet.Aug.53

name	sex	culture	method	motive	accomplishment	reality	source
Teutonum uxores	f	n	various means	*pudor*	+	+	Flor.1,38,17
Teutonus	m	n	hanging	*desperata salus*	–	+	Front.Strat. 4, 7, 5
Theano	f	G	weapons	*desperata salus*	+	?	Hyg.Fab.186
Thelesinus	m	R	weapons	*fides*	?	+	Val.Max.6, 8, 2
Themisto	f	G	?	*dolor*	+	?	Hyg.Fab.1,2
Themistoclis mater	f	G	?	*pudor*	+	?	Plout.Them.2,6
Themistokles	m	G	poison	*pudor*	+	+	Thouk.1,138, 4
Theon	m	G	*inedia*	*dolor*	–	+	P.Oxy 1,119,r.14/15
Therykion	m	G	weapons	*pudor*	+	?	Plout.Kleom.31,12
Thisbe	f	n	weapons	*desperata salus*	+	+	Ov.Met. 4,162
Thrasea Paetus	m	R	weapons	*necessitas*	+	+	Tac.An.16,35, 2
Thrasyllos	m	G	?	*exsecratio*	–	+	Fox, p.143
Thrasyllus	m	G	*inedia*	*mala conscientia*	–	–	Apul.Met. 8,14
Tiberius	m	R	*inedia*	*exsecratio*	+	+	Suet.Tib.10
Tigellinus	m	R	weapons	*necessitas*	+	+	Tac.Hist.1,72, 4
Tigurinorum uxores	f	n	various means	*pudor*	+	+	Oros.Hist.5,16,13
Timagoras	m	G	jumping	*iactatio*	+	+	Paus.1,30,1
Timanthes	m	G	fire	*pudor*	+	+	Paus.6, 8,4
Timarchos	m	G	hanging	*pudor*	+	+	Plout.Mor.841A
Timokrates	m	G	weapons	*pudor*	+	+	Thouk.2,92, 3
Timoleon	m	G	*inedia*	*dolor*	–	+	Plout.Tim.5
Titinius	m	R	weapons	*fides*	+	+	Vell.2, 70,3
Titius Aristo	m	R	?	*inpatientia*	–	+	Plin.Ep.1,22,7–12
Titius Rufus	m	R	?	*pudor*	+	+	Cass.Dio 59,18,5
Trebellenus Rufus	m	R	?	*pudor*	+	+	Tac.An. 6,39, 1 (6,45,1)
tribuni militum quidam	m	R	?	*desperata salus*	+	?	Liv. 4,51, 3
Tullius Marcellinus	m	R	various means	*inpatientia*	+	+	Sen.Ep.77,5–9

Name							Source
Turannius	m	R	inedia	*pudor*	–	–	Sen.Brev.20,3
Tyrakinos	m	G	hanging	*pudor*	+	+	Cic.Verr.2,3,56/129
Ulpius Optatus	m	R	weapons	*pudor*	+	?	CLE 520
Urbinii servus	m	R	weapons	*devotio*	+	+	Val.Max.6, 8, 6
uxor Ketei iunior	f	n	fire	*fides*	+	+	Diod.19, 34,1–6
uxor mariti absentis	f	R	jumping	*fides*	–	–	Sen.Rhet.Contr.2,2
uxor mulierum osoris	f	G	hanging	*dolor*	?	?	Philogelos 248
Vaccaei	?	n	?		+	+	Liv.Per.57
Valentinianus II	m	R	hanging	*desperata salus*	+	?	Oros.7,35,10
Valeria Tusculanaria	f	R	jumping	*desperata salus*	+	?	Plout.Mor.311B
Valerius Asiaticus	m	R	weapons	*pudor*	–	+	Tac.An.11, 3, 2
Valerius Severus	m	R	weapons	*necessitas*	+	+	Lact.Mort.persec.26,11
Valerius Tusculanarius	m	R	jumping	*necessitas*	+	?	Plout.Mor.311B
Vari tribuni militesque	m	R	weapons	*desperata salus*	+	+	Cass.Dio 56,21,5/22,1
Varonilla	f	R	?	*necessitas*	+	+	Suet.Dom.8
Varus I	m	R	weapons	*desperata salus*	+	+	Vell.2,119,3
Varus II	m	R	weapons	*desperata salus*	+	+	Vell.2, 71,2
Varus III	m	R	weapons	*desperata salus*	+	+	Vell.2,119,3
Velleius Paterculus	m	R	weapons	*fides*	+	+	Vell.2, 76,1
Vescularius Flaccus	m	R	?	*necessitas*	+	+	Tac.An. 6,10, 2(6,16,2)
Vestalis	f	R	?	*pudor*	+	+	Plout.Fab.Max.18,3
Vetti socii	m	R	weapons	*desperata salus*	+	+	Diod. 36,2,6
Vettii servus	m	R	weapons	*fides*	+	+	Sen.Ben.3,23,5
Vettius, Titus	m	R	weapons	*pudor*	+	+	Diod.36,2,6
Vibius Marsus	m	R	inedia	?	–	+	Tac.An. 6,48, 1 (6,54,1)
Vibius Virrius & senatores	m	n	poison	*desperata salus*	+	+	Liv.26,14, 3–5
Vibulenus Agrippa	m	R	poison	*pudor*	+	+	Tac.An. 6,40, 1 (6,46,1)
Victomelani	?	n	fire	*desperata salus*	+	+	Diod.25, 17
Vidacilius	m	n	poison	*desperata salus*	+	+	App.Emph.1, 6,48

name	sex	culture	method	motive	accomplish-ment	reality	source
Vinicianus, Annius	m	R	?	pudor	+	+	Cass.Dio 60,15,5
Vipsania Agrippina	f	R	inedia	taedium vitae	+	?	Tac.An. 6,25, 1 (6,31,1)
vir auro privatus	m	G	hanging	desperata salus	+	-	A.P. 9,44+45
vir aurum inveniens	m	G	hanging	desperata salus	-	-	A.P. 9, 44+45
vir cui laqueus incisus	m	R	hanging	dolor	-	-	Sen.Rhet.Contr.5,1
vir e fico	m	G	hanging	?	+	+	Diog.Laert.6, 61
vir laqueum inveniens	m	G	hanging	desperata salus	+	-	A.P. 9, 44+45
vir nomine privatus	m	G	hanging	desperata salus	+	+	Artem.Oneir.1,4
vir se ipso usus	m	G	?	pudor	+	+	Artem.Oneir.5,31
vir somniens	m	G	?	pudor	+	+	Artem.Oneir.5,33
viri boni	m	R	?	necessitas	+	+	Cass.Dio 63 (62), 17,2
viri coniugum amantes	m	R	?	dolor	+	+	Lact.Mort.persec.38,3
Vistilius	m	R	weapons	pudor	+	+	Tac.An. 6, 9, 4 (6,15,4)
Vitellii Germanus	m	R	weapons	fides	+	+	Cass.Dio 65 (64), 21, 1
Vitellius	m	R	weapons	pudor	-	+	Tac.An. 5, 8, 3 (6,3,3)
Volumnius	m	R	weapons	dolor	+	+	Val.Max.4, 7, 4
Vulteii commilitones	m	R	weapons	pudor	+	+	Luc.Phars.4,546–549
Vulteius	m	R	weapons	pudor	+	+	Luc.Phars.4,545
Zarmaros	m	n	fire	iactatio	+	+	Cass.Dio 54, 9,10
Zenon Eleates	m	G	provocation	devotio	+	+	Diod.10, 18,6
Zenon Stoicus	m	G	inedia	iactatio	+	+	A.P. 7,118
Zeuxis	m	G	hanging	?	-	+	P.Oxy.VI, 850

APPENDIX B:
PROFILE OF ANCIENT
SELF-KILLING

1. TOTALS

884 cases[1] of individual self-killing
                        countable individuals: 854[2]
  76 cases of collective   self-killing[3]
                        countable individuals: 8785
_____
960 cases   9639 individuals

2. SUICIDE COMMITTED AND ATTEMPTED

777 cases of suicide committed (9481 individuals)
183 cases of attempt/contemplation/wish (158 individuals)

ratio between cases of suicide committed and attempts/contemplation/wishes: 4:1

3. SELF-KILLING COMMITTED AND HISTORICAL (HARD NUCLEUS)

494 cases of individual suicide committed and historical
                              countable individuals: 481
  70 cases of collective suicide committed and historical[4]
                              countable individuals: 7775
_____

564 cases of suicide committed and historic with 8256 individuals

233

4. BARBARIANS–GREEKS–ROMANS[5]

a. barbarians

78(58) cases of individual self-killing
                countable individuals: 76   (57)
35(35) cases of collective self-killing
                countable[6] individuals: 6355(6355)
_____

113(93) cases = 12% (16%) of the total with   6431(6412) individuals

b. Greeks

386(124) cases of individual self-killing
                countable individuals: 383(132)
 17 (13) cases of collective self-killing
                countable[7] individuals:1010(0)
_____

403(137) cases = 42% (24%) of the total with   1393(132) individuals

c. Romans

420(312) cases of individual self-killing
                countable individuals: 395 (292)
 24 (22) cases of collective self-killing
                countable[8] individuals:1420(1420)
_____

444(334) cases = 46% (60%) of the total with   1815(1712) individuals

5. DISTRIBUTION OF CASES OVER PERIODS[9]

		cases	countable individuals
a.	Mythical (–750 BC)	125 (0)	130 (0)
b.	Archaic (750–500 BC)	38 (18)	44 (20)
c.	Classical (500–336 BC)	78 (54)	74 (50)
d.	Hellenistic (336–27 BC)	105 (59)	95 (50)
e.	Early Rome (–500 BC)	13 (4)	14 (2)
f.	Early Republic (500–200 BC)	39 (32)	74 (69)
g.	Late Republic (200–27 BC)	164(133)	2433(1408)
h.	Early Empire (27 BC–192 AD)	255(202)	6624(6575)
i.	Late Empire (from 192 AD)	51 (41)	71 (61)

6. METHODS (IN ORDER OF DIMINISHING FREQUENCY)

a. In numbers of cases with specified methods

	barbarians		Greeks		Romans		total	
	man	woman	man	woman	man	woman	man	woman
weapons	*29*[10]		*66*		*153*		*248(179)*[11]	
	21	4	48	18	135	17	204	39
hanging	*7*		*81*		*27*		*115 (38)*	
	5	2	33	44	18	8	57	54
jumping	*17*		*55*		*30*		*102 (47)*	
	8	4	30	23	20	7	58	34
poison	*10*		*23*		*20*		*53 (37)*	
	8	2	13	10	19	1	40	13
inedia	*3*		*26*		*22*		*51 (30)*	
	2	1	22	3	15	7	39	11
fire	*15*		*12*		*8*		*35 (23)*	
	7	2	9	3	3	2	19	7
provocation	*1*		*8*		*13*		*22 (15)*	
	1	0	8	0	13	0	22	0
	82		*271*		*273*		*626(363)*	
	52	15	164	101	2223	42	439	158
varia							*52*	
							34	10
unknown							*282*	

total number of cases   *960*

b. Specified methods in percentages[12]

Nota bene: of course the small percentages, based on a few cases, do not have real statistical significance in this or in the other tables.

	barbarians		Greeks		Romans		total	
	man	woman	man	woman	man	woman	man	woman[13]
weapons	*35%*		*24%*		*56%*		*40% (48%)*	
	40%	27%	29%	18%	61%	40%	46%	25%
hanging	*9%*		*30%*		*10%*		*18% (10%)*	
	10%	13%	20%	44%	8%	19%	13%	34%
jumping	*21%*		*20%*		*11%*		*16% (13%)*	
	15%	27%	18%	23%	9%	17%	13%	22%
poison	*12%*		*8%*		*7%*		*8% (10%)*	
	15%	13%	8%	10%	9%	2%	9%	8%
inedia	*4%*		*10%*		*8%*		*8% (8%)*	
	4%	7%	13%	3%	7%	17%	9%	7%
fire	*18%*		*4%*		*3%*		*6% (6%)*	
	13%	13%	5%	3%	1%	5%	4%	4%
provocation	*1%*		*3%*		*5%*		*4% (4%)*	
	2%	0%	5%	0%	6%	0%	5%	0%

± 100%

7. MOTIVES (IN DIMINISHING ORDER OF FREQUENCY)

a. In numbers of cases

	barbarians		Greeks		Romans		total	
	man	woman	man	woman	man	woman	man	woman
pudor		*38*		*117*		*141*	*296(192)*	
	29	8	69	47	114	24	212	79
desperata salus		*40*		*66*		*98*	*204(133)*	
	22	3	43	16	81	8	146	27
dolor		*10*		*85*		*30*	*125 (32)*	
	4	5	40	44	19	11	63	60
necessitas		*1*		*7*		*50*	*58 (52)*	
	1	0	3	4	41	8	45	12
devotio		*7*		*20*		*25*	*52 (30)*	
	7	0	12	8	23	2	42	10
fides		*4*		*10*		*31*	*45 (30)*	
	3	1	3	7	20	11	26	19
inpatientia		*2*		*19*		*23*	*44 (26)*	
	2	0	18	1	22	1	42	2
iactatio		*2*		*20*		*7*	*29 (21)*	
	2	0	17	2	3	0	22	2
taedium vitae		*1*		*6*		*13*	*20 (11)*	
	1	0	6	0	11	2	18	2
exsecratio		*1*		*13*		*5*	*19 (6)*	
	1	0	9	4	4	1	14	5
furor		*2*		*10*		*5*	*17*	
	1	0	8	3	5	0	14	3
conscientia		*3*		*8*		*2*	*13 (4)*	
	3	0	3	5	2	0	8	5
specified		*111*		*382*		*430*	*923(547)*	
	76	17	231	141	345	68	652	226

b. In percentages

(Note the warning on small percentages under 6 b)

	barbarians		Greeks		Romans		total	
	man	woman	man	woman	man	woman	man	woman[14]
pudor	34%		31%		33%		32%	(35%)
	38%	47%	30%	33%	33%	35%	33%	35%
desperata salus	36%		17%		23%		22%	(24%)
	29%	18%	19%	11%	23%	12%	22%	12%
dolor	9%		22%		7%		13%	(6%)
	5%	29%	17%	31%	6%	16%	10%	27%
necessitas	1%		2%		12%		6%	(10%)
	1%	0%	1%	3%	12%	12%	7%	5%
devotio	6%		5%		6%		6%	(5%)
	9%	0%	5%	6%	7%	3%	6%	4%
fides	4%		3%		7%		5%	(5%)
	4%	6%	1%	5%	6%	16%	4%	8%
inpatientia	2%		5%		5%		5%	(5%)
	3%	0%	8%	1%	6%	1%	6%	1%
iactatio	2%		5%		2%		3%	(4%)
	3%	0%	7%	1%	1%	0%	3%	1%
taedium vitae	1%		2%		3%		2%	(2%)
	1%	0%	3%	0%	3%	3%	3%	1%
exsecratio	0%		3%		1%		2%	(1%)
	1%	0%	4%	3%	1%	1%	2%	2%
furor	2%		3%		1%		2%	(2%)
	1%	0%	3%	2%	1%	0%	2%	1%
conscientia	3%		2%		0%		1%	(1%)
	4%	0%	1%	4%	1%	0%	1%	2%

±100%

8. RELATIONS BETWEEN METHOD AND MOTIVE[15]

a. In numbers of cases

	weapons	hanging	jumping	poison	*inedia*	fire	provoca-tion	total
pudor	86	33	26	19	8	7	5	184
desperata salus	56	25	30	14	4	11	0	140
dolor	23	24	16	0	15	2	0	80
necessitas	18	3	2	3	1	0	0	27
devotio	10	1	7	1	0	3	15	37
fides	27	0	2	4	0	4	0	37
inpatientia	7	1	4	5	8	1	0	26
iactatio	3	1	4	4	5	6	0	23
taedium vitae	1	3	0	2	4	0	1	11
exsecratio	7	4	1	0	1	0	1	14
furor	3	4	6	1	0	1	0	15
conscientia	2	3	2	0	2	0	0	9
totals	243	102	100	53	48	35	22	603

b. Relation between motive and method in percentages

	weapons	hanging	jumping	poison	*inedia*	fire	provo-cation	
pudor	35%	32%	27%	36%	17%	20%	23%	(32%)[16]
desperata salus	23%	25%	30%	26%	8%	31%	0%	(22%)
dolor	10%	24%	15%	0%	31%	6%	0%	(13%)
necessitas	7%	3%	2%	6%	2%	0%	0%	(6%)
devotio	4%	1%	7%	2%	0%	9%	68%	(6%)
fides	11%	0%	2%	8%	0%	11%	0%	(5%)
inpatientia	3%	1%	4%	8%	17%	3%	0%	(5%)
iactatio	1%	1%	4%	8%	10%	17%	0%	(3%)
taedium vitae	0%	3%	0%	4%	8%	0%	5%	(2%)
exsecratio	3%	4%	1%	0%	2%	0%	5%	(2%)
furor	1%	4%	5%	2%	0%	3%	0%	(2%)
conscientia	1%	3%	2%	0%	4%	0%	0%	(1%)

±100%

c. Relation between motive and method

	weapons (40%)[17]	hanging (18%)	jumping (16%)	poison (10%)	*inedia* (8%)	fire (6%)	provo-cation (4%)	
pudor	47%	18%	14%	10%	3%	4%	3%	±100%
desperata salus	40%	18%	21%	10%	3%	8%	0%	
dolor	29%	30%	20%	0%	19%	3%	0%	
necessitas	67%	11%	7%	11%	4%	0%	0%	
devotio	27%	3%	19%	3%	0%	8%	41%	
fides	73%	0%	5%	11%	0%	11%	0%	
inpatientia	27%	4%	15%	19%	31%	4%	0%	
iactatio	13%	4%	17%	17%	22%	26%	0%	
taedium vitae	9%	27%	0%	18%	36%	0%	9%	
exsecratio	50%	29%	7%	0%	7%	0%	7%	
furor	20%	27%	40%	7%	0%	7%	0%	
conscientia	22%	33%	22%	0%	22%	0%	0%	

9. SELF-KILLING OBSERVED AMONG THE LOWER CLASSES

64(40) cases of individual self-killing
                                countable individuals: 62   (37)
23(21) cases of collective self-killing
                                countable[18] individuals: 2429(1429)

___

87(61) cases with (countable)   2491(1466) individuals

238

10. MEN AND WOMEN (AND NON-HUMAN SELF-KILLING)

a. Numbers

I. Reckoned as cases

	men	women
barbarians	78 (65)	17(10)
Greeks	246 (95)	143(33)
Romans	358(269)	69(48)
total	683(429)	229(91)

cases of (exemplary) self-killing of non-human beings 4(1)

II. Reckoned as countable individuals

	men	women
barbarians	156 (144)	314(307)
Greeks	1233 (96)	156 (36)
Romans	1727(1643)	88 (69)
total	3117(1883)	555(412)

b. Ratios of the sexes in percentages

I. Reckoned as in cases

	men	women
barbarians	82%(87%)	18%(13%)
Greeks	63%(74%)	38%(26%)
Romans	84%(85%)	16%(15%)
total	75%(83%)	25%(17%)

II. Reckoned as countable individuals

	men	women
barbarians	33%(32%)	67%(68%)
Greeks	89%(73%)	11%(27%)
Romans	95%(96%)	5%(4%)
total	85%(82%)	15%(18%)

c. Ratios of the methods (absolute numbers under 6a)

	barbarians		Greeks		Romans		total	
	man	woman	man	woman	man	woman	man	woman
weapons	84%	16%	73%	27%	89%	11%	84%	16%
hanging	71%	29%	43%	57%	69%	21%	51%	49%
jumping	67%	33%	57%	43%	74%	26%	63%	37%
poison	80%	20%	56%	44%	95%	5%	75%	25%
inedia	67%	33%	88%	12%	68%	32%	78%	22%
fire	78%	22%	75%	25%	60%	40%	73%	27%
provocation	100%	0%	100%	0%	100%	0%	100%	0%

d. Ratios of motives (absolute numbers under 7a)

	barbarians		Greeks		Romans		total	
	man	woman	man	woman	man	woman	man	woman
pudor	78%	22%	59%	41%	83%	17%	73%	27%
desperata salus	88%	12%	73%	27%	91%	9%	84%	16%
dolor	44%	56%	48%	52%	63%	37%	51%	49%
necessitas	100%	0%	43%	57%	84%	16%	79%	21%
devotio	100%	0%	60%	40%	92%	8%	81%	19%
fides	75%	25%	30%	70%	64%	36%	58%	42%
inpatientia	100%	0%	95%	5%	96%	4%	95%	5%
iactatio	100%	0%	89%	11%	100%	0%	92%	8%
taedium vitae	100%	0%	100%	0%	85%	15%	90%	10%
exsecratio	0%	0%	69%	31%	80%	20%	74%	26%
furor	100%	0%	73%	27%	100%	0%	82%	18%
conscientia	100%	0%	37%	63%	100%	0%	62%	38%

11. CASES OF SELF-KILLING AMONG THE YOUNG

a. Recorded cases

young women	82(20)
young men	84(25)
total plus one group and one horse	168(47)

b. Specified methods (in order of diminishing frequency)

jumping	37(31%)
hanging	36(30%)
weapons	31(26%)
inedia	7 (6%)
poison	5 (4%)
fire	3 (3%)
provocation	1 (1%)
cases with methods specified:	120

c. Specified motives (in order of diminishing frequency)

pudor	50(31%)
dolor	47(29%)
desperata salus	24(15%)
devotio	13 (8%)
fides	8 (5%)
exsecratio	6 (4%)
necessitas	5 (3%)
furor	3 (2%)
inpatientia	2 (1%)
conscientia	2 (1%)
taedium vitae	1 (1%)
iactatio	1 (1%)
cases with motives specified:	162

12. CASES OF SELF-KILLING AMONG THE OLD

a. Recorded cases

old men	74(49)
old women	13 (5)
total	87(54)

b. Specified methods (in order of diminishing frequency)

inedia	18(30%)
weapons	13(21%)
poison	11(18%)
hanging	6(10%)
fire	5 (8%)
jumping	5 (9%)
provocation	3 (5%)
cases with methods specified:	61

c. Specified motives

inpatientia	21 (24%)
pudor	17 (20%)
iactatio	11 (13%)
taedium vitae	11 (13%)
dolor	10 (11%)
desperata salus	8 (9%)
necessitas	5 (6%)
devotio	2 (2%)
fides	1 (1%)
exsecratio	1 (1%)
furor	0
conscientia	0
cases with motives specified:	87

APPENDIX C:
SUICIDAL VOCABULARY OF GREEK AND LATIN

a. Greek

term	place
aera helkein	Philem.frg. 119 (Edmonds)
angchomai	Hipp.Parth.
angchonas kraino	Hipp.Parth.
angchone	Eur.Hel.200/201
anachraomai heauton	Cass.Dio 52,17,4
anaireo heauton	Parth.Erot.path.48,2
anairetes heautou	Vettius Valens 2,40
anakremannumi heauton	Diod.4,62,3
analiskomai	Thouk.3,81,3
anartao heauton	Artem.1,4
apallage biou	Hipp.Epid.7,89
apallattomai psuches	Eur.Hip.726
apallattomai tou biou	Eur.Hip.356
apallatto heauton tou zen	Diod.20,21,1
apamao laimon	Hom.Il.18,34
apangchomai	Her.2,131
apangchonizomai	Hipp.Parth.
apangchonizo	A.P.11,249
apartaomai	P.Oxy.I,50
apechomai siton	Louk.Hist.21 (pos dei..)
apechomai trophes	Louk.Makrobioi 19
aperchomai tou biou hekon	Louk.Dem.4
aphiemi heauton (epi kephalen)	Her.3,75
aphiemi psuchen autocheiriaai	Paus.8,51,8
aphiemi ten zoen	Ach.Tat.2,30,2
aphistamai tou biou	Dion.Hal.Rom.Arch.9,27,5
apoche siton	Dion.Hal.Rom.Arch.9,27,5
apochraomai heauton	Cass.Dio 57,15,5
apodidomi heauton eis sphagen	Diod.21,6,2
apokartereo	Hipp.Sark.19
apokarteresis	Quint.8.5.23
apokremnizo heauton	Ktesias 4 Koenig (Photios)

apokteino heauton	Dio Chrys.64,3
apokteino limoi	App.Emph.4,4,23
apoktinnumi heauton	Cass.Dio 72,17,3 ?
apoluo hauton ek ton tou somatos	desmon Ael.Poik.hist.5,6
aponechomai tou somatos	Plout.Mor.475D–476A
apophthinomai	Hom.Od.10,52
apopnigo heauton	Diog.Laert.7,28
apopnigo heauton di'angchones	Diod.25,15
aporregnumi bion	Eur.Iphigen.Taur.974
aposphattomai	Xen.Kour.3,1,25
aposphatto heauton	Diod.16,16,3
apostasis biou	Eur.Hip.277
apotemno ton laimon autos	Cass.Dio 65,16,4
apotemno ton pharugga	Hipp.Sark.18
apotheo zoen	A.P.7,731
apothneisko huph'heautou	Plout.Fab.18,3
artao deren	Eur.Andr.811
asiteo	Eur.Hip.277
asitia	Eur.Hik.1105
autagretos leipo heliou phos	Semonides Frg.1,19
autepiboulos	Hesychios s.v.
authairetos thanatos	Xen.Hell.6,2,36
authentes	Suidas s.v.
autocheir	Aristot.frg.502
autocheir sphage	Eur.Phoin.331
autocheiriai apothneisko	Cass.Dio 51,26
autocheri katathneiskomai	A.P.7,517
autoentes	Cass.Dio 58,15,4
autokritos apothneisko	Philodemos Than.6,10/11
autoktonia	P.G.2,312C
autoktonos	Aisch.Agam.1635?
automatos erchomai	A.P.7,118
autophoneus	Hesychios autoepiboulos
autophoneutes heautou	Eus.H.E.2,7
autophoneutos	Schol.rec.Aisch.Hepta 735
autophonia	Schol.Aisch.Eum.337
autophonos	Opp.Kyn.2,480
autophontes	Schol.El.272?
autosphages	Suidas s.v.
autothanatos	Plout.Mor.293E
autothelei Haidan erchomai	A.P.7,470
biaiothanasia	Paul.Al.ed.Boer p.66 r.13
biaiothanatos(›biothanatos)	Paul.Al.ed.Boer p.46 r.23
biothanatos(‹biaiothanatos)	SHA Hel.33,2
brochizo heauton	P.Oxy.I,850
cheira heautoi prosphero	Diod.13,89,2
cheiras epiphero heautoi	Aretaios,Ait.3,6,5
cheiras prosago	P.Mich.5.231
damnamai heauton	A.P.7,233

diacheirizomai heauton	Aristot.frg.502
diachraomai heauton	App.Emph.4,4,21
diaphtheiro heauton	Pol.8,20,6
diergazomai heauton	Her.1,213
ekbaino ek tou zen (hekon)	Athen.Deipn.4,157D
ekleipo to zen	Diod.20, 71,5
ekleipo ton bion	Louk.Makrobioi 19
eleutheros potmos	A.P.7,493
empimpremi heauton	App.Emph.2,15,105
empipto (eis phrear/potamon)	Louk.Het.Logoi 12,2
endeia	Diod.34/35,4,1
epididomi hauton hekon	Athen.13,602D
epididomi to zen	Diod.10,21,1
epikatasphazo heauton	Her.1,45
episphazo heauton	Plout.C.Gracch.17,3
ethelontedon teleutao	Cass.Dio 58,15,4
ethelontes apothneisko	Cass.Dio 69,83
ethelonti diaptheiromai	Cass.Dio 58,24,3
exago heauton	A.P.7,95
exago heauton tou biou	Diog.Laert.7,130
exago heauton tou zen	Plout.Mor.1076B
exagoge eulogos	Plot.1,9
exapto brochon amphi deiren	Eur.Ion 1065
haireomai ton thanaton	Diod.20,21,2
hallomai	Hipp.Parth.
hekonti diaphtheiromai	Joseph.Pol.Ioud.1,594
hekontos apothneisko	Cass.Dio 58,16,3
hekon apothneisko	Cass.Dio 60,3,5
hekousiaai gnomei heauton exagagein	Paulus Aegineta 5,29
hekousios proiemi ton bion	Plout.Cat.Min.73,4
hekousios apothneisko	Thouk.1,138,4
hekousios thanatos	Plout.Them.2,6
huph'heautou apothneisko	Cass.Dio 58,24,3
hupopheugo	A.P.7,107
idia teleute	Diod.11,58,3
idios thanatos	Phil.231
karteria	Philostr.Bioi Soph.2,24
katachraomai heauton	Cass.Dio 60,15,5
kataka(i)o heauton	Pol.16,34,9
katakremannumai	Phil.183
katakremnizo heauton	Pol.16,34,10
kataleipo ton bion	Ach.Tat.7,6,4
katasphazo heauton	Diod.17,79,6
katastrepho (without "bion")	Stob.Eklog.3,7,5
katastrepho bion (agchonei)	Diod.4,34,7
katastrepho ton bion brochoi	Plout.Mor.314C
katastrophen tou biou poieomai	Diod.17,101,4
katecho to stoma kai pneuma	App.Emph.4,1,4
kathiemi heauton es potamon	Schol.Hom.Il.9,537

kremannumi heauton	Aristoph.Batr.122
kteino heauton	App.Emph.3,13,92
laimotomeo heauton	Plout.Otho 2
lambano thanaton	Eur.Hel.200/201
methiemi soma	Eur.Hip.356
methistemi hauton (ek) tou zen	Plout.Mor.774B
methistemi heauton ek tou zen	Diod.12,11,2
nestis boras thneisko	Eur.Iphigen.Taur.973
otheo heauton es to pur	Her.7,167
paio epar xiphei	Eur.El.688
pateo lax zoen	A.P.9,574
peripipto toi xiphei/beloi	Aristoph.Sphek.523
phleba anateino	Cass.Dio 72,26,4
phlebas entemno	App.Emph.1,8,74
phlebas epitemno	Cass.Dio 78,16,6a
phlebas schazo	Cass.Dio 63,17,4
phlebas temno	Cass.Dio 77,5,6
phoneuo heauton	Hesychios s.v.
autocheir phthano ten heimarmenen	Joseph.Pol.Ioud.1,594
phtheiro heauton	Cass.Dio 54,8,1
plesso heauton	Joseph.Ioud.Arch.14,356
pnigetos	Hesychios s.v.angchone
proanalisko heauton	Cass.Dio 59,18,4
proapochraomai heauton	Cass.Dio 57,15,5
proaposphatto heauton	Cass.Dio 65,10,1
proiemi to zen	Diod.17,117,3
proiemi ton bion	Plout.Mor.146D
prosballo toi xiphoi	Philodemos Than.28,22/23
ripto heauton	App.Emph.5,9,82
ripto heauton apo petron	Plout.Mor.1069D–E
ripto soma	Eur.Hip.356
sphagen parecho	Plout.Luc.18,6
sphazo heauton	Hipp.Sark.
sterisko heauton tou zen	Diod.4,52,5
teleutao (brochoi)	Plout.Mor.311C
teleutao ton bion	Artem.1,4
therizo heautou ton trachelon	Diod.25, 13

b. Latin

abicere se (muro)	Cic.Tusc.1,34
abominare vivere	CIL IX 2229
abrumpere momentum extremae lucis	Luc.Phars. 4,483
abrumpere vitam	Sen.Ep.78,2
abstinentia	Sen.Ep.70,9
abstinentia cibi	Tac.An.6,26,1
absumere se (veneno)	SHA Did.Iul.8,7
accersita mors	Plin.Ep.1,12,2
adprehendere ultro mortem	Sen.Rhet.Suas.6,8

adsciscere sibi mortem	Lex coll.fun.Lanuvini
appetere mortem	Sen.Ep.24,23
approbare mortem sibi?	Sen.Ep.70,12
arcessere mortem	Plin.Ep.1,12,2
armare manus in pectus	Sen.Rhet.Suas.6,2
assassinius sui/suipsius	not ancient
caelum bibere	Lucilius frg. 615 (Edmonds)
cervicem alicui praebere	Vell.2,6
claudere animam	Ov.Met.7,604
collum laedere	Hor.Carm.3,27,60
conficere se	Hier.Chron.197
consciscere sibi letum	Lucr.3,81
consciscere sibi mortem	Liv.34,17,6
consciscere sibi necem	Gell.6,18,11
consulere extremis rebus	Luc.Phars. 4,477
consulere suae vitae durius	Caes.Civ.1,22,6
consumere se (suspendio)	Val.Max.5,8,3
corrumpere se	Flor.1,22,6
deicere se	Amp.8,4
deicere se praecipitem	C.I.L.XIII,7070
deliberata mors	Sen.Ep.77,5
desciscere e vita	Cic.Fin.3,18
desilire	Hor.Ep.17
destinare mori	Suet.Aug.53
destinata mors	Tac.An.15,632
discedere e vita	Cic.Tusc.1,84
effundere animam	Carm.de Bell.Aeg.49?
egestas cibi	Tac.An.6,23,1
elidere spiritum	Sen.Ep.70,20
emittere se	Sen.Ep.70,5
eripere spiritum	Val.Max.6,1 ext.3
exanimare se	Caes.B.G.6,31
excedere e vita	Cic.Fin.3.18
eximere se	Flor.2,9,15
exire	Sen.Ep.70,24
exire vita	Val.Max.9,12 ext.1
exprimere spiritum	Tac.An.15,57,3
extortor animae suae	Aug.Gaud.1,27,31?
extrahere se rebus humanis	Dig.21,1,23,3
fabricare sibi mortem suis manibus	Apul.Met.6,32,2
fauces secare	Suet.Cal.23
ferrum adigere in viscera	Sen.Ep.1,4,4
ferrum in ilia demittere	Ov.Met.4,119
ferrum transadigere	Ap.Met.8,14
festinare ad mortem	Aug.Gaud.1,6,7?
festinare mortem in se	Tac.An.4,28,2
finem vitae facere	Liv.3,58,9
finem vitae sibi ponere	Tac.An.5,8,3
finem vitae suae imponere	Sen.Vit.19,1

finire se	Sen.rhet.Contr.10 praef.7
finire spiritum	Tac.An.14,51
finire vitam	Plin.N.H.6,66
fodire viscera ferro	Lucanus 4,512
fugere in mortem	Tac.An.6,26,2
gladio percutere pectus suum	Val.Max.4,6,2
gladio se transfigere	Vell.2,63,2
gladio se transigere	Tac.An.14,37,6
gladio sibi necem manu sua consciscere	Gell.13,20,3
gladio transverberare praecordia sua	Val.Max.3,2,13
gladio uti adversus se ipsum	Val.Max.5,8,4
gladium agere per sua praecordia	Val.Max.6,8,3
gladium in pectus abdere	Sen.Rhet.Suas.6,2
homicida in se	Sen.Rhet.Contr.8,4
iacere e saxo	Prop.2,17,13
iacere se in praeceps	Tac.An.6,49,1
ictibus mutuis procumbere	Tac.An.4,73,7
ictus sibi dirigere in viscera	Tac.An.2,31,3
immittere se in medios hostes	Cic.Tusc.1,48,116
incisione venarum	Hier.Chron.211
incubare ferro	Sen.Phaedr.259
incumbere in gladium	Lucil.601
induere se in laqueum	Plaut.Cas.113
inedia	Gell.3,10,15
inicere semetipsum profundo mari	(Ps) Clem.Recogn.7,13
inrogare sibimet mortem	Tac.An.4,10,3
inserere se in laqueum	Cic.Verr.4,37
interemptor ipse sui	Sen.Ep.70,14
interficere se	Hier.Chron.194,1
interimere se	Serv.Verg.Aen.12,603
interimere se vita	Plaut.Cist.711
irrogare sibi mortem	Digesta 48,21,3,5
iudicare de semetipso	Tert.Apol.4,6
iugulare se	Ov.Am.3,8,21
iugulo ferrum adigere	Suet.Nero 49
iugulum alicui dare	Cic.Mil.31
iugulum porrigere	Hor.?
iugulum praebere	(Ps) Quint.
laqueo animam claudere	Ov.Met.7,604
laqueo collum implicare	Ov.Her.2,142
laqueo nexili se suspendere	Apul.5,16,4
laqueo se suspendere	Matth.27:5
laqueum nectare	Calpurnius Ecl.3,87
laqueum torquere	Dig.21,3,23,3
liberum mortis arbitrium permittere	Suet.Dom.8
manu sua cadere	Tac.An.3,42,4
manu sua gladio sibi necem consciscere	Gel.13,20,3
manus sibi afferre	Sen.Ep.70,10
manus sibi inferre	Dig.47,2,36 pr.

migrare de/e vita	Cic.Fin.1,62/3,18
mittere animam	Ennius,Ann.210 Vahlen
mittere se	Flor.1,21,17
necare se	Serv.Verg.Aen.12,603
nectere vincula gutturi suo	Hor.Ep.17,72
occidere se (ipsum)	Plaut.Trin.1,2,92
occupare mortem manu	Flor.2,13,83
offerre se ad mortem	Cic.Tusc.1,31
oppetere mortem	Cic.Fin.3,18,64
parere sibi letum manu	Verg.Aen.6,434/5
percellere se sua manu	Oros.Hist.7,35,19
perdere se	Cic.Fin.1,46
perimere se	Flor.1,34,17
perimere semetipsum	(Ps) Clem.Recogn.7,14
petere mortem	Cic.Fin.2,19,61
potiri mortem	C.I.L.IX,1164
praebere . . . brachium	Hier.Chron.210,3
praecipitare se	Dig.15,1,9,7
praecipitem se mittere	Dig.21,1,23,3
praecipitio uti	(Ps) Clem.Recogn.1,13
praecipitium	(Ps) Clem.Recogn.7,14
privare se anima	Enn.Scen.198
privare se vita	Cic.De or.3,3,9
proicere se in puteum	Amp.2,6
propria manu se . . .	Hier.Chron.204,3
quaerere mortem	Tac.An.1,5,4
quaerere sortem manu	Luc.Phars.7,309
renuntiare vitae	Suet.Galba 11
saevire in se	Dig.29,5,1,22
saevire in suum corpus	Dig.15,1,9,7
sanguinem per venas mittere	Tac.An.13,30,4
spontana mors	Aug.Gaud.30,34
sponte decedere	Plin.Ep.1,22,8
sponte exire	Plin.Ep.1,22,8
sponte moriri	Sen.Rhet.Suas.6,9
sponte mortem sumere	Tac.An.4,22,1
statuere aliquid non ignave de spiritu	Sen.Rhet.Contr.8.4
statuere de se	Tac.An.6,29,2
suae manus occidunt aliquem	Sen.Rhet.Contr.Exc.8,4,3
sumere mortem	Tac.An.13,30,3
suspendere se	Matth.27:5
suspendio perire	Oros.4,5,9
suspendio vitam finire	Dig.48,21,3,2
suspendiosus	AE 1971,88 col.II r.22?
torquere laqueum	Dig.21,1,23,3
tradere se aliciu iugulandum	Cic.Mil.11,31
transigere viscera	Luc.Phars.4,545
tumultuarius mors	Apul.Met.1,16
ultimum consilium	Sen.Nat.Quaest.4A praef.

venas abrumpere	Tac.An.6,29,1
venas abscindere	Tac.An.15,69,3
venas intercidere	Tac.An.16,14,6
venas porrigere	Tac.An.16,35,2
venas praebere exsolvendas	Tac.An.6,38,4
venas resolvere	Tac.An.6,48,5
veneno vitam finire	Sen.Helv.10,9
venenum haurire	Tac.An.16,14,6
venis ictum inferre	Tac.An.5,8,3
vim sibi adferre	Tac.An.16,17,9
vim vitae suae adferre	Tac.An.6,38,4
vim vitae suae inferre	Tac.An.6,38
vitae mortisque consilium suscipere	Plin.Ep.1,22,10
voluntaria mors	Liv.8,39,14
voluntarius exitus	Tac.An.6,40,3
voluntarius finis	Tac.An.4,19,7
voluntate exanimare	Hier.Chron.189,4

NOTES

LESS THAN AN ANIMAL, MIGHTIER THAN A GOD

1 *Naturalis historia*; in denoting ancient sources in the main text and the notes titles are given in a more extended version than is usual among Classicists and Ancient Historians. In the text the work is only denoted by an Anglicized name, if this English name is common; the notes give title and author in Latin or in Greek transcriptions.

2 L. D. Hankoff ('Flavius Josephus: Suicide and Transition' in *New York State Journal of Medicine* 79 (1979) pp.937–42) observed 'a preoccupation or perhaps obsession with suicide' in Josephus: not only does he often mention cases of self-killing, but there is a specific pattern in his descriptions, in Hankoff's words there are 'standard plots': first there is the speech of a leader. Then it is decided by lot who will have to kill the others before he is allowed to lay hands upon himself. There are always a few who hide in a cave or something of that kind to escape the mass suicide and these few survivors are characterized by Josephus as people of more than average status and intelligence. In an earlier publication (1977) Hankoff called Josephus a 'cunning man' who preferred survival above ideology and principles.

3 Flavius Josephus, *Polemos Ioudaikos* 3,8,5; The Greek *physei*-argument for Josephus is only complementary to his main plea: the soul is the divine part of the body which God has committed to us. Destroying this is an act of injustice to the lawful owner, God. Fugitive slaves are punished rightly – a allusion to the ancient idea that a *fugitivus* steals himself? Is it not a crime to run away from God? After death the soul of a suicide has lost the opportunity to return to chaste bodies – the idea of metempsychosis. The darker regions of the nether world receive the souls of those who have laid mad hands upon themselves.

4 Aristoteles, *Historia zoön* 9,47. In reality lemmings die involuntarily when they respond to the urge to look for new territories; in their excitement they often plunge into waters they are unable to cross. It is a mistaken idea to assume that whole groups of lemmings jump into the fjords and in this way sacrifice themselves for the well-being of the species. Another species which in antiquity is said to commit suicide

251

is the tiger; when tigers have been driven mad by drums they tear themselves (Ploutarchos, *Moralia* 144D and 167C); the bird called porphyrion was believed to draw the attention of his master to the infidelity of his wife by strangling itself (Athenaios, *Deipnosophistai* 9,388C).

5 'Judging whether life is worthwhile or not is answering the essential question of philosophy. And if Nietzsche is right in stating that a philosopher, in order to have authority, must set the example, one sees the importance of the answer, because the decisive act is required.' From the opening lines, under the subtitle 'The absurd and suicide', of Albert Camus's *Le Mythe de Sisyphe*, Paris 1942.

6 Ambrose Bierce, *In the Midst of Life*. Tales of Soldiers and Civilians, Secausus (N.J.)1974, p.112.

7 The Dutch writer whose death raised controversy 46 years afterwards was Menno ter Braak who died 14 May 1940; mockery of Fannius: Martialis, *Epigrammata* 2,80; the expression dying by a Roman death, *Romana morte*, figures in *Epigrammata* 1,78 with respect to one Festus. Possibly this Festus is not a fictitious person but Gaius Calpetanus Rantius Quirinalis Valerius Festus (J.-L. Voisin, 'Apicata, Antinous et quelques autres', in *Mélanges d'archeologie et d'histoire de l'école française de Rome*, 99.1 (1987), p.272).

8 See Porterfield in J. P. Gibbs, *Suicide*, New York 1968, p.36; In the Introduction to her work Anderson rightly states that there is very little valid investigation into the history of suicide except for its role in literature and moral philosophy (Olive Anderson, *Suicide in Victorian and Edwardian England*, Oxford 1987, p.1). The only study of medieval suicide – apart from its role in literature – is an article by Schmitt about some fifty cases, J.-L. Schmitt, 'Le suicide au Moyen Age' in *Annales Économies Societés Civilisations* 31 (1976) pp.3–28.

9 See II.4.A *suicidum*, a non-word.

1 CASUS MORIENDI

1 In antiquity Hyginus the mythographer has made handy lists of *Men who killed themselves* and *Women 'quae se ipsae interfecerunt'* (*Fabulae* 242 and 243).

2 Y. Grisé, *Le suicide dans la Rome antique*, Montreal/Paris 1983. The study on which Grisé leans heavily is A. Bayet, *Le suicide et la morale*, Paris 1922; for ancient sources this book makes use of nineteenth-century studies with referencing conventions which have gone out of use. Some examples of mistakes in Grisé: 'Les deux Ignatii' who are mentioned as having committed suicide in 43 BC to 'échapper aux siccaires'(p.27) in reality were called Egnatius and according to Appianos they 'died by one blow' (*Emphylika* 4,4,21) in a series of political murders; there is no reason to surmise a case of suicide. C. Judacilius who should be found in *Emphylika* I,*V*,48 appears in I,*VI*,48 as Vidacilius. In *Emphylika* IV,VIII,62 the Dolabella indicated (p.29) is not present. Aquilius Florus was not the 'fils', but the 'père' (p.42;

31 BC). There is no indication for suicide by Martina the poisoner in Tacitus, *Annales* 3,7,2. When it is said of Sextilia, mother of Vitellius the emperor, that she died 'in an opportune death', *opportuna morte*, no doubt a natural death occurring at the right moment is meant, not suicide (p.50; 69 AD); Grisé calls self-killing a possibility. It is not only persons in ancient sources that have suffered from carelessness. This kind of error is almost inevitable when many data have to be processed, as I found out myself: in my Appendix A Caecilius Classicus is recorded twice. Trusting her communication that Caramuel formed *suicidium* as a Latin neologism in the '*XVIIIe* siécle' (p.22) I made the observation in my 'Antieke zelfdoding tussen honor en horror', *Hermeneus* 59.1(1987) 8-17, that we had here the interesting case of latinizing the French learned word 'suicide'. But in fact Caramuel published his *Theologia moralis fundamentalis* in the *seventeenth* century; the revised edition, in which *suicidium* and *suicida* occur, was published in Rome in 1656 (the Leuven edition of 1643 does not have the words). Professor IJsewijn in Leuven called my attention to this fact; see our discussion in *Hermeneus* 59.4(1987)250. Most annoying is a mistake when Grisé mentions a rare inscription in which a self-killing occurs as published in the *Corpus Inscriptionum Latinarum* VI 12469; finally I discovered that two figures had been transposed: the correct number is 12649. But in that inscription there is no deed of despair by a 'père par la perte de sa fille' (p.30); it is questionable whether the father who speaks to us had already died from grief when the tomb was made *for his daughter*. The only reference to self-killing is a malediction addressed to a former slave of the family to whose 'guile' the death of the girl is attributed. See for this text, which is interesting for other reasons than Grisé gives, p.5.

3   Aigner's *Der Selbstmord im Mythos*, Graz 1982, pointed the way to many a mythical case. However I did not include all his instances, for he regards an utterance such as 'Would that I were dead' already as a suicide contemplated.

4   It is debatable whether attempts are the key to the understanding of suicidal motivation. P. Moron, *Le suicide*, Paris 1975, p.34, stresses that 'para-suicide' ought to be the most important clue for the suicidologist. But are the driving forces of those who failed to commit suicide the same as those who were 'successful'? Was the 'failure' not a calculated risk? There is another objection: will not the surviving self-killer himself try to discover a logical structure in his own behaviour to satisfy himself and the psychiatrist who sits at his bedside? Even there a strong need to interpret will be operative. On the ratio of suicides committed to attempted suicides see Matthÿs, p.77.

5   Seneca, *Epistulae* 78,2: 'Saepe impetum cepit abrumpendae vitae: patris me indulgentissimi senectus retinuit.' Augustinus, *Confessiones* 4,6,11: 'et taedium vivendi erat in me gravissimum et moriendi metus . . . bene quidam dixit de amico suo: dimidium animae suae'. Every educated reader of the *Confessiones* would immediately recognize Horace's phrase, applied to Virgil in the *Carmina* 1,3,8.

6 *Corpus Inscriptionum Latinarum* VI 12649, *Atimetus libertus* in line 14.

7 'sine alimentis deficiens in puteum se proiecit'; Ampelius 2,6; other fictional cases of non-human self-killing are: the Sphinx and *dikaios logos* in Aristophanes; the case of the Scythian stallion (*equus Scythicus*) is presented by Aristoteles as a scientific fact and is regarded as 'hard' in this study.

8 *Nephelai* 988.

9 Émile Durkheim, *Le suicide*, 1897; third edn, Paris 1930, p.5.

10 So suicide in accordance with Deshaies' definition: 'l'acte de se tuer d'une manière consciente en prenant la mort comme un moyen ou un fin' (quoted by Moron, op. cit., p.4). A modern definition was formulated by Diekstra for the World Health Organisation, *Suicide and its Prevention*, p.53: (a) an act with a fatal outcome; (b) that is deliberately initiated and performed by the deceased him- or herself; (c) in the knowledge or expectation of its fatal outcome; (d) the outcome being considered by the actor as instrumental in bringing about desired changes in consciousness and social conditions.

11 *Anabasis* 4,7,13.

12 In fact Saul is mentioned by Flavius Josephus who in his *Ioudaike Archaiologia* also mentions other cases taken from the Old Testament: Abimelech, Samson, Saul's armourbearer, Ahitophel and Zimri. This author, who stands between Judaic and Graeco-Roman culture, has been used only as a source for cases for which he relies on sources nearer to his time or on personal research.

13 Other groups with exact numbers are: 1000 soldiers of Opitergium, 1000 fellow-slaves of Satyros and 400 Roman soldiers who did not wait to be killed by the Frisians.

14 England has 9 suicides per 100,000 persons each year; the Netherlands (1983) and the USA 12 per 100,000, the German Federal Republic 21 and France 22; Hungary is 'in the lead' with 55; Mediterranean countries like Italy and Greece produce as official rates 5 to 10. *Nature* (May 1983) 303,3.

15 S. Labovitz, 'Variation in Suicide Rates' in Gibbs, op. cit. pp.57-73, especially p.60 and 63; E. Westermarck 'Suicide: A chapter in comparative ethics', *Sociological Review* 1 (1908), p.12, had already indicated the great varieties; Durkheim op. cit., (p.215) takes a growth during human evolution for granted; for the significance of modern suicide statistics: S. Taylor, *Durkheim and the Study of Suicide*, London, 1982, p.31.

16 S. Taylor, op cit., p.74:

> A historical account therefore, whether of the French Revolution or Joe Soap's sudden and unnatural death, is a selective reconstruction: an *interpretation* of past events shaped first by the (acknowledged) availability of evidence and second, by the (less commonly acknowledged) values, beliefs, theories, common-sense understandings, etc. of the observer. [also p.93]

17 See Theodore Crane, *The Imagery of Suicide in Lucan's 'De Bello Civili'*, Diss. The University of North Carolina at Chapel Hill 1964.

18 Durkheim, op. cit., p.216: 'Toutes les révolutions qui ont eu lieu en France au cours de ce siècle ont diminué le nombre des suicides au moment où elles se sont produites'.

19 Apart from the *Vulteii commilitones* (Livius, *Periochae* 110): Caesar's soldiers in 54 BC when they were beleaguered unexpectedly by Ambiorix: until dark they offered resistance, but during the night they killed themselves to the last man 'despairing of deliverance' (Caesar, *De Bello Gallico* 5,37,6; Cassius Dio 40,6); after the catastrophe at Lake Trasymene (217 BC; Polybius 3,84,10); Crassus' soldiers after Carrhae (53 BC; Cassius Dio 40,25,2); Pompeius' soldiers after Corfinium (49 BC; Caesar, *De Bello Civili* 1,22,6); troops of Gaius Antonius, Caesar's loyal partisans, after Coructae (Cassius Dio 41,40,2).

20 13(4) and 39(32) cases; see Appendix B 5.

21 This is an era which also is an area – the Greek East of the Mediterranean; chronologically there is an overlap with Early and Late Republic.

22 For instance Agathonike; see p.195.

23 See Jean-Pierre Vernant, *Mythe et société en Grèce ancienne*, Paris 1974 (English edn London 1980).

24 1635 individuals in 248 cases.

25 Tacitus, *Annales* 16,16 and 6,29. In my 'Van mors voluntaria tot suicidium', *Tydschrift voor Geschiedenis* 101 (1988), pp.17–35, I wrongly stated that the total was not so impressive.

26 Cassius Dio 51,26; 69,83; 58,16,3; 58,15,4; 60,35; 77,5,6; 78,16,6a; 72,26,4; 63,17,4.

27 Durkheim, op. cit., p.46; K. Matthijs, *Zelfdoding*, Leuven 1985, p.25; Labovitz in Gibbs, op. cit., p.69: '. . . suicide rates are highest in the most and the least prestigious occupations . . . and lowest in the intermediate occupations'.

28 See for the function of the Roman arena as a 'domesticated battlefield' Keith Hopkins' 'Murderous Games' in *Death and Renewal*, Cambridge 1983, pp.1–30.

29 D. Gourevitch, *Le triangle hippocratique dans le monde Greco-Romain. Le malade, sa maladie et son médecin*, Paris/Rome 1984, p.177, is wrong in stating that Seneca's descriptions of suicides by slaves are contemptuous; equally contestable is the general pronouncement: 'Mais chez Sénèque lui-même tant de respect et d'admiration pour les esclaves est bien rare.'

30 A gladiator who had been sent forth to the morning exhibition was being conveyed in a cart along with other prisoners; nodding as if he were heavy with sleep, he let his head fall over so far that it was caught in the spokes; then he kept his body in position long enough to break his neck by the revolution of the wheel (*Epistulae* 70,23); during a sham sea-fight one of the barbarians sank deep into his own throat a spear which had been given him for use against his foe (*Epistulae* 70,26).

31 'Tarquinii plebeii' in Plinius, *Naturalis Historia* 36,107; Servius specifies their method as hanging in his *Commentarii in Vergilii ad*

Aeneidem 12,603 (see p.104); according to him it was Tarquinius *Superbus* who forced his people to work on the sewers.

32 Suetonius, *Otho* 10; Ploutarchos, *Otho* 15.

33 Tacitus, *Historiae* 3,54.

34 Where a name is unknown a Latin pseudonym is given in Appendix A; this is mentioned in the main text, sometimes in brackets.

35 *Epistulae* 70,25.

36 Aristophanes, *Hippeis* 83; Acroteleutium and Staphyla in Plautus; the case of Staphyla is of some socio-historical interest for it demonstrates that at the beginning of the second century BC the public was assumed to know its letters.

37 By counting the cases in *Dictionnaire de la mythologie grecque et romaine* by Pierre Grimal, Voisin (Le suicide d'Amata, *Revue des études grecques*, 57 (1979), p.257 n.2) also established an excess of female suicide in myth: 50 against 40 male suicides. As he does not give names his data cannot be compared with mine. In my list of 71 cases (with 56 women who actually killed themselves) are Aglauros and Herse, Aithra, Alkestis, Alkinoe, Althaia, Amophinome, Amphinomene, Antigone, Antikleia, Antipoinos' daughters, Apriate, Arachne, Arganthone, Ariadne, Britomartis/Diktynna, Byblis, Deianeira, Elektra, Erechtheus' daughters, Erigone, Euadne (Kapaneus' wife), Euadne (Pelias' daughter), Europa, Eurydike (Kreon's wife), Halia, Harpalyke, Hekabe, Helena (4 times), Hermione, Hiketides, Hippodameia, Ilione, Ino, Iokaste (Epikaste), Iole, Kallirhoe (Lykos' daughter), Kalypso, Kanake, Kleite, Kleoboia, Klytaimnestra, Kreusa, Kyane, Laodameia, Leda, Makaria, Medeia, Menippe and Metiche, Molpadia and Parthenos, Mykerinos' daughter (a somewhat dubious case as the story is set in Egypt), Myrrha (Smyrna), Neaira, Niobe, Ochne, Oinone, Parthenope, Pelopeia, Phaidra's nurse, Phaidra (2x), Phyllis, Polyxena, Selene, Skylla, Stheneboia, Theano and Themisto. The 51 male mythical cases, including 37 actual self-killers, are: Achilles, Admetos, Adrastos, Agrios, Aiax, Aigeus, Althaimenes, Ameinas, Antilochos, Assaon, Astyanax, Bytes, Dionysos, Euenos, Glaukos, Haimon, Herakles (2x), Hipponoos, Iason, Iphias, Iphis, Kaineus, Kalchas, Kambles, Kastor and Pollyx, Kinyras, Klymenos, Kodros, Kyanippos, Kyklops, Leukippos, Lykourgos (Dryas' son), Maion, Makareus, Melikertes, Menelaos (2x), Menestratos, Menoikeus, Narkissos, Nisos, Odysseus, Oidipous, Oinomaos, Orestes (3x), Philoktetes, Pylades, Solois.

38 See Mary Lefkowitz, *Women in Greek Myth*, London 1986; G. Steiner, *Antigones. The Antigone Myth in Western Literature, Art and Thought*, Oxford 1984, p.242.

39 In 1963 in France the men-women ratio was still 2:1. French women are assumed to make more attempts than men, in a proportion of 5:2 according to A.-P. Fabre, *Aspects medico-sociaux de l'intoxication aiguë volontaire*, Thèse de médecine, Toulouse 1968 (in Moron, op. cit., p.54); data for the nineteenth century in Durkheim, op. cit., pp.38 and 168.

40 T. Asuni, 'Suicide in Western Nigeria', *British Medical Journal* 1962.2,

pp.1091–7; M. Gelfand, 'Suicide and Attempted Suicide Among the Shona: Research Report', in *Zambezia* 2.2 (1972), pp.73–8; J. H. M. Beattie, 'Homicide and Suicide in Bunyoro', in Bohannan, P. (ed.), *African Homicide and Suicide*, Princeton N.J. 1960, p.143, on Bunyoro: thirty-seven men against twenty-four women; P. Bohannan, 'Patterns of Murder and Suicide' in Bohannan, ibid., p.261 on three Bantu tribes in Uganda: 2:1; figures on fifty-four cases of suicide in the Middle Ages in J.-C. Schmitt, 'Le suicide au Moyen Age', in *Annales Économies Sociétés Civilisations* 31 (1976), p.5.

41 E.g. see the discussion about the frequency of hanging in section I.2.G.

42 Helen King, 'Bound to Bleed: Artemis and Greek Women', in A. Cameron and A. Kurt (eds), *Images of Women in Antiquity*, London 1983.

43 *Anthologia Palatina* 5,297.

44 Sophokles, *Antigone* 654, 816, 917/8; Euripides, *Iphigeneia he en Aulidi* 461; *Medeia* 985; *Hekabe* 416, 612; complaint of Phrasikleia in P. A. Hansen, *Carmina Epigraphica Graeca*, Berlin 1983, no.24; see also M. Lefkowitz, op. cit., p.51.

45 Even in this century Greek women are known to have killed themselves for this reason. Striking parallels are also present in suicides among young women in modern India. See A. J. F. M. Kerkhof and S. S. Nathawat, 'Suicidal behaviour in India and the Netherlands' in R. F. Diekstra (ed.), *Suicide and its Prevention*, Leyden 1989, pp.144–59, esp. p.168.

46 Hyginus includes Alkestis among the 'Women who have killed themselves' (*Fabulae* 243,4).

47 Anthologia Palatina 9,245.

48 Line 13/14 of the inscription as published by Lebek, *Zeitschrift für Papyrologie und Epigraphik* 59(1985) pp.7–8.

49 Philostratos, *Heroikos logos* 51, pp.2–6. Hyginus does record the romantic suicide of Stheneboia because of her unreturned love for Bellerophon (*Fabulae* 57,5).

50 Homeros, *Odysseia* 10; Euripides, *Aiolos;* Suetonius, *Nero* 21 and Cassius Dio 63,10.

51 E. Eyben, *De jonge Romein volgens de literaire bronnen der periode ca. 200 v.Chr. tot ca.500 na Chr.*, Brussels 1977; *De onstuimigen*, Antwerp/ Kampen 1987. Debate between Pleket and Eyben about the latter's view that there was such a thing as Roman youth in *Lampas* 14.2(1981) pp.133–43.

52 Dolabella had had his share of life – including being married to Cicero's daughter Tullia – when he chose death. Both with respect to age (26) and knowledge of life he can hardly count as a youth. Lucanus was already 25 when he ended his life on the orders of Nero.

53 Stephen Kern, 'Explosive Intimacy; Psychodynamics of the Victorian Family', *History of Childhood Quarterly* 1.3 (1974) pp.437–61.

54 Propertius 2,17,line 13/14.

55 In Phrygia houses and people disappeared in a fissure. The oracle said that the evil would only end when the most precious thing was

sacrificed. Midas' son Anchouros realized that human life was meant and he jumped into the cleft, a parallel to Curtius the Roman (Ploutarchos, *Moralia* 306F). The Roman Aquilius was seized by the Lesbians and was meant as a magnificent and welcome gift for king Mithridates. 'He, however, *though a very young man*, had the courage to perform a heroic deed. Forestalling the men who were about to arrest him, he chose death in preference to ill-usage (*hybris*) and a shameful execution'. Diodoros uses the word *deinotes*, which is both 'terribleness' and 'grandeur' for denoting Aquilius' behaviour (37,27,2).

56   Ploutarchos, *Moralia* 234C; Seneca, *Epistulae* 77,15; there is a neat parallel to this story for a Spartan female in Ploutarchos, *Moralia* 242D.

57   T. Fusé, 'Modernization and Suicide in Japan: A Comparative Approach', in *Cultures et développements* 12.1 (1980), pp.52 and 54.

58   J. P. Sartre, *Les mains sales*, Paris 1960, p. 137: Hoederer:

'La jeunesse, je ne sais pas ce que c'est: je suis passé directement de l'enfance à l'âge d'homme'. Hugo: 'Oui. C'est une maladie bourgeoise (Il rit). Il y en a beaucoup qui en meurent'.

59   Apuleius, *Metamorphoses* 4,7.

60   *Metamorphoses* 6,30.

61   See J. N. Bremmer, 'Oude vrouwen in Griekenland en Rome', *Lampas* 17.1 (1984) pp.96–113; English version 'The Old Women of Ancient Greece' in Josine Blok and Peter Mason (eds), *Sexual Asymmetry. Studies in Ancient Society*, Amsterdam 1987, pp.191–216; Anton J. L. van Hooff, 'Oud-zijn in het oude Hellas,' in *Tijdschrift voor Gerontologie en Geriatrie* 14 (1983) 4.

62   Staphyla in Plautus' *Aulularia* 77.

63   *Facta et dicta memorabilia* 2,6,8.

64   Imperial *pudor* was not the sole motive; she also had a cancer of the breast (Cassius Dio 78(79),23,1).

65   E. Le Roy Ladurie, *Montaillou, village occitan de 1294 à 1324*, Gallimard, Paris 1982, p.337.

66   The other cases are Argos' father, *Argi pater* in Appendix A, Lysidamos and Antipater. Antipater had been the teacher of the Severian brothers Caracalla and Geta. When the latter had found his Cain in Caracalla the former consul, aged sixty-eight, wrote a letter full of reproofs to the fratricide. 'He is said to have died rather from *karteria* (fasting till death) than because of illness.'

67   For the 'Keion nomimon' pp.32 and 167.

68   Gourevitch, op. cit., p.172: 'Le suicide rationnel du malade se présente donc essentiellement comme une conduite de vieux.' For stylizing of death by philosophers, see Johannes Hahn, *Der Philosoph und die Gesellschaft*, Stuttgart 1989, esp. pp.202–3 on the significance of a dignified end.

69   *Digesta* 28,3,6,7.

70   Diogenes Laertios 8,74.

71   Aelianus, *Poikile historia* 2,41,5; according to Chares 35 participants in

the drinking competition died immediately as a consequence of hypothermia, six died afterwards in their tents (Athenaios, *Deipnosophistai* 10,437A); a more positive picture of the same scene is presented by the same Aelianus at another place (5,6): here Alexander declares that Kalanos – as such his name is given here – had fought opponents more formidable than he had done: 'I fought Taxila and Dareios, but Kalanos pain and death'.

72 Strabo 15,1,73; 'Zarmaros' in Cassius Dio 54,9,10.
73 Contra M. I. Finley, 'Les personnes âgées dans l'Antiquité classique', *Communications* 37 (1983) 31–45.
74 Corellius Rufus in Plinius, *Epistulae* 1,12,1–11; Silius Italicus, *Epistulae* 3,7,1.
75 See p.153; J.-L. Voisin, 'Apicata, Antinous et quelques autres' in *Melanges d'archéologie et d'histoire de l'école française de Rome* 99.1 (1987), pp.257–80, p. 276 argues that Bassulus' age must have been between seventy and eighty.

2 MODI MORIENDI

1 Seneca, *De Providentia* 6,9.
2 'Gamble with death': S. Taylor, *Durkheim and the Study of Suicide*, London 1982, p.140 ff.; 'Ordeal': p.161 ff.
3 De mortibus non vulgaribus, *Dicta et facta memorabilia* 9,12.
4 Y. Grisé, *Le suicide dans la Rome antique*, Montreal/Paris 1983, p.93.
5 Seneca, *De ira* 3,15,4.
6 Valerius Maximus is not to be taken too seriously when he apparently contests the exaggerated attention devoted to method when arguing for a reappraisal of the case of Coma the slave. He was the brother of Kleon the leader of the Sicilian Slave Revolt. Caught by the Romans, he was interrogated about the power and the strategy of the fugitives. He took his time, apparently to gather his thoughts, pressed his knees against his breast and held his breath. Valerius (9,12, ext.1) praises his audacity: 'let them whet iron, mix poison, seize ropes, look for impressive height – as if grandiose tools or exquisite methods are needed'.
7 Grisé, op. cit., p.118; the passages quoted are Ovid, *Fasti* 6,373 and Ammianus Marcellinus 17,9,4; I do not believe that Thrasyllus' decision to end life by starvation and not by the sword proves the infamy of *inedia*. There are more debatable points in the section 'Le suicide par inanition': Megara does not speak of a *wish* to die from hunger, but in the place in Seneca's *Hercules Furens* 419/20 which Grisé indicates on page 119, she expresses her firm determination to remain loyal to her husband even if pressure is put on her by chains or starvation: 'I will, Alcides, die as your wife'.
8 Cicero, *Tusculanae disputationes* 1,34,84; this case is a rare instance of greater tendency for self-murder among young men, even to the extent of constituting an epidemic, cf. p.129.

9   *Peri thanatou* 4,6,r.10/11; more about Philodemos and Epicureanism on p.185. In Bassi's edition it reads 'it is a deed of utter madness to die voluntarily by starving oneself'.

10 War as something of prehistory: Aristeides, *Eis Romen* 70; Loukianos, *Pos dei historian syngraphein* 21.

11 Ploutarchos, *Moralia* 690A/B; Corpus Hippocraticum, *Peri Sarkon*, Littré 8, p.610; Aulus Gellius, *Noctes Atticae* 3,10.

12 Corpus Hippocraticum, *Peri diaites oxeon* 15, Littré 2, p.344.

13 Athenaios, *Deipnosophistai* 2,46.

14 *Hiketides* 1104-8.

15 *Satyricon* 111; when the pair have been enjoying love in the vault for several nights a disaster occurs: one day one of the crosses is found without a corpse. The soldier tells the lady that he will not wait for a court-martial, but will punish his negligence with his own sword. But then the widow puts the corpse of her husband at his disposal as a substitute for the missing bandit.

16 In 1774 David painted the scene of Erasistratos' diagnosis; Julian, *Eis tous apaideutous kunas*, 198D; about Julian's curious asexual interpretation of the orgiastic Cybele: Dario M. Cosi, *Casta Mater Idaea*, Venice 1986.

17 It is somewhat disturbing that the *Su(i)da(s)*, the Byzantine lexicon of the tenth century, calls an *Apokarteresanta* somebody who 'leads himself out of life' by hunger *or the rope*.

18 James Joyce, *Ulysses*, Harmondsworth 1968, p.556.

19 Corpus Hippocraticum, *Peri sarkon* 18. Littré 8, p.609.

20 J. de Romilly, 'La tragédie grecque et l'idéal héroïque', *Didactica Classica Gandensia* 22 (1982) 27; Sophokles, *Aias* 815–22.

21 Calpurnia, Antistius' wife, stabbed herself with a sword after her husband had been killed.

22 *Historia ekklesiastike* 8,14.

23 *Incisio venarum, praebere brachium, sanguinem per venas mittere, venas abrumpere/abscindere/intercidere/porrigere/praebere exsolvendas/resolvere, venis ictum inferre.*

24 *Phleba(s) anateino/entemno/schazo/temno.*

25 Suetonius, *Nero* 37,2.

26 Anderson, *Suicide in Victorian and Edwardian England*, Oxford 1967, pp.373–4: young women from the working class drowned themselves when deceived in love; the depressed middle-aged woman took poison, couples in love concluded a 'narcotic suicide pact' and the older businessman threw himself in the way of a train, a method which became common only after 1868.

27 *Epistulae* 70,16: 'non opus est vasto vulnere dividere praecordia: scalpello aperitur ad illam magnam libertatem via.'; *Naturales Quaestiones* 3,15: 'Ergo, ut in corporibus nostris sanguis, cum percussa vena est, tam diu manat, donec omnis effluxit . . . ita in terra, solutis ac patefactis venis, rivus aut flumen effunditur. Interest quantum aperta sit vena; on pneumatism': J. Godderis, *Galenos van Pergamon Over psychische stoornissen*, Leuven/Amersfoort 1988, p.20.

28 The assistance of others at the death of Brutus and Cassius is

explained by Florus (2, 17, 15) as a further proof of their adherence to philosophical principles: they were unwilling to stain their own hands with blood, although their decision to die was an act of their own free will; Cicero, *Philippicae* 2,6,12; Vergilius, *Aeneis* 8,670.

29 Ph. Pinel, *Traité médico-philosophique sur l'aliénation mentale ou la manie*, Paris 1801, pp.54–7, mentioned by Godderis, op. cit., p.108.

30 *Anthologia Palatina* 7,233;7,234;11,354.

31 *Digesta* 49,16,6,7.

32 Émile Durkheim, *Le suicide*, 1897; Second edn: Paris 1930, p.3.

33 Kodros as a beggar in Pherekydes, *Fragm.Griech.Hist.* 4 F 125; Hellanikos, *F.G.H.* 3 F 154; Lykourgos, *Leokr.*84 sqq.; Iustinus 2,6,16. This historian may be the source for the pun in *Fas et nefas* (*Carmina Burana* 19) when the poet says that he, albeit more Codrian than Codrus, will have plenty of everything if his protector will look after him (strophe 5, line 5/6: *quia Codro Codrior/omnibus habundas*).

34 Tacitus, *Historiae* 4,34,4.

35 'Probably the most profound emotional shift concurring with the transition from Republic to Principate is the transfer of popular affection from state to princeps, which is closely bound up with the personalization of sovereignty', H. S. Versnel, 'Destruction, *Devotio* and Despair in a Situation of Anomy: the mourning for Germanicus in triple perspective', in *Perennitas. Studi in onore di Angelo Brelich*, Rome 1980, p.562.

36 See for this my 'Het Romeinse moordspel' (The Roman murderous game), in *Kleio* 28.9 (November 1987) pp.9–17.

37 The idea of *suicides obsidionaux* in Durkheim, op. cit., p.118: under Decius the aged Apollonia freed herself from her executioners and threw herself into the fire, AD 250.

38 Diodoros Sikoulos 19,34,1–6; it is probably these scenes that caused Aelianus in his *Poikile historia* 7,18 to generalize: 'among the Indians women are subjected to the same fire as their men; the women dispute the honour of the fire; finally the one who is selected by lot is burned with the man'.

39 Philostratos, *Eikones* 2,30,2; older version in Euripides, *Hiketides* 1016.

40 Herakles' triad is not identical with the other instances of the three *Selbstmordwege*, as Fraenkel holds, E. Fraenkel, 'Selbstmordwege', in *Philologus* 87 (1932), 470–3; in a scholion on Pindaros' *Olympionikai* 1,97 a noble method is mentioned first before the disgraceful ones: sword, rope and ravine. The *malus servus*: *Digesta* 21,1,23,3.

41 See for the controversy about Demosthenes' death: Ploutarchos, *Demosthenes* 30,4; on the availability of hemlock: H. Aigner, *Der Selbstmord im Mythos*, Habilitations-Schrift, Graz 1982, p.203.

42 Livius 8,18,8; why should this, as Grisé, op. cit., p.109 n.116, asserts, be 'une ordalie'? The *matronae* do not subject themselves to a divine judgement: they only react to their desperate situation.

43 On opium and other drugs see D. Gourevitch, *Le triangle Hippocratique dans le monde Greco-Romain, le malade, sa maladie et son médecin*, Paris/Rome 1984, p.181 n.32.

44 Plinius Maior, *Naturalis Historia* 24,163.

45 Helena in Sophokles frg.178 (Pearson = 663 Nauck) and in Aristophanes' *Hippeis* 83.

46 Plinius Maior, *Naturalis Historia* 28, 147, who says that bull's blood is reckoned one of the poisons, except at Aigeira (in Achaia). For there the priestess of the Earth, when about to prophesy, drinks bull's blood before she goes down into the cave.

47 Livius 31,18,7.

48 Stories of this type exist about the Jews when Jerusalem was captured, about the Stoeni, Gallaeci, Segestani and the women of the Teutons.

49 Suetonius, *Vita Tiberii* 61.

50 'De mortibus non vulgaribus' in Valerius Maximus, *Facta et dicta memorabilia* 8,12.: Herennius Siculus, Iulius Celsus and Caldus Caelius.

51 *Odysseia* 22,462.

52 Pausanias, *Periegesis tes Hellados* 8,23,6–7; Artemis as the sinister Hekate 'who jumps from the rope': Ploutarchos, *Moralia* 170B; on the Aiora: Suidas s.v. *eidolon* = Aelianus, *Poikile historia* 13,24.

53 Sophokles, *Oidipous Tyrannos* 1033–1041; Seneca *Phaedra* 1177.

54 Servius, *Commentarii in Vergilii Aeneidem*, ad 12,603 says that in the old books of the priests it was ordered to throw away the body of a suicide; he quotes Varro as saying that the ghosts of those who had hanged themselves were placated by hanging masks (on trees?) in imitation of their death (see also pp.17 and 164 for this important text).

55 Diogenes' misogynist reaction has already been mentioned on p.20; Euadne in Philostratos, *Eikones* 2,30,2.

56 Aristoteles, *Problemata* 954 B 35; on *Peri parthenion*, p.22.

57 *Corpus Inscriptionum Latinarum* I, 1418 = *C.I.L.I.*[2], 2123 = *C.I.L.* XI,6528 = *Inscriptiones Latinae Selectae* 7846 = *Inscriptiones Latinae Liberae Rei Publicae*[2] 662 = J.-L. Voisin, 'Apicata, Antinous et quelques autres', in *Mélanges d'archéologie et d'histoire de l'école française de Rome*, 99.1 (1987), pp.257–80, Annexe no.1.; comment in the same article.

58 Voisin, ibid., p.261; Wacke too assumes that hanging was far less frequent than in modern Germany, where the method accounts for 40 per cent of all self-killings. The inscription about the regulations with regard to the manceps can be found in *l'Année épigraphique* 1971, no.88, col.II r.22.

59 The sentence, not well formed with two occurrences of 'war' close to each other, has been translated literally: *Vita Maximi et Balbi* 4,3.

60 Theokritos, *Eidyllia* 23,36 sqq.; a well-balanced book on 'l'amour grec' is K. J. Dover, *Greek Homosexuality*, Cambridge Ma. 1978 (paperback: Vintage Books, New York 1980); for the element of revenge in ancient suicide see under *exsecratio* in I 3e.

61 Among the 13 cases of female suicide which J. Schmitt, 'Le suicide au Moyen Age', in *Annales Économies Sociétés Civilisations* 31 (1976), collected, hanging was the method 8 times (p.5).

62 For Rhodesia/Zimbabwe: M. Gelfand, 'Suicide and attempted suicide

among the Shona', in *Zambezia* 2.2 (1972), p.74; for Western Nigeria: Asuni; for Bunyoro: J. H. M. Beattie in P. Bohannan, *African Homicide and Suicide*, Princeton N.J., 1960, p.143; identification of hanging with suicide: P. Bohannan, 'Homicide and Suicide in North Kavirondo' in Bohannan, ibid., p.175; generalization about hanging: P. Bohannan, 'Patterns of Murder and Suicide' in Bohannan, ibid., p.263; remark about Busoga: Fallers in Bohannan, ibid., pp.70 and 75; for Gisu: J. La Fontaine, 'Homicide and Suicide among the Gisu' in Bohannan, ibid., p.116; about England: Anderson, op. cit., pp. 119 and 172; for methods in the Middle Ages: Schmitt's (op. cit.) statistics on p.5; for France: P. Moron, *Le suicide*, Paris 1975, pp.35–6; only Prussia in the last decades of the eighteenth century does not fit the pattern with 136 cases of drowning, 53 hangings, 42 uses of fire-arms and 8 throat-cuttings: H. Brunschwig, *La crise de l'état prussien à la fin du XVIIe siècle et la genèse de la mentalité romantique*, Thèse Lettres, Paris 1947, p. 267, explains the deviations by pointing to the pre-romantic climate and the over-representation of soldiers (with 50%) in his collection.

63 Rescript by Antoninus Pius: *Digesta* 48,21,3,2; for mourning: *Digesta* 3,2,11,3.

64 Anderson, op. cit., p.373.

65 *Digesta* 21,1,23,3 about the methods supposed to be used by slaves; Aristophanes, *Batrachoi* around line 122: rope and ladder, jump from tower and hemlock; comparable to Aristophanes' joke is what Euripides' admirer (*Euripidis admirator* in Appendix A) says in fragment 130 (Edmonds) of Philemon: 'If it were true what some assert that a dead person sees, I would have hanged myself to see Euripides'.

66 Semonides 1,18/19. In the Archaic and Early Classical Periods in Greece there looms a syndrome of deep pessimism in which the irrelevance of life is stressed: better not to have been born at all. And having been born the best thing is to die as soon as possible. The story of Kleobis and Biton fits this pattern well: in answer to their mother's prayer Hera gave them the best gift she could give – death. Whereupon Herodotos' comments in 1,31: 'And the god clearly demonstrated in this way that for a human being death is preferable above life'; other instances of archaic pessimism in Hesiodos, *Erga kai hemerai* 174–5 and Theognis 181–2 and 425–8.

67 *Asinaria* 816; more instances taken from Roman comedy in Grisé, op. cit., p.108 n.103. Exclamations like these are modelled on similar self-cursing in Attic comedy, e.g. in Philemon frg.103 (Edmonds).

68 Athenaios, *Deipnosophistae*, 9,396A; comedy of Krobylos mentioned by Athenaios in 3,109D6 and 248B; a cook who was confronted with the price of one drachme for a fish called *trachelos* would have preferred to hang himself by the neck (= *trachelos*): Athenaios, *Deipnosophistai* 7,294B.

69 Other examples: Deinarchos the niggard wanted to *hang* himself, but discovering that a rope cost six copper coins he desisted. Menophanes owned such a little piece of land that he had to use another man's tree when he *hanged* himself because of hunger. An Abderite, the ancient

prototype of a stupid person, wanted to *hang* himself, but the rope broke. He went to the doctor and then hanged himself with plaster and all. A sick person consulted a practitioner: 'Doctor, I cannot stand or sit'. 'Why not try *hanging*?' (*Philogelos* 183). Aristeides represents in no less than three epigrams of the *Anthologia* (9,149, 150 and 255) the wretched suicide: after the loss of his only animals, one sheep and one cow, he *hanged* himself with the strap of his knapsack on a pear-tree (140) or in the empty stable (150); more on the *Philogelos* in II.4.B.

70 Corpus Hippocraticum, *Peri topon* 39 (Littré 6,329); *Aphorismoi* 2,43 (Littré 4,482).

71 For Hierax and other cases in papyri more in II.4C. The conversion of the robber on the cross is told by Luke 23:39–43; the story elaborates on Matthew 27:44 and Mark 15:32 where it is said that all, including the robbers, abused Jesus. In medieval representation Judas' soul can only escape by his bottom because his neck was strung tight.

72 *Oneirokritika* 2,50; recent translations: Artemidoros von Daldis, *Das Traumbuch*, DTV, Munich 1979 (hardbound: Artemis, Zürich); *The Interpretation of Dreams*, Robert J. White, *Oneirocritica by Artemidorus*, Park Ridge N.J. 1975; the meaning of hanging in dreams in *Oneirokritika* 2,50; for Timon: Ploutarchos, *Antonius* 70.

73 Moron, op. cit., p.36.

74 Stesichoros (ca. 600 BC) told in a poem about Kalyke's unhappy love for Euathlos; when Aphrodite did not answer her prayer and the young man 'overlooked her' (*hypereiden*), she threw herself from the Leucadian rocks; the Cyclops in Euripides' satyr-play says that he is willing to jump from the Leucadian cliffs as long as he may get drunk; so at least in the fifth century BC the syndrome had been established.

75 See for this element: H. S. Versnel, 'Self-Sacrifice, Compensation and the Anonymous Gods', in *Le sacrifice dans l'antiquité*, Entretiens sur l'antiquité classique 27, Geneva 1981, p.154.

76 Another story where the (attempted) murder-weapon is probably used as the tool for self-killing is told by Cicero: Marcus Marcellinus was unexpectedly attacked with a dagger by Magius Cilo, a close friend. He was wounded in his belly and head; there were good prospects for survival, but Magius killed himself.

77 Aelianus, *Poikile historia* 8,14; there is some controversy in antiquity about the exact method of the great Cynic's suicide: in another reading he held his breath.

78 The same applies to Alcinoe and the *matrona ornata*, the rich Byzantine lady who was kidnapped by partisans of the Blue Circus Faction; from their ship she addressed her husband: there was no need for him to be afraid of her being violated. Having said that she jumped into the sea.

79 Groups of beleaguered people who threw themselves from walls: *Poeni obsessi, milites esurientes, perfugae, fugitivi Sicilienses*; for jumping into death by Christians: Eusebios, *Historia ekklesiastike* 8,12; about the Patriciani Filastrius tells in his *Diversarum haereseon liber* 62(34)$\frac{1}{2}$:

Further there are the Patriciani, a name derived from one Patricius who lived in the city of Rome. They assure that the human flesh was not wrought by God, but they hold it to have been made by the devil. This they think must be condemned and rejected by all means, so that even some among them did not hesitate to lay hands upon themselves.

On the Donatists see p.196.

80 Elias Bickerman, 'Consecratio', in: *Le culte des souverains dans l'empire romain*. Entretiens de la Fondation Hardt 19, Geneva 1973, p.12; M. F. Griffin, *Philosophy*, Oxford 1976, p.66.

81 S. Taylor, *Durkheim and the Study of Suicide*, London 1982, pp.141 and 143; elsewhere he uses such forms of words as 'risk-taking exercises', 'contest', 'game', 'ordeal' and 'ludenic behaviour'; for self-killing in the English countryside: Anderson, op. cit., p.420.

3 CAUSAE MORIENDI

1 O. Anderson, *Suicide in Victorian and Edwardian England*, Oxford 1987, pp.66–7.

2 R. Aron, *Main Currents of Sociological Thought*, vol. 2, London 1968, p.34, quoted by S. Taylor, *Durkheim and the Study of Suicide*, London 1982, p.21.

3. É. Durkheim, *Le suicide*, 1897; second edn: Paris 1930, p.365: 'L'hypercivilisation qui donne naissance à la tendance anomique et à la tendance égoiste'.

4 In spite of incidental scepticism: 'Ce qu'on appelle statistique des motifs de suicides, c'est en réalité une statistique des opinions que se font de ces motifs les agents, souvent subalternes, chargés de ce service d'informations', Durkheim, op. cit., p.144.

5 J. P. Gibbs, *Suicide*, New York 1968, Introduction p.17: 1. the greater the incidence of disrupted social relations in a population, the higher the suicide rate of that population; 2. all suicide victims have experienced a set of disrupted social relations that is not found in the history of non-victims.

6 Taylor, op. cit., p.192.

7 See E. Jonker, *De sociologische verleiding (The Temptation of Sociology)*, Dissertation, Utrecht, Groningen 1988, p.9: 'sociologie als wereldbeeld' (sociology as an image of a world).

8 R. G. Collingwood, *The Idea of History*, Oxford 1946; a recent interpretation of Collingwood's thoughts: W. J. van der Dussen, *History as a Science. Collingwood's Philosophy of History*, Dissertation, Leyden 1980.

9 Even if the structures of motivation for 'para-suicide' were the same as for accomplished self-killing, the unsolvable question remains whether somebody who is being interviewed by a psychiatrist does not give the answer wanted, or does not try to impose a logical structure on his behaviour himself.

10 *Digesta* 3,2,11,3; 28,3,6,7; 29,5,1,23; 49,14,45,2; 49,16,6,7; *Codex Iustinianus* 9,50.

11 *Digesta* 29,5,1,23; 49,14,45,2; 49,16,6,7.

12 *Digesta* 49,14,45,2.

13 *Digesta* 49,16,6,7; Ruffus, *Leges militares* 24.

14 *Digesta* 28,3,6,7: 'iactatione ut quidam philosophi'.

15 *Digesta* 49,16,6,7.

16 Digesta 3,2,11,3; 29,5,1,23. alternatives: because of having committed an outrage (*ob admissum flagitium*) and 'from consciousness of crimes' (*conscientia scelerum*; Livius 31,31,14).

17 Tacitus, *Annales* 6,23,1; also 'ordered death', *mors iussa* (Tac., *An.*16,17,2) or 'enforced death', *mors coacta* (Tac.,*An.*16,19,2).

18 My list of 12 ancient motives more or less is similar to that of J. Bayet, *Croyances et rites dans la Rome antique*, Paris 1971, p.278: dévotio, désir d'expier, d'éviter l'infamie, du supplice, de fuir la maladie, la souffrance, la vieillesse, de ne pas survivre à un être cher, de prévenir ou de laver un outrage, de ne pas tomber aux mains de l'ennemi, dégoût de la vie, par ordre, suicides politiques.

19 *De bello Gallico* 5,37,6.

20 In Appendix A cases of *suicides obsidionaux* under Abydeni, Agrigentini, Indi obsessi, Isauri, Iudaei, milites Caesaris, *milites esurientes*, Poeni obsessi, Saguntini, Segestani, senes Athenienses, Sidones, Taochoi, Vibius Virrius and senatores Capuenses.

21 Diodoros 36,3,6.

22 He has therefore been classified as a case of *desperata salus* whereas his noble father and his followers are to be found under the heading *pudor*.

23 Other instances of suicides by commanders out of despair: Cornutus, Roscius, Laelius (all three BC 43), Fuficius Phango, Demochares, Arruntius Furius – when his soldiers proved unwilling to support him in his undertakings against Claudius.

24 Lucretius, *De rerum natura* 3,72; earlier in the *Kyroupadeia* (3,1,25) Xenophon has Tigranes say: 'some, for fear that they will be caught and put to death, in terror take their own lives before their time – some by hurling themselves over a precipice, others by hanging themselves, others by cutting their own throats'.

25 One example from the Greek world: when the regime and the life of Aristotimos had been finished off, the tyrannicides came to his house. Aristotimos' wife bolted the door and hanged herself.

26 Cannutia Crescentina and Floronia.

27 Her motivation therefore has not been 'established' as despair, but as *pudor*.

28 Seneca Rhetor, *Controversiae* 5,1.

29 J.-C. Schmitt, 'Le suicide au Moyen Age', *Annales Économies Sociétés Civilisations* 31 (1976), pp.12 and 4.

30 In Tychon's comedy *Stratiotes*, Athenaios, *Deipnosophistai* 3,103F.

31 *Kathistemi es anangken hekousiou thanatou; ad mortem voluntariam cogere*.

32 Dio Chrysostomos, *Oratio* 43,11; Suetonius, *Domitianus* 9.

33 I therefore do not see much room for doubt about the 'motive' for Asinius Gallus' suicide. He died by *inedia*. Ancient observers wondered whether he *sponte* or *necessitate* came to the deed. The method seems inadequate for an enforced self-killing, unless no other means was available or if the self-killing was meant as a demonstration, but in the latter case he would not have left his public in doubt as to his purpose.

34 The case of the Persian Bogoas also has little to suggest suicide. Having attempted to poison Darius he was invited for dinner and then forced to drink his own mixture (Diodoros 17,5,6).

35 Tertullianus, *Apologeticum* 6,4; the eight Roman women are: Antonia, Cornificia, Ennia, Messalina, the two sisters Ocellatae Servilia and Varonilla.

36 The victim of this peculiar jealousy was Servianus; a few years before, in AD 132, Hadrian had forced Marcellus – probably C. Publicius Marcellus – 'into a free death' (*ad mortem voluntariam coegit*).

37 Magnentius and Decentius.

38 Seneca Rhetor, *Controversiae* 3,9.

39 Taylor, op. cit., p.113: 'This is not to dispute that suicide is associated with various forms of mental disorder, but simply to argue that the official rates are systematically biased in that direction.'; Joost Meerloo, *Suicide and Mass Suicide*, New York 1968: ancient *furor* would also comprise Meerloo's 10 per cent cases of suicide by impulse.

40 Roman law about *furor*: 'aliqua furoris rabie constrictus se praecipitem dedit' (*Dig*.6,22,2); see for the distinction between *furor* and *insania*: Cicero, *Tusculanae disputationes* 3,7-11; see J. Godderis, *Galenos van Pergamon over psychische stoornissen*, Leuven/Amersfoort 1988, for the little attention paid to psychic imbalance; two kinds of *mania* in Aretaios, *Peri aition kai semeion oxeon pathon*, 3,6,5; one has the duty to prevent a friend from plans of self-killing which he conceived in his *athumia*: Xenophon, *Apomnemoneumata Sokratous* 4,2,17.

41 Herodotos 6,75 and 84.

42 Philemon, frg.106 (Kock; Ploutarchos, *Moralia* 102C).

43 J. Bels, 'La mort volontaire dans l'oeuvre de Saint Augustin', in *Revue de l'histoire des religions*, 187 (1985), pp.147–80; Schmitt, op. cit., p.7.

44 On the development of the story of Aiax see A. C. Pearson in the Introduction of his edition of the Aias, *The Ajax of Sophocles*, Cambridge 1907, pp.x–xvii; in our classification *pudor* has been taken as the primary motive; in a similar way the frenzy of Heracles is seen as a complementary reason for a self-killing primarily explained by *inpatientia doloris*.

45 Dio Chrysostomos, *Oratio* 11,126 and 152; *Or*.8,34; 60; 78,44; for the 'recycling' of the myth of Heracles: P. Desideri, *Dione di Prusa*, Messina/Firenze 1978, p. 491 sqq. 'Miti nuovi e miti riciclati'.

46 See the legal texts where *inpatientia*, *taedium* and *dolor* overlap each other.

47 Unless Dido is to be regarded as a historical case; the women meant are: Acroteleutium, Anthia, Ariadne, Byblis, Chloe, Kalypso, Phaidra, *puella in pictura*, Stheneboia.

48 Men with suicidal pangs of love: Antiochos, Chaireas (5x), Dionysios *erastes*, *eromenos*, Koresos, Leucippos, Lycidas, Onnes, Polemon, Propertius, *puer in pictura* and Solois.

49 *Oratio* 32,50.

50 See note 87. In modern cases suicide notes are written by approximately 15% of those who end their lives (E. S. Shneidman, 'Approaches and commonalities of suicide', in R. F. W. Diekstra (ed.) *Suicide and its Prevention*, Leyden 1989, pp.14–36, esp. p.19.

51 *Anthologia Palatina* 5,297 (also on p.23); a lesbian experience is hinted at in one of Loukianos' *Hetairikoi dialogoi* (5): Klonarion and Leainia.

52 Kallisthenes and Straton.

53 Chaireas 1, Habrokomes 3 and 4, Kleitophon 1 and 3.

54 Philostratos, *Eikones* 2,30,5.

55 *Heroikos* 51,2-6; the same story in *Bios Apolloniou* 4,16 by the same Philostratos. My attention was drawn to this version by my colleague Jaap-Jan Flinterman who is preparing a dissertation on this representative of the Second Sophistic Movement.

56 Aithra, Antikleia, Argos' father, Arruntius' wife, Eurydike, wife of Kreon, Gordianus, Hampsicora, Iason, Kios, Neaira, Sisyngambris.

57 Self-killings because of a lost brother: Althaia, Basilo, Ligarius, Selene.

58 One of Pompey's soldiers and one of Strabo's.

59 The age is not indicated in the text: he is denoted as the oldest of the *paidia*, which suggests twelve to fourteen years.

60 Josine Blok and Peter Mason, *Sexual Asymmetry. Studies in Ancient Society*, Amsterdam 1987.

61 Seneca Rhetor, *Controversiae* 8,1.

62 Element of revenge in contemporary self-killing: P. Moron, *Le suicide*, Paris 1975, p.70; 'Samsonic': M. P. Jeffreys, 'Samsonic Suicide or Suicide of Revenge Among Africans', in *African Studies* 11.3 (1952) 1118-22; Ajax invokes the Erinyes in Sophokles, *Aias* 835 sqq; the woman who met the wish of her father: the Elder Seneca, *Controversiae* 10,3; psycho-analytic view: H. Musaph, *Doden met verlof Depressie en doodsdrift*, Baarn/Antwerp 1972, p.21 referring to Freud and Bernfeld.

63 E. Westermarck, 'Suicide: a chapter in comparative ethics' in *Sociological Review*, 1 (1908), p.13; J. La Fontaine, 'Homicide and Suicide among the Gisu', in P. Bohannan (ed.), *African Homicide and Suicide*, Princeton N.J., 1960, p.113; J. H. M. Beattie, 'Homicide and Suicide in Bunyoro', in Bohannan, op. cit., p.146; G. M. Wilson, 'Homicide and suicide among the Joluo of Kenya', in Bohannan, op. cit., p.193 (Joluo): 'the threat of suicide is an effective technique used by the Joluo to achieve goals or to avoid distasteful consequences'; Westermarck's further order is: Japan, India, Old Testament, Islam, Greeks, Rome, Christianity (p.18 sqq.).

64 Euripides, *Iphigeneia he en Taurois* 973 sqq.; to be compared with this behaviour is the magic pressure which is sometimes exerted on statues of the saints: by laying them face to the ground people 'force' them to make it rain; about suicide as an instrument of the weak: M. Delcourt, 'Le suicide par vengeance dans la Grèce ancienne', in *Revue de l'histoire des religions*, 119 (1939), p.166.

65 Cicero, *Epistulae familiares* 7,3,3.

66 Taylor, op. cit., p.134 about the characteristics of a social group with a special code. On guilt and shame: G. Piers and M. B. Singer, *Shame and Guilt. A Psychoanalytic and a Cultural Study*, New York 1971; A. W. H. Adkins, *Moral Values and Political Behaviour in Ancient Greece*, London 1972; Peter Walcot, *Envy and the Greeks*, Warminster 1978.

67 Beattie, op. cit., on shame in Africa: p.146; in Luo male suicide is usually caused by loss of status, according to Wilson, op. cit., p.194, but Beattie op. cit. (p.144) only saw 2 self-killings from shame among the 28 cases where a motive could be established; on the role of lost status in Japan: T. Fusé, 'Modernization and Suicide in Japan: a comparative approach', in *Cultures et développements* 12.1 (1980), p.150.

68 *Panegyrici Latini* II (XII) 41,4.

69 Aischines 3,212; Dover, p.168.

70 Cicero, *De officiis* 1,31; Herodotos 5,66; Demosthenes 9,31; *Anthologia Palatina* 7,148.

71 Diodoros 31,9,3–7; Ploutarchos, *Moralia* 198B and *Aemilius* 34,3.

72 Diodoros 20,61,8.

73 Roman soldiers in captivity 'did away with themselves from shame'; Onomarchos feared the disgrace (*aikian*) that results from captivity; the same motive is attributed to Philistos who transfixed himself. Lucanus stylizes the suicides of the last republicans in the Civil War as martyrs: in the *Pharsalia* Vulteius makes a complete speech aboard his ship to prove that it is disgraceful to survive a defeat. His comrades follow him in voluntary death.

74 See 'Murderous Games' in Keith Hopkins, *Death and Renewal*, Cambridge 1983; refusers are the Saxon gladiators of Symmachus and the Germans in Seneca's letter 70 (p.17); unwilling Roman gladiators are Satyrus and his thousand comrades.

75 As early as BC 413 some anonymous military tribunes are said to have withdrawn from a legal hearing by killing themselves.

76 Cassius Dio 58,15,2.

77 I have counted 15 to 20 individual cases, e.g. Pompeius Macer and son, Proculus and Rufus Scribonius, Spurius Oppius, Statilius Taurus, Trebellenus Rufus, Vistilius.

78 In the case of Fabius Maximus doubt existed whether losing the favour of the emperor had caused him to die. Pomponius Labeo opened his veins when he had lost the emperor's friendship.

79 Orgetorix is said to have killed himself when he was formally accused of striving for tyranny. Sulpicius Galba did not get 'his' province. Banishment caused Agrios to kill himself. Turannius started on a hunger-strike because he – at 90 years of age – was

bereft of his political function. Scipio Aemilianus could not live up to his promises.

80   *Digesta* 49,14,45,2: 'pudore aeris alieni'.

81   Artemidoros, *Oneirokritika* 5,31 and 33; Theognis 1,173-176.

82   Horatius, *Carmina* 1,37,29.

83   I. Donaldson, *The Rapes of Lucretia. A Myth and its Transformations*, Oxford 1982, p.8; Augustine's interpretation on p.196.

84   Bohannan, op. cit., p.176 about North-Kavirondi.

85   Around line 1369 of the *Oidipous Tyrannos*.

86   Sophokles, *Oidipous Tyrannos* 981/2.

87   Quintilianus, *Institutio Oratoria* 4,2,69.

88   Letters written by suicides mainly occur in the sources in the world of the Macedonians. Another instance: the Greek Dioxippos had defeated a Macedonian in a duel. To avenge him his comrades had hidden a beaker in Dioxippos' luggage and accused him of theft. Dioxippos wrote a letter to Alexander and 'removed himself from life'. Dimnos is a third suicidal letter-writer I know of apart from the special cases of Petronius and Antipater.

89   *Digesta* 3,2,11,3; very clear in *Digesta* 28,3,6,7 'because of guilt over a (military) dereliction' (*ob conscientiam delicti*).

90   Musaph, op. cit., p.23; G.Simpson, 'The Aetiology of Suicide', Introduction to Durkheim's *Suicide*, London 1952, p.24: 'the suicide murders the introjected object and expiates guilt for wanting to murder the object. The ego is satisfied and the superego mollified through self-murder'.

91   Musaph, op. cit., p.24.

92   Atratinus opened – very sophisticatedly – his veins in the bath: he had become tired of his diseases.

93   The other one in our material is the fictitious old crone, the *anus* in Apuleius.

94   Stoic justification of suicide when the quality of existence is in danger: Seneca, *Epistulae* 30,2; on self-killing from medical reasons in Africa: Beattie, op. cit., p.144 (Bunyoro); the old African woman in Joluo: Wilson, op. cit., p.213.

95   Vergilius, *Aeneis* 4,653.

96   *Anthologia Palatina* 9,354; for the first century AD Festus is a concrete example of a Roman soldier who only wants to die in his bed by his own sword (p.54).

97   Aelianus, *Poikile historia* 10,11.

98   *Naturalis Historia* 25,23.

99   See for this syndrome H. S. Versnel, 'Self-sacrifice, Compensation and the Anonymous Gods', in *Le sacrifice dans l'antiquité*, Entretiens sur l'antiquité classique 27, Geneva 1981, pp.135–94 especially p.163; the Decii, father and son, bought Roman victories with their life having devoted themselves in a formal ritual; the formula (*carmen*) was still extant in the time of Plinius Maior, *Naturalis historia* 28,12. A self-killing in the last decades of the seventh century BC still had all the marks of myth: when the Alcmeonids had killed the

partisans of Kylon, the would-be tyrant, in the holy precinct, a curse came over Attica. Thereupon 'Kratinos willingly gave himself up on behalf of her (Attica) who had fed him'; Aristodemos, his lover, died with him (Athen.14,619E); for suicide in military circles: Durkheim, op. cit., p.260: 'Tout prouve donc que le suicide militaire n'est qu'une forme du suicide altruiste'; a higher frequency among professional soldiers: p.253; among special corps: p.258.

100 See H. S. Versnel, 'Vrouw en vriend', in *Lampas* 17.1 (1984) pp.28–45 (published in English as 'Wife and Helpmate') in: Josine Blok and Peter Mason, op. cit., pp.59–86; in 1912 the Japanese general Noji committed suicide at the death of the emperor; about the *soldurii/silodouroi*: Caesar, *De bello Gallico* 3,22,2 and Athenaios, *Deipnosophistai* 6,249B; about free death for a price: *ibidem* 4,154C.

101 *Facta et dicta memorabilia* 6,7 and 8.

102 Seneca Rhetor, *Controversiae* 2,2 and 2,5,8.

103 Arria demonstrated to Paetus that it did not hurt and Paxea shared with her husband death and the means of death.

104 Martial 1,8.

105 *Digesta* 28,3,6,7.

106 Athenaios, *Deipnosophistai* 4,155E.

107 A. Bayet, *Le suicide et la morale*, Paris 1922, p.272; Cicero, *Tusculanae disputationes* 1,74.

108 Durkheim, op. cit., about marriage: p.208; protestantism has 'une superiorité . . . au point de vue de suicide' because as a church it is less integrated than catholicism (p.222), which is called by Durkheim elsewhere (p.173) 'une société'.

109 In Gibbs, op. cit., p.37.

110 P. Bohannan, 'Theories of Homicide and Suicide', in Bohannan, op. cit., p.9; 'Patterns . . .', ibid., p.266.

4 SUICIDE IN WORDS AND TEXTS

1 Quoted by P. Moron, *Le suicide*, Paris 1975, p.16.

2 Bernardus O. F. M. Alaimo, 'De suicidii nomine et quibusdam eius definitionibus', in *Antonianum* 31 (1956), p.194: 'Primus qui, quantum hodie scitur, vocem "suicidium" cum respectiva "suicida" usurpavit fuit Caramuel'.

3 'nec strictius teneris te non occidere, quam proximum'.

4 I did also consult the Caramuel's first Leuven edition of 1643, but I could find neither theme nor words; on *suicidium* in Browne's work: M. F. Griffin, Greece and Rome 33–1, p.68; having already completed the manuscript I discovered that *suicida* is more than 450 years older than is hitherto supposed: it already occurs in Gauthier of Saint-Victor, *Contra Quatuor Labyrinthus Franciae* 4,2 of 1177/78; more on this word history in 'A longer life for *suicide*', to be published in Romanische Forschungen.

5 The English translation of Comenius' text is taken from the London

edition of 1777, of which a facsimile edition was published in the Osborne Collection of Early Children's Books, Holp Shuppan Publishers, Tokyo 1981; a facsimile of the original edition is available in the German collection of 'Die bibliophilen Taschenbücher', Harenberg Kommunikation, Dortmund 1978, 1985 (ISBN 3.921846.30.7; on Donne's plea for legitimate self-killing: G. Highet, *The Classical Tradition*, Oxford 1985 (second edn), p.170.

6 Y. Grisé, *Le suicide dans la Rome antique*, Montreal/Paris 1983, p.23 thinks the absence remarkable and meaningful in the light of compounds like homicidium, matricidium, fratricidium, infanticidium, tyrannicidium: 'On s'étonne alors que les Romains n'aient pas cherché à former sur ces modèles quelque dérivé approprié', whereas the suffix -cidium is so productive that it allows for funny words such as 'purse-killer' (*perenticida*; Plautus *Epidicus* 352) and 'sack-killer' (*utricida*; Apuleius, *Metam*.3,18,7). Only late Latin has as Christian literal translations from biblical Greek two words for 'to appropriate': *suificere* and *propriificere*, where the pronouns *suus* and *proprius* are used as prefixes.

7 Euripides, *Andromache* 172.

8 'You at least were the *autocheir* of your mother'; Euripides, *Alkmaion*, frg 358 (Nauck; Plutarch, *Moralia*, 89A); with respect to *autocheir* in a papyrus (*P. Giss. Univ.* V col.2.10): A. von Premerstein, *Schriften der Ludwigsuniversität zu Giessen*, 1936, no.46 with note; Haimon as an *autocheir*: Sophokles, *Antigone* 1175/6.

9 To kill oneself: *apokteino heauton, apoktinnumi heauton, kteino heauton, phoneuo heauton*; to do away with oneself: *anachraomai heauton, apochraomai heauton, diachraomai heauton, katachraomai heauton*; to destroy oneself: *anaireo heauton, analiskomai, apophthinomai, diaphtheiro heauton, phtheiro heauton*; destroyer of oneself: *anairetes heautou*; to bereave oneself of life: *sterisko heauton tou zen*; to put an end to one's life: *teleutao (ton bion)*.

10 *katastrophen tou biou poieomai, katastrepho ton bion.*

11 *conficere se, eximere se, finire se, finem vitae facere, interficere se, interimere se, necare se, occidere se, perdere se, perimere se(metipsum).*

12 *absumere se, appetere/oppetere mortem, conficere se, consulere extremis rebus/vitae (durius), discedere e vita, effundere animam, emittere se, exanimare se, exire (vita), exprimere spiritum, extrahere se rebus humanis, festinare mortem in se, fugere in mortem, inrogare sibimet mortem, offerre se ad mortem, privare se anima/vita, quaerere mortem, saevire in se.*

13 *vim sibi adferre, vim vitae suae adferre/inferre.*

14 The same expressions figure in the works of Aulus Gellius and Ausonius, authors who will never choose the common word when an exotic one is available.

15 Athenaios, *Deipnosophistai* 4,157B.

16 *Pro Cluentio* 61,171.

17 *Institutio Oratoria* 9.2.86.

18 *Institutio Oratoria* 8,5,22/23; Dio Chrysostomos, *Oratio* 74,5.

19 Sophokles, *Philoktetes* 999–1002 and 1208–9.

20 This figure of 37 applies only to those cases where ancient drama is

the primary source. Ajax for instance is not included in this number, because his suicide is already alluded to in Homeros.

21 The 11 cases are: Antigone, Astyanax, Deianeira, Euadne, Eurydike, Herakles, Iphis, Kanake, Leda, Menoikeus and Phaidra.

22 'It is surprising to what degree the . . . generally accepted results of modern suicidology are applicable to the Sophoclean Ajax.' B. Seidensticker, 'Die Wahl des Todes bei Sophokles' in *Sophocle*, Entretiens Fondation Hardt 29, Geneva 1983, p.140.

23 Euripides, *Hippolytos* 728–31.

24 Euripides, *Herakleidai* 501–34.

25 R. Garland, *The Greek Way of Death*, London 1985, p.97 commenting on an earlier saying of Tekmessa: 'There is no criticism of suicide as such, merely an appeal for the avoidance of an action bound to react harmfully upon family and friends'.

26 Philostratos, *Heroikos* 35,15.

27 *Aias* 466 sqq., 966 sqq. and 1415 are the relevant passages.

28 Suetonius, *Augustus* 85,2; Cassius Dio 58,24,4 (34 AD).

29 This, at least, is Ploutarchos' interpretation of Aiantis' place in the Tribal Cycle of Athens in *Moralia* 629A.

30 Passages in *Herakles* relevant to the argumentation are: 1243 sqq., 1254, 1348; in Plato's *Phaidon* 62B Sokrates says that mankind is shut up in a kind of jail and that one is not allowed to free oneself from it or escape: the word *apodidraskein* which is used here is the technical word for running away by slaves.

31 A. W. H. Adkins, *Moral Values and Political Behaviour in Ancient Greece*, London 1972, chapter 5.

32 Seidensticker, op. cit., pp.108–9, n.1. Deianeira, Antigone, Haimon and Eurydike.

33 Euripidis admirator, Dionysos, Acroteleutium, Koneiazomenai, Lysidamos, Polemon, servus II, Staphyla.

34 Chariton, *Chaireas and Kallirhoe* 8,1,4; about ancient novel: Thomas Hägg, *The Novel in Antiquity*, Oxford 1983.

35 Ploutarchos, *Moralia* 633B.

36 Anaxagoras, Aristoteles, Empedokles, Epikouros, Zeno; most often those poems of the Greek Anthology were composed by Diogenes Laertios who mentions them with much self-satisfaction in his *Bioi kai gnomai ton en philosophiai eudokimesanton*.

37 Voisin has a small corpus of this material in an annex to his article 'Apicata', J.-L. Voisin, 'Apicata, Antinous et quelques autres' in *Mélanges d'archéologie et d'histoire de l'école française de Rome*, 99.1 (1987), pp.273–80; Peter van Minnen of Leyden University called my attention to this recent publication.

38 *Vivere non potui plures XXX per annos/nam eripuit servos mihi vitam et ipse/ praecipitem sese deiecit in amnem (Corpus Inscriptionum Latinarum XIII 7070)*; as a poem it has been included in the *Carmina Epigraphica Latina* (1007).

39 *Corpus Inscriptionum Latinarum* IV 1864: *Samius/Cornelio/suspendre.*

40 *C.I.L.XIV* 4533 col.II r.17/18: *VII K. November Apicata Seiani se occidit.* The sequence of the facts recorded in the inscription means that Cassius Dio's information (58,6,11) has to be corrected: He says that

Apicata only committed suicide *after* her children had been killed. Voisin, op. cit., p.273, rightly comments that the Fasti of Ostia 'célèbrent comme une victoire le suicide en 31 ap. J.-C. d'Apicata, l'épouse de Séjan'.

41 Voisin, ibid., p.267 ff. referring to the cases of Cn. Calpurnius Piso and P. Palpellius Clodius Quirinalis.

42 Henry Seyrig, 'Les combats de gladiateurs à Thasos', in *Bulletin de correspondance hellénique* 52 (1928) 388 ff., especially pp.390–1; *idios thanatos* as self-killing in Philemon frg. 231. Louis Robert is right in explaining *idio(i) ethanon* as '. . . il est mort de sa belle mort'; note 4 justifies his interpretation of a 'natural death' referring to *Supplementum Epigraphicum Graecum* VI 274: a soldier in Lycia who died *eidioi thanatoi* and Dessau *Inscriptiones Latinae Selectae* 5106: a gladiator who 'sua morte obit' (*Les gladiateurs dans l'orient grec*, Paris 1940, p.114).

43 *Anthologia Palatina* 10,59; see Bianca Hafen, *Griechische Epigramme auf Selbstmörder*, Dissertation, Munich 1979.

44 *C.I.L.* X 5920 = *Carmina Latina Epigraphica* 423 = Voisin, op. cit., no.21.

45 L. Alfonsi, 'Un "protrettico" epigrafico di età imperiale', in *Epigraphica* 26 (1964–5), pp.59–67, recognizes pieces of Sallustius and Terentius in the text and discovers the Stoic doctrine of the supreme importance of the quality of life in line 15: *sed iam valete, donec vivere expedit*. I think he is overstressing the point: these addresses are commonplace.

46 *C.I.L.* IX 1164: *verum vexatus animi curis/non nullis etiam corporis doloribus/ utrumque ut esset taediosum ultra modum/optatam mortem sum potitus*; J. Berlage, 'Ziekten en sterfgevallen in de brieven van Plinius de Jongere', in *Hermeneus* 9 (1938–9), pp.66–73.

47 *C.I.L.* V, 5278; Voisin, op. cit., p.277 n.8; text of the inscription: 'morborum vitia et vitae mala maxima fugi nunc careo poenis pace fruor placida'.

48 *Papiri della Società Italiana* (*P.S.I.*) III,177; second/third century AD; *The Oxyrhynchus Papyri* (P.Oxy.) 1,119, l.14–15; the case of Thrasyllos is mentioned by R. Lane Fox, *Pagans and Christians*, Harmondsworth 1986, p.143.

49 *P.Oxy.* VI, 850: *ennounta brochisai heauton*.

50 See J. and L. Robert, 'Bulletin épigraphique', in *Revue des études grecques* (1977) p.572, with respect to *Ostraka Florida* 7 with a reference to the 'Bulletin épigraphique' 1974 p.331, for *idios thanatos*; see above note 42; also in the *Poimandros* 22 of the *Corpus Hermeticum*, *idios thanatos* undoubtedly means natural (= personal) death.

51 H. C. Youtie, *Transactions and Proceedings of the American Philological Association* 98 (1967) pp.512–13, advocates this interpretation; *cheiras prosago* for 'to lay hands upon oneself' is an uncommon phrase. Youtie gives *autocheir* as a cognate expression. Maybe *cheiras epiphero* said by Aretaios is a better parallel. Could it not be that a Latinism – cf. *manus ad/inferre* – penetrated the bureaucratic Greek of Roman Egypt? The whole text is very formal.

52 *P. Oxy.* I, 51; because no criminal context is indicated, this case usually is regarded as an instance of suicide.

NOTES

5 EXPERTS, LAW-GIVERS AND ARTISTS

1 Hippokrates, *Aphorismoi* 2,43 (Littré 4, p.482), earlier discussed on p.72.
2 Corpus Hippocraticum, *About places (peri topon)* 39 (Littré 6, p.329).
3 On the oath and medical ethics: D. Gourevitch, *Le triangle hippocratique dans le monde Greco-Romain. Le malade, sa maladie et son médecin*, Paris/ Rome 1984, pp.204–5.
4 *thanasimon pharmakon hekousiai gnomei dia to exagagein heautous*, Paulus Aegineta 5,29.
5 Paulus Alexandrinus, ed. Ae. Boer 1958 (Teubner), p.46, l.23.
6 Ptolemaios, *Tetrabiblos* 201 (4,9).
7 Vettius Valens 2,40; the passages referred to are in Kroll's edition on page 130, line 16; p.126 l.21 ff. p.127, l.18 ff.
8 *Oneirokritika* 2,50 and 51.
9 The cases mentioned in this section are to be found in Appendix A under pseudonyms: *vir somniens, vir se ipso usus, femina somniens*.
10 *Oneirokritika* 1,4.
11 Dio Chrysostomos, *Oratio* 64,3 and 4; Zenobios, *Providentia* 6,17.
12 J. Ferguson, *Utopias of the Classical World*, London 1975.
13 Vergilius, *Aeneis* 4,384 e.v.
14 F. Cumont, *Lux perpetua*, Paris 1949, especially pp.334–8; Lasch, R. 'Die Verbliebsorte der abgeschiedenen Seele der Selbstmörder', *Globus* 77 (1900) 110 sqq., here cited according to Garland.
15 Xenophon, *Kyroupaideia* 3,1,25.
16 Macrobius, *Commentarii in Somnium Scipionis* 1,13,10; Vrught-Lenz, pp.26/27.
17 Aischines, *Oratio* III, 244; Flavius Josephus, *Polemos Ioudaikos* 3,8,5; on violating a person murdered by *maschalismos*, M. Delcourt, 'Le suicide par vengeance dans la Grèce ancienne', in *Revue de l'histoire des religions*, 119 (1939), p.161; *Su(i)da(s)* under 'Kynegion'; Ploutarchos, *Themistokles* 22; excluding some of the dead from the community of the *Manes*: J. ter Vrught-Lenz, op. cit., p.74.
18 Vergilius, *Aeneis* 6,434; *Semahot* II, 2, 44a3, II, 1, 44a3 and II, 4, 44a3; my attention was called to these regulations by the (unpublished) thesis of one of my students Cas Nelisse, *Apologia pro vita sua. Gedachten over zelfbehoud en zelfvernietiging in het werk van Flavius Josephus (Thoughts about self-preservation and self-destruction in Flavius Josephus' work)*, Nijmegen 1989.
19 On the separation of self-killers: E. Westermarck, 'Suicide: a chapter in comparative ethics', in *Sociological Review* 1 (1908), p.16; fear of evil spirits: G. M. Wilson, 'Homicide and Suicide among the Joluo of Kenya', in P. Bohannan (ed.), *African Homicide and Suicide*, Princeton N.J. 1960, p.184; burning of hut or tree: L. A and M. C. Fallers, p.70; purification of the hut among the Gisu and the dog's burial: Fallers, op. cit., pp.111–12; a rational explanation for the removal of the tree: P. Bohannan, 'Homicide and Suicide in North Kavirondo', in Bohannan, op. cit., p.177; naming a brother's son after a suicide:

NOTES

Wilson, op. cit., p.195 on Joluo; on medieval practices: J.-C. Schmitt, 'Le suicide au Moyen Age', in *Annales Économies Sociétés Civilisations* 31 (1976), p.11.

20   Quintilianus, *Institutio Oratoria* 7,3,7; Plinius, *Naturalis historia* 14, 119; Servius, *Commentarii in Vergilii Aeneidem* 12,603 says it was Tarquinius Superbus, mentioning Cassius Hemina as his source (more on p.17); Diogenes mocked even with this common belief: when he was told that the tree from which he was plucking the figs, had recently been used by someone to hang himself, the Cynic said: 'Very well, then I purify the tree from murder' (*vir e fico*) .

21   *C.I.L.* XI 6528 = I.L.S.7846 = Bruns, *Fontes* (7), p.381,35 = Arangio-Ruiz, *Negotia*, p.249,9. The text about the exclusion of the hanged is : 'exauctorateis et quei sibi laqueo manu(m) attulissent'. The community could be defiled by the *miasma* caused by hanged persons who were not cut down. An ancient commentator on Euripides, *Hippolytos* 780 says: 'For they thought to share the defilement (*miasma*) in as far as they did not cut the nooses of the hanged'.

22   C. O. Müller (ed.), *Festus. De Verborum Significatione*, Leipzig 1880, p.64: 'carnificis loco habetur is qui se vulnerasset ut moreretur'.

23   *C.I.L.* XIV, 2112, col.II, 1.5–6 = *I.L.S.* 7212; Voisin, op. cit., pp.262–6, asserts that the Lanuvian regulations indirectly deny the supposed suicide of Antinous. The collegium was under the patronage of Hadrianus' beloved boy (and of Diana); see also A. Wacke, 'Der Selbstmord im römischen Recht und in der Rechtsentwicklung' in *Zeitschrift der Savigny-Stiftung für Rechtsgeschichte-romanistische Abteilung* 97 (1980), p.48.

24   9,873 C–D; Plato excepts suicide on judicial order, because of pain or in order to save one's honour. It does not have much significance either that a commentator on Plato's *Phaidon* writes in the second half of the sixth century that 'they' did not wash the *biothanatoi* and that 'they' honoured the souls of the dead in three degrees: for the all-holy priest differently from the *biothanatoi* and also differently from the mass (Olympiodoros, *In Platonis Phaedonem commentaria*, ed.Norvin 243.22).

25   Diodoros 3,33,5; Prokopios, *Hyper ton polemon* 6,14; Diodoros 17,91,3.

26   On the *Keion nomimon*: Valerius Maximus 2,6,7–8; Strabo 10,5,6; *Anthologia Palatina* 7,470 (p.36); Aelianus, *Poikile historia* 3,37; on Marseille: Valerius Maximus 2,6,8; the proverb *sexagenarii de ponte* W.Otto, *Die Sprichwörter der Römer*, Leipzig 1890 under *sexagenarii*; the rational explanation is that it was a cry to exclude the old men from the voting bridge.

27   Quintilianus, *Declamationes* 4 and 337; Wacke, op. cit., p.48.

28   Libanios, *Declamationes* 30,61 (also *Decl.*26,29 and 35); Aristoteles, *Ethika Nikomacheia* 5,11.

29   Suetonius, *Claudius* 16,3; Livius 39,19; *Digesta* 48,3,14,3.

30   Quintilianus, *Institutio Oratoria* 7,4,39; Tacitus, *Annales* 6,29: 'eorum qui de se statuebant humabantur corpora, manebant testamenta'; see for the 'Timing of Suicide' the article of this title by A. R. Hands in *Proceedings of the African Classical Association* 5 (1962), pp.27–31.

31   *Digesta* 48,21,3; Wacke, op. cit., p.56.

32 *Digesta* 48,9,8; 48,21,3,1.
33 *Digesta* 48,21,3,4 and 5.
34 *Digesta* 49,14,45,2; 29,5,1,23; 28,3,6,7.
35 *Digesta* 48,21,3,8; *Codex Iustinianus* 6,22,2.
36 *Digesta* 21,1,23,3; the same *ausurus* in Seneca Rhetor, *Controversiae* 8,4: 'Nihil non ausurus fuit qui se potuit occidere'.
37 *Digesta* 48,19,38,12; 49,16,6,7.
38 *Digesta* 48,8,7 pr.; J.-C. Schmitt, 'Le suicide au Moyen Age', in *Annales Économies Sociétés Civilisations* 31 (1976), p.6; É. Durkheim, *Le suicide*, 1897, second edn: Paris 1930, pp.384, 432, 442 and 450.
39 Appianos, *Emphylika* 2,101.
40 Apart from personal discoveries material from Aigner and Touchefen has been used; Papastakos's article was not at my disposal.
41 Segment 145 of the relief; see Florea Bobu Florescu, *Die Trajanssäule*, Bucharest-Bonn 1969, Illustr.116; the soldier who cut off Decebalus' head was called Tiberius Claudius Maximus and he reported it as the main deed of his life on his tomb; he was promoted by Traianus (the text has Troianus) to the rank of decurio 'because he had caught Decebalus and brought his head to him (Tr.) in Ranisstorum' (*AE* 1969–70, 583); the famous head was later carried around in the triumphal procession (Cassius Dio 68,14,3); my colleague Rien Polak called my attention to the scene on the cup of Lucius Cosius from La Graufesenque: A. Vernhet, 'Un four de la Graufesenque', in *Gallia* 39 (1981), p.33.
42 Philostratos, *Eikones* 1,4.
43 *Eikones* 2,30,2; 2,9,4/5.
44 *Eikones* 1,12–13; this case, (already mentioned on p.76), in Appendix A as *puella/puer in pictura*; for 'shinju' Porterfield in J. P. Gibbs, *Suicide*, New York 1968, p.40.
45 The same moment is chosen in three other pictures which prove Ovid's popularity; see J. Baldassare, 'Piramo e Tisbe: dal mito all 'immagine', in *L'art decoratif à Rome à la fin de la République et au début die Principat*, Rome 1981, pp.337–51. Ploutarchos, *Moralia* 674A. The scene in Euripides' *Phoinissai* 1455 where Jokaste stabs herself with one of the swords of her sons, Polyneikes and Eteokles who fought each other to the death is represented on a relief cup now in Halle, see James Blitz, 'Tragedies van Euripides op Macedonische reliëf-bekers', *Hermeneus* 62.2 (1990), pp.113–19, esp. pp.113–14. There does also exist a painting of another famous female suicide in tragedy, Phaidra. One of my students, Sjors van Hoof, brought to my notice the drawing in S. Reinach Répetoire de peintures, Paris 1922, p.209, where one sees 'Fedra', depicted with the rope in her hand. Dido in the *Virgilius Vaticanus*, Cod.Lat.3225, f.40; Herakles on a pelice, Munich (2360 = J 384) from Vulci painted by Cadmos ca.450 BC in J. D. Beazley, *Attic Red-Figure Vase Painters* vol. 2, Oxford 1963, p.1186,30; R. Flacelière and J. Devambez, *Héracles, Images et récits*, Paris 1966, pl.23; P. Mingazzini, 'La rappresentazione vascolare del mito dell'apoteosi di Herakles', in *Atti dell'Accademia Nazionale dei Lincei. Memorie classe di scienze moralï, storiche e filologiche*, Ser.6,1 (1925) pp.413–90.

46 Even the fury that preceded the final deed was depicted in a series of pictures: Plinius Maior, *Naturalis historia* 35,136; Philostratos, *Bios Apolloniou* 2,22.

47 Plinius, *Naturalis historia* 34,28 says that there was no Lucretia among the statues voted to Roman heroes and heroines; I. Donaldson, *The Rapes of Lucretia. A Myth and its Transformations*, Oxford 1982, p.14 only mentions and describes the depictions, but gives no details of their whereabouts; Saul in a window of Chartres cathedral and in a miniature that illustrates Boccaccio's *De casibus virorum illustrium* made by Laurent de Premserfait between 1409 and 1419; in the same manuscript figure Hannibal, Hasdrubal's wife, Marcus Antonius and Cleopatra, Diocletianus (with a knife!) and Lucretia; a selection of the rich iconography of Lucretia: Botticelli's painting in the Isablla Stewart Gardener Museum in Boston, a piece made by Guido Reni in the Sala di Ercole in the Capitoline Museum in Rome; in the Staatliche Kunstsammlungen in Kassel, the painting of Hans Makart; in the Szépmüvészeti Museum, Budapest, that of the Master of the Holy Blood; pictures in Petty Bange, *Tussen heks en heilige. Het vrouwbeeld op de drempel van de moderne tijd, 15de/16de eeuw* (Between Witch and Saint. The Image of Women at the Threshold of Modern Time, 15th/16th Century), SUN, Nijmegen 1985, pp.136–43 and 212–13.

48 Chapeaurouge points the way to medieval representations; for the temptation of suicide in the Artes moriendi: L. Breure, *Doodsbeleving en levenshouding*, Hilversum 1987; the *patientia* in Comenius' *Orbis Sensualium Pictus* in the London edition of 1777 on pages 145–6 (see note 5 of II.4 for the data).

6 PHILOSOPHERS AND THEOLOGIANS

1 *Polemos Ioudaikos* 3,8,5; 7,9,1.

2 *Peri apoches empsychon* 2,47.

3 H. Diels, *Fragmente der Vorsokratiker*, Berlin 1922, 22,121.

4 Diogenes Laertios 6,52; *Praxeis (Acts)* 16:27–28.

5 *Clementina Homilia* 12,13/14 (*Patrologia Graeca* 2,312 b and c).

6 Diogenes Laertios 7,31; 7,130; 10,119; Seneca, *Epistulae* 4,4; 30,12; 24,24–26; *De tranquillitate animi* 2,14–15; *De ira* 2,36,5–6; M. F. Griffin, *Seneca. A Philosopher in Politics*, Oxford 1976, p.196.

7 Musonius Rufus frg.29H; Epiktetos, *Diatribai* 1,9,10–17; Porphyrios, *Bios Pythagorou* 57 (Herakleides, *Epitome biôn Satyrou*).

8 On perverted self-love in self-killing: Aristoteles, *Ethika Nikomacheia* 5,11, 1138A and 9,4, 1166B and Ploutarchos, *Moralia* 497D: *kakia* a weed next to virtue; in this context Ploutarchos mentions Hegesias as the one who in an evil way drove many of his listeners to suicide; ailments and mental illness in which people destroy themselves are deviations from the natural state; Cicero about Epicurean lightheartedness: *Tusculanae disputationes* 5,118; the authentic Epicurean

view in the Philodemos-papyrus from Herculaneum, *Peri thanatou* 15,5–6; Epikouros on the loss of eye-sight: Diogenes Laertios 10, 119.

9 Diodoros 2,57,5; 3,5,2; 3,6,2.

10 *Nomoi* 9,871A–3D.

11 *Phaidon* 62A; Sokrates argues that for him dying is inevitable at that specific moment.

12 P. Moron, *Le suicide*, Paris 1975, p.100.

13 Antisthenes: Athenaios 4,157B; *Ajax* or *Ajax's Speech* by Antisthenes is mentioned by Diogenes Laertios 6,15; Antisthenes and Diogenes in Julianus, *Eis tous apaideutous kunas* 181B; Antisthenes addressing himself to the Eleusinian priest in Diogenes Laertios 6,4; the noose seen as a therapy against love by Krates in Diogenes Laertios 6,86, quoted by Julianus, *Eis tous apaideutous kunas* 198D (already quoted on p.46); mocking with fear of death in Dio Chrysostomos: *Oratio* 6,42; more stories about the view on suicide among Cynics in Diogenes Laertios 4,3; 6,18; 6,24; 6,77; 6,95; Aelianus, *Poikile historia* 8,14; 12,11.

14 See Johannes Hahn, *Der Philosoph und die Gesellschaft. Selbstverständnis, öffentliches Auftreten und populäre Erwartungen in der hohen Kaiserzeit*, Stuttgart 1989, for the subtle dynamics in the relationship between philosophers and the general public.

15 Lucretius 3,79; it is an old paradox: Xenophon already has it in his *Kyroupaideia* 3,1,25; Diogenes the Cynic says in Dio Chrysostomos' *Oratio* 6,42 that in case of a shipwreck and encirclement many anticipated the end (*proelabon*); Seneca, *Epistulae* 24,33: 'it is ridiculous that some are driven to death from fear of death'.

16 *Vivere cum dolore* is the worst evil: L. Manlius Torquatus in Cicero, *De finibus bonorum* 1,9; *neglegit mortem*: 1,41; *aequo animo e vita, cum ea non placeat, tamquam e theatro exeamus*: 1,49.

17 Diogenes Laertios 7,28; a different story which has him die from starvation in 7,31.

18 Ploutarchos, *Moralia* 1076B ; the remark of Plinius Maior with which we opened this study thus seems to reflect a Stoic idea; criticism on the Stoic points of view in *Moralia* 1039D–1040A, 1042D, 1060C–D, 1070B and 1076B.

19 Epiktetos 1,9,16; Cicero, *Tusculanae disputationes* 1,74; Griffin, op. cit., 1976, p.374: 'Seneca is less explicit than Epictetus about the need for a sign'; anticipating a strict necessity: Seneca, *Epistulae* 58,34; *non sumus in ullius potestate, cum mors in nostra potestate est*: Seneca, *Epistulae* 91,21; about Seneca's desire of death: *Epistulae* 54,1–2; 77,9.

20 Griffin, *Philosophy*, p.67; *contraria* and *molesta tranquillitatem turbantia*: Cicero, *De finibus* 3,60; 'Whenever the sage comes across something he cannot avoid, the harbour is near and he may swim thither, away from his body, as though from a small boat that takes in water'; Ploutarchos, *Moralia* 476A; Seneca, *Epistulae* 70,5; *vincula servitutis*: Seneca, *Epistulae* 70,12; Seneca's approval for Lucilius' behaviour in *Naturales Quaestiones* 4A praefatio; Griffin, p.196 and 198.

21 Five degrees in causation of death: 'Olympiodoros philosophus', *In Phaedonem commentaria*, p.243 (ed. W. Norvin, Teubner Leipzig 1913);

the secret doctrine in *Phaidon* 62B; about Plato's relations with Orphism and Pythagoreanism: J. C. G. Strachan, 'Who did forbid suicide at Phaedo 6213?' in *Classical Quarterly N.S.*, 20 (1970), p.220; the Pythagorean Philolaos about suicide: Diels, op. cit., p.315 (Philolaos 14); the Pythagorean taboo on suicide in Macrobius, *Commentum in Ciceronis Somnium Scipionis* 1,13,9; it is forbidden to leave the position determined by god: Cicero, *Somnium Scipionis* 3.

22 Brutus' suicide is called *ouch hosion*: Ploutarchos, *Brutus* 40,4; against *pudor* as a sufficient ground for Academics: Diogenes Laertios 9,120; philosophers must always be prepared to counter all the tricks of death like an accomplished strategist, but they must wait for the right opportunity to die, so that they be not taken off their guard, *'nor like suicides rush into death'* (Philostratos, Ta es ton Tyanea Apollonian 7,31).

23 *Enneades* 1,9; R. Garland, *The Greek Way of Death*, London 1985, apparently overlooks the links between Neo-platonic and Christian doctrine of the soul saying that Greek popular religion has hardly any trace of the view that God has laid down a certain length of time for life (p.97); Julianus' last words in Ammianus Marcellinus 25,3; Prudentius, *Psychomachia* 142–161 and 348–410 (*patientia* and *ira*); for pictures illustrating Prudentius: Chapeaurouge; Comenius takes the line of this tradition with his depiction of despair.

24 Tertullianus, *Apologeticum* 4,6; 46,14; 50,5 and 7; on the rediscovery of Lucretia as a virtuous heathen: I. Donaldson, op. cit., p.26; Shakespeare's Lucretia constitutes a new stage in the evaluation: his story is no longer one of moral certainties. Lucretia seems unsure of the moral consequences both of rape and of suicide, hesitantly debating her way towards death. 'Once again', Donaldson comments on p.47, 'the simpler code of honour is complicated by newer.'

25 M. Bayet, *Le suicide et la morale*, Paris 1922, pp.227–8, 245, 237, 251–2; on *ultro se offerre*: Acta Cypriani 1,5; Cyprianus, *Epistulae* 81; Clemens Alexandrinus, *Stromateis* 4,4,17,1 appealing to Plato's *Politeia*.

26 Bayet, ibid., pp.227–8, 251–2; *Acta Sanctorum Martyrum: Karpos, Papylos et Agathonike* 42–3; Hieronymus, *Adversus Iovinianum*, Migne *Patrologia Latina* 23,284; Hieronymus has *seven* girls, whereas the poem of the *Anthologia Palatina* 7,492 has only three; one document that dates from the time shortly after the Great Persecution of 306 does not yet give evidence of a principled rejection: Petros, bishop of Alexandria, argues that priests who had defected should not be punished too severely, for otherwise they 'might hasten their death by violence'. Such a *biothanasia* is evidently regarded as the nadir of despair – not of sin. The argument is still pastoral, not moral.

27 Quintilianus, *Institutio Oratoria* 7,3,7; Lactantius, *Institutiones divinae* 3,15–24.

28 For the relation between Neo-Platonism and Lactantius' and Augustinus's theology see P. W. v.d. Horst; 'Jewish justification of self-killing in order not to sin', in *Mishnah Sanhedrin* 73a, VIII 7; on Donatist suicides: P. MacKendrick, *The North African Stones Speak*, London 1980, p. 263; the Circumcelliones (here called Circuitores) were even said to force passers-by to kill them and to seek death by

brigandage (Filastrius, *Diversarum haereseon liber* 85(57)½. Augustinus on suicide: *De civitate Dei* 1,17-27; disapproval of the Donatist attitude: 'confessores. . .vestri quando se ipsos praecipitant, cui ducunt martyrium, utrum Christo qui talia suggerentem diabolum reppulit, an potius ipsi diabolo qui talia Christo faciendo suggessit?' (*Comm.litt.Petr.* 2,49,114; Hieronymus, *In Ionam* 1,12: 'it is not allowable to die by one's own hand during a persecution *except when chastity is threatened*'; about the significance of Augustine's polemics against the Donatists about suicide: J. Bels, 'La mort volontaire dans l'oeuvre de saint Augustin', in *Revue de l'histoire des religions*, 187 (1975), pp.150, 154 and 161; Augustine brings suicide, which in the traditional view lies in the sphere of sacrifice, into that of homicide, with the disgust that accompanies murder: Bels, ibid., p.180.

29 Council of Orléans, AD 533, Canon 15; Council of Braga, AD 563, Canon 16.

APPENDIX B: PROFILE OF ANCIENT SELF-KILLING

1 In this study the reckoning is quite deliberately in cases (see p.8); one case may comprise more than one individual, even large groups, or it may refer to a renewed attempt/contemplation by an individual who was already been counted as one case.

2 The difference between this figure and that of individual self-killing (884) is caused by the fact that sometimes a single person – especially in fiction – is said to have contemplated suicide more than once. On the other hand one case of individual self-killing may comprise several persons.

3 The following have been counted as group suicides (the numbers of persons involved in the 11 cases of mass suicide where a number is given in the sources is given in brackets): Abydeni, Aeginetae, Agrigentini multi, Ardiaii, Argivi *nobiles*, Campani, christiani Antiocheni, christiani Nicomedenses, Crassi tribuni militum, Euni socii, fugitivi Sicilienses, Gallaeci, Galli, Galli morientes, Gamalani (5000), Hierosolymitae a.Chr.63, Hiketides (10), Hispani captivi, Hispani multi, Indi obsessi, Iotapatae superstites (38), Isauri, Iudaei, Kerkyraioi 1, Kerkyraioi 2, Kleomenis amici, Koneiazomenai, legionarii legionis Martiae, Lycii, *magistratus curules*, Masadani (960), *matronae venenum terentes* (20), milites Antonii, milites Caesaris, milites Crassi, *milites esurientes*, milites ex Venetis, milites Gaii Antonii, milites Iotapatae, milites Opitergini (1000), milites Othonis, milites Pompeii, milites post Trasymenum, milites Romani CCCC (400), milites Romani pauci, Montani, mulieres Ardubenses, nautae Ioppae, Numantini, Othonis amici, Pantheiae eunuchi, Patrenses, perfugae, Persae, Poeni obsessi, Rhodii, Rhodii quidam, Romani quidam, Saguntini, Satyri socii (1000), Saxones gladiatores (29), Segestani, senes Athenienses, senes Trinacienses, *servi multi*, Sidones, Stoeni,

Taochi, Teutonum uxores, Tigurinorum uxores, Vari tribuni militesque, Vetti socii, Vibius Virrius & senatores (28), Victomelani, Vulteii commilitones.

4 In nine cases an 'exact' number is given.

5 Ratios between men and women under b 10.

6 There are six barbarian cases where a specific number is given for the participants in a mass suicide.

7 There are two Greek cases where a specific number is given for the participants in a mass suicide.

8 There are three Roman cases where a specific number is given for the participants in a mass suicide.

9 The total of cases is less than under Appendix B 1, because for some case – for instance the fictional – the period cannot be established.

10 The totals may be bigger than the sum of the cases of men and women because there are cases of group suicide in which mixed groups were involved.

11 The hard cases are given in brackets.

12 'Varia' and 'unknown' have not been taken into account.

13 Ratios for the sexes under 10 c.

14 Ratios of the sexes for each motive under 10 d.

15 Of course only those cases could be taken into account where both a method and a motive was given.

16 Percentage of motives in general appears in brackets; compare with table 7 b.

17 Percentage of methods in general appear in brackets; compare with table 6 b.

18 There are 4(3) cases of collective self-killing among the lower classes where an 'exact' number is given.

BIBLIOGRAPHY

Adkins, A. W. H. *Moral Values and Political Behaviour in Ancient Greece*, London 1972.

Agostino, V. d' 'Plinio il Giovane e il problema del suicidio', in *Studi sul neostoicismo: Seneca, Plinio il Giovane, Epitteto, Marco Aurelio*, Turin 1962, pp.62–89.

Aigner, H. *Der Selbstmord im Mythos*, Habilitations-Schrift, Graz 1982.

Alaimo, Bernardus, O. F. M. 'De suicidii nomine et quibusdam eius definitionibus', in *Antonianum* 31 (1956) pp.189–214.

Alfonsi, L. 'Un "protrettico" epigrafico di età imperiale', in *Epigraphica* 26 (1964–5) pp.59–67.

Anderson, Olive *Suicide in Victorian and Edwardian England*, Oxford 1987.

Baechler, J. *Les suicides*, Paris 1975.

Bartel, R. 'Suicide in Eighteenth-Century England: The Myth of a Reputation', in *Huntington Library Quarterly* 23 (1959–60) pp.145–158.

Baumhauer *Veterum philosophorum doctrina de morte voluntaria*, Dissertation, Trier 1842.

Bayet, Albert *Le suicide et la morale*, Paris 1922.

Bayet, J. *Croyances et rites dans la Rome antique*, Paris 1971.

Bayet, J. 'Le suicide mutuel dans la mentalité dans la Rome antique', in *Année Sociologique* 3, ser.5 (1951) pp.35–89.

Beattie, J. H. M. 'Homicide and Suicide in Bunyoro', in P. Bohannan (ed.), *African Homicide and Suicide*, Princeton N.J., 1960, pp.130–53.

Bels, J. 'La mort volontaire dans l'oeuvre de saint Augustin', in *Revue de l'histoire des religions* 187 (1975) pp.147–80.

Berlage, J. 'Ziekten en sterfgevallen in de brieven van Plinius de Jongere', in *Hermeneus* 9 (1938–9) pp.66–73.

Berlage, J. 'Excursus over de opvattingen omtrent zelfmoord in de Grieks-Romeinse oudheid', in *Hermeneus* 12 (1939–40) pp.89–121.

Blok, J. and Mason, P. *Sexual Asymmetry. Studies in Ancient Society*, Amsterdam 1987.

Bohannan, P. (ed.) *African Homicide and Suicide*, Princeton N.J. 1960.

Bohannan, P. 'Homicide and Suicide in North Kavirondo', in P. Bohannan (ed.), ibid., pp.154–78.

Bohannan, P. 'Patterns of Murder and Suicide, in P. Bohannan (ed.), ibid., pp.230–66.

Brehart, J. and Roger, J. 'Le suicide du Noir Africain', in *La nouvelle presse medicale* (1973.2) pp.863–4.

Brunschwig, H. *La crise de l'état Prussien à la fin du XVIIIe siècle et la genèse de la mentalité romantique*, Thèse Lettres, Paris 1947.

Camus, Albert *De myte van Sisyfus. Een essay over het absurde*, Amsterdam 1962 (originally published as *Le Mythe de Sisyphe*, Paris 1942).

Caramuel, L.J. *Theologia moralis fundamentalis*, second edn: Rome 1656.

Chapeaurouge, Donat de 'Selbstmorddarstellungen des Mittelalters', in *Zeitschrift für Kunstwissenschaft* 14 (1960) pp.135–46.

Choron, J. 'Notes on Suicide Prevention in Antiquity', in *Bulletin of Sociology* (July 1968) pp.46–8.

Coquelin de Lisle, A. 'Le suicide à Rome', in *Du Suicide et de la participation au suicide d'autrui*, Rennes 1928, pp.23–32.

Crane, Theodore *The Imagery of Suicide in Lucan's 'De Bello Civili'*, Dissertation, The University of North Carolina at Chapel Hill 1964.

Cumont, F. 'Comment Plotin dé tourna Porphyre du suicide', in *Revue des études grecques* 32 (1919), pp.113–20.

Cumont, F. *Virgile et les morts prématures*, Paris 1945.

Cumont, F. *Lux Perpetua*, Paris 1949, pp.334–8.

Davies, M. I. *Studies on the Early Traditions of the Oresteia Legend in Art and Literature with Related Studies on the Suicide of Ajax*, Dissertation, Princeton 1971.

Delcourt, M. 'Le suicide par vengeance dans la Grèce ancienne', in *Revue de l'histoire des religions* 119 (1939) pp.154–71.

Deshaies, G. *La psychologie du suicide*, Paris 1947.

Diekstra, R. F. *Crisis en Gedragskeuze: Een theoretische en empirische bijdrage tot het zelfmoordprobleem*, Amsterdam 1973.

Diekstra, R. F. *Over suicide. Zelfdestructie, zelfbehoud en hulpverlening*, Alphen aan den Rijn 1981.

Diekstra, R. F. (ed.), *Suicide and its Prevention*, Leyden 1989.

Donaldson, I. *The Rapes of Lucretia. A Myth and its Transformations*, Oxford 1982.

Dover, K. J. *Greek Popular Morality*, Oxford 1974.

Durkheim, Émile *Le suicide*, 1897; second edn: Paris 1930.

Edelstein, L. *Ancient Medicine*, Baltimore 1967.

Eijk, W. J. *De zelfgekozen dood naar aanleiding van een dodelijke en ongeneeslijke ziekte*, Brugge 1987.

Eyben, E. *De jonge Romein volgens de literaire bronnen der periode ca. 200 v. Chr. tot ca. 500nna Chr.*, Brussels 1977.

Eyben, E. *De onstuimigen*, Antwerp/Kampen 1987.

Faber, M. D. *Suicide and Greek Tragedy*, New York 1970.

Fallers, L. A. and Fallers, M. C. 'Homicide and Suicide in Busoga', in P. Bohannan (ed.), *African Homicide and Suicide*, Princeton N.J., 1960, pp.65–93.

Fenton, W. N. 'Iroquois Suicides', in *Anthropological Papers* 14 (1941) p.79.

Fontaine, J. La 'Homicide and Suicide among the Gisu', in P. Bohannan (ed.), ibid., pp.94–129.

Fontenrose, J. *The Delphic Oracle*, Berkeley, Los Angeles and London 1978 (Paperback edn 1981).

Fontinoy, C. 'Les causes du suicide des veuves', in *Mélanges Fohalle*, Gembloux 1969, pp.195–204.

Fox, R. Lane *Pagans and Christians*, Harmondsworth 1986.

Fraenkel, E. 'Selbstmordwege', in *Philologus* 87 (1932) pp.470–3.

Frend, W. *The Donatist Church*, Oxford 1952.

Fühner, H. 'Der Tod des Themistokles. Ein Selbstmord durch Stierblut', in *Rheinisches Museum N.F.* 91 (1942) pp.193–9.

Fusé, Toyomasa 'Modernization and Suicide in Japan: A Comparative Approach', in *Cultures et développement* 12.1 (1980) pp.45–80.

Galinsky, H. *Der Lucretia-Stoff in der Weltliteratur*, Breslau 1932.

Garland, R. *The Greek Way of Death*, London 1985.

Garland, R. 'Death without dishonour. Suicide in the Ancient World', in *History Today* 33.1 (1983) pp.33–7.

Garrison, G. *Le suicide dans l'antiquité et dans les temps modernes*, Paris 1885.

Geiger, K. A. *Der Selbstmord im klassischen Altertum*, Augsburg 1888.

Gelfand, M. 'Suicide and Attempted Suicide Among the Shona: Research Report', in *Zambezia* 2.2 (1972) pp.73–8.

Gibbs, J. P. 'Testing the Theory of Status Integration and Suicide Rates', in *American Sociological Review* 47.2 (1982) pp.227–37.

Gibbs, J. P. and Martin, W. T. *Status Integration and Suicide*, Oregon 1964.

Gibbs, J. P. (ed.) *Suicide*, New York 1968.

Glotz, G. *La solidarité de la famille (dans le droit criminel) en Grèce*, Paris 1904.

Godderis, Jan *Galenos van Pergamon over psychische stoornissen*, Leuven/Amersfoort 1988.

Gourevitch, D. *Le triangle hippocratique dans le monde Greco-Romain. Le malade, sa maladie et son médicin*, Paris/Rome 1984.

Gourevitch, D. 'Suicide Among the Sick in Classical Antiquity', in *Bulletin History Medicine* 43 (1969) pp.501–18.

Green, P. D. *Long Lent Loathed Sight: A Study of Suicide in Three English Nondramatic Writers of the Sixteenth Century*, Dissertation, Harvard 1971.

Griffin, M. F. *Seneca. A Philosopher in Politics*, Oxford 1976.

Griffin, M. F. 'Philosophy, Cato and Roman Suicide I & II', in *Greece and Rome* 33.1 (April 1986) pp.64–77 and 33.2 (October 1986) pp.192–202.

Grisé, Y. *Le suicide dans la Rome antique*, Montreal/Paris 1983.

Grisé, Y. 'Pourquoi "retuer" un mort? Un cas de suicide dans la Rome royale', in *Mélanges Lebel*, pp.267–81.

Grisé, Y. 'Les modes de suicide à Rome I–II', in *Cahiers des études anciennes* 8 (1978) pp.27–48 and 11 (1980) pp.45–79.

Grisé, Y. 'De la fréquence du suicide chez les Romains', in *Latomus* 39 (1980) pp.17–46.

Gunning, J. 'Zelfmoord in de Oudheid', in *Hermeneus* 12 (1939–40) pp.130–2.

Haegg, Tomas *The Novel in Antiquity*, Oxford 1983 (Swedish edn 1980).

Hafen, Bianca *Griechische Epigramme auf Selbstmörder*, Dissertation, Munich 1979.

Hahn, J. *Der Philosoph und die Gesellschaft. Selbstverständnis, öffentliches Auftreten und populäre Erwartungen in der hohen Kaiserzeit*, Stuttgart 1989.

Hands, A.R. 'The Timing of Suicide', in *Proceedings of the African Classical Association* 5 (1962) pp.27–31.

Hankoff, L. D. 'Flavius Josephus: Suicide and Transition', in *New York State Journal of Medicine* 79 (1979) pp.937–42.

Hankoff, L. D. 'Flavius Josephus: First-Century AD View of Suicide', in *New York State Journal of Medicine* 77 (1977) pp.1986–92.

Hankoff, L. D. 'The Theme of Suicide in the Works of Flavius Josephus', in *Clio Medica* 11 (1976) pp.15–24.

Hankoff, L.D. and Einsiedler, B. *Suicides*, Littleton (Ma.) 1979.

Henry, A. F. and Short, J. F. *Suicide and Homicide*, Glencoe 1954.

Hertog, M. M. den *De zedelijke waardering van den zelfmoord*, Dissertation, Utrecht 1913.

Hirzel, R. 'Der Selbstmord', in *Archiv für Religionswissenschaft* 11 (1908) pp.75–104, 243–84, 417–76; reprinted Darmstadt 1966.

Historia, 'Le dossier du suicide, numéro special 388', 1979.

Hooff, Anton J. L. van 'Van mors voluntaria tot suicidium', in *Tijdschrift voor Geschiedenis* 101 (1988) pp.17–35.

Hooff, Anton J. L. van 'Antieke zelfdoding tussen honor en horror', in *Hermeneus* 59.1 (February 1987) pp.8–17.

Hooff, Anton J. L. van 'De gewone vrouw moest hangen', in H.I.N.T., 'Tijdschrift Geschiedenis Studentenvereniging', Nijmegen, 1.7 (November 1984) pp.11–14.

Horst, P. W. v.d. 'A Pagan Platonist and a Christian Platonist on Suicide', in *Vigiliae Christianae* 25 (1971) pp.282–8.

Horstmanshoff, H. F. J. *De pijlen van de pest. Pestilenties in de Griekse wereld, 800–400 v.Chr.*, Dissertation, Leiden, Amsterdam 1989.

James, C. 'Whether 'tis nobler. Some Thoughts on the Fate of Sophocles' Ajax and Euripides' Heracles', in *Pegasus* 12 (1969) pp.10–20.

Jeffreys, M. P. 'Samsonic Suicide or Suicide of Revenge Among the Africans', in *African Studies* 6.3 (1952) pp.118–22.

Jeorger, M. e. a. 'L'histoire du suicide', in *Histoire* 27 (1980) pp.37–55.

Kany, J. *Le suicide politique à Rome et en particulier chez Tacite*, thèse de 3e cycle, Reims 1970.

Katsouris, A. G. 'To motibo tes autoktonias sto archaio drama', in *Dodone* 4 (1975) pp.203–34/Engels: 'The Suicide Motive in Ancient Drama', in *Dionysio* 47 (1976) pp.5–36.

Kern, Stephen 'Explosive Intimacy: Psychodynamics of the Victorian Family', in *History of Childhood Quarterly* 1.3 (1974) pp.437–61.

King, Helen 'Bound to Bleed: Artemis and Greek Women', in Cameron, A. and Kurt, A., *Images of Women in Antiquity*, London 1983.

Kuiper, T. *Philodemus Over den dood*, Amsterdam 1925.

Lasch, R. 'Die Verbleibsorte der abgeschiedenen Seelen der Selbstmörder', in *Globus* 77 (1900) pp. 110–15.

Lefkowitz, Mary, *Women in Greek Myth*, London 1986.

MacDonald, M. 'The Inner Side of Wisdom: Suicide in Early Modern England', in *Psychological Medicine* 7 (1977) pp.565–82.

Martino Fusco, M. di 'Il suicidio nelle dottrine di Cicerone', in *Mouseion* 1 (1923) pp.95–8.

Masaryk, T. G. *Suicide and the Meaning of Civilization*, University of Chicago Press 1970.

Matthijs, K. *Zelfdoding*, Leuven 1985.

Matzneff, G. 'Le suicide chez les Romains', in *Le défi*, Paris 1959, pp.105–43.

Meijer, M. J. 'The Price of a P'Ai-Lou', in *T'oung Pao* 67.3/5 (1981) pp.288–304.

Mommsen, T. *Römisches Strafrecht*, Graz 1955 (=1899).

Moron, P. *Le suicide*, Paris 1975.

Muriel, Jeorger e. a. 'L'histoire du suicide', in *Histoire* 27 (1980) pp.37–55.

Musaph, H. *Doden met verlof. Depressie en doodsdrift*, Baarn/Antwerpen 1972.

Papastakos, A. 'He autoktonìa eis tèn archaìan parastatikèn tèchnen', in *Archaìkogikon Deltìon* 25 (1970–1) p.36 e.v.

Parke, H. W. and Wornell, D. E. *The Delphic Oracle I–II*, Oxford 1956.

Piers, G. and Singer, M. B. *Shame and Guilt. A Psychoanalytic and a Cultural Study*, New York 1971.

Pinguet, M. 'Hara-kiri: l'art del l'éventrement au Japon', in *Histoire* 31 (1981) pp.10–18.

Pollard, J. *Seers, Shrines and Sirens. The Greek Religious Revolution in the Sixth Century*, London 1965.

Potthoff, Th. *Euthanasie in der Antike*, Dissertation, Münster 1982.

Rist, J. M. *Stoic Philosophy*, Berkeley/Los Angeles 1978.

Rolfs, D. J. jr. *The Theme of Suicide in Italian Literature: From the Middle Ages to the Late Renaissance*, Dissertation, Berkeley 1972.

Romilly, J. de 'Le refus du suicide dans l'Heracles d'Euripides', in *Archaiognoosia* 1 (1980) pp.1–10.

Romilly, J. de 'La tragédie grecque et l'idéal heroïque', in *Didactica Classica Gandensia* 22 (1982) p.27.

Rose, A. R. 'Seneca and Suicide. The End of the Hercules Furens', in *Classical Outlook* 60 (1983) pp.109–11.

Rose, H. I. *Hygini Fabulae*, Leiden 1963.

Rosen, G. 'History in the Study of Suicide', in *Psychological Medicine* 1 (1971) pp.267–85.

Rost, H. *Bibliographie des Selbstmords*, Augsburg 1927.

Schadewaldt, B. H. 'Historische Betrachtungen zum Alterssuizid', in *Aktuelle Gerontologie*, 7 (1977) pp.59–66.

Scherer, G. *Das Problem des Todes in der Philosophie*, Darmstadt 1988[2].

Schmidt, B. 'Der Selbstmord der Greise von Keos', in *Neue Jahrbücher Klass.Alt.* 11 (1903) pp.617–28.

Schmitt, J.-C. 'Le suicide au Moyen Age', in *Annales Économies Sociétés Civilisations* 31 (1976) pp.3–28.

Seidensticker, B. 'Die Wahl des Todes bei Sophokles', in *Sophocle*, Entretiens Fondation Hardt 29, Geneva 1983, pp.105–44.

Spero, M. H. 'Samson and Masada: Altruistic Suicides Reconsidered', in *Psychoanalytical Review* 65 (1978) pp.631–9.

Starobinski, J. 'L'épée d'Ajax', in *Trois fureurs*, Paris 1974, pp.11–71.

Steiner, G. *Antigones. The Antigone Myth in Western Literature, Art and Thought*, Oxford 1984.

Strachan, J. C. G. 'Who did forbid suicide at Phaedo 62B?', in *Classical Quarterly N.S.* 20 (1970) pp.216–20.

Tadic-Guilloteaux, N. 'Sénèque face au suicide', in *Antiquité Classique'* 32 (1963) pp.541–51.

Taylor, Steve, *Durkheim and the Study of Suicide*, London 1982.

Thalheim 'Selbstmord', in Pauly-Wissowa, *Realencyclopädie der classischen Altertumswissenschaft*.

Thomas, C. 'First Suicide Note?' in *British Medical Journal* 281 (1980) pp.284–5.

Thomas, C. 'Inde: le pays du suicide?' in *Histoire* 30 (1981) pp.81–3.

Touchefen, O. 'Ajax' in J. Boardman (ed.) *Lexicon Iconographicum Mythologiae Classicae* I, Zürich 1981.

Versnel, H. S. 'Destruction, Devotio and Despair in a Situation of Anomy: The Mourning for Germanicus in Triple Perspective', in *Perennitas Studi in onore di Angelo Brelich*, Rome 1980.

Versnel, H. S. 'Self-sacrifice, Compensation and the Anonymous Gods', in *Le sacrifice dans l'antiquité*, Entretiens sur l'antiquité classique 27, Geneva 1981, pp.135–94.

Versnel, H. S. 'Two types of Roman devotio', in *Mnemosyne* 29 (1976) pp.364–410.

Veyne, Paul 'Suicide, fisc, esclavage, capital et droit romain', in *Latomus* 40 (1981) pp.217–68.

Voisin, J.-L. 'Le suicide d'Amata', *Revue des études grecques* 57 (1979) pp.254–66.

Voisin, J.-L. 'Apicata, Antinous et quelques autres', in *Mélanges d'archéologie et d'histoire de l'école française de Rome*, 99.1 (1987) pp.257–80.

Vrught-Lenz, J. ter *Mors immatura* (dissertation Leyden) Groningen 1960.

Wacke, Andreas 'Der Selbstmord im römischen Recht und in der Rechtsentwicklung', in *Zeitschrift der Savigny-Stiftung für Rechtsgeschichte-Romanist.Abteilung* 97 (1980) pp.26–77.

Walcot, Peter *Envy and the Greeks*, Warminster 1978.

Walcot, Peter 'Suicide. A Question of Motivation', in *Studies in Honour of T. B. L. Webster I*, Bristol 1986, pp.231–7.

Westermarck, E. 'Suicide: A Chapter in Comparative Ethics', in *Sociological Review* 1 (1908) pp.12–33.

Wilie, R. 'Views on Suicide and Freedom in Stoic Philosophy and Some Related Contemporary Points of View', in *Prudentia* 5 (May 1973) pp.15–32.

Wilson, G. M. 'Homicide and Suicide among the Joluo of Kenya', in P. Bohannan, *African Homicide and Suicide*, Princeton, N.J. pp.179–213.

Young, Lung-Chang 'Altruistic Suicide: A Subjective Approach', in *Sociological Bulletin* (India) 21.2 (1972) pp.103–21.

Youtie, H. C. 'Notes on Papyri', in *Transactions and Proceedings of the American Philological Association* 98 (1967) pp.512–13. (P. Mich. V, 231).

Zilboorg, G. 'Suicide among Civilised and Primitive Races', in *American Journal of Psychiatry* 92 (1935–6) pp.1347–69.

INDEX

289